ART IN WALES

ART IN WALES

An Illustrated History 1850 – 1980

Eric Rowan

Welsh Arts Council
University of Wales Press
Cardiff
1985

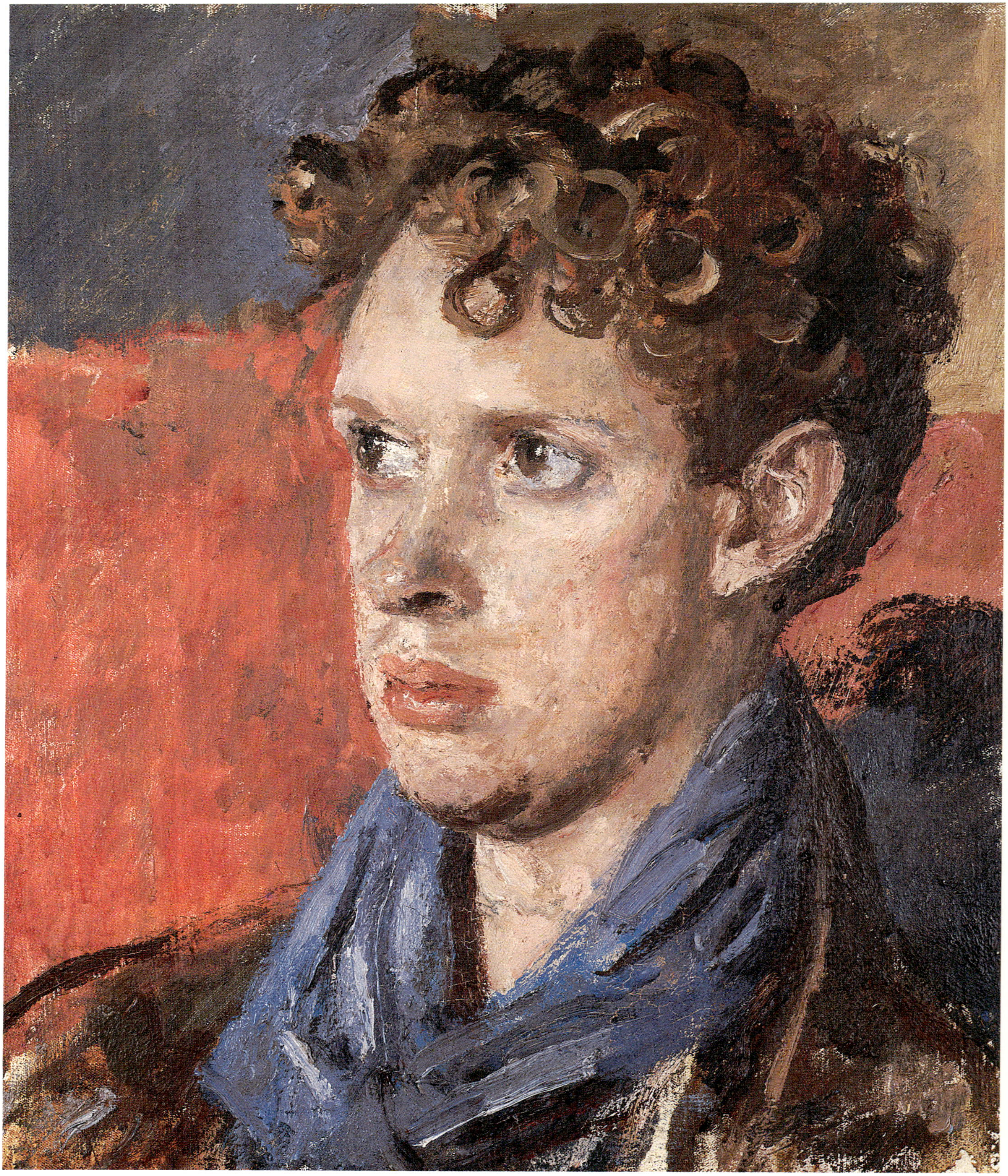

The first volume of *Art in Wales* was a conspectus of four millennia of the visual arts through the eyes of five observers. In this second volume, a different approach has been taken in finishing the account up to the present decade. It brings into much closer focus a period of a hundred and thirty years as seen by one author.

The Art Committee of the Welsh Arts Council and the University of Wales Press thus complete this joint venture, believing that it offers, not indeed the whole story of art in Wales, but a bird's-eye view which we trust will stimulate the reader to investigate more fully and widely.

We again thank Eric Rowan, the editor of the first volume and author of this one, the designer, the printers, and all whose co-operation has enabled us to share this part of our visual heritage with a wider public.

Peter Jones, *Art Director, Welsh Arts Council*
John Rhys, *Director, University of Wales Press*

Portrait of Dylan Thomas by Augustus John

CONTENTS

FOREWORD

This book is a continuation and a culmination of the story that began in the first volume on the history of Welsh art, *Art in Wales 2000 BC - AD1850*. The first book was based on the catalogue of an exhibition originally mounted in 1964, then brought up to date, edited and published in September 1978. Because it began life as a catalogue, it was rooted in a display of art objects and thus had a strong visual emphasis, manifested in the large number of illustrations. In this second volume I have tried to preserve the same form of historical account, not only because it ensures continuity of style, but also because it appears to be the most informative way of telling the history of the visual arts.

The first volume concentrated between its covers a period of nearly 4000 years of continuous history; yet this second volume, of similar size, covers only 130 years. The explanation of this apparent discrepancy in the time scale is that much more art has been preserved and recorded in this short period of modern history than in any comparable period in the more distant past. What is more, time is the greatest arbiter in matters of art, determining what is excellent and eliminating what is insignificant. In the modern period this determining factor becomes less reliable and more confusing the nearer we approach our own day. This is further complicated by the fact that, in the last 30 years or so, there has been a plethora of artistic ideas and forms, bursting through the traditional boundaries of art, and making selection and definition even more difficult.

And so the focus of this history of art in Wales increases progressively until it covers the widest angle that is compatible with the limitations of a single book. As we approach contemporary events, more detail is included because we do not have the assistance of hindsight in our selection. It therefore becomes necessary to present a broad picture, so that current artistic events can be recorded in order to inform a more discriminating posterity. Even so, there has persisted the daunting problem of what to include and what to eliminate, for it was essential to produce from a disparate spate of achievement a coherent and continuous narrative.

As a guide through this problem, I recalled that, in his celebrated television lectures on *Civilisation*, Sir Kenneth Clark described them as a 'personal view'. At the time I thought this was an unjustifiable conceit; a piece of egotism which attempted to convey the whole of European culture from a single, subjective viewpoint. But that was before I began writing this book. Since then I have come to realise that a broad treatment of history cannot be finally resolved, it cannot be determined individually and yet objectively, neither can it be selected by committees. So I have become more tolerant towards the 'personal view', indeed I have come to regard it as an essential restriction in dealing with a work of this kind. For though the history of the visual arts in Wales from 1850 to the present day is a more modest subject than the whole of the civilisation of Europe, it demands the same attitude and imposes similar restrictions. It is too diffuse, too complex and too variegated a subject to be treated with complete objectivity. There are too many events, too many personalities, too many conflicting opinions on those events and personalities for the whole to be compressed into one short, comprehensive account. So this book is presented with proper humility as a personal view, a review of the last century and a quarter, approached with the maximum possible detachment, but nevertheless seen from one point of view.

In this approach I have relied on the impersonal attitude of the art historian, and on my experience of looking at the art of the period, of lecturing on it, and of writing about it. And not only the art of Wales, but that of Europe and America. For it seemed to me, in the outline proposed by the Welsh Arts Council and the University of Wales Press, that the most rewarding attitude would be to regard art in Wales as part of the general development of Western art. To do this meant avoiding an insular, regional viewpoint by placing Welsh art in an international context. I chose this perspective because I believe that the visual arts in Wales merit such distinction; that the contribution from this country has been important enough for it to be evaluated by the highest possible standards.

And just as the art of the Roman invaders, and that of visitors such as Cox and Turner, were seen to be relevant in the first volume, so I have thought fit to include artists who were not born in Wales, or whose stay here has not been of long duration. The deciding factor has been the individual's contribution to the total Welsh contribution to the mainstream of Western art in the period of the survey. This means that many outstanding artists, working in a highly individual way or making only incidental or random contributions to the general picture, have been omitted or mentioned only in passing. Such discrimination in no way diminishes their ability or their achievement, it simply means that they were not easy to categorise in the progression of what was intended as a relatively generalised account. These omissions have been made only after careful deliberation and often with some regret. But it was not possible — without producing an over-detailed and interminable catalogue — to include all the artists working within the confines of the period.

If further justification is needed for this selective method, it lies in the fact that there are virtually no other books on the subject. The outstanding exception is David Bell's excellent summary, *The Artist in Wales*, which has been of considerable help to me, not only for the information it contains but in the attitude it adopts and the priorities it defines. However, Bell's book was published in 1957, it had a much wider historical scope than this volume, it included more categories of creative endeavour, and it was consequently even more selective.

This present survey is confined to the so-called 'fine arts', though it is not seen as a definitive history of such art in Wales. It is, rather, an attempt to map out the salient features of a world that has become increasingly important; a pioneering expedition into territory that has been neglected by the wider world of scholarship. That it is fertile territory has become a conviction of mine which has grown during the writing of this book. The exploration has been rewarding, and I am grateful to the Welsh Arts Council and the University of Wales Press for giving me the opportunity to undertake it. I hope and expect that subsequent students of the subject will investigate those alluring but outlying areas which have not fitted into the scope of this survey, and examine in more detail those landmarks which I have located but which deserve more attention in their own right.

Finally, I should like to record my gratitude to the many organisations and individuals who have freely given me advice and help. These include the compilers of the innumerable catalogues I have consulted, the staff and archives of the Welsh Arts Council, the National Museum of Wales, the National Library of Wales, the many galleries and museums throughout the Principality, and others in Europe and America. My thanks are also due to those who have generously given permission to use photographs of their possessions, and whose names are recorded in detail in the list of illustrations.

Eric Rowan
March 1984

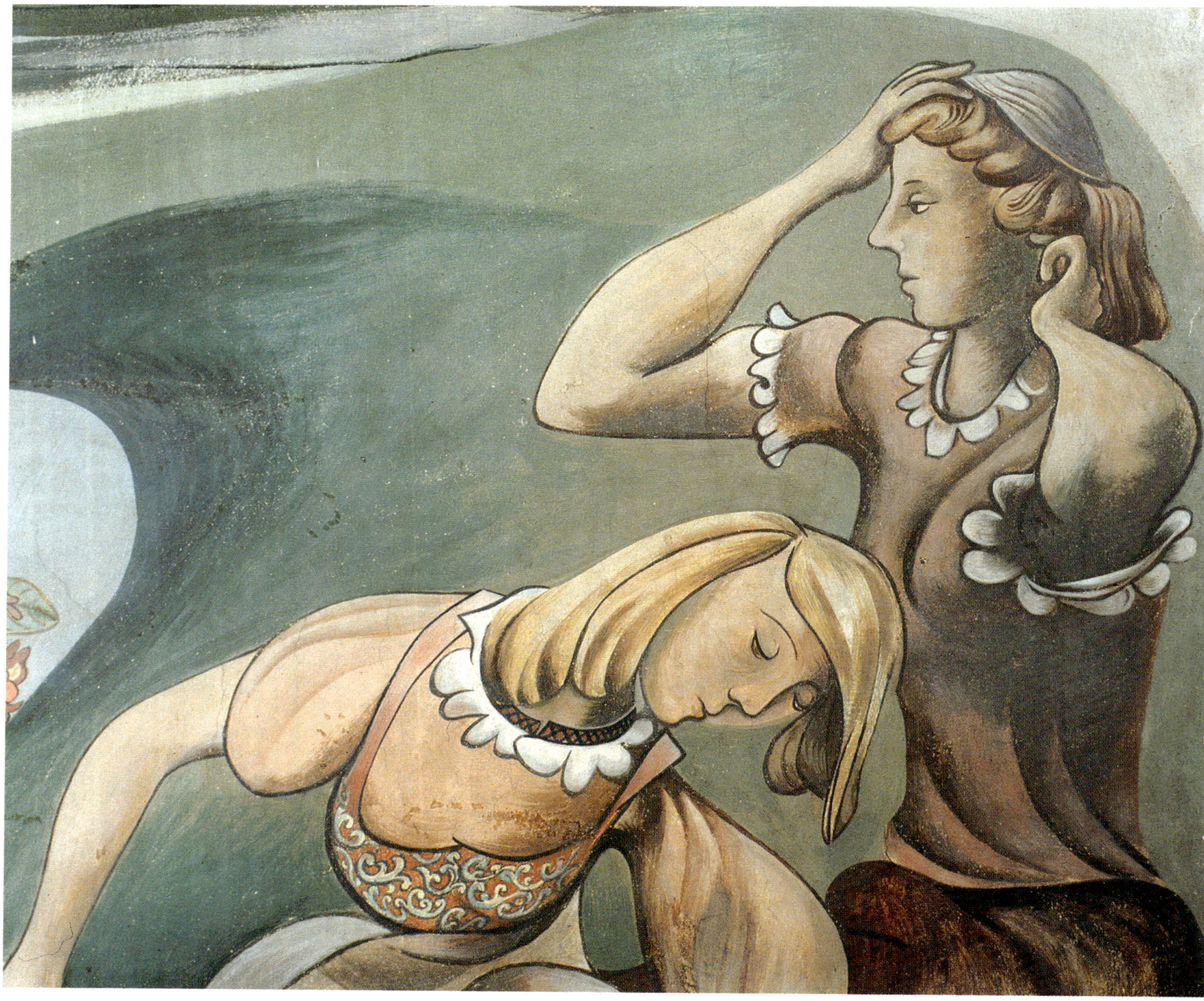

Detail of the 'Norwegian' murals by Ceri Richards

INTRODUCTION

By the middle of the nineteenth century the traditional social pattern of Wales had changed completely. The rapid growth of industry and the coming of the railways meant that the old rural pattern of squire and peasant gave way to an urban culture dominated by a new and prosperous middle class. It also meant that the geographical isolation was overcome by the introduction of quick and easy travel. However, the effects of this change on the art of Wales were not as immediate nor as drastic as they were on other aspects of society. By the time the initial pioneering conditions had improved, and there was time to think of art, the wealthy industrialists became patrons in their turn. The third generation of Crawshays, for example, 'discovered' Penry Williams in the drawing office of their iron works at Cyfarthfa, and paid for his training at the Royal Academy in London. But the only material difference between the patronage of Williams and that of Richard Wilson a century before, was that the former's came from iron and the other's came from land.

It is also true that the industrial entrepreneurs were mainly English, and if they had cultural pretensions then, like the landed gentry, they too looked to the Royal Academy and the London establishment for their art. The same preference was adopted by the new managerial class and it was, no doubt, often a case of prejudice and snobbery. There was, however, some justification for such a preference, for in the middle years of the nineteenth century there was no indigenous Academy in Wales, no art schools with professional standards, no art societies of high quality, no regular exhibitions, no galleries to hold such exhibitions and virtually no resident Welsh artists of any distinction. There was also, about this time, a general decline in the popularity of landscape as subject-matter in favour of historical figure painting, anecdote and medievalism. This meant that, although travel was easier, fewer artists came to paint in Wales and there was little in terms of commissions or important exhibitions to attract them for other reasons.

So the traffic in talent was from Wales to England. The first art schools in Wales were not founded until 1853 — in Swansea and Caernarfon — followed by Cardiff in 1865. But these were small and simple places and any prospective Welsh artists with ability and ambition went straight to the Royal Academy schools in London. If successful there, they would either go on to Rome or stay in London, for they were the places where a living could be made from art. Once established there, it seems there was little incentive to depict Welsh history or legend in their work. The main themes were from classical antiquity or English history and literature, since these were the principal demands of the art market. For by this time, not only was portraiture suffering from the competition of the camera, but the tradition of direct personal patronage was declining in favour of the practice of buying, at choice, from large annual exhibitions.

And even in this respect, Welsh artists were unfortunate. In 1870, The Fine Art and Industrial Exhibition was held at the Drill Hall in Cardiff, showing paintings alongside sewing machines and other such mechanical marvels. The Cardiff Art Society hung its first exhibition in 1879, but there were no regular annual exhibitions of professional, contemporary art in Wales until 1884 when The Fine Art Loan Exhibition was held in the Cardiff Public Hall. This was an ambitious venture, promoted by the Royal Cambrian Academy and its circumstances are indicative of the ideals and realities of Welsh art of this period.

The Cambrian Academy was founded in 1881 and, a year later, Queen Victoria allowed it to become Royal. The primary aim of the Royal Cambrian Academy was to establish a permanent institution in Cardiff with galleries, studios, a lecture hall and an art school which would be free to all students passing the entrance examination. There were to be facilities for painting, sculpture, architecture, the performance of music and an annual exhibition of fine art. This proposed home of national culture was sponsored by the Duke of Beaufort, the Marquis of Bute, the Earl of Cawdor, all the MPs and mayors of Wales, and it was supported by artists as eminent as Sir Frederick Leighton, PRA, Alma-Tadema, Millais and Herkomer. It was proposed that the costs should be met by the profits from an annual exhibition, of which the first one, The Fine Art Loan Exhibition of 1884, showed *avant-garde* artists of the status of Sickert and Watts. But if the ideal was intoxicating, the realities were sobering. The public was interested but the profits were negligible. The creation of a Royal Academy of Wales, along the line of the one in London, remained a dream and, after 1884, the disillusioned RCA retired with its annual exhibitions to Conwy and did not hold another exhibition in Cardiff for a further eighty years.

Such a grandiose failure did not prevent other groups from forming. The Swansea Art Society started in 1886 and the South Wales Art Society was launched two years later with Goscombe John as a founder member. These societies still flourish but they have always been relatively local groups with a bias towards the amateur, and as such they did not command the confidence of the collecting class. The South Wales Art Society held its first annual exhibition in 1888, also in the Cardiff Public Hall, and it realised a profit of £49. This contrasts significantly with the legacy of £32,000 bequeathed twenty years earlier by an expatriate Welsh sculptor, John Gibson, to his Alma Mater, the Royal Academy in London. But, although two more art schools had opened — at Carmarthen in 1880 and at Welshpool in 1883 — there was still no establishment with national and professional standards of a quality which could form the basis of a national academy. Perhaps art education never had a high official priority: as late as 1928, twenty years after its foundation, Llanelli School of Art was still confined to one room in Coleshill Terrace — and that room also served as the local synagogue on Saturdays.

This lack of opportunity, and the consequent emigration of talent, created a paradoxical situation. Because there were few opportunities to support full-time artists, when such opportunities did occur there were few local artists to call on. When a commission of any importance was forthcoming in Wales it was usually offered to artists in England. This was the case during the restoration of Llandaff Cathedral in the 1850s when the architect and Chapter commissioned Rossetti, William Morris, Thomas Woolner and Burne-Jones to carry out the more important features of decoration. One talented native artist, Milo ap Griffith, who worked on the carvings of the cathedral, gained no reputation from his efforts and he later emigrated to California where he became a professor in San Francisco. And in the 1870s, when William Burges was building Cardiff Castle and Castell Coch, he complained that it was almost impossible to find good sculptors, and he had to import those that he could find from England.

Such examples can be multiplied and they underline the fact that, in the second half of the last century and in the first quarter of this, there was no pool of indigenous professional artists that could form a 'School of Wales' or could be drawn upon to meet important commissions. In spite of the growing towns and the spate of public buildings, in spite of burgeoning civic pride and the wish to manifest it in works of art, and in spite of the obvious creative potential, there was in Wales no national institution for art education, no established class of patrons, no dealers or private galleries and no public gallery of any consequence until the opening of the National Museum in 1927.

It is tempting to suggest that the cause of these deficiencies was the lack of a metropolitan focus. Until 1955 there was no designated capital city; the largest towns had been, in turn, Swansea, Merthyr Tydfil and Cardiff, and at the turn of the century the population of Cardiff was only 164,333. Such a handicap was highlighted by the absurd rivalry which broke out around 1904 as to which town in Wales should harbour the National Library and the National Museum.

This hypothesis also gains force if two other points are considered. The first is that what art activity did take place in Wales was concentrated mainly in the south-east, which was the most urbanised part of the country. The second point is that if Cardiff — as the *de facto* capital and the largest town — is compared contemporaneously with Edinburgh or Dublin, then there is a striking discrepancy in achievement. Most national art groups have a nucleus within a large capital city which maintains an established cultural tradition — and Wales had no such city.

The alternative suggestion, untenable to most Welshmen, is that there were not enough competent Welsh artists to form a national school. The answer to this contention has been clouded by the emigration of native artists to England and by the traffic of foreign artists to Wales, so that it is not easy to establish a reliable definition of a Welsh artist. The author of an earlier survey of this subject, the Reverend T. Mardy Rees[1], solved the problem with a directness and authority that Duchamp would have envied. He simply designated certain artists as Welsh, mainly on the strength of their names, their family history or their own wishes. Thus, he included in his catalogue: William Morris, Owen Jones, Burne-Jones, G.F. Watts and Frank Brangwyn. An impressive list for a national school, but not supported by anything but the most rudimentary qualifications.

To some extent the problem of identification besets this present survey, though it has been partly resolved by usage since the days of the Reverend T. Mardy Rees. So that now, by almost common consent, Brangwyn is considered Welsh while the others listed above are not. This is a crude and somewhat arbitrary form of qualification but it does leave open the possibility of electing — even posthumously — new members to the ranks of Welsh artists. To take one example, there is the interesting case of Arthur B. Davies, hitherto regarded as an American painter and one of the moving spirits behind the New York Armory Show of 1913. Yet Davies's father was born in Carmarthenshire, was Welsh-speaking and became a Welsh preacher at Utica, NY. So that, by pedigree, Davies has just as valid a claim to Welshness as his contemporary Brangwyn and has, moreover, a greater claim on the rather tenuous basis of stylistic qualifications. Davies's haunting, poetic paintings, in an attenuated symbolist style, are closer to what many Welshmen would consider to be the Welshness of Welsh art than are Brangwyn's confident, objective and sometimes imperialistic canvases. Brangwyn, on the other hand, is well-represented in Wales, particularly in the vast Empire Panels in Swansea — though these were originally designed for the House of Lords in London.

However, the principle of qualifying by common agreement has been consolidated through the increasing and accelerating activity manifest in Welsh art since the 1930s. On all levels: individual, commercial, educational and political, there has been a growing concern for the role and status of the visual arts in Wales. In 1937, the Contemporary Art Society for Wales was founded, under the chairmanship of Lord Howard de Walden, and its first acquisition, a painting by David Jones, was donated by the Contemporarty Art Society in England. The CASW was modelled on the English prototype and though relatively under-financed, has certainly provided material and psychological encouragement among artists in Wales. The National Museum, by absorbing the contents of the old Cardiff museum, by acquisitions, donations and loans has created an outstanding collection of European painting and sculpture which is impressive even by international standards, and which incidentally spares Cardiff the burden of supporting a municipal gallery of its own.

The museum is admirable as a repository of art history, but in the common function of a national museum as a focus for information, influences and ideas for that nation's artists, it is inadequate. Allowing for the superb representation of Impressionism and Post-Impressionism, there is a gradual decline through modernism, and any Welsh artist relying on his own national museum for seminal encounters with modern art would be sadly out of date.

There is no equivalent to a Museum of Modern Art in Wales and the task of keeping the public and the artists informed about current ideas is effected through the medium of touring exhibitions. By far the greatest part of this service is provided by the Welsh Arts Council which, with its gallery in Cardiff, Oriel, provides permanent premises for temporary exhibitions in the capital city.

It would be difficult to imagine modern art existing on any worthwhile scale in Wales without the massive support of the Arts Council. Indeed, there is evidence to suggest that, if such public patronage were to be withdrawn, living art in Wales would quickly decline. Private galleries, dependent on the sale of modern art, which opened, flourished, faded and died in Cardiff and Swansea during the 1950s and 1960s have not been replaced. Their role has been more than amply filled by galleries belonging to various public bodies — by 1976 there were six such galleries in Cardiff alone. The system of granting substantial bursaries to individual artists or of sponsoring large commissions for public places, is also financed by the Welsh Arts Council. Even the enterprise of artistic groups like the Association of Artists and Designers in Wales, which provides studio space for some of its members, is supported by the Council.

Yet, in another sector, official attitudes towards the arts in Wales have been less than helpful. Of the seven art schools of Wales which contributed to a joint exhibition in 1955, only two, Cardiff and Newport, had retained recognition of degree courses by 1965. The other five — Swansea, Carmarthen, Llanelli, Wrexham and Connah's Quay — were demoted to providing vocational courses and supplying the two survivors with pre-diploma students. And the autonomy, and possibly the standards, of these two have been sacrificed to the official policy of integrating them with other colleges of higher education into larger institutes of general learning. So that, by 1976, there was not one autonomous art school offering high level specialist courses in the whole of Wales — and the old ideal of a national academy remains as remote as ever.

It appears, then, that while art in Wales has prospered enormously in the last 50 years, there is little cause for complacency, particularly as it is, collectively, hermetic and inward-looking. The Welsh Arts Council regularly sends exhibitions around Great Britain but it has no power to invade the international arena, while the British Council is reluctant to promote indigenous Welsh exhibitions for showing abroad. This is left to private enterprise, mainly in the form of *56 Group Wales*, a collection of about twenty individual artists, who are supported by the Welsh Arts Council, but who determine their own policy and elect their own members. It has been said that the group is a rather complacent, exclusive, establishment club — and none too progressive at that — but there is no doubt about its proselytising activities. Since its formation in 1956, it has regularly sent selections of modern Welsh art all over Britain. It also appears to be the only organisation extroverted enough to promote Welsh painting and sculpture abroad. As a result, exhibitions of contemporary Welsh art have been seen in Holland, Ireland, Germany, France and Italy.

This raises the question of national identity in the visual arts and poses the final problem concerning this survey: whether there is a school of modern art that can be unequivocally labelled as Welsh in an international context. There is, as yet, no conclusive evidence to support such a thesis, certainly not enough to convince the British Council which sees Welsh art as a regional offshoot of British Art. And the synthetic attempts by some Welsh artists to graft ancient Celtic forms onto a modernistic idiom do nothing to refute this contention. Nor could any common identity for Welsh art be based on characteristics of the typical Welsh temperament (if such a thing exists), since many artists in Wales are not of Welsh origin. Neither is Welsh subject-matter, as a whole, adequate to sustain a separate category. There is a Welsh literature because there is a Welsh language with its unique formal attributes, but the visual arts operate without the restrictions of national language barriers and, particularly in contemporary Western art, it is not usually possible to determine the origin of a work of art.

In his Reith Lectures of 1955, Nikolas Pevsner attempted to define the Englishness of English art[2]. In the United States during the first half of this century, writers, artists and critics struggled to identify a truly American idiom and believed they succeeded with Abstract Expressionism. But the English argument is entirely retrospective, and hardly touches the twentieth century, while the American case is, in effect, an *a posteriori* definition. Neither thesis is entirely convincing and it is extremely difficult to apply their criteria to art in progress and virtually impossible to apply them to the relatively tiny output of modern art from Wales. It would be more reasonable to paraphrase Jackson Pollock's celebrated dictum about the art of America: 'the idea of an isolated [Welsh] painting ...seems absurd to me, just as the idea of creating a purely [Welsh] mathematics or physics would seem absurd'[3].

So, until time and effort and imagination might identify a recognisably national style, we should regard Welsh art as a small but vigorous tributary to the mainstream of modern art. And this sums up the scope of this survey which is not to establish a case for the recognition of an autonomous Welsh art, but to summarise the activities of outstanding artists — Welsh or foreign — who have worked in Wales, and of Welsh-born artists who have worked outside Wales, from 1850 until the present day.

1. *Welsh Painters, Sculptors and Engravers, 1527–1911*. Rev. T. Mardy Rees. Caernarvon, 1912.
(Rees was equally simplistic in his analysis of style: 'Ecstatic joy alone can account for the superb reproductions of some of the Welsh painters and sculptors'.)

2. Published by the Architectural Press in 1956 under the title: *The Englishness of English Art*.

3. Jackson Pollock: 'A Statement on his paintings'. *Art and Architecture* LX I., February 1944.

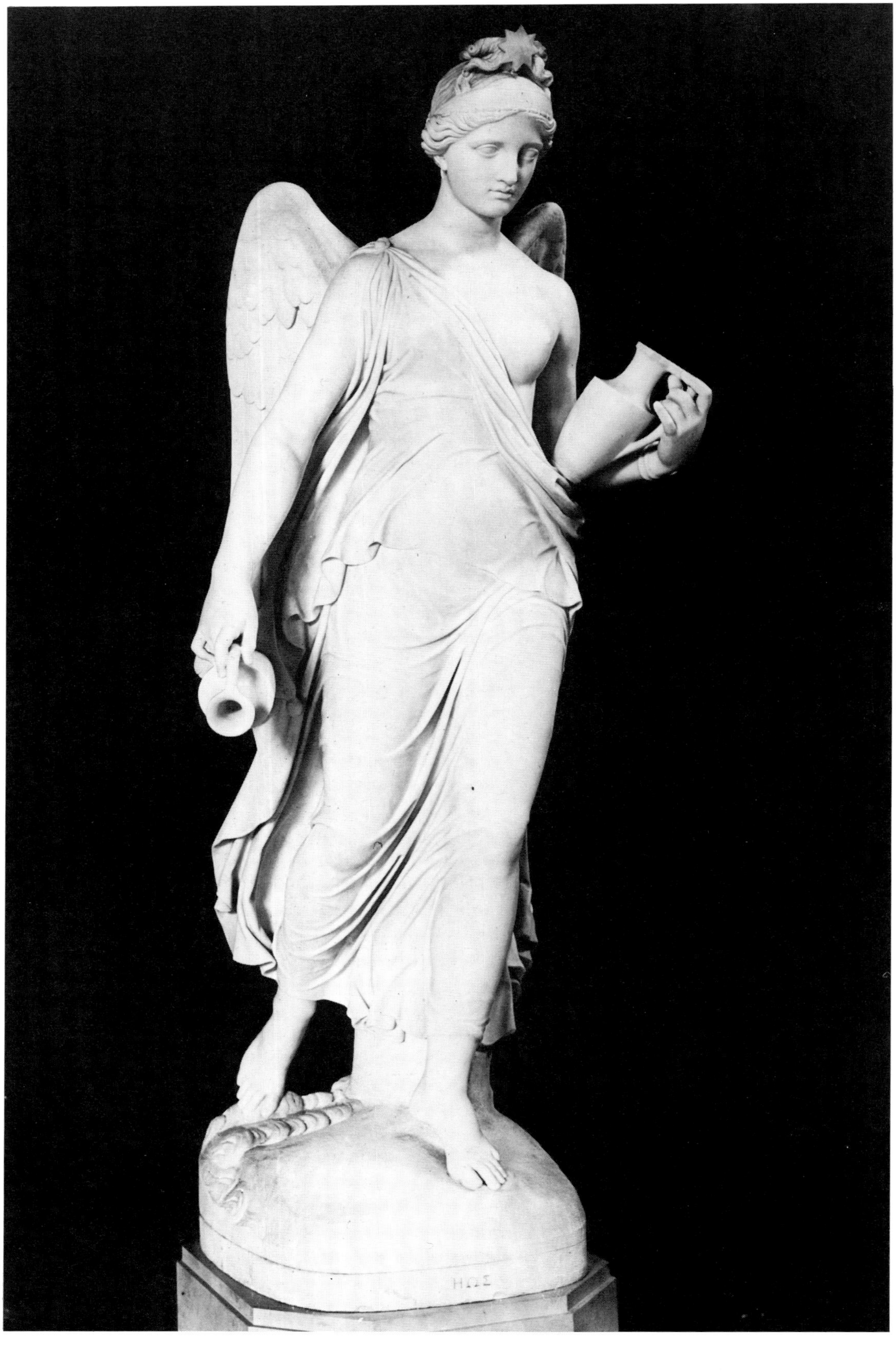

THE NINETEENTH CENTURY

Chapter One

In the second half of the nineteenth century, British artists achieved a status in society unparalleled before or since. Frederick Leighton, PRA, was the first and last painter to be made a lord, and his pictures sold for vast sums. In London, Leighton, G.F.Watts, William Burges, Luke Fildes and other successful artists and architects built themselves studio-mansions in the Melbury Road area of Kensington. At the beginning of the period, Rome was still the centre of European art, and its leading light was John Gibson, the neo-classical sculptor, once described as 'a God in his studio'. Gibson's studio was the fashionable cultural venue of Rome, and his circle included the young Leighton, Thackeray, Robert Browning and his wife Elizabeth, as well as assorted British and Italian aristocrats. In Wales, meanwhile, there was a forlorn struggle to found a national academy of arts; but there was no money, and those eminent artists who might have become founder-members had all migrated to London or Rome.

1. John Gibson 1790 - 1866
Aurora (1848) Marble height 1.75m
National Museum of Wales

Born near Conwy, Gibson often referred to himself as 'John of Conwy'. Towards the end of his life he declared, 'I am a member of eleven academies, also of the Legion of Honour - I am a Welshman'. Gibson was the last of the great neo-classical sculptors. He had worked in Canova's studio in Rome for three years, and had been helped and advised by Thorwaldson. This statue belonged to his Welsh patron, Mr. Sandbach, who also owned his 'Hunter and Dog', now in the National Museum of Wales. In 1861, Sandbach also commissioned a large marble relief of the subject of 'Christ Blessing the Children'.

In the 1850s and 60s, the most eminent sculptor of modern times (according to his obituary in the *Art Journal* for 1866) was a Welshman. He was John Gibson, born at Y Gyffin, near Conwy, who at the age of nine was sent to Liverpool to find his fortune. There he was apprenticed to a sculptor, a position that required much effort and little imagination. Gibson, however, was ambitious and gradually began to produce his own work in his own time, and to study anatomy with a surgeon, Dr Vose. Gibson acquired a first-rate, indeed a first-hand, knowledge of anatomy for he admitted that, with other students, he went grave-robbing in search of specimens.

1 In Liverpool, he also moved into the more intellectual circle of William Roscoe, a
patron and collector of art, who recommended the young Welshman to Fuseli at the
Royal Academy schools in London . This was Gibson's first step on the road to success
for, after his period at the Royal Academy, Fuseli recommended him, in turn, to Flaxman
and Canova, the two neo-classical sculptors then both at the height of their fame and it
was Flaxman who directed Gibson towards Rome. In Rome, Gibson spent three years in
Canova's studio before setting up his own studio under the advice of Thorwaldson.

With these influences, and with his experience of anatomy, it was not surprising that Gibson should become a convinced neo-classicist. He carved the statues of both Peel and Huskisson garbed in togas: 'the human figure concealed under a frock coat is not a fit subject for sculpture' he declared. Taking the principles of neo-classicism even further, to their obvious conclusion, he believed that modern marble statuary should be coloured, in imitation of that of ancient Greece.

Gibson produced a coloured statue of Queen Victoria for the grand staircase of
2 Buckingham Palace, and two painted figures of Pandora, though his most famous work
in this medium was his *Tinted Venus*. Starting in 1833, he carved and coloured at least five
versions of this figure, working on them until his death in 1866. 'Here is a little nearer
approach to life', he said of them, suggesting that his neo-classicism was taking a turn
towards naturalism. The version illustrated here was exhibited with great pomp at the
London International Exhibition of 1862, where it was displayed in a Greek temple
specially designed by Owen Jones, and where it caused a sensation.

By 1850, Gibson had spent 32 years in Rome, and he was to pass the remaining 16
years of his life there. They were years that were both prolific and profitable, for he
3 amassed a personal fortune, leaving £32,000 and the contents of his studio to the Royal
Academy 'that the students might benefit'. In Rome he knew two fellow-contrymen,
Penry Williams and Thomas Brigstocke, and it appears that they formed a
4 Welsh-speaking clique there. It is recorded, for instance, that Cardinal Mezzofanti, who
admired Brigstocke's work, offered to teach him Italian if the painter would teach him
Welsh in return.

Brigstocke stayed only 10 years in Rome, but Gibson and Williams remained close and faithful friends. Together they shared the dangers and excitements of Garibaldi's *Risorgimento*, Gibson nursed Williams through the frightening experience of an eye disease, while Williams attended Gibson through his last, fatal illness. And because he was a member of the Legion d'Honneur, Gibson was given a full military funeral by the French in Rome.

Penry Williams, the house-painter's son from Merthyr Tydfil who was taken up by the Crawshays of Cyfarthfa, passed the greater part of his life in Rome — nearly 60 years. In his Roman period, corrupted perhaps by his own facility and academic training,
5 Williams painted rather stereotyped, topographical views of Rome and the Campagna. These are more ambitious than his earlier, Welsh paintings, and more in the spirit of the second half of the nineteenth century. But he never again attained the freshness of vision or the tenderness that had enlivened his paintings of the ironworks and the workers of Cyfarthfa, nor did he match the intensity to be found in the small, meticulous watercolours of his native town, Merthyr Tydfil.

These artists, however, represent the end of a tradition, and the new feeling of the 1850s was to be found in the work of the Pre-Raphaelites. The principal artists of the Brotherhood and their followers used both figures and landscape with equal emphasis in their work, but the literary-historical content was rarely concerned with Wales, while their preferences in landscape were not for the sublime heroics of untamed nature, but for the ordered details of a more domesticated countryside.

Some landscape painters with affiliations to the Pre-Raphaelite ideals did work in
6 Wales, often following the influence of David Cox. George Pryce Boyce and Alfred William Hunt were two such artists, and it was during a sketching trip through Wales that Boyce first met Cox. Hunt initially painted dramatic, panoramic views of the Welsh mountains in the manner of Cox, but a more modern feeling, invested with careful detail, appears in his quieter, pastoral scenes.

With easier travel into the heart of Wales, the laborious and lengthy peregrinations of the pre-railway era were replaced by the custom of short holiday visits. From Boyce's diaries, it appears that Betws-y-Coed was a favourite gathering place, and he mentions a meeting with William Burges and his relations there one summer.

William Dyce was another painter who spent working holidays in Wales, and into
7 topographical mountain views he interpolated 'narrative' figures. These were sometimes elevated in sentiment, with such titles as *The Man of Sorrows* or *David in the Wilderness*, though they were, on occasion, more deliberately quaint, showing figures in Welsh costumes. Perhaps this was because, as Dyce said, 'I expected to pay for the trip with my paintings'.

One native Welsh painter who was close to the Pre-Raphaelites through his friendship with Ford Madox-Brown, was Henry Mark Anthony. Although he was born in Manchester, Anthony came of Welsh parents who moved to Cowbridge during his youth. He had a considerable influence on Madox-Brown who described him in his diaries as
8 '...like Constable only better by far'. From such a description, it is clear that Anthony's style was broader in handling than was usual with the Pre-Raphaelite masters. It had, in fact, been formed during his period with the Barbizon school in the 1830s, when he had been particularly friendly with, and influenced by, Corot. Though he was never a committed Pre-Raphaelite, Anthony was generally admired by Ruskin and the Brotherhood and he was considered by William Michael Rossetti to be 'the outstanding landscape painter in England'.

Probably the most famous Pre-Raphaelite painting with a Welsh connection is Dante Gabriel Rossetti's triptych *David Rex*, commissioned for Llandaff Cathedral in

9 1856. In March of that year, Rossetti accepted the commission and wrote to Llandaff asking £400 for the three panels (£200 for the centre, and £100 each for the wings). Periodically throughout the rest of the 1850s he was either waiting for, or asking for, money from the cathedral authorities or was, once more, about to start work on the triptych.

In spite of its troubled and spasmodic gestation, the alterpiece is one of the most successful of Rossetti's large paintings. Although the three parts do not fit together quite comfortably in stylistic terms, each panel is accomplished in its own right. It also contains, as was the habit among the Pre-Raphaelites, portraits of the artist's friends as the principal characters, including William Morris and his wife Jane.

Apart from Llandaff Cathedral, the direct influence of William Morris and his partners was not widespread in Wales, probably because there was proportionately less church building or restoration in the nineteenth century than was the case in England. And, even then, much of Morris and Company's work for the cathedral was destroyed by German bombs during the second world war. Burne-Jones's six ceramic panels on *The Creation of the World* were not specifically designed for the cathedral but were a later
10 donation. He did, however, design some stained glass windows for Llandaff and produced other commissions in the same medium, notably for the parish church at Hawarden.

But the greatest concentration of the Pre-Raphaelite influence in Wales is to be found in the two architectural masterpieces of William Burges: Cardiff Castle and Castell Coch, both commissioned by the third Marquess of Bute. As a young man, Burges was an enthusiastic member of the Pre-Raphaelite circle and was particularly friendly with Ford Madox-Brown and Dante Gabriel Rossetti. Yet though he admired Rossetti's Llandaff triptych for its intrinsic merits, he considered it unsuitable for its setting and made no attempt to commission work from his friend. Burges also had firm ideas about the work he wanted from his artists, as was evident in an earlier commission of his, the refurbishing of Worcester College Chapel in Oxford, when he rejected Millais's designs for the stained glass windows.

So it is unfortunate for Wales that, by the 1870s, when he was occupied with the decorations of the two castles, Burges could neither afford nor accommodate the work of his more talented contemporaries. Generally speaking, all the mural paintings in the castles are mediocre works by Westlake, Lonsdale and other relatively obscure artists. As
11 some compensation, however, the cycle of murals in the banqueting hall of Cardiff Castle is one of the largest and most systematic treatments of an historical theme by a nineteenth - century medievalist.

The total effect of Burges' imaginative reconstruction of thirteenth-century domestic interiors is breathtaking. Almost every surface, every piece of furniture, is covered with historical, allegorical or moral lessons with innumerable figures, birds, beasts, reptiles, plants and abstract decoration distributed lavishly throughout the interiors. Inevitably, the result is less a reproduction of genuine medieval taste than an embodiment of high Victorian design. Burges' early attachment to the theories of Ruskin and the Pre-Raphaelites, combined with his admiration for Pugin and Viollet-le-Duc, resulted in a style that is a unique blend of detailed nineteenth-century naturalism, medievalist fantasy and historical reconstruction.

Where the fine arts are applied to the decorations in the two castles, it is the
12 sculpture that is outstanding, and it forms what is probably the largest collection of a late
Pre-Raphaelite style of sculpture in Britain. After Woolner's period in Australia there
were few sculptors working in the Pre-Raphaelite idiom, and even fewer with any
individual talent, so that Burges was fortunate to acquire the almost exclusive services of
Thomas Nicholls, who became the architect's favourite sculptor.

Very little is known about Nicholls, except that he was a student at the Royal
13 Academy School of Architecture, and exhibited at the Royal Academy in 1864. A
retiring but conscientious man, he seems to have had little more status than that of a
jobbing architectural sculptor. Yet his work is a cut above that of other stone carvers of
the gothic revival and though at times insipid, at its best it captures some of the sentiment
and poetry often concealed in nineteenth-century medievalism and naturalism.

By the 1870s, the decorative work was in progress at both castles though this, in turn, was an end rather than a beginning. For by that time the Gothic Revival and the Pre-Raphaelite movement had both passed their peaks, and 1874 saw the first exhibition of Impressionism in Paris. There was also a small exhibition of Impressionism in London in 1882, the year that marked the first birthday of the Royal Cambrian Academy.

The academy started with high hopes but was beset by frustrating realities. With the
failure of its plans for a comprehensive national academy of the arts in Cardiff, it moved
14 to Conwy in 1884. It never became a teaching institution and its exhibitions have been
almost entirely of members' work. In Conwy, through the generosity of Lord Mostyn, it
was granted the lease of Plas Mawr at a peppercorn rent. Plas Mawr is a magnificent
Elizabethan building, virtually unchanged throughout the centuries, and it has remained
the headquarters of the Royal Cambrian Academy since 1884. In its limited way, the RCA
has modelled itself on the RA in London, and is now both a charity and a limited
company. Its annual exhibitions (which are still hung in the ancient rooms of Plas Mawr)
have had little or no effect on the development of modern art in Wales, and it has
remained academic in every sense of the word. Even Impressionism made a late
appearance there, though the same could be said of the rest of Wales.

There is one remarkable exception to this generalisation and it marks the high point
of Impressionism in Wales. This was Alfred Sisley's visit to Glamorgan in 1897. He came
under the patronage of his friend, the industrialist François Depeaux, and he painted at
15 Penarth and on the Gower peninsula. Sisley ignored the more grandiose features of the
south Wales landscape, preferring the less spectacular coastline.

He painted at least five pictures at Penarth, all showing the sea, and with the pier,
the cliffs or the shipping to enliven it. He was clearly enchanted by Penarth and wrote to
16 his friend, the critic Gustave Geffroy: 'I am materially very well off here: "in lodgings"
with worthy people, the climate is very mild, even too warm these present days ... I hope
to be able to tear myself away from what I see around me and return home ... around the
month of October'.

From Penarth, Sisley moved to Langland Bay on the Gower coast, where he stayed at the Osborne Hotel. Here he completed thirteen paintings, showing Langland Bay,

Lady's Cove within the bay, and Storr Rock within the cove. He caught all the subtle effects of light in all its changing summer moods: *Before the Storm, Sea Rising, South-West Gale, The Wave, Morning.*

17 Sisley's Welsh period occurred during the last two years of his life, when he was already ill with cancer, and the paintings and drawings produced then form the last important group of works, his first and last attempt to paint the sea. They mark his nearest approach to pure Impressionism, and it is interesting to compare them with his earlier paintings and to observe the general loosening of technique, the growing disregard for detail and the move towards a minimal composition, already apparent at that time in the work of Monet.

In effect, the Welsh summer of Alfred Sisley coincided with both the end of the nineteenth century and the first stirrings of modern art. But before modernism took hold in Wales, the old style had one last monumental fling.

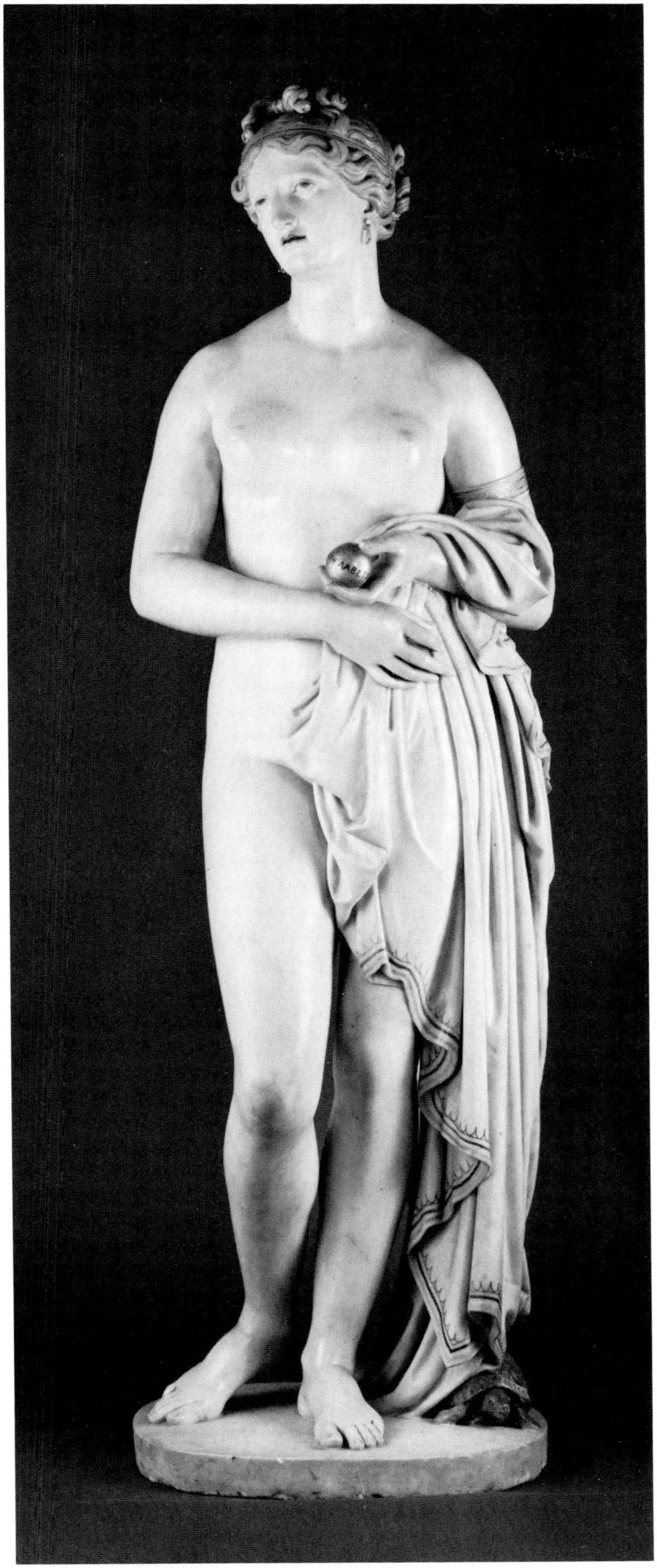

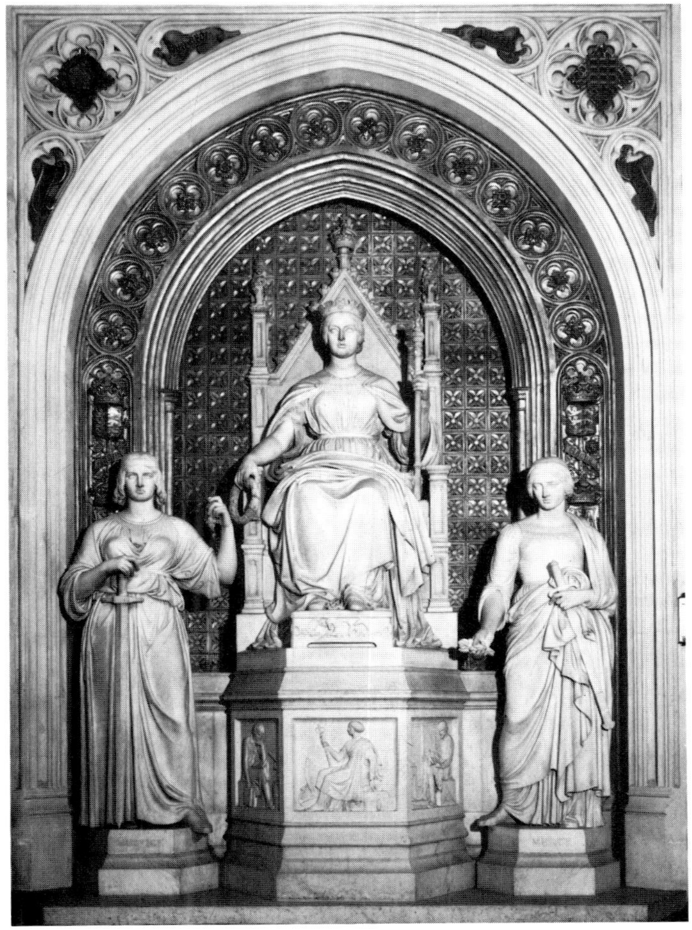

2. John Gibson
Tinted Venus (1851 - 3) Painted marble life size
Walker Art Gallery, Liverpool
Lord Lytton once said of Gibson, 'In you we behold the three great and long undetected principles of Grecian Art, Simplicity, Calm and Concentration'. Commissioned by Robert Preston of Liverpool, this version of the Tinted Venus was completed in 1853. It shows the goddess, coloured in naturalistic flesh tones, holding an apple inscribed, 'To the Most beautiful'. On the tortoise is written (in Greek), 'Gibson made me in Rome'.

3. John Gibson
Queen Victoria Flanked by Justice and Mercy (1856)
Marble total height 2.44 m
House of Lords, London
Commissioned by Queen Victoria, and set in an interior designed by Pugin, this sculptural group dominates the Prince's Chamber in the House of Lords. On 4 September 1856, Gibson wrote to his friend, Mrs Bunbury, '...they are now placing my statue of the Queen at the Parliament House and two other statues belonging to the group have just arrived from Rome and I am obliged to go there often until the affair is all finished. I fear this business will keep me late in Town indeed it may prevent me from fulfilling my promise to go to Wales'.

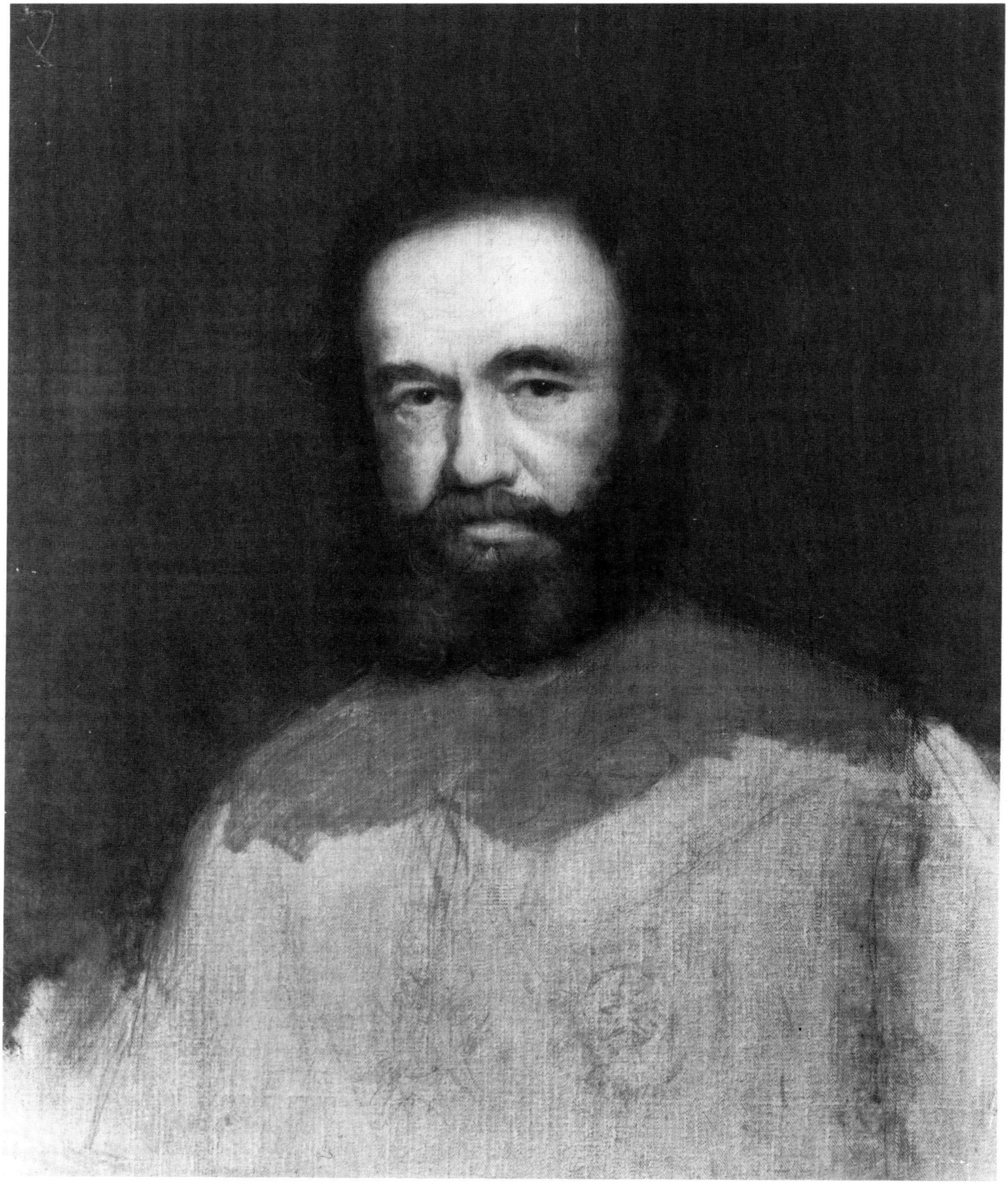

4. Thomas Brigstocke 1809 - 91
General Sir James Outram, Bt, 1803 - 63 (c.1863)
Oil on canvas 69.5 x 50.5cm
National Portrait Gallery
Born in Carmarthen, Brigstocke studied at the Royal Academy Schools in London before going on to Italy. He spent about ten years in Rome where, together with John Gibson and Penry Williams, he was part of a Welsh group with eminent friends and patrons. Brigstocke later returned to England and thereafter painted mainly portraits and animal studies in the manner of Landseer. Sir James Outram was one of the heroes of the relief of Lucknow in 1857.

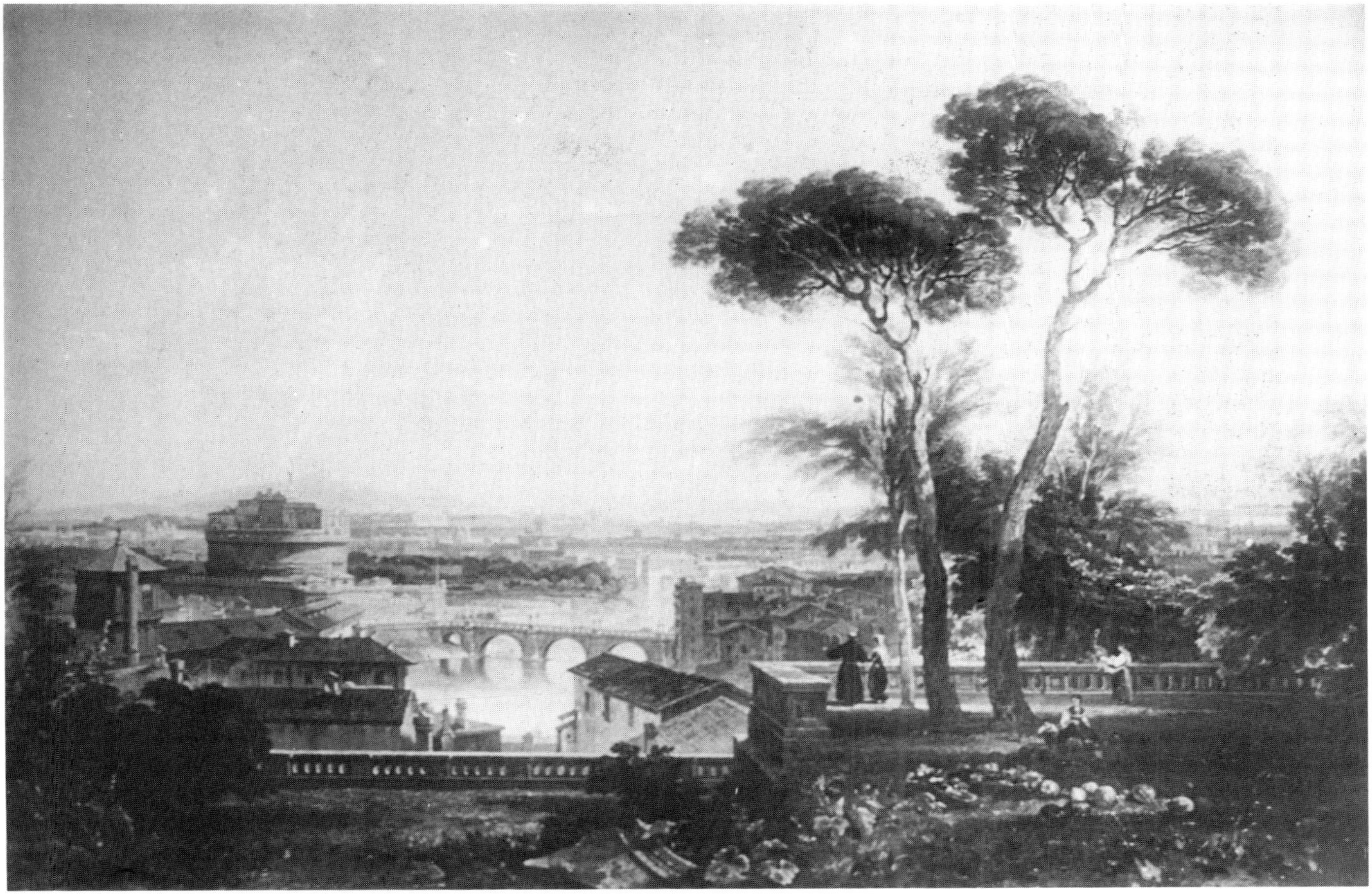

5. Penry Williams 1800 - 85
View of Rome (undated) Oil on canvas 21 x 31 cm
National Museum of Wales

Like his friend Gibson, Williams became an Italianate Welshman, spending the greater part of his life in Rome. During his sixty years there, Williams painted festivals, famous monuments and genre scenes, as well as landscapes that had been depicted by a fellow Welshman, Richard Wilson, a hundred years before. Williams's landscapes are less 'ideal' than Wilson's and are coloured by the intervening discoveries of the Nazarenes and the Pre-Raphaelites.

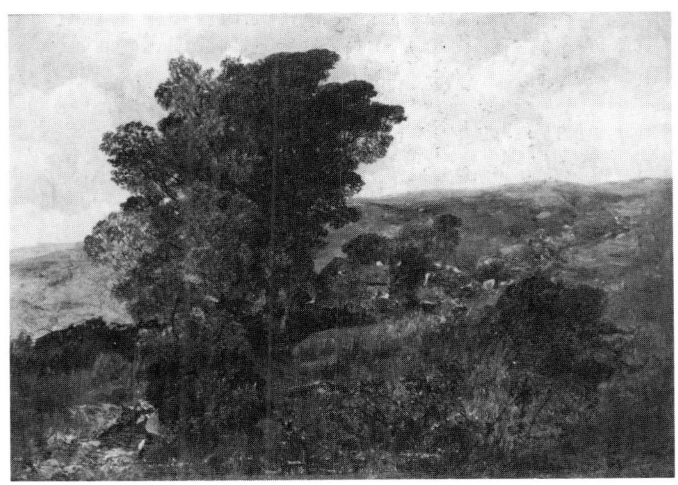

6. Alfred William Hunt 1830 - 96
View of Nantlle, Gwynedd (1855) Oil on canvas 26 x 36 cm
Ashmolean Museum, Oxford

Hunt was born in Liverpool and became one of the flourishing group of artists who worked there during the second half of the nineteenth century. His earlier works dealt with the dramatic power of the north Wales landscape, particularly around Snowdon, and are outstanding for their sublime qualities. Hunt's work subsequently drew high praise from Edmund Gosse and Roger Fry, as well as from his contemporary Ruskin, who described one of Hunt's Caernarvonshire scenes as 'the best landscape I have seen in the [RA] exhibition for many a day - uniting most subtle finish and watchfulness of nature with a real and rare power of composition'.

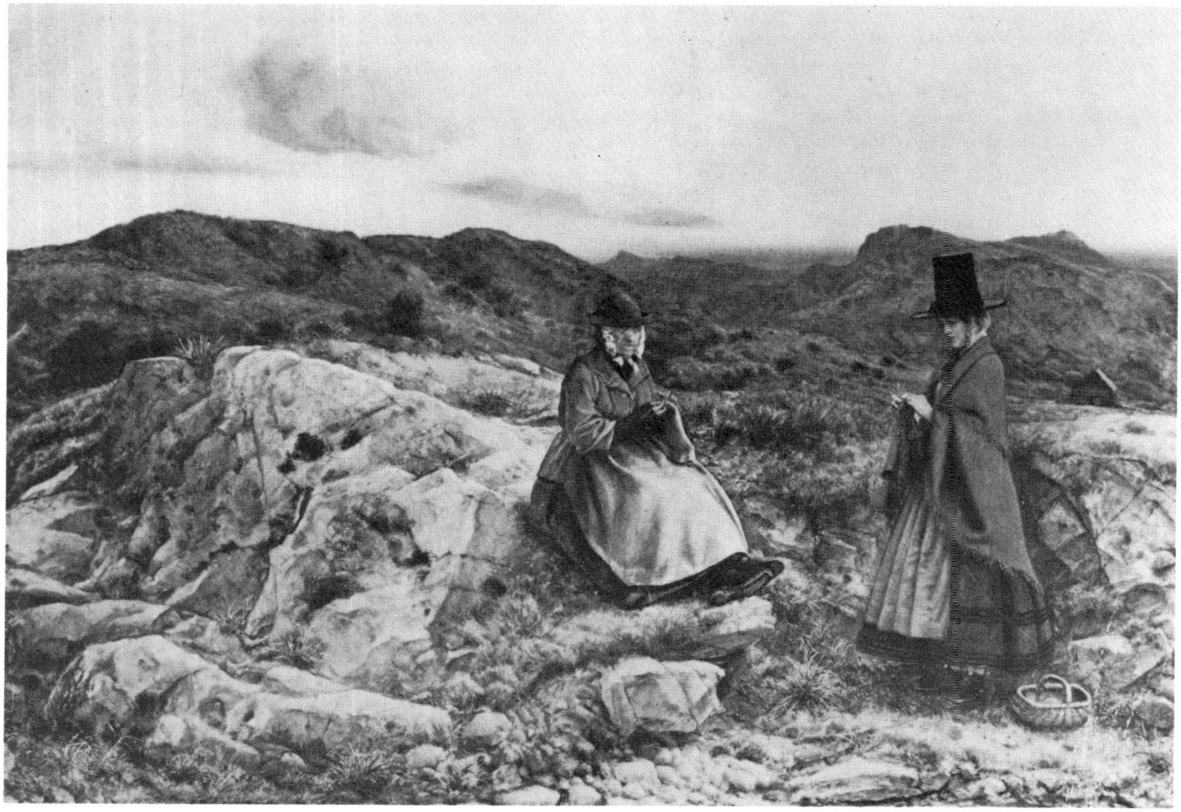

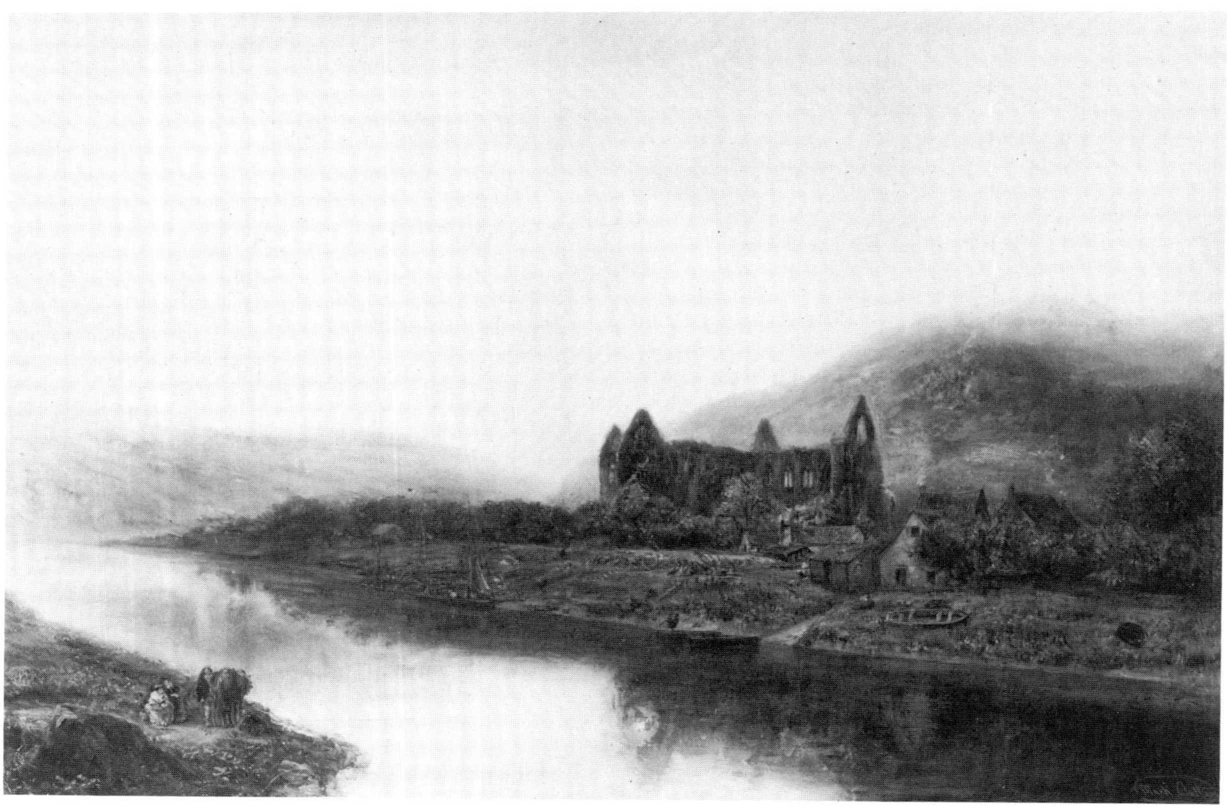

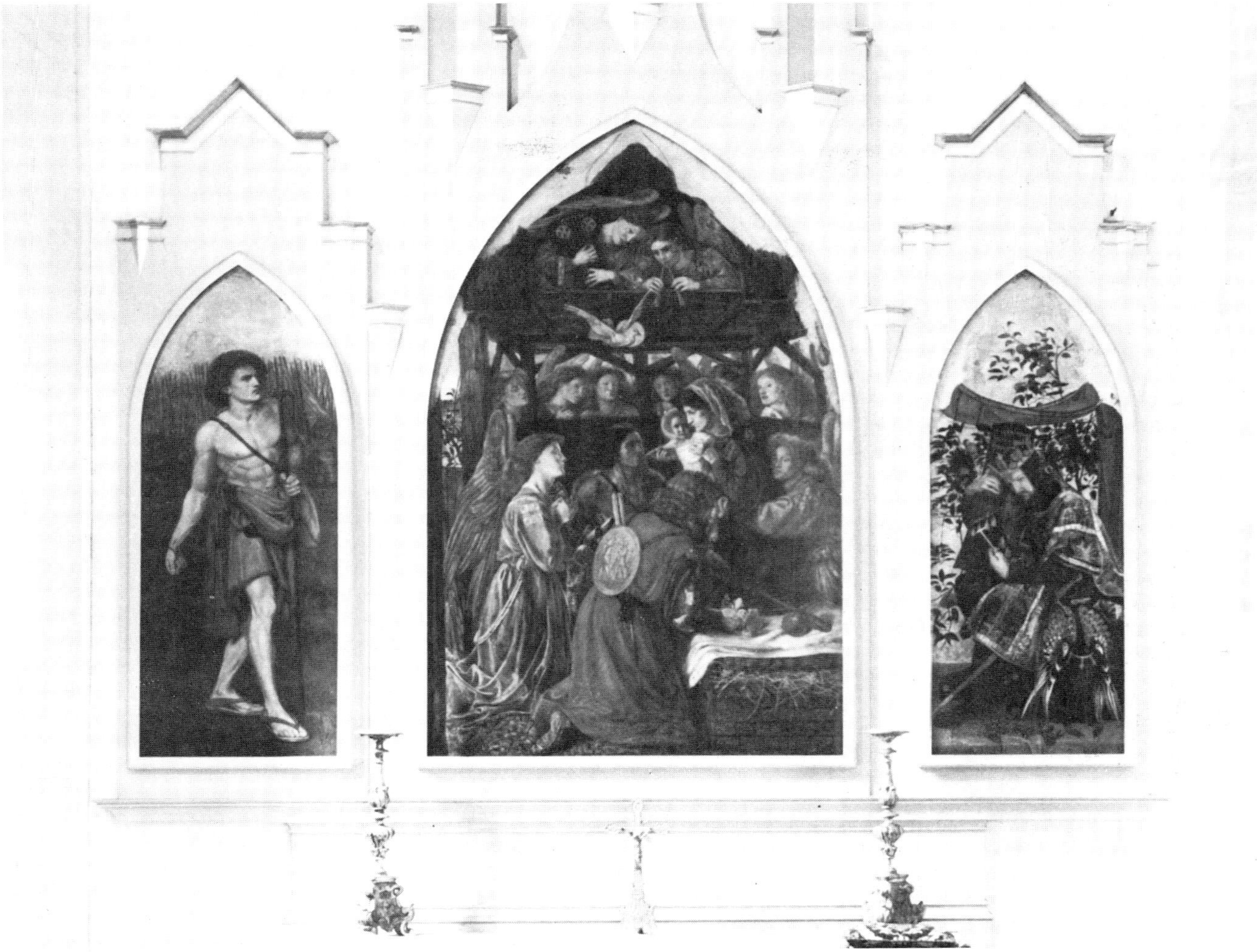

7. William Dyce 1806 - 64
Welsh Landscape with Figures (1860) Oil on board
35.3 x 50.5 cm
Private Collection
Dyce is often regarded as the link between the Nazarenes and the Pre-Raphaelites, and in his later work developed a detailed form of Pre-Raphaelitism. His masterpiece in this style is 'Pegwell Bay, Kent', though he painted landscapes in both Scotland and Wales. Of the two he preferred Wales and its mountains, 'more awful and terrific looking than anything I know of in Scotland'.

8. Henry Mark Anthony 1817 - 86
Tintern Abbey (undated) Oil on canvas 63.5 x 93.5 cm
National Museum of Wales
Although he came of Welsh parents and passed his youth in Cowbridge, Anthony spent much time abroad, and this is one of his rare paintings with a Welsh subject. He lived in France from about 1834 to 1841 and at Barbizon he knew both Corot and Dupré. Anthony's work has an affinity with Dupré's, and his subsequent paintings reflect the influence of the mid-nineteenth century landscape style from Barbizon. He later became close to the Pre-Raphaelites though he never adopted their precise realism but kept the broader handling that he had learnt in France.

9. Dante Gabriel Rossetti 1828 - 82
David Rex (1856) Oil on Panel
Llandaff Cathedral
Now known as The Seed of David (Rossetti himself always referred to it as David Rex), this painting was greatly admired by William Burges, who saw it in various stages of completion in Rossetti's studio. According to tradition, Swinburne posed for the figure in the left panel, though this is now disputed, William Morris sat for the figure in the right panel, while the Madonna in the centrepiece is a portrait of Morris's wife, Janey, with whom Rossetti had a stormy love affair.

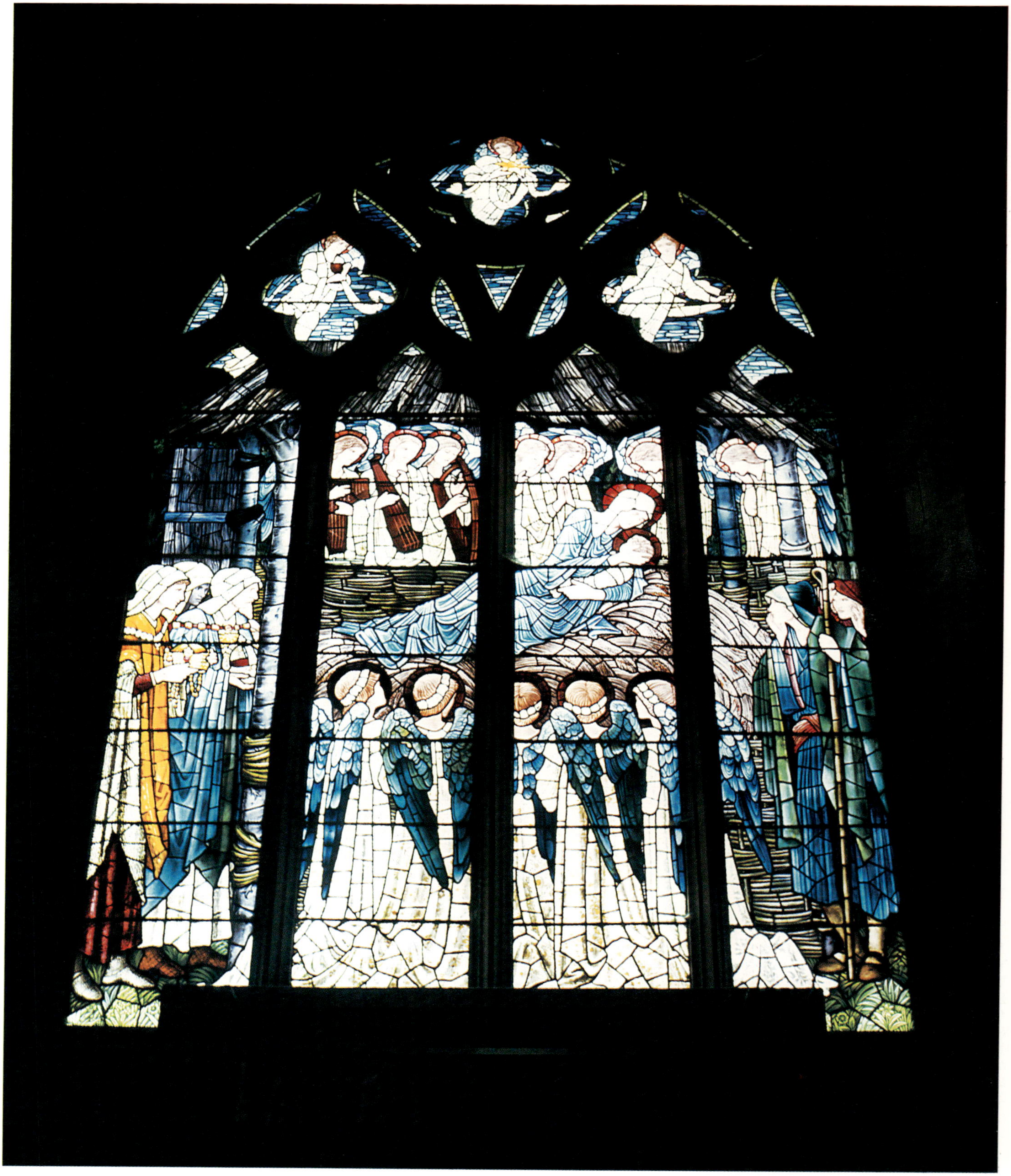

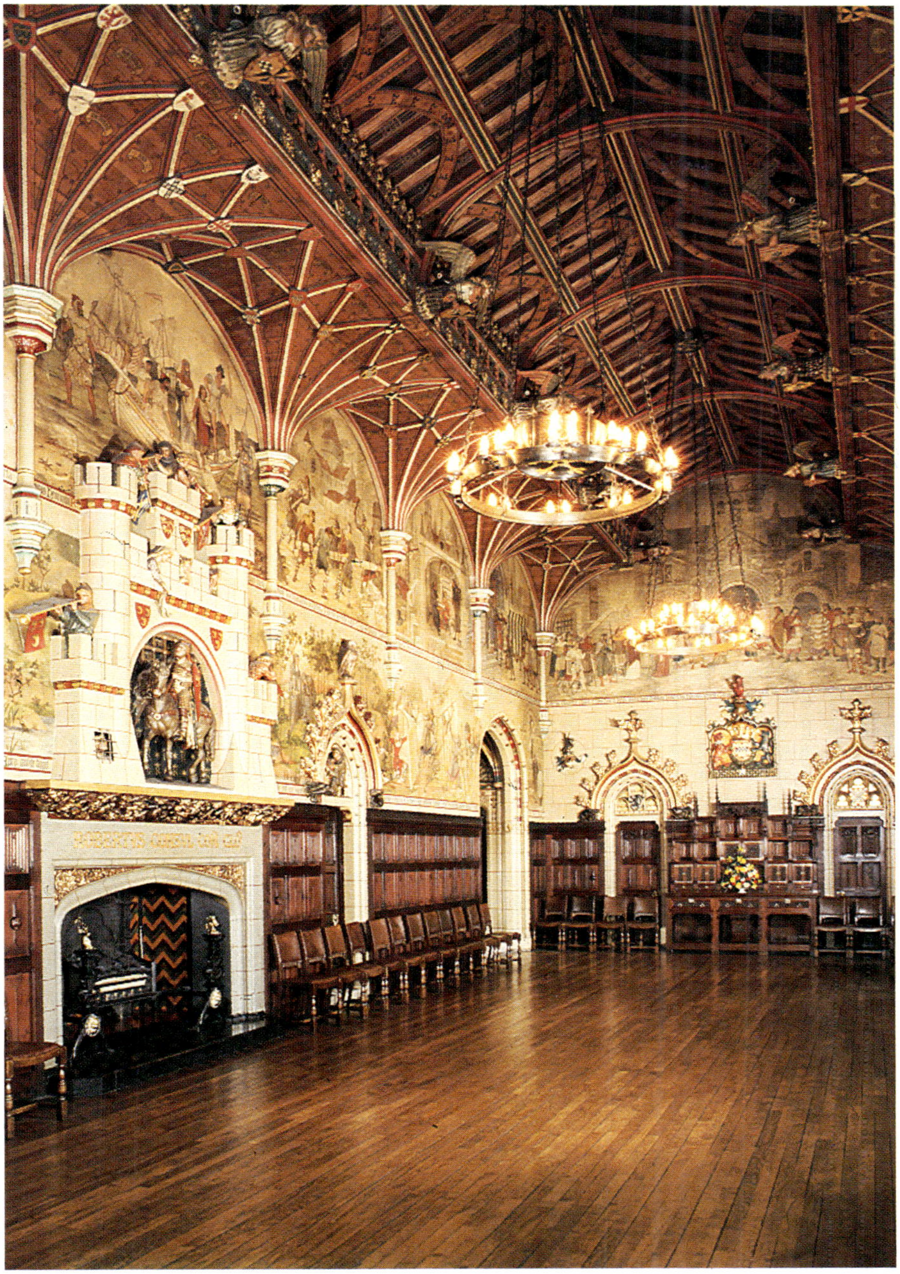

10. Edward Burne-Jones 1833 - 98
The Nativity (1897 - 8) Stained glass
West window St. Deiniol's Church, Hawarden

One of Burne-Jones's last works, this window was designed in 1897 and erected in the following year by Gladstone's children, in commemoration of their father's 'long and splendid life'. The scale of the figures is larger than in the traditional treatment of west windows, while the angels in the upper traceries, larger even than their settings (an unusual and effective device), appear to be looking into the church from the sky outside.

11. Horatio Walter Lonsdale 1844 - 1919
Scenes from the life of Robert Earl of Gloucester (c.1875)
Oil and gold leaf on canvas
Banqueting Hall, Cardiff Castle

These murals, executed by Lonsdale, contain details traceable to the architect, William Burges. These include copies from Viollet-le-Duc's architectural restorations at Carcassone, intended by Burges to be built at Castell Coch, but here inserted as features in the pictorial narrative. No precise date has been found for the murals, but in Burges's letters and drawings there are several instructions to both Lonsdale and Nicholls about the decorative scheme for the hall, and a series of watercolour designs by Lonsdale dated May 1875. Robert of Gloucester was the natural son of Henry 1, and half-brother to Queen Matilda. The murals depict the struggle for the crown of England between Matilda and her brother Stephen, and the part played by Robert.

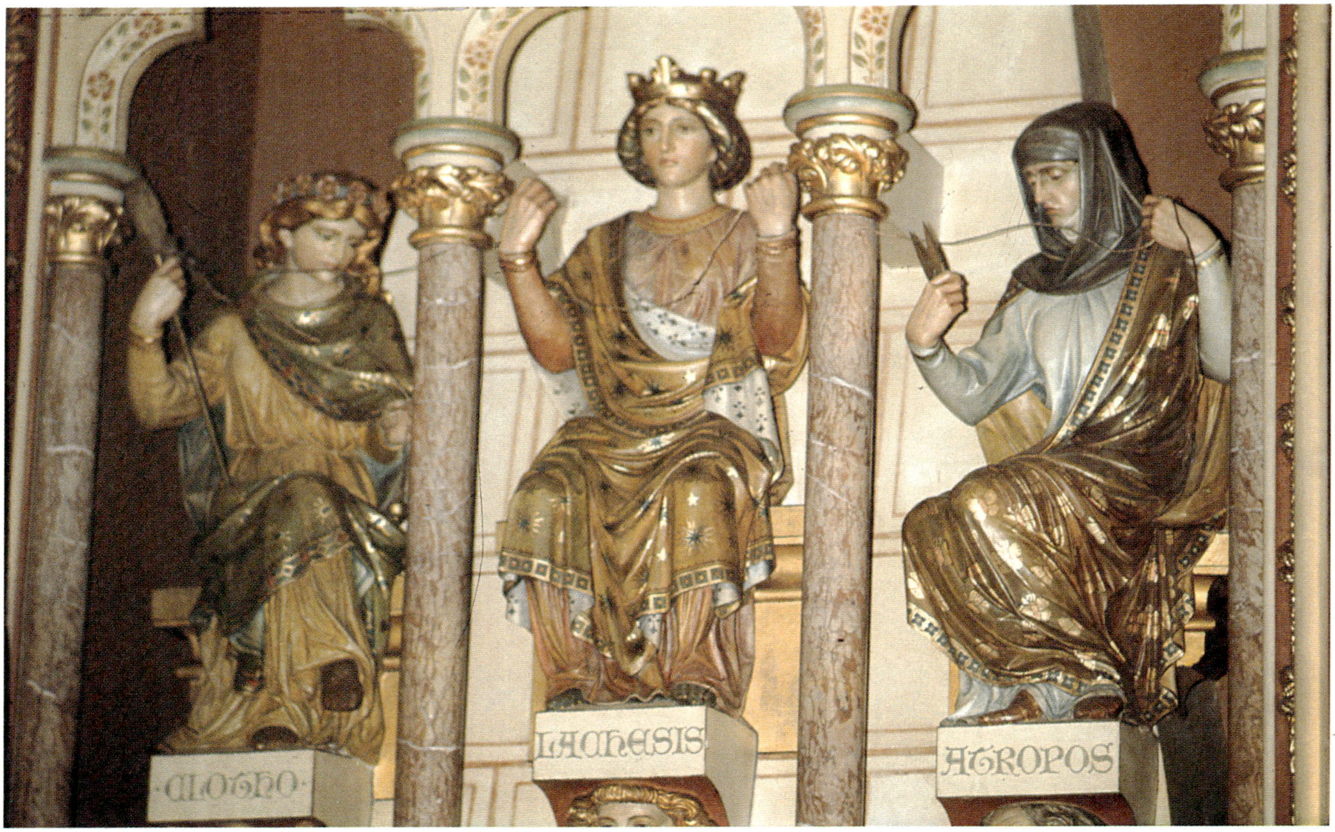

12. Thomas Nicholls 1817 - mid 1890s
The Three Fates (c.1880) Carved and painted stone
Castell Coch, South Glamorgan

The monumental fireplaces (see previous illustration) were a dominant feature of Burges's interiors and often served as a vehicle for allegorical or moralistic story-telling. The designs, with their incongruities of scale between figures and settings, derived from medieval manuscripts which Burges copied in the British Museum. He would frequently dictate the design to Nicholls, about whom little is known, except that he exhibited in the Royal Academy in 1864 and that, apart from the huge body of work he did for Burges, he also worked for Butterfield at St. Augustine's College, Canterbury, and Pearson at St. Augustine's Church, Kilburn.

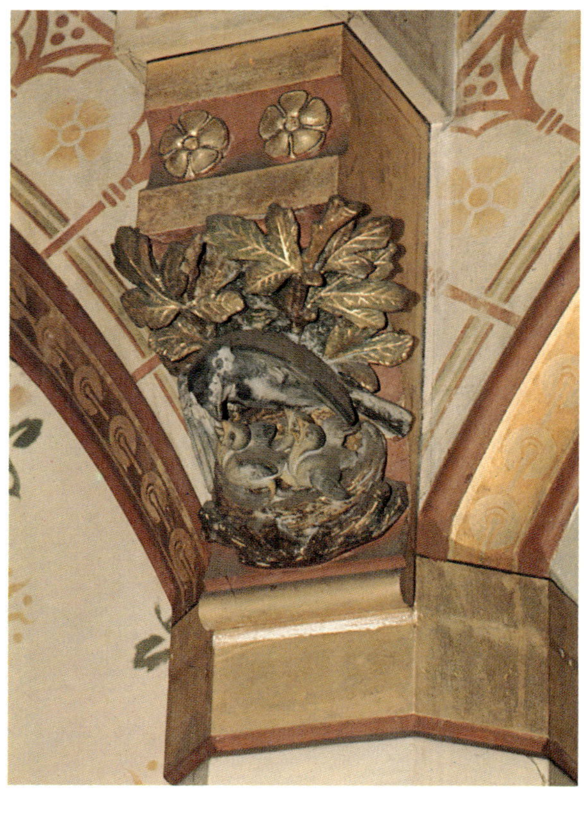

13. Thomas Nicholls
Bird with Fledglings (c.1880) Carved and painted stone corbel
Castell Coch, South Glamorgan

As well as grandiose themes, intended as prompts to elevated conversation, Burges also delighted in simple decorative features, derived from nature and influenced by his friends in the Pre-Raphaelite circle. With these details, which adorn the interiors of his two castles in unrelieved profusion, Nicholls was probably given more freedom of choice and execution.

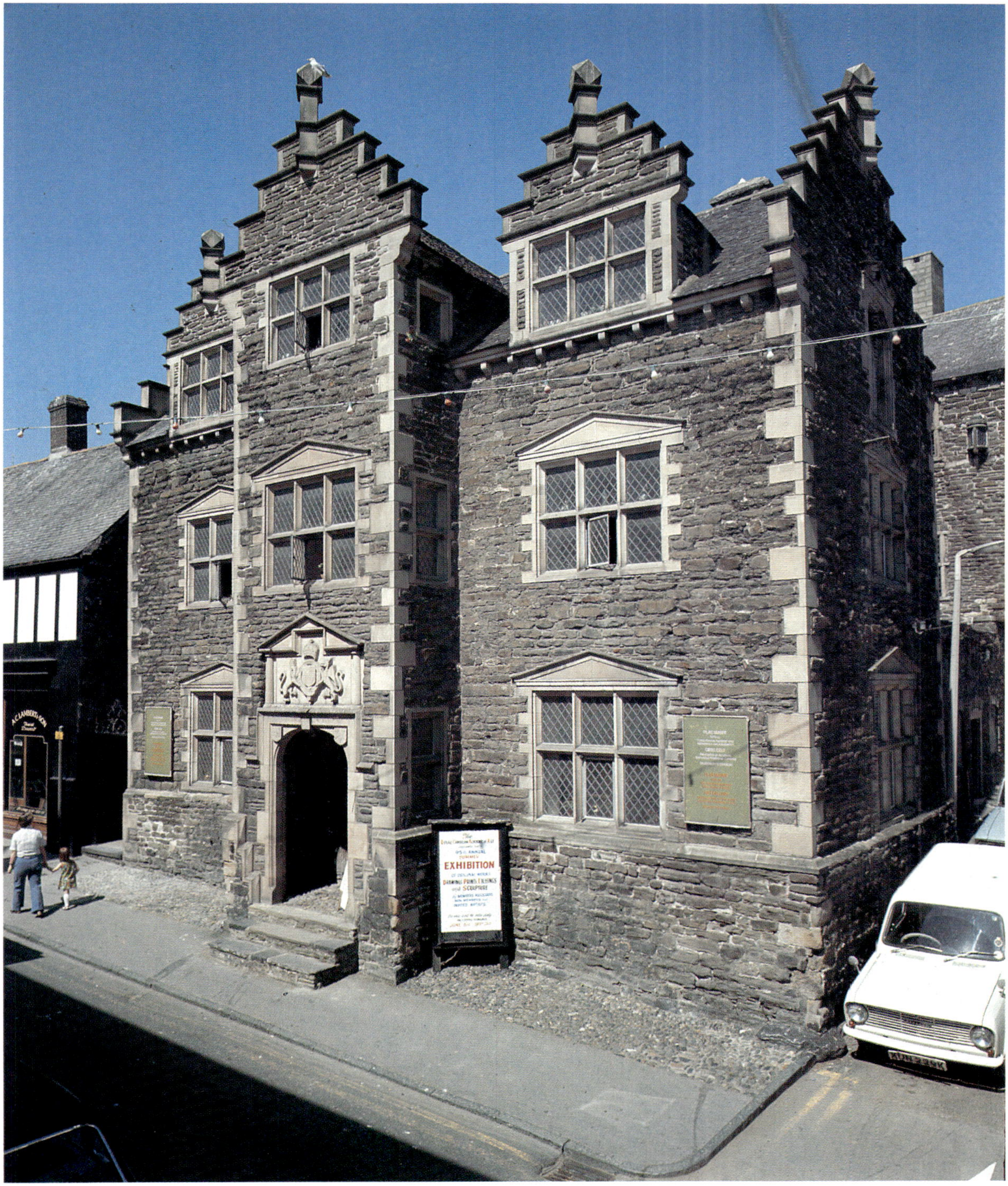

14. Plas Mawr, Conwy
Headquarters of the Royal Cambrian Academy
The Cambrian Academy, founded in 1881, became Royal the following year. Its purpose was to establish in Cardiff an institution similar to the Royal Academy of Arts in London, with studios, galleries, a lecture hall, a concert room and an annual exhibition. All this was to be paid for by a Fine Art Loan Exhibition held in Cardiff in 1884. The exhibition was, financially, a disaster and, in the same year, the Royal Cambrian Academy moved to these premises in Conwy. Here is preserved, in an attenuated form, the original ideals, with art classes during spring and autumn, and an annual exhibition during the summer.

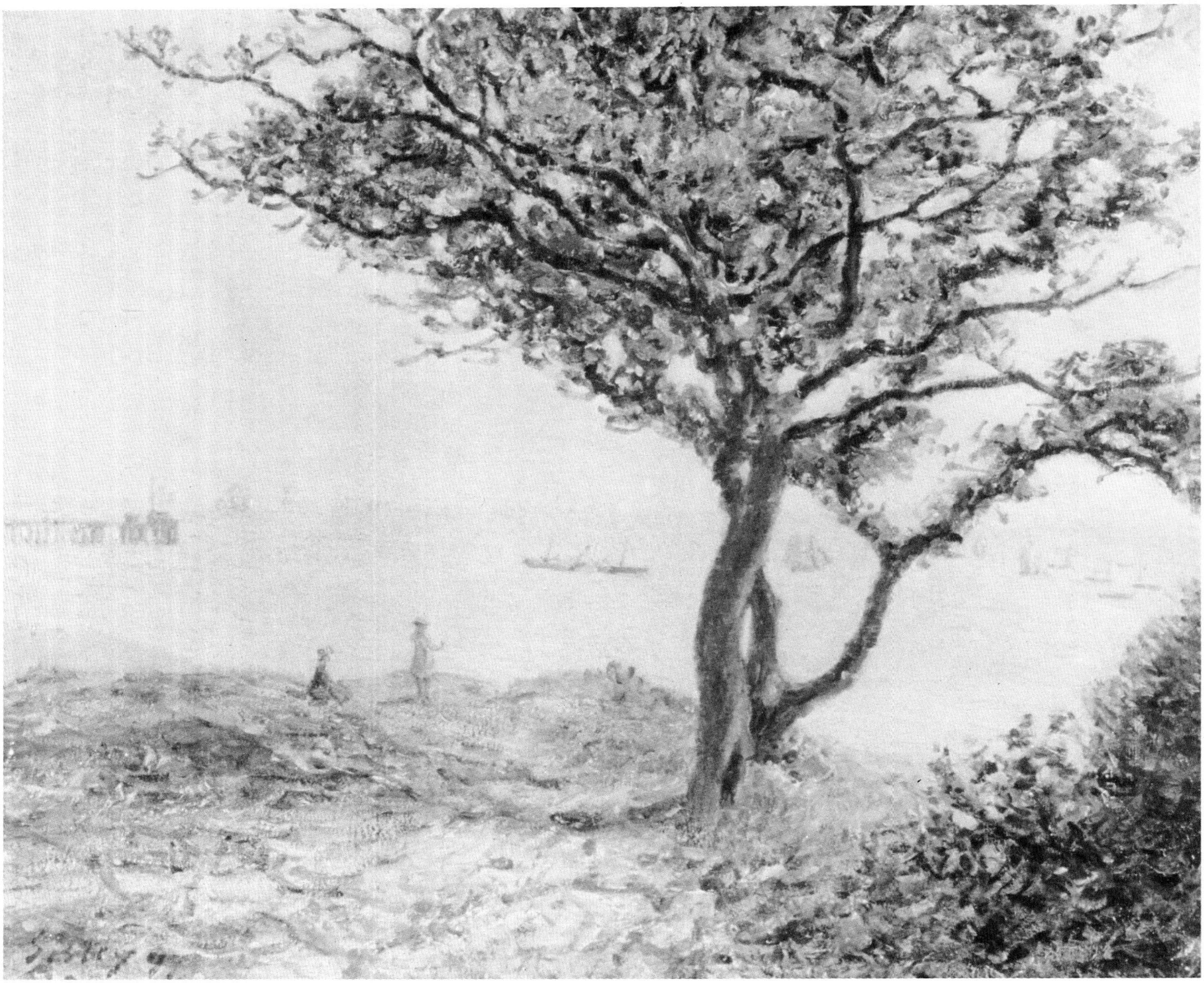

15. Alfred Sisley 1839 - 99
Cardiff Shipping Lane with Penarth Pier (1897) Oil on canvas 54 x 65 cm
Musée Saint-Denis, Reims
Sisley arrived in Penarth about 9 July 1897 and wrote to his friend, the critic Gustave Geffroy, 'The country is pretty and the shipping-lane with the great boats that go in and out of Cardiff is superb...'

16. Alfred Sisley
Bristol Channel, Evening Effect (1897)
Oil on canvas 60.3 x 73 cm
Allen Memorial Art Museum, Oberlin College, Ohio
Another view of the Bristol Channel, taken from the same point on the cliffs at Penarth, this time looking westward towards Sully Island. According to the Daulte Catalogue Raisonné, Sisley painted a total of 17 views of the Welsh coast at Penarth, Langland Bay and Storr Rock in Lady's Cove (Daulte 865 - 881). Sisley also made many preparatory drawings for his Welsh series and one of them, a study for this painting in coloured chalks, is now in the Musée du Petit Palais, Paris.

17. Alfred Sisley
Storr Rock, Lady's Cove, Langland Bay (1897)
Oil on canvas 46 x 61 cm
Musée de Rouen
During his long summer in south Wales, Sisley moved from Penarth to the Gower Peninsula, where he painted and drew many views of Langland Bay in all kinds of weather and with all the subtle and constantly changing effects of light. Whilst there he stayed at the Osborne Hotel and there exists a drawing of the interior of the hotel. From the windows of the hotel (now modernised) it is possible to see the views that fascinated Sisley, and which inspired his first, and last, series of paintings about the sea.

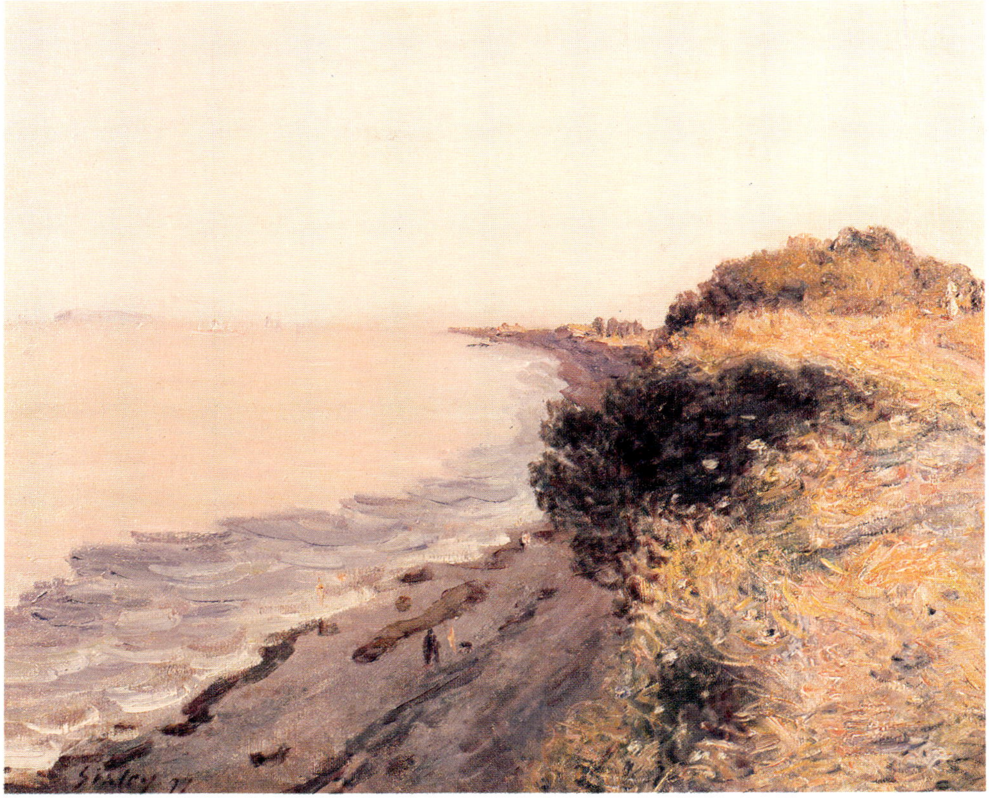

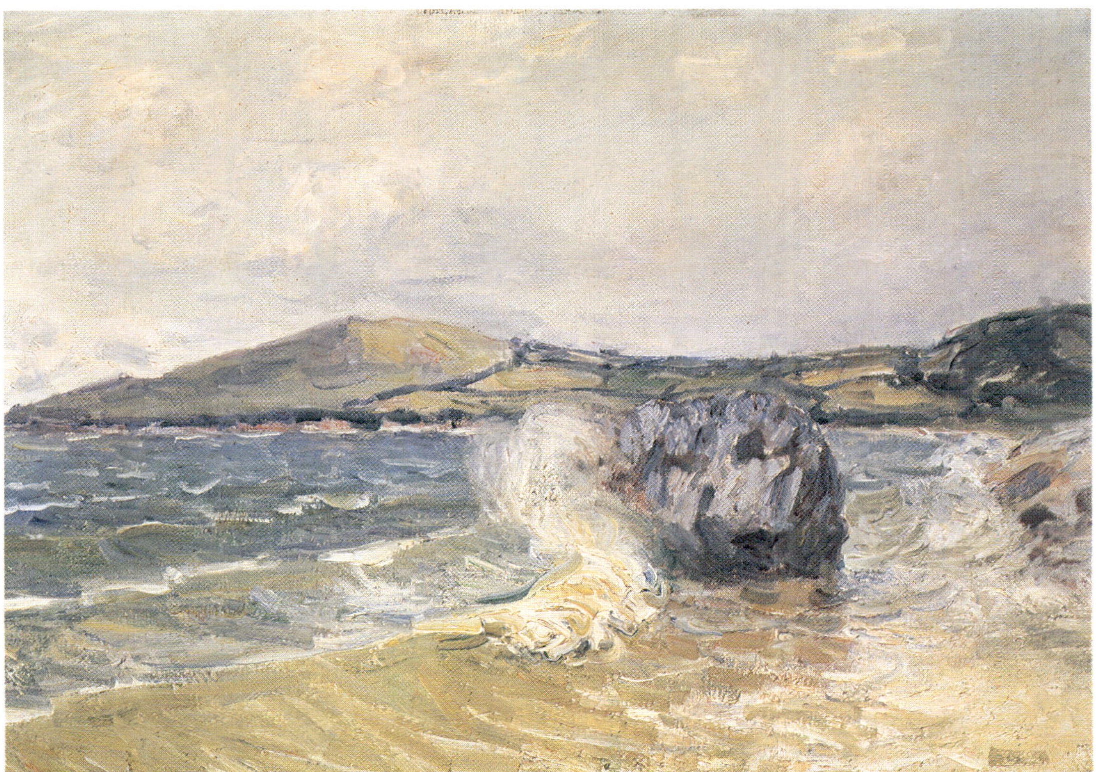

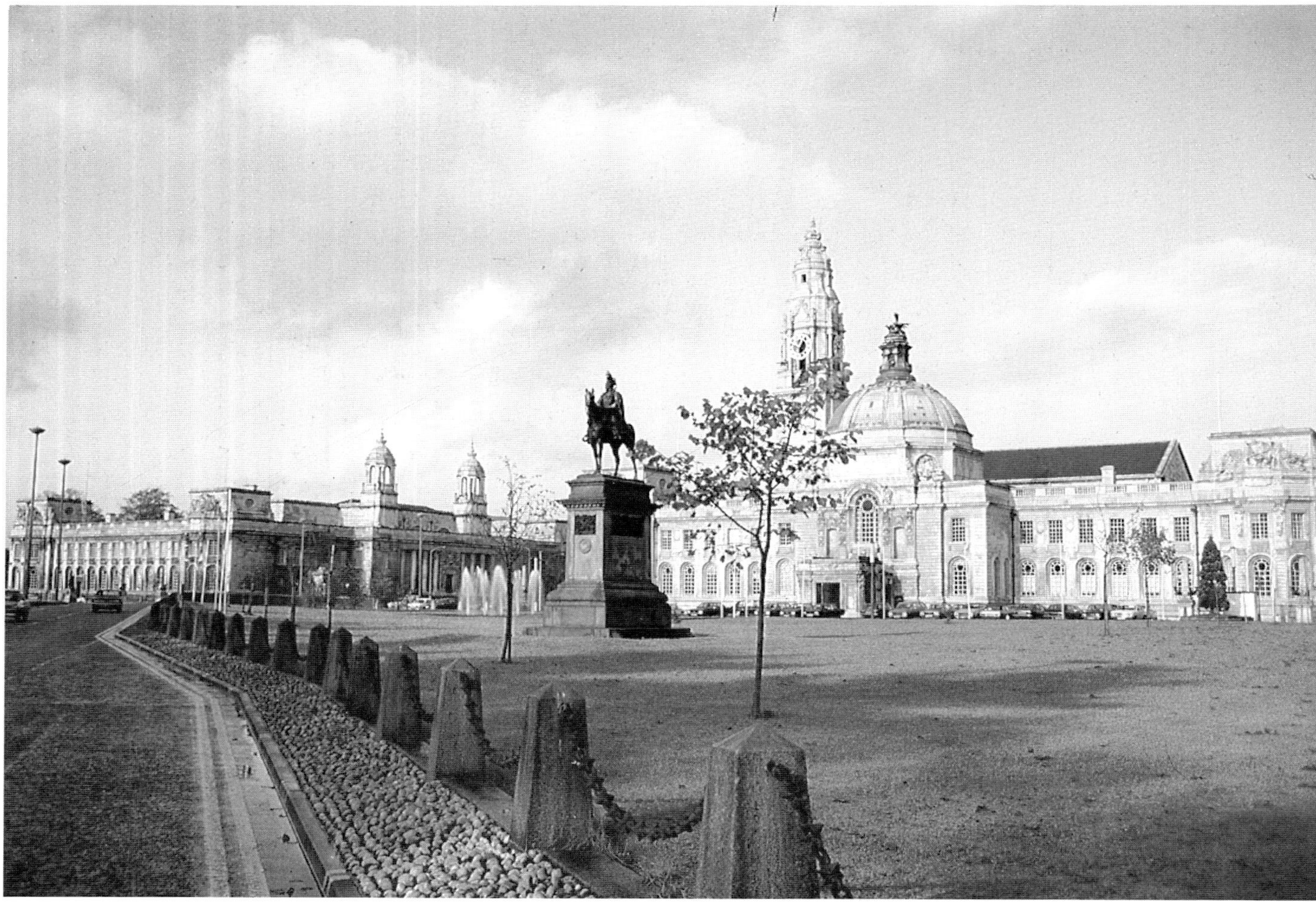

CIVIC PRIDE

Chapter Two

Around the turn of the century, there were rumblings of national pride in Welsh culture. The idea of a national library was first raised at the Eisteddfod at Mold in 1873. The concept of a museum of Wales was first mooted in 1876 and re-asserted in 1890, while in 1900 the Cardiff Museum was astutely re-named the Welsh Museum. In 1904 a deputation was sent to the Chancellor of the Exchequer in London to demand a museum and a library for Wales. In 1907 the National Museum of Wales was founded in Cardiff by Royal Charter of King Edward VII. By that time, the Civic Centre at Cardiff was well under way; an architectural enterprise of a scope unprecedented in Wales since the building of the castles 600 years before by Edward I. It was, perhaps, no more than the spirit of the age that the creation of Cardiff's imposing centre occurred at the same time as prestigious enclaves of British Imperialism were being built at Canberra and New Delhi. Whatever the actual promptings, the nucleus of the future capital of Wales was more or less complete with the formal opening of the National Museum of Wales in 1927 by the King-Emperor, George V.

18. Civic Centre, Cardiff
Law Courts and City Hall, South Front (1906)
Though each of the three buildings on the south side of the Civic Centre have different designs, they are unified by the applied sculpture, which culminates in a monumental climax on the City Hall in the centre (right in photograph).

At the beginning of the twentieth century, Cardiff was the largest and most important town in Wales. Within the space of fifty years its polulation had increased ninefold, and by 1901 it numbered 164,333. The city had grown proportionately, with concentric arcs of Victorian dwellings spreading out to form new suburbs that enclosed the city centre and the dockland that supplied its lifeblood. It had grown quickly and, though small in comparison with the major cities of other countries, it already had aspirations to capital status and sufficient confidence to assert its status in prestigious public buildings. So that, when fine new buildings were planned to constitute a grandiose civic centre, it was decided to adorn them with works of art appropriate to their scale and magnificence.

On and around the three buildings that form the south front of the civic centres are distributed allegorical sculptures representing a judicious mixture of material and intellectual values — covering every aspect of national life. The exterior of the city hall has decoration of an abundance, if not quite of a standard, that would have graced a Renaissance city. The building itself, opened in 1906, is in a grandiose form of Edwardian
18 baroque, typical of public buildings of the period. For the purpose of decoration, the main front of the hall was conceived as one unit with the adjacent law courts, and the two buildings have related themes.

From west to east, the four main groups on the two buildings represent: *Science and*
19 *Education, Commerce and Industry, Poetry and Music,* and *Unity and Patriotism*. The two large groups flanking the *porte cochère* of the city hall symbolise the sea receiving the three rivers of Cardiff — the Taff, the Ely and the Rhymney — while the dome is crowned with a great lead dragon, a weighty image of Welsh national pride, executed by a Frenchman, H.C. Fehr.

One distinguishing feature about the appearance of these groups of statuary is that, although they were executed by several different artists, there is a remarkable similarity of style about them. It suggests that there was either an unusual affinity of ideas among
20 the artists, or that the iconography and details were precisely determined beforehand by a committee.

The same characteristics distinguish the sculptures that surround the exterior of the National Museum of Wales on the east side of the city hall. These are of a later date and have a more pronounced twentieth-century look about them, for although the museum was founded by Royal Charter in 1907, the foundation stone was not laid until 1912, construction was interrupted by the war, and the building was not formally opened until 1927. Nevertheless, its sculptures perpetuate the allegorical fixation of the other two
21 buildings, and the museum establishes a satisfying visual balance with the Law Courts on the west side. Altogether, five artists worked on the carvings that adorn the museum, and reading around the building from east to west the groups represent: *Mining and Shipping,*
22 *Stone Age, Bronze Age and Iron Age, Coal Age, Learning, Art,* and *Music.*

The other outstanding groups of monumental statuary that grace Cardiff's Civic
23 Centre stand at each end of the stylobate of the County Hall. They are both by Albert Hodge, and, though carved around 1912, have an archaic quality of mood. There is something of the dramatic romanticism of Fuseli about the strained, histrionic poses of

24 the figures and the horses, with their contorted neo-classical features, staring eyes and parted lips. They too are allegorical and represent such mundane activities as *Navigation* and *Mining* , occupations which Hodge invested with a sublime terror.

Inside the buildings, the sentiment becomes less pretentious and a more human note is struck. And, once again, the sculpture of the civic centre reaches its climax in the middle of the City Hall. At the top of the main stairs, on the *piano nobile* , is a large area known as the Marble Hall. When the hall was completed in 1906, there were ten empty plinths lining the balustrades at the top of the stairs, obviously intended to hold sculpture. Eight years later, D.A. Thomas, who was created Lord Rhondda in 1916, gave
25 £15,000 to pay for statues to stand on these plinths, and a competition was arranged. The theme was to be that of great Welsh heroes, with J. Havard Thomas as adviser to a committee, chaired by the future Lord Rhondda, and with designs invited from members of the Royal Society of Sculptors. But, before the competition was completed, the committee summarily changed its mind and decided on ten direct commissions from members of the Society, with Havard Thomas retained as consultant.

This decision caused an uproar at a special meeting of the Royal Society of Sculptors, where a resolution was put forward condemning Havard Thomas for his complicity in the new arrangement. The council — five members of which had been granted the new commissions — supported him in his revised role. Whereupon, the members reacted violently and vociferously, the council resigned and walked out, and the meeting ended in chaos.

The society suffered a severe trauma over the Cardiff project, and it was some time before it recovered its dignity and prestige. The commissions, however, were upheld and an extra statue — that of Queen Boadicea — was added. But the way was not entirely clear for the chosen few. They were given biographical and historical details of their allotted subjects, and from these they had to produce drawings and a scale model of their proposed design. These, in turn, were considered and amended by Lord Rhondda's committee before the work could be started.

The unhappy circumstances of the project and the uninspiring process of arriving at its details might account for the final appearance of the statues which, though impressive
26 in their total ensemble, are individually rather stilted and contrived. Even the material from which they were carved does little to enliven them, for though the serravezza marble was expensive, it has a durable, soapy texture which effectively prohibits any crispness of
27 detail. This is the case even with the centrepiece 'Dewi Sant', which is by the best known of all the artists, William Goscombe John. Compared with some of his work in bronze, it is a flabby creation and appears decidedly academic when compared with Rodin's carvings of the same period.

Goscombe John was a native of Wales who struggled to establish a career in fine art, and who became one of the most prolific and most successful British sculptors of his generation. In his day, this involved working on private and public commissions to celebrate or commemorate important events and individuals. The impressive list of such commissions that John acquired, his diligence in executing them, and his capacity to work on any scale from a medal to a war memorial, all testify to the strength of his ambitions and the degree of his success.

He was born in Cardiff in 1860, the son of a woodcarver, Thomas John. At the age of fourteen he started to train under his father who by then was employed at the Bute Workshops in Cardiff, which had been set up by William Burges to provide the enormous amount of decorative work required for Cardiff Castle. It was through his father's acquaintance with Burges, and the latter's connection with Thomas Nicholls, that young Goscombe John progressed from craftsman to artist.

In 1881 he left Cardiff to work in Nicholls's studio in Lambeth, where he remained for five years. Such was his determination that, while still working for Nicholls, John also enrolled as a student at the Royal Academy schools and worked there in the evenings. Encouragement and practical support from friends and patrons in Wales helped to promote his career, and by 1889 he was skilled enough to win the biennial Gold Medal of the RA.

28 This award took him on an extensive tour throughout Europe and North Africa, and culminated in a year spent in Paris. There, he was at the centre of European art, an opportunity he did not waste, for he saw and appraised the work of leading French sculptors, among them Rodin whose studio the young Welshman would frequently visit. The influence of some of these French artists, in particular that of Rodin, can be discerned in Goscombe John's work of this period, though its freshness began to wane with the passing of time and the more conservative tastes of his British patrons.

29 After his stay in Paris, he returned to England and set up a studio in London. Now aged 31, he set about establishing his practice, rapidly gaining commissions, and becoming an accepted figure on the more respectable side of the Bohemian fringe. Election to the Royal Academy came in 1909, and in 1911 he was knighted at the Investiture of the Prince of Wales at Caernarfon Castle.

Like his fellow-countryman, namesake and contemporary, Augustus John, Goscombe John seemed to become creatively atrophied by the success that he struggled to achieve. A long line of monuments, memorials, medallions, regalia, metalwork and the like, and over one hundred and fifty portraits, ensured his material comforts, though they did not guarantee a lasting and influential artistic reputation.

But there is no doubt that Goscombe John was a sincere champion of the cause of Welsh Art, especially of the National Museum of Wales. And not the least of his achievements is that he showed how a Welsh artist, once he had made his mark in the world, could command loyal patronage from his native land. John's works in Wales are
30 numerous and widespread and, by now, so familiar that they are overlooked, though their conventional dignity adds a civilized note to the many public places where they are located.

The other outstanding Welsh figure in the art establishment of this period, and one with a wider reputation, was Frank Brangwyn. Though he was not born in Wales, Brangwyn has now been successfully, and perhaps inextricably, accepted as a Welsh artist. He was also, single-handedly, responsible for the other large decorative scheme for a public building in Wales, which appeared eighteen years after Cardiff's Marble Hall was opened. Brangwyn's British Empire Panels, which now hang in Swansea's Guildhall, were begun in 1925 — about the same time as the sculptures of the National Museum of Wales — and the original idea had been suggested a year earlier, ten years before they finally appeared in Swansea.

This followed a decision in the House of Lords in 1924 to provide a memorial to those peers, or relatives of peers, who had died in the First World War. Lord Iveagh agreed to commission the work and offered Brangwyn a fee of £20,000. The artist set to work immediately and his first design dealt with the obvious realities of war: guns, soldiers, tanks, and all with a theatrical air of combat. Brangwyn soon rejected this concept as too
31 illustrative and too poignant — gave what panels he had completed to the National Museum of Wales — and started again. His second scheme was more decorative, more allusive, less realistic and consisted of virtually abstract, heraldic designs. This idea was even more quickly abandoned, the third scheme was fixed upon, and the preparatory cartoons were started.

This final solution, the one we see in Swansea today, was for a series of panels depicting the glories of the Empire for which the dead had given their lives. It is a great, sprawling, ambitious scheme, claustrophobic in its effect, and with all the lush colour and obsessive detail that is typical of Brangwyn's public works. Typical also is the thoroughness and zest with which Brangwyn tackled his enormous labour. He prepared
32 a vast collection of preparatory sketches: plants, people, animals, birds, buildings, and, with little regard for geographical contiguity, welded them all into a stupendous series of compositions. So crowded are the panels that it is not easy to detect the structure behind the details. This is more evident in the cartoons, which show more of the geometry behind the teeming forests.

But there is no narrative in the Empire Panels, they are a biological, zoological, anthropological kaleidoscope, a patchwork of the symbols and images of imperial possessions, a passing parade of the exotic elements that were so dear to Brangwyn. And,
33 as such, they are immensely effective. It is clear from the false starts he made that the commission meant much to Brangwyn, and he obviously regarded it as the pinnacle of his career. The sustained invention and vigour of the huge panels are extraordinary for an artist who was 65 when they were completed.

So it was a bitter blow to Brangwyn when they were rejected, as unsuitable for their location, by the Royal Fine Art Commission. When the rejection was made public, an offer of £40,000 for the panels came from America, where Brangwyn's work was held in high esteem. But, after their brief appearance at The Ideal Home Exhibition of 1933, the artist gave them to Swansea Corporation which had offered to alter the plans of its new
34 Guildhall to accommodate them. It was some comfort to Brangwyn to find a welcoming home for his greatest series of paintings, which, he said dolefully, 'represent the work of seven years of a life the sands of which are running low'.

Even then, Brangwyn's life had not been without success. As a young man he had worked as a designer for William Morris and his company, where he had reinforced the belief in sound craftsmanship already acquired from his father, Curtis Brangwyn. The elder Brangwyn was an architect–designer, of Welsh extraction and with a Welsh wife, who had established a practice in Bruges, where his son Frank was born. Even while he was working as a designer, the young Brangwyn was already painting, and though he is now chiefly remembered as a painter, his contribution to design in the form of stained glass, carpets, jewellery, furniture, metalwork and domestic interiors is also considerable.

But apart from a brief return in the 1930s, he gradually abandoned his career as a designer, and from the turn of the century he concentrated his energies on painting, gaining a reputation for large mural decorations. His first venture into this competitive and demanding specialisation came in 1895 when he was commissioned by Samuel Bing to paint a frieze and two large panels for his shop in Paris, *Hotel de l'Art Nouveau*. The skill and speed with which he completed this commission confirmed his predeliction for public art on a monumental scale and, during the next forty years, Brangwyn produced decorative schemes for many buildings: in Japan, America, Canada and England.

His prestige was based on his traditional approach to subjects, usually of a celebratory nature, and it was their decorative treatment that ensured his success. Indeed, the accelerating success of his style hampered his development as an artist, and there is little significant change between the style of his Art Nouveau murals and that of his Empire Panels.

This consistency is all the more remarkable when it is remembered that the period of Brangwyn's career witnessed the most significant changes in art that had occurred since the Renaissance. While Brangwyn toiled at his massive paintings, he was too busy and too withdrawn to notice that the old, stable world of his youth was crumbling about him, and that a new and revolutionary spirit was changing the arts of Europe.

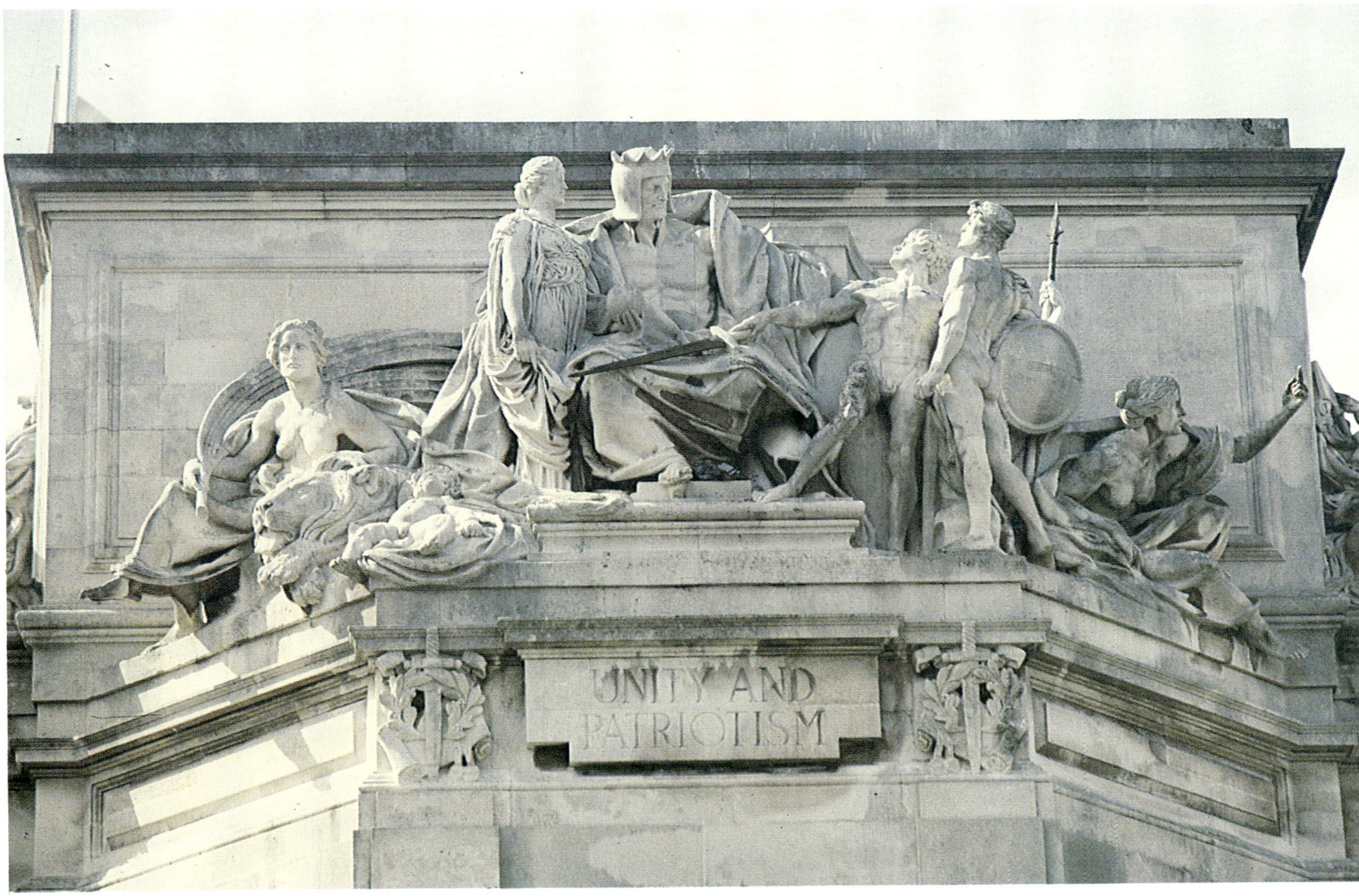

19. Henry Poole 1873 - 1928
Unity and Patriotism (1906) Stone
City Hall, Cardiff

Most of the artists who worked on the sculptures at Cardiff's Civic Centre were young men, in their early thirties at the time of the commission. In spite of this, there is an academic consistency of style about their work that is due either to the conservative state of British sculpture at the time, or to the demands of public commissions - or possibly to both. Henry Poole, who was elected an ARA in 1927, had previously worked under Harry Bates and G.F.Watts.

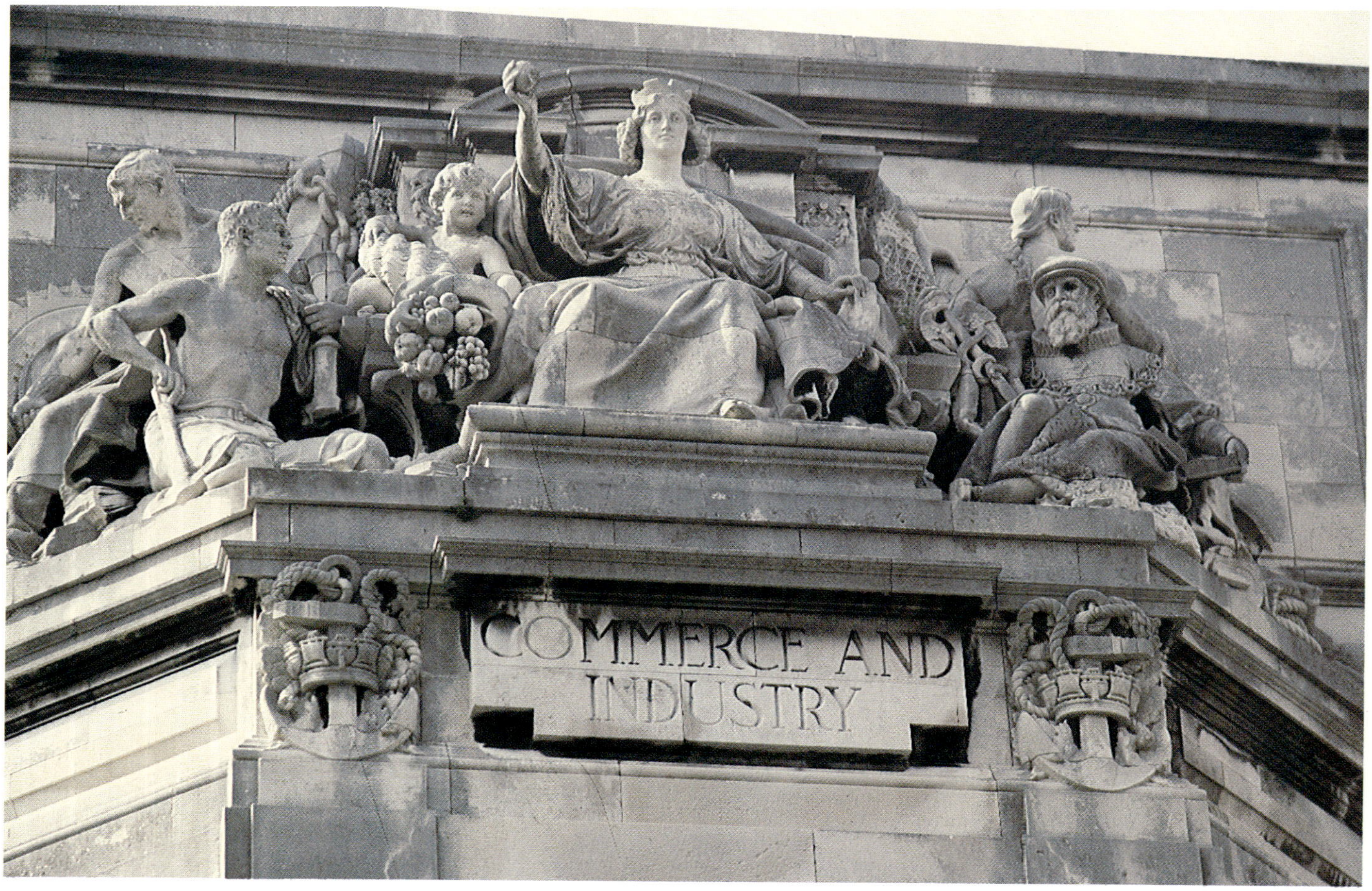

20. Paul Montford 1868 - 1938
Commerce and Industry (1906) Stone
Law Courts, Cardiff

Two groups by Paul Montford provide the bridge between the south fronts of the Law Courts and the City Hall. On the west wing of the City Hall is his group 'Music and Poetry', which is balanced on the neighbouring east wing of the Law Courts by this ensemble representing 'Commerce and Industry'. Although they are not integrated into the building, as was the style of Gothic architecture, they fit admirably into their setting, mainly by the device of allowing the drapery to overflow onto the architectural mouldings.

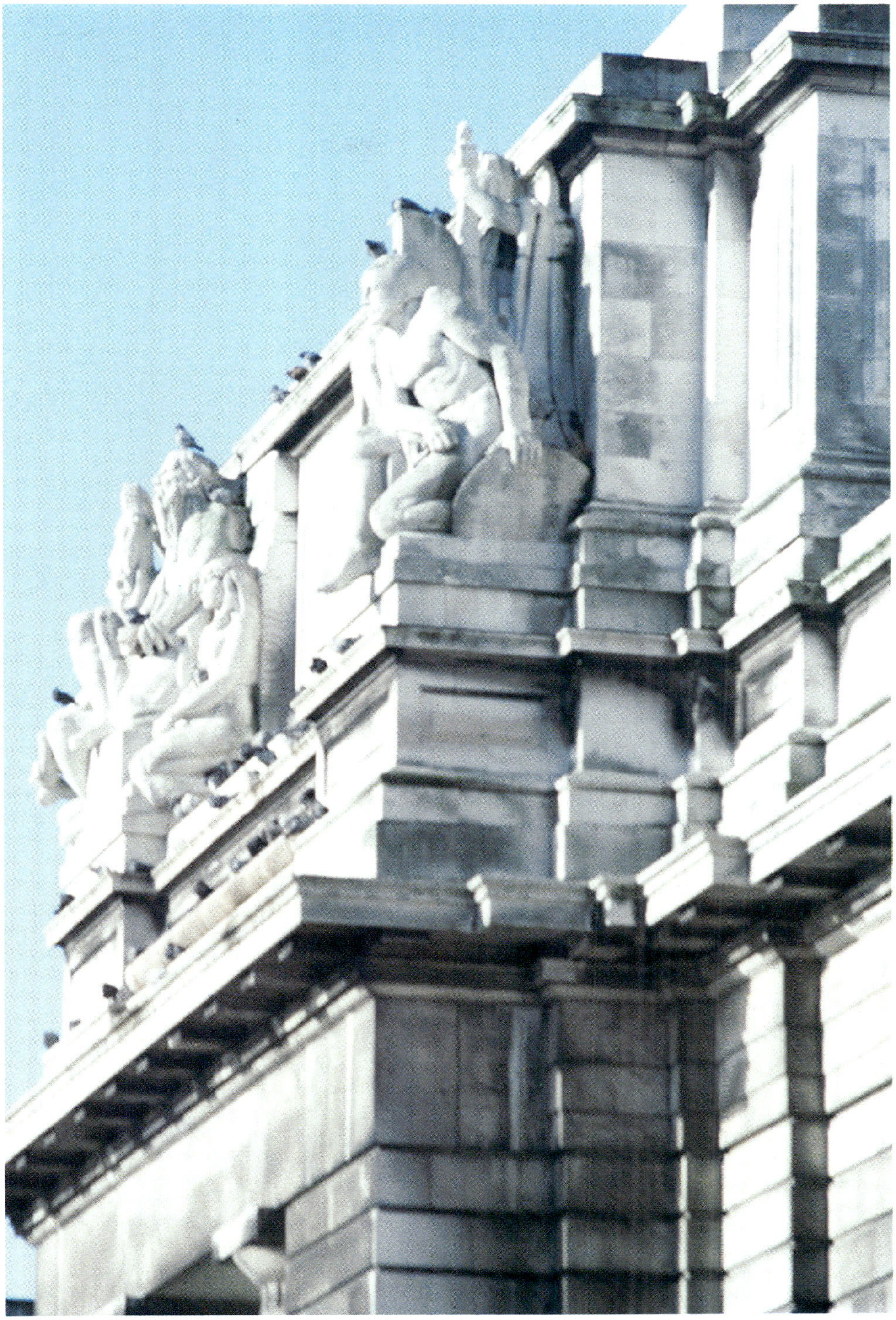

21. Gilbert Bayes 1872 - 1953
The Prehistoric Period (L), The Classic Period (R) (1915)
Stone, South Front, West Wing, National Museum of Wales

Although the building was opened twenty years after the City Hall, the sculptures on the National Museum preserve the convention of personifying human endeavours and historical periods. In 1913, on the advice of Goscombe John, a limited competition was arranged for sixteen groups of sculpture - four to each front - to represent the Arts, The Sciences, The Industries of Wales, and the four ages of technology (Stone, Bronze, Iron, Coal). The following year the titles were changed and Gilbert Bayes was commissioned to carve these two groups: 'Stone Age' having become 'The Prehistoric Period', and 'Bronze Age' renamed 'The Classic Period'.

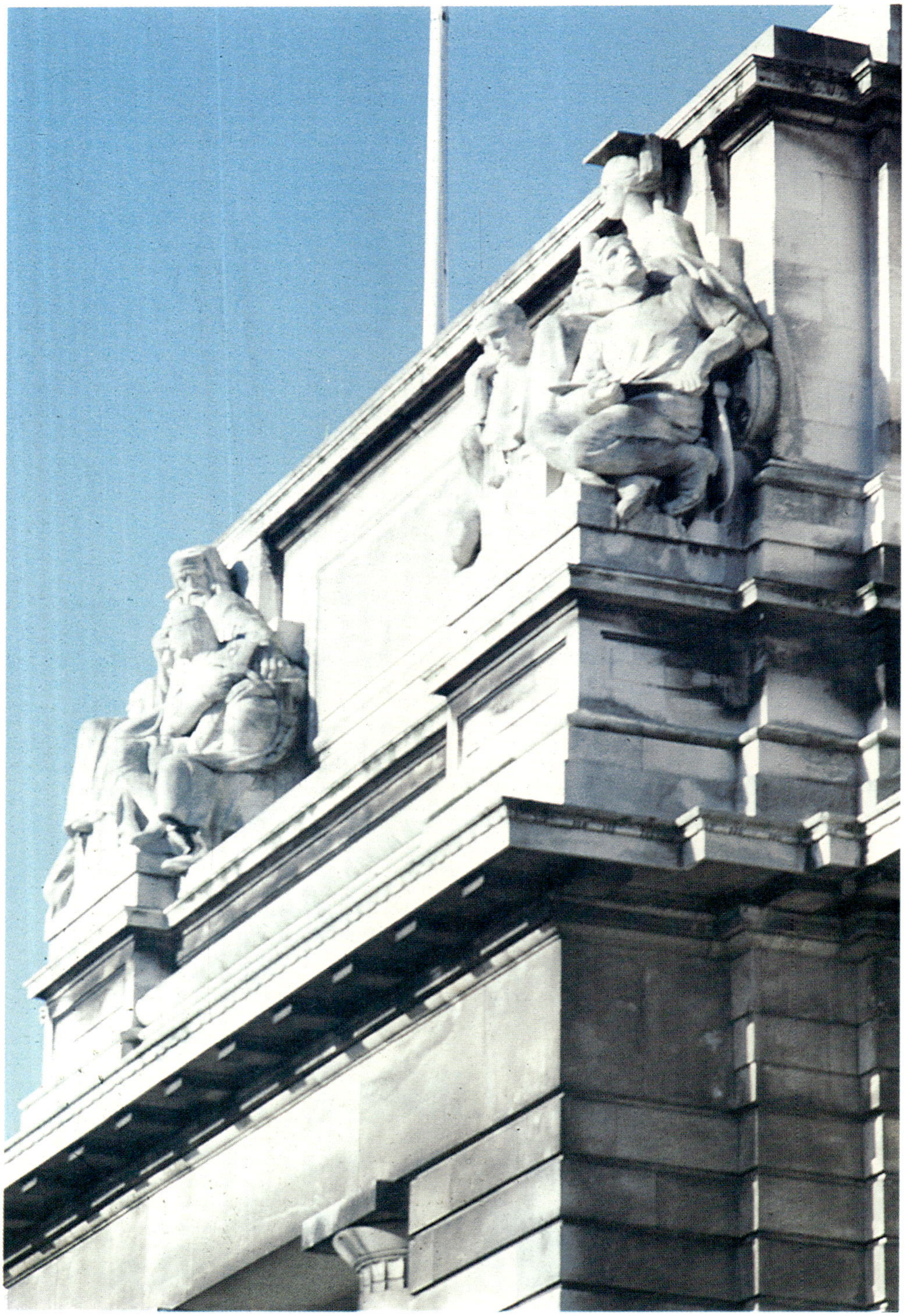

22. Louis Richard Garbe 1876 - 1957
The Medieval Period (L), The Modern Period (R) (1915)
Stone, South Front, East Wing, National Museum of Wales

The original title for 'The Modern Period' was 'The Coal Age', nominated as the fourth and last in the great epochs of civilisation. It was an allegorical conceit that symbolised Cardiff's faith in a source of wealth and of advanced technology that was already dwindling when the sculpture was made. From the confident strength of the carvings it would seem that no premonitions of decline troubled the patrons or the artists. There is, indeed, a feeling of continuity with the sculptures on the City Hall (No. 19) and the Law Courts (No. 20), though there is also a more modern touch in the relatively geometrical treatment of the figures on the museum that reflects the advances made in academic monumental art during the early decades of the twentieth century.

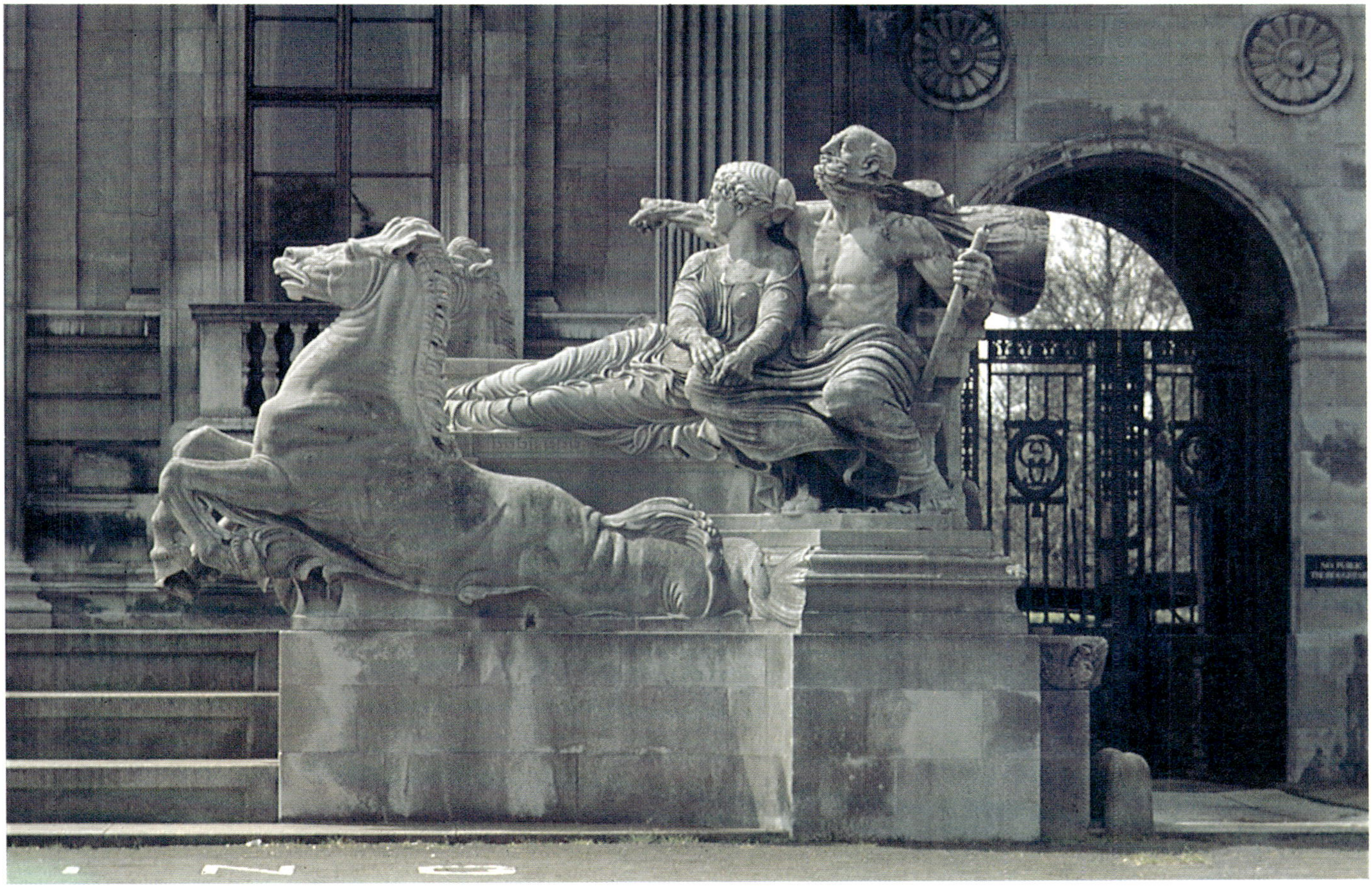

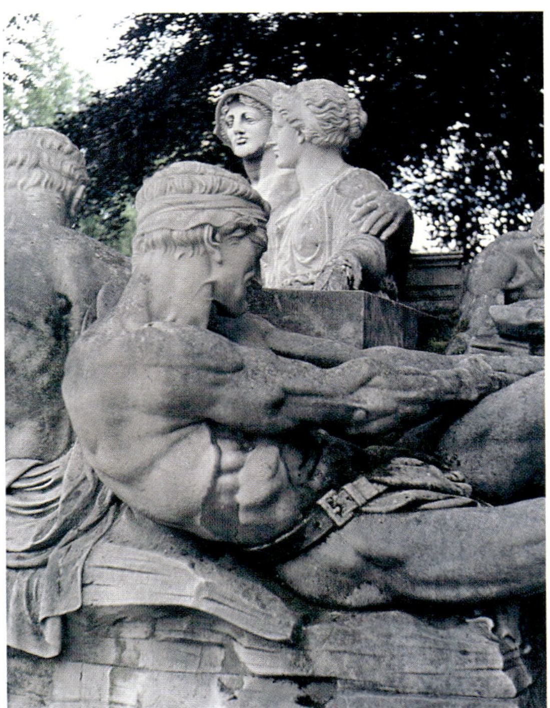

23. Albert Hemstock Hodge 1875 - 1918
Navigation (1912) Stone
County Hall, Cardiff

Appearing in time between the sculptures on the City Hall and those on the National Museum, the carvings on the stylobate of the County Hall are unlike either. Without the lyrical grouping of the former or the calm dignity of the latter, they are more violent interpretations of similar themes: 'Navigation' and 'Mining'. Historically, they are oddities, for the style has more in common with eighteenth-century romanticism than with twentieth-century objectivity, and it would seem that the artist was less concerned with the subject-matter than with making dramatic figure compositions.

24. Albert Hemstock Hodge
Mining (1912) Stone, County Hall, Cardiff

Seen from the side facing the building, the sculptures of County Hall reveal an even more dramatic treatment, unsuspected from the front. The muscular strainings and the controposto of the figures seems to suggest the influence of Michaelangelo and the Mannerists. All the sculptures on the east front were by Hodge, who was also responsible for the figures on the wing walls, and the druid and bard in the Council Chamber. The central feature on the west front was carved by Arthur Broadbent.

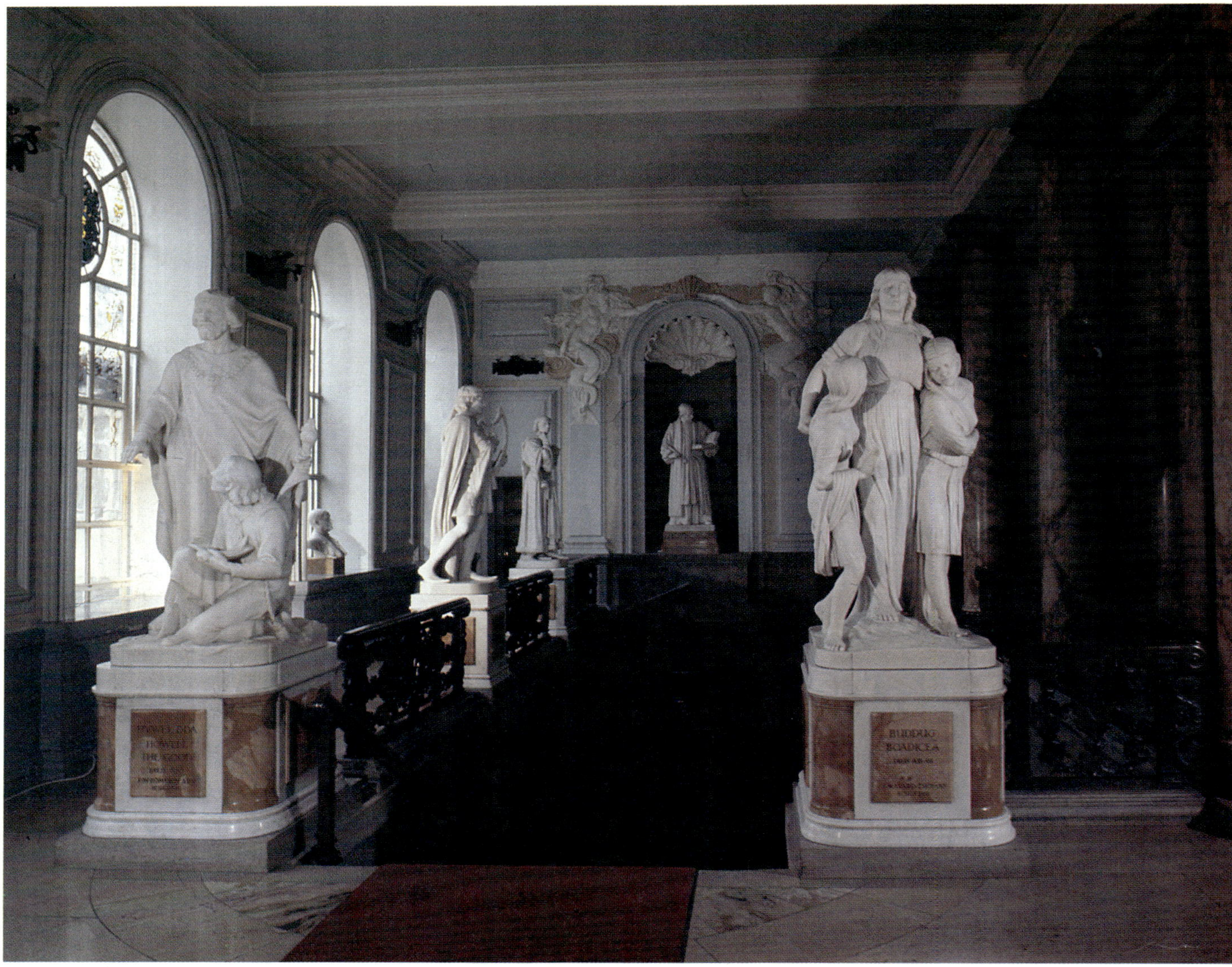

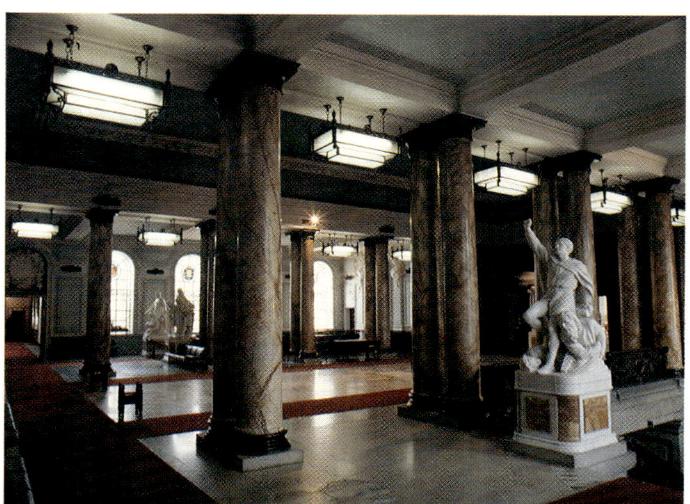

25. Various artists
Marble Hall, City Hall, Cardiff
(a) West Staircase
(b) View from South east

The eleven statues of Welsh heroes in the Marble Hall were unveiled on 27 October 1916 by Lloyd George, who was then Secretary of State for War. The eleven heroes are: Howell the Good (F.W. Pomeroy), Prince Llewellyn (Henry Pegram), Henry VII (Ernest S. Gillier), Bishop Morgan (T.V. Clapperton), Pantycelyn Williams (L.S. Merrifield), Dafydd ap Gwilym (W.W. Wagstaff), Giraldus Cambrensis (Henry Poole), Owen Glyndŵr (Alfred Turner), Sir Thomas Picton (T. Newburn Crook), Boadicea (J. Havard Thomas) and Dewi Sant (Goscombe John).

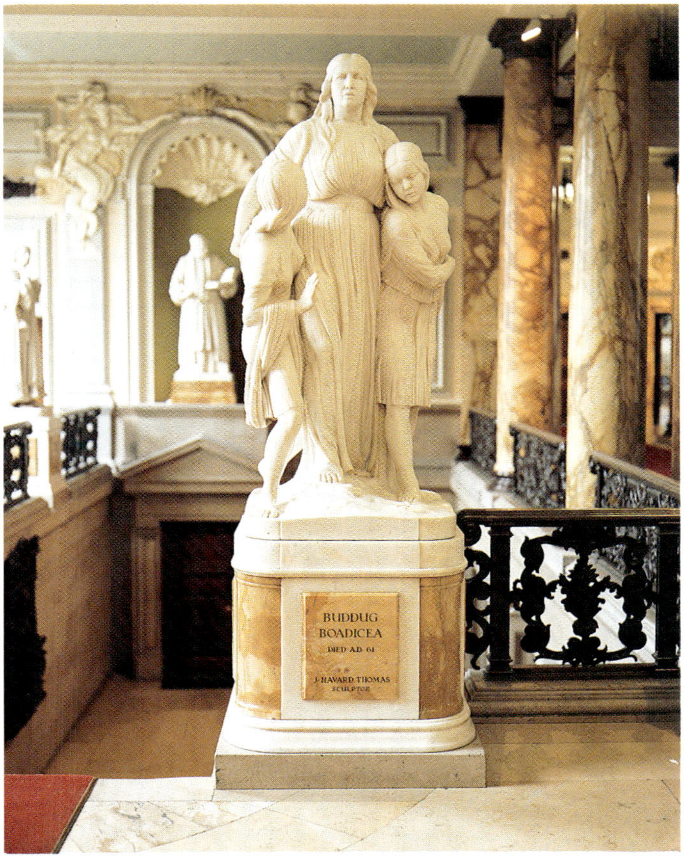

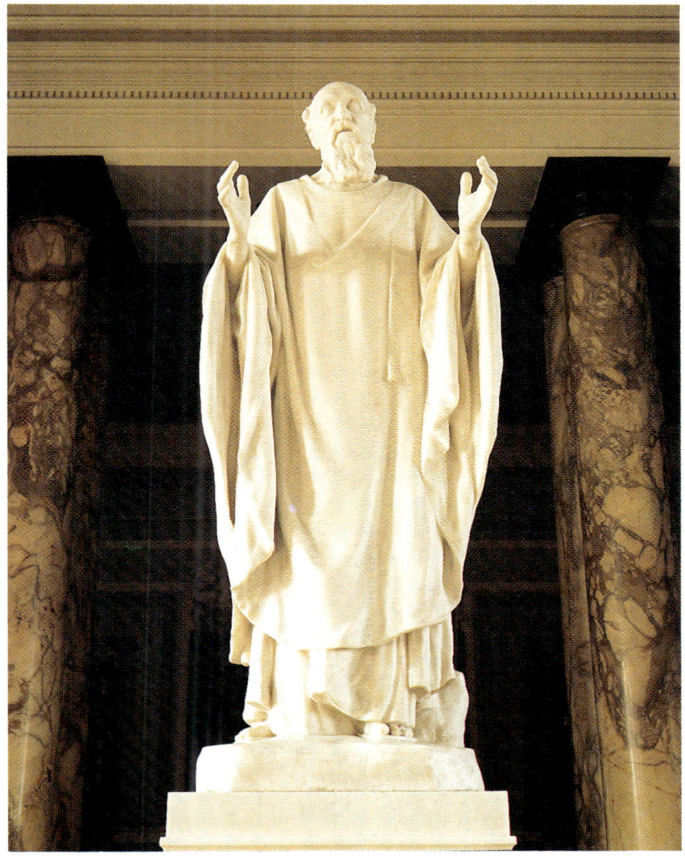

26. J. Havard Thomas 1854 - 1921
Queen Boadicea (1916) Marble life size
City Hall, Cardiff

This statue, a late addition to the pantheon of Welsh heroes, stretched the definition to include a woman who was one of the earliest and best-known of the Celtic fighters for liberation. It was carved by the artistic adviser to the selection committee and was described in the 'Architectural Review' (October 1916) as 'a masterpiece of modern sculpture' and 'a thing of extraordinary beauty'. Havard Thomas was born in Bristol and, in the year this carving was made, had been appointed Professor of Sculpture at the Slade School.

27. William Goscombe John 1860 - 1952
Dewi Sant (1916) Marble life size. City Hall, Cardiff

Goscombe John, as the most celebrated living Welsh sculptor, an RA and a newly-created knight, was consulted by D.A. Thomas (Lord Rhondda) about the project for the hall of sculpture in Cardiff's new City Hall. John, a founder member of the Royal Society of British Sculptors, was one of the artists given a commission, and his statue of Saint David takes pride of place in the ensemble of Welsh heroes. Two other sculptors who were given commissions, Clapperton and Merrifield, had both been assistants in John's London studio - another measure of his status as an artist.

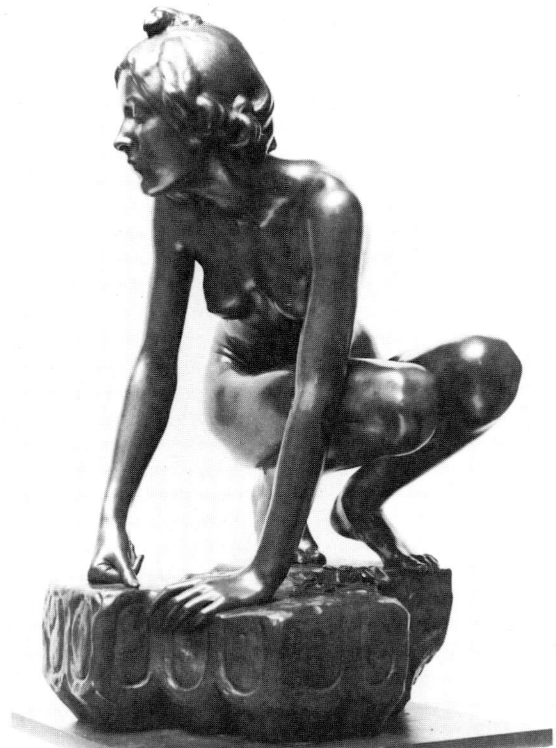

29. William Goscombe John
The Elf (1898) Bronze height 101.5 cm
Welsh Folk Museum, St. Fagan's, Cardiff

This was one of Goscombe John's most popular works, and it was very favourably received when the plaster cast was first exhibited at the Royal Academy in 1898. It shows John at his most sensitive and inventive, before the dead hand of public commissions vitiated his style. 'The Elf' was obviously a work which the artist himself held in high esteem, for a stylised line engraving of it appeared forty-four years later on the plinth of his self-portrait bust (1942). There are also smaller versions of 'The Elf' in Newport Art Gallery and in the Cyfarthfa Museum, Merthyr Tydfil.

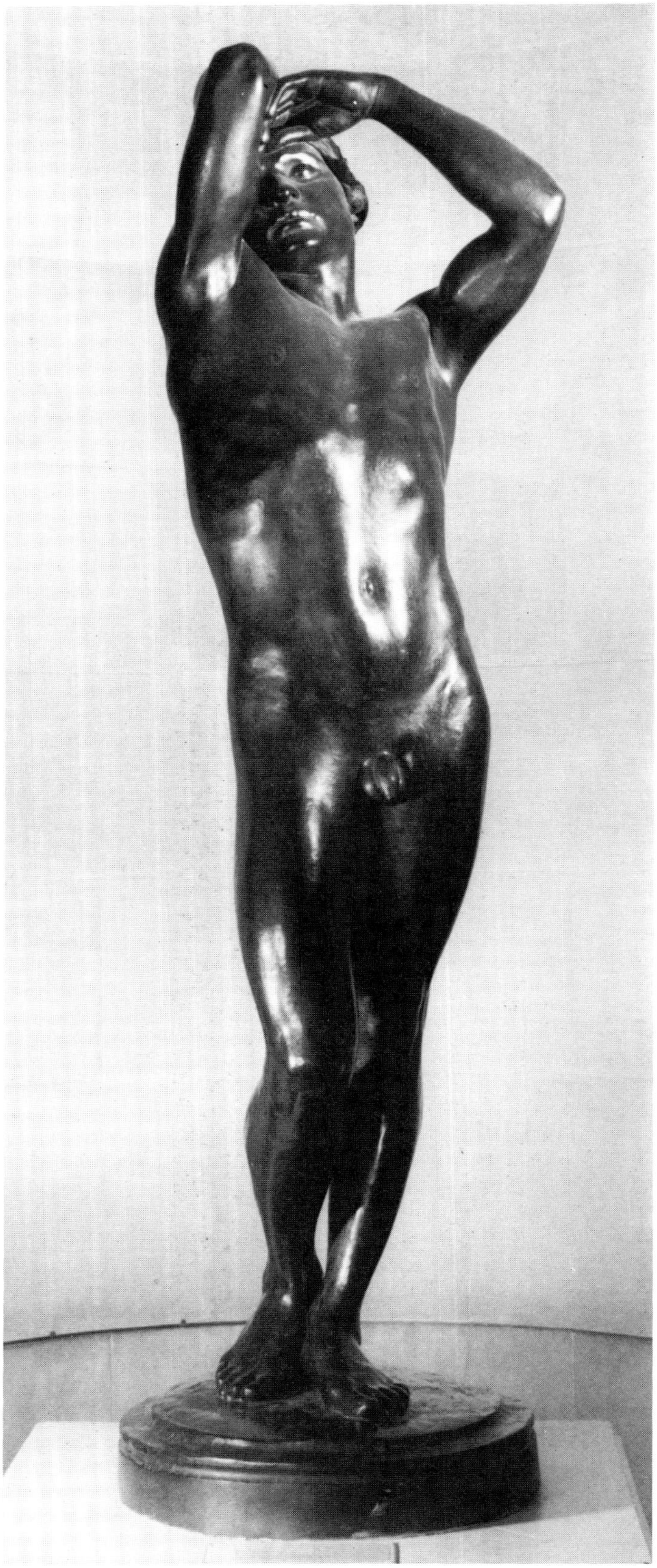

28. William Goscombe John
Morpheus (1890) Bronze height 168 cm
National Museum of Wales

This figure from classical mythology was modelled during John's stay in Paris during 1890. At that time, John was regularly visiting Rodin and watching him at work in his studio. So it is not surprising that the powerful influence of the Frenchman should affect the young Welshman, as is evident in this figure of Morpheus. At the time John left Paris, Rodin was beginning work on his controversial statue of Balzac, though this work by John is more akin to Rodin's 'Age of Bronze' (1877), which had been exhibited in London in 1884, the year John first enrolled at the Royal Academy schools.

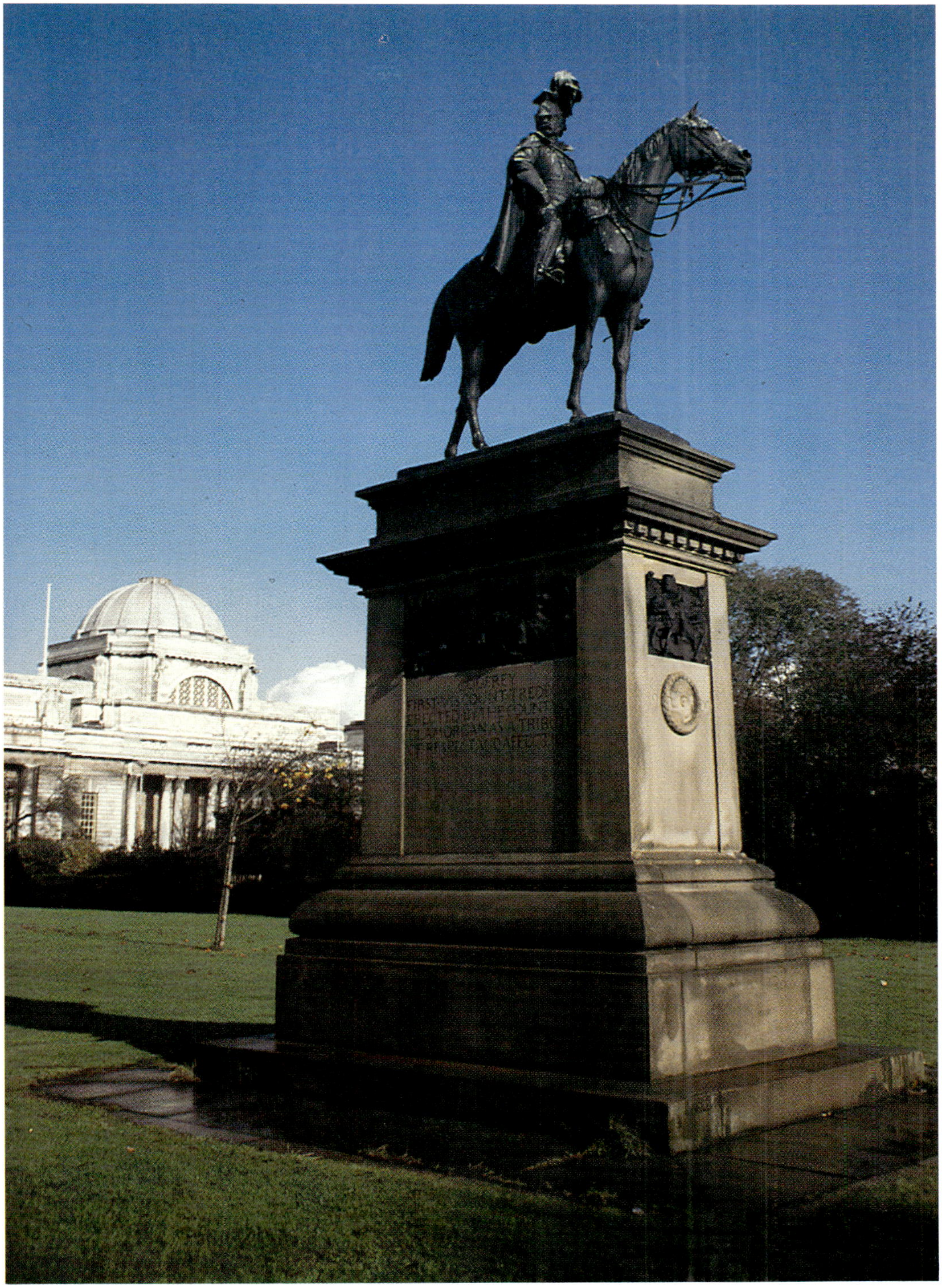

30. William Goscombe John
Viscount Tredegar (1906) Bronze
Boulevard de Nantes, Cardiff

This was John's first equestrian portrait, a convention in which he quickly became an expert. Others include that of Lord Minto (1913) in Calcutta, and one of King Edward VII (1911) for Liverpool. The commission to commemorate Lord Tredegar was won by John in circumstances not entirely to his credit, and are described by Fiona Pearson in her book on the artist. Lord Tredegar was a veteran of the famous charge at Balaclava, and here he wears the uniform of the Light Brigade. Situated in what was once a quiet park in the civic centre of Cardiff, the site has been invaded by a four-lane carriageway, so that Lord Tredegar and his horse now gaze bravely down at the traffic which volleys and thunders across their path.

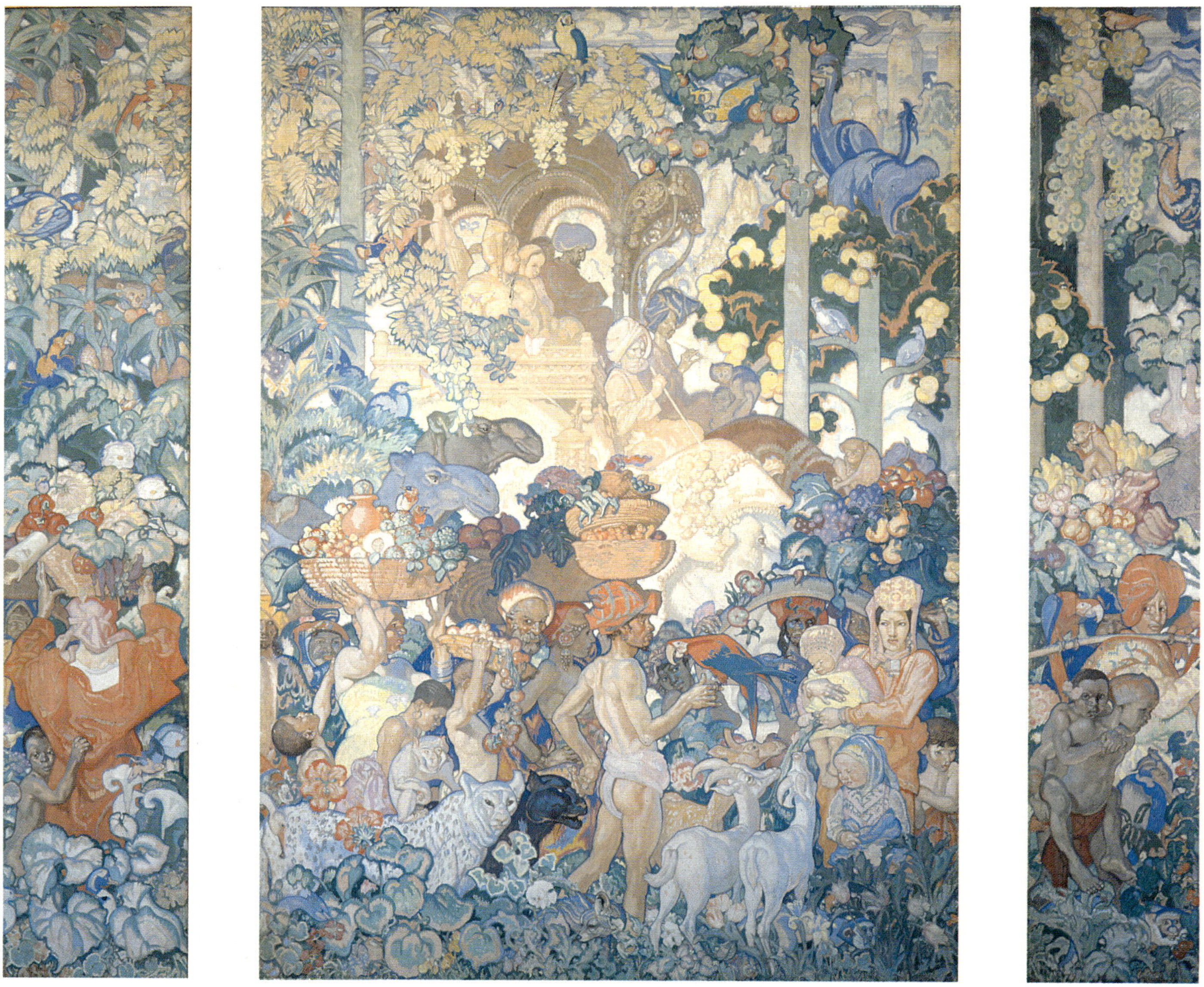

31. Frank Brangwyn 1867 - 1956
British Empire Panels, centre section of large panel, south wall
(1925 - 32) Oil on Canvas 610 x 371 cm
Guildhall, Swansea
Brangwyn prepared two earlier schemes for the Empire Panels, and rejected both in favour of the scheme which can be seen today in the Guildhall at Swansea. This final scheme consists of eight large panels, of which this is one, and ten smaller panels, about twelve by thirteen feet in size (No.34). Also at the Guildhall are the studies, sketch designs and cartoons for the panels; a prodigious amount of work, showing how thorough and consistent was Brangwyn's approach to this tremendous commission.

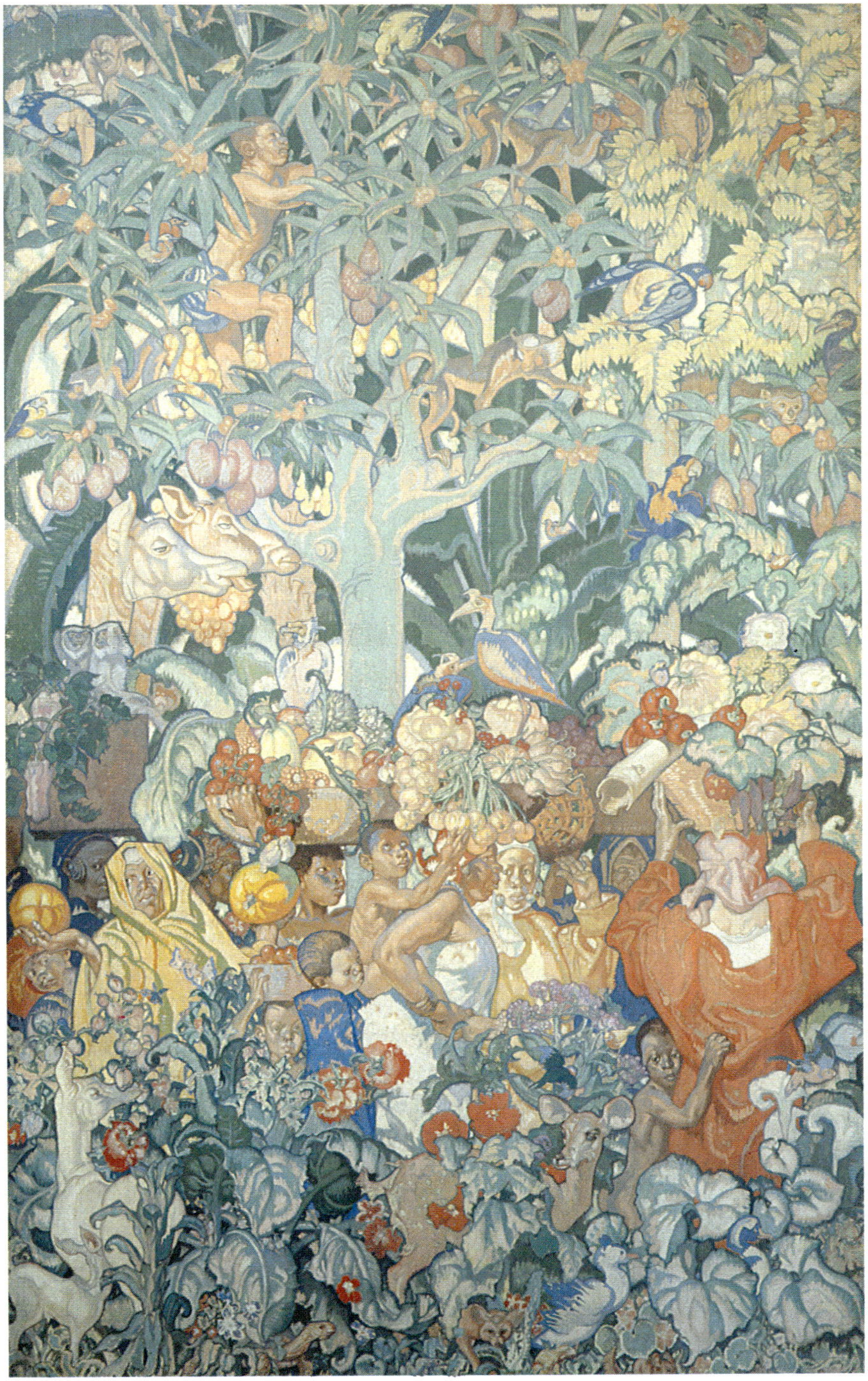

32. Frank Brangwyn
British Empire Panels, left-hand section of large panel, south wall (1925 - 32) Oil on canvas 610 x 371 cm
Guildhall, Swansea

The third of Brangwyn's schemes for the Empire Panels was originally commissioned for the House of Lords, though it was rejected before it was even completed, by the Royal Fine Art Commission in 1930. This was probably not so much a criticism of Brangwyn's work as of the unsuitability of style for the proposed setting. As works of art, they were highly esteemed. Frank Rutter, in his book on Brangwyn, breathless with admiration, described the panels as 'the most splendid and distinguished unit of decorative painting executed in Europe since Tintoretto ceased his work in the Doge's Palace at Venice'.

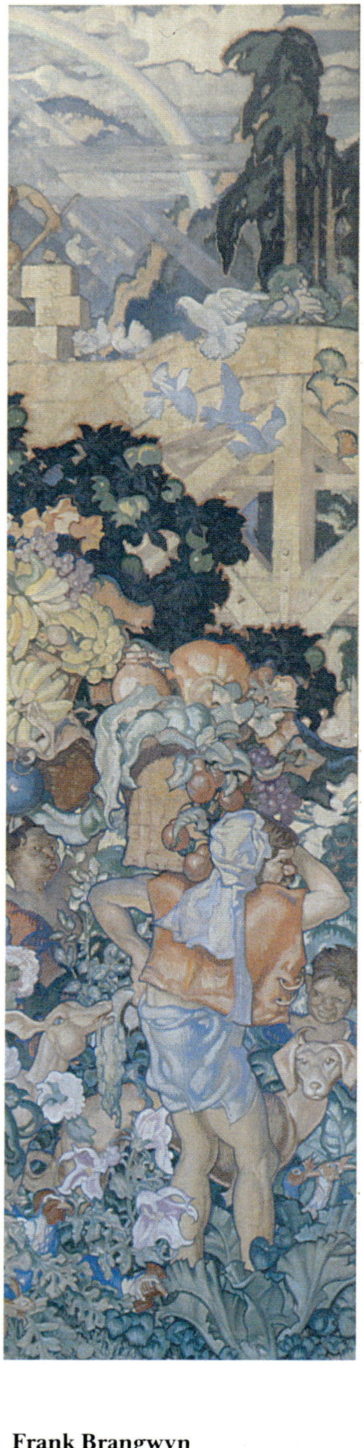

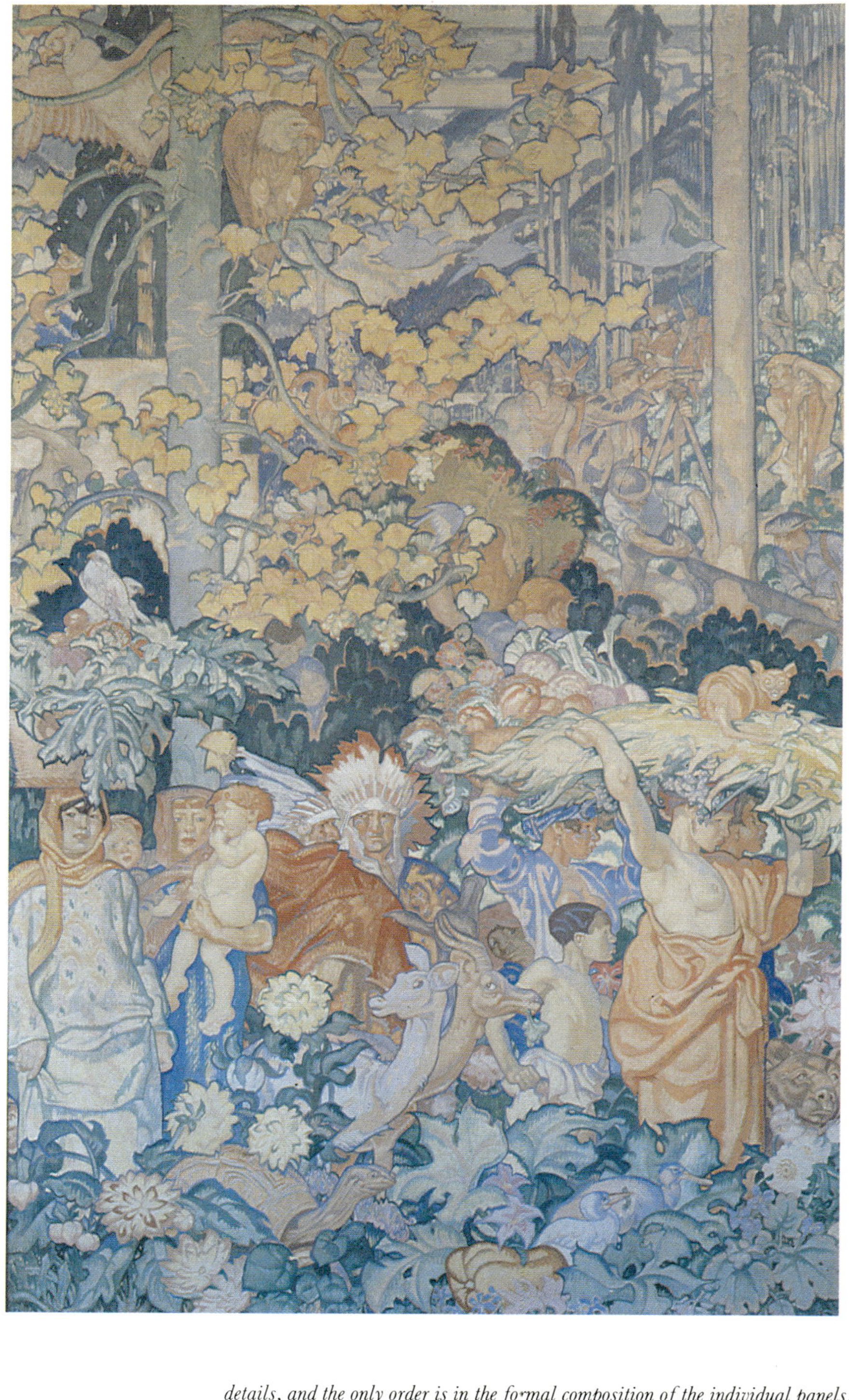

33. Frank Brangwyn
British Empire Panels, right section of large panel, north wall (1925 - 32) Oil on canvas 610 x 371 cm
Guildhall, Swansea

There is no narrative thread to Brangwyn's Empire Panels, no sequence of thematic treatment, no geographical categories; the content is a pot pourri of details, and the only order is in the formal composition of the individual panels. And just as the style of these panels belonged to an earlier period, so did the mood. Although the British Empire reached its territorial peak around 1933, there were serious strains in its administration, and forebodings about its future - none of which is hinted at in Brangwyn's sprawling tribute to imperial splendour.

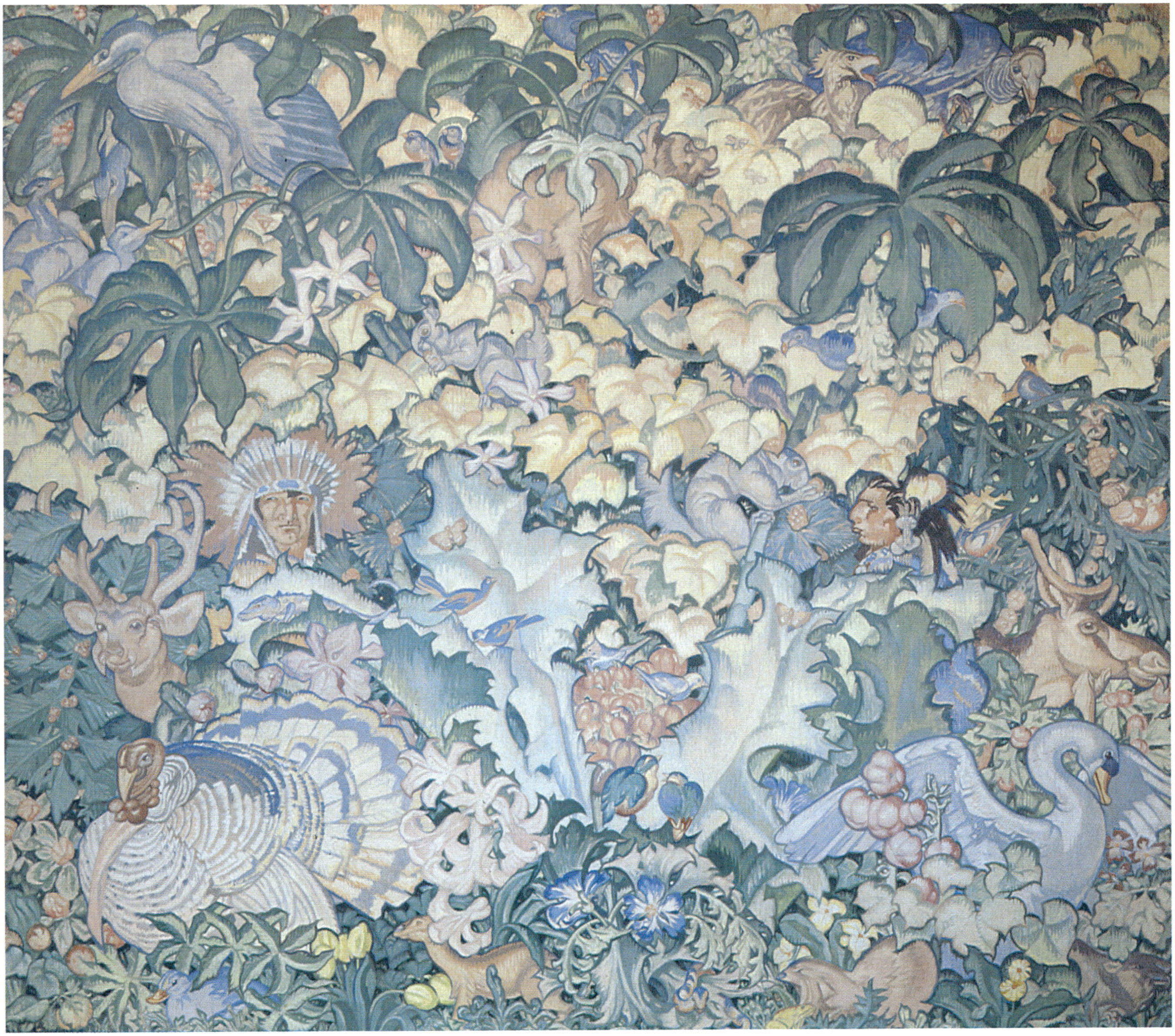

34. Frank Brangwyn
British Empire Panels, small panel 2, north wall (1925 - 32)
Oil on canvas 366 x 406 cm
Guildhall, Swansea
The more decorative of the Empire Panels, luxuriating in exotic plant life, resemble overblown William Morris designs into which have strayed various human and animal creatures. In their debt to the Arts and Crafts movement of the nineteenth century (Brangwyn worked for a while as a designer with Morris & Co.) they show how little Brangwyn's style had developed since his first mural commission, for Hôtel de l'Art Nouveau, more than thirty years before.

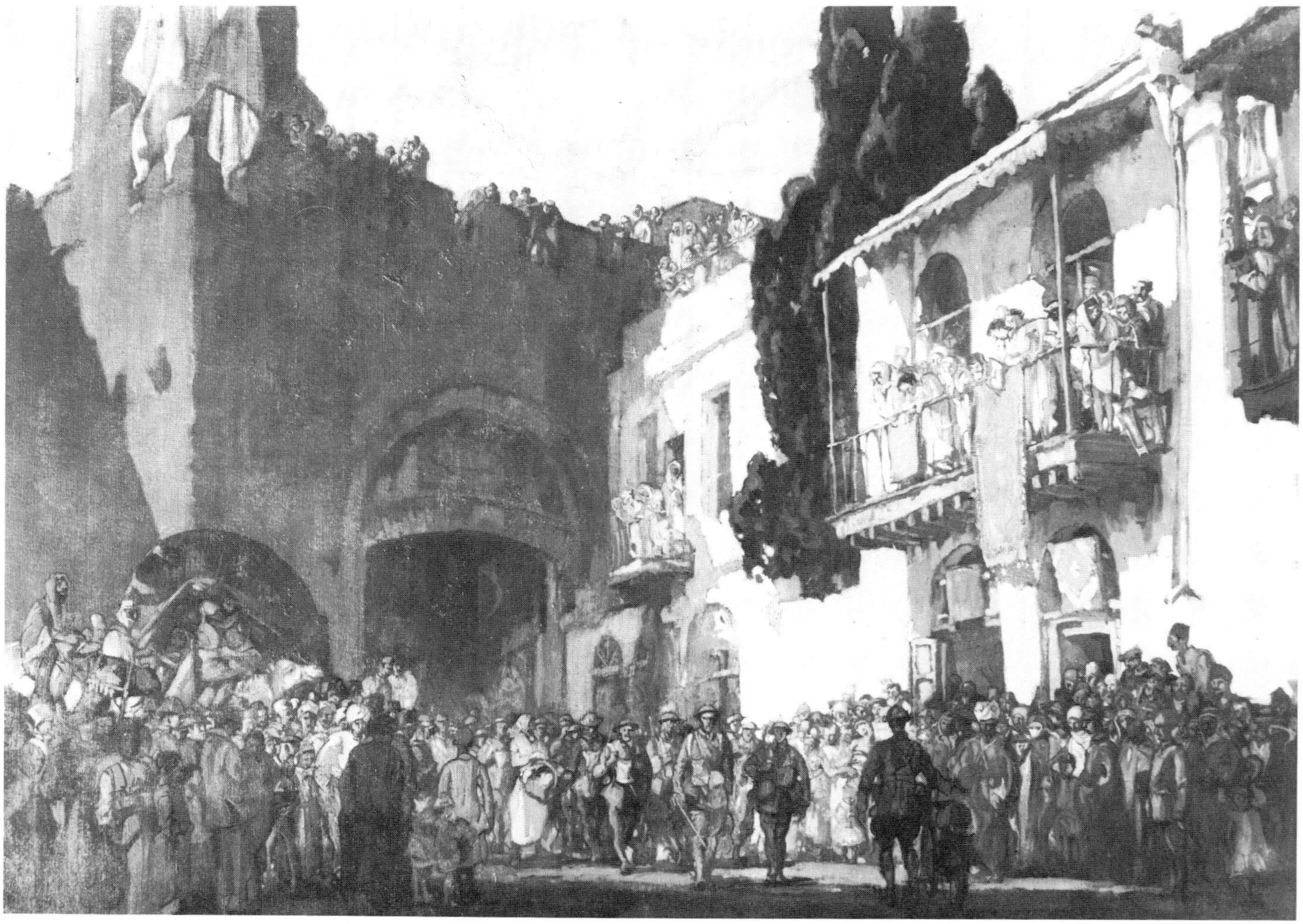

A TIME OF REVOLUTIONS

Chapter Three

During the creation of Wales's national cultural institutions, the Museum, the Library and the University, no one seriously suggested a national college of art and design. The most successful Welsh artists continued to be expatriates who bestowed the benefit of their talents on other countries. Even there, however, they seemed to be inhibited about committing themselves to the *avant-garde*, and they did not conform to any dogma, revolutionary or otherwise. Paris had now replaced Rome as the centre of western art, and it was more accessible to British artists. In Paris, in 1907, Augustus John's encounter with Picasso and the birth-pangs of Cubism led to no more than half-hearted pastiches in the style of Picasso's Blue Period. Gwen John lived and worked in Paris from 1903 until 1939, serenely indifferent to the revolutionary ideas that abounded there. J.D. Innes first painted at Collioure in 1908, three years after Matisse, another regular visitor, had invented Fauvism there. Innes never ventured into pure Fauvism, merely allowing its influence to colour his own version of Post-Impressionism.

35. Frank Brangwyn
Entry of the Welsh Division into Jerusalem (1931) Oil on canvas
104 x 143.5 cm
National Museum of Wales

This painting commemorates the capture of Jerusalem in December 1917, which was the climax to Lord Allenby's campaign in Palestine. In 1931, Brangwyn was commissioned by the War Memorial Committee of the National Museum of Wales to paint a war picture with a specific Welsh theme, and this picture was the outcome. Brangwyn, however, was not satisfied with the progress of the picture and did not want to complete it, offering the Committee a more general and much larger cartoon of soldiers working a gun. The Committee insisted on the Jerusalem picture, which Brangwyn eventually completed, and which was unveiled in April 1932 by Major General Motte, who had commanded the 53rd Welsh Division, and who is presumably the figure in the lead. The Committee was delighted with the painting though Brangwyn, as consolation, gave the 'Guns' cartoon to the Museum along with a companion drawing, 'Tanks'.

While Cardiff was celebrating its prosperity in traditional forms, the years before the First World War saw an astonishing change in European art. Ideas were in a ferment, and almost without pause — co-existing in a climate of sustained excitement — new movements appeared in rapid succession: Cubism, Fauvism, Expressionism, Suprematism, Constructivism, Futurism, and the daring plunge into abstract art.

For reasons that have never been convincingly explained, most British artists held back at first from the revolutions going on in Europe. It was not that they were isolated from them, for Paris was still their Mecca; nor were they completely immune, as was proved by the excursion into Vorticism. It just seemed that they were immersed in their own radicalism, directed against the Royal Academy, and had little use for the new aesthetics. In Wales the immunity was more complete, for any contemporaneous effects of the new ideas have never been detected.

The main instrument of revolt against the Royal Academy, with its ideals of attenuated Pre-Raphaelitism, was the New English Art Club. Founded in 1885, the NEAC was committed to new ideas in art, which meant, in effect, traditional English subject-matter enlivened with the 'realism' of Manet, Degas and Bastien-Lepage. In Wales, it had no counterpart, but among Welsh artists who regularly exhibited with the NEAC in London were Frank Brangwyn, Augustus John, Gwen John and J.D. Innes.

By the turn of the century Brangwyn was already launched on his career as a painter
of mural decorations, though he continued to produce easel paintings which allowed him
complete freedom of style and content. His earlier canvases have a broad, muted tonality
derived from Whistler and with subject-matter related in style — and sometimes in place
36 — to that of the Newlyn School. After his period in Cornwall, when he was also 'sowing
his wild oats' with Impressionism, Brangwyn's style matured, and on to Whistler's broad
masses he grafted a range of exotic colours. This heightened chromatism was combined
35 with a quick, sure graphic technique, developed from his experience as a journalistic
illustrator, which allowed him to depict dramatic scenes with great bravura and facility.
Once formed, this style remained relatively unchanged for almost fifty years. He
appeared untouched by the manifold developments of modern art, and there is little
37 significant change between a painting of 1900 and one completed in 1946.

A contemporary of Brangwyn's was Augustus John, who suffered from the opposite
defect: he never quite found his own individual style. John's eclecticism came from many
sources — often the one that he had most recently seen — and was mainly confined to the
old masters. The nearest he ever came to the mainstream of modern art was during a brief
38 encounter with Picasso's blue and rose periods around 1907.

Augustus John, did, however, make a personal, if transient, contribution to modern
art. This was with a group of small landscapes from Wales, France and Ireland, produced
in the years before the First World War. These quick, bright panels, full of colour and
light, were a brief flowering of native Post-Impressionism. Like other northern artists —
39 like Van Gogh, who had painted in the same area, sometimes from the same motifs —
John was intoxicated by the atmosphere of Provence. Then in his early thirties, he
responded directly to sensory stimulation and, freed from the obligation to paint finished
40 exhibition pictures, he produced this dazzling series of spontaneous studies. It was an

experience that was soon to enable him to depict the Welsh landscape in an entirely novel manner.

There is no telling where British art would have gone if John had pursued this promising innovation. The paintings sometimes move very near to abstraction; the heightened colour was applied in broad strokes which, denied his facility of draughtsmanship, became almost geometrical. But John was inconstant as an artist and the innovation came to a premature end.

In fairness to John, it must be remembered that portraiture was more profitable than landscape painting — and he had two families to support. He applied his abundant
41 energy to portrait painting and this, together with his inimitable flair for catching a likeness, earned him an international reputation and a comfortable income. Almost single-handed, he changed the tradition of English portraiture from the formality of Sargent's society portraits to a style that gave life and character to his sitters. The best by
42 far of all his portraits are those of the people close to him: his wife, his children, the women in his life, friends for whom he felt a special affinity. More than any other artist, of any time, he painted his family, as direct portraits or interpolated into figure compositions. The most striking of these imaginative compositions is *Lyric Fantasy*, painted while he was living in Dorset around 1911. A large unfinished canvas, it also
43 show's John's sentimentality, his yearning for another place, another time, a retreat from the world of fashionable society that he despised and yet could not resist.

This ambivalence is also evident in John's attitude to his native land. He was born in Tenby, in 1878, the son of a Pembrokeshire lawyer, and his decision to become an artist meant that he had to leave Wales. After an indifferent first year at the Slade School in London, he suddenly blossomed both as a Bohemian personality and as a draughtsman of precocious talent. For the rest of his life he kept a studio in London, though he travelled widely and restlessly, as if in search of some place that would suit the conflicting demands of his complex nature. But he never settled in Wales, though at the time of his friendship with Dylan Thomas he did search for a home somewhere in Pembrokeshire.

44 He also visited north Wales on at least two historic expeditions. The first was in 1901, when he went in search of the gypsies, in the company of John Sampson, the Librarian at Liverpool University and an authority on the Romany culture. Augustus John's second important visit was more fruitful for his art and his companion on this occasion was a fellow Welsh artist, James Dickson Innes.

Nine years younger than John, Innes was born in Llanelli and, after a year at Camarthen School of Art, also went to the Slade School. He and John first met when Innes was a student, though it was not until 1910 that a firm and mutually beneficial friendship
45 developed between the two artists. Innes was a consumptive and had all the febrile energy that the disease imparts to its victims. He travelled frequently in Spain and France, and spent some time at Collioure, a small, picturesque fishing town, south of Perpignan and near the Pyrenees. It was a place favoured by Matisse and Derain, as well as other Fauve artists, and Matisse spent several summers painting at Collioure during the periods when Innes was also there. It is not known whether the two artists ever met, though there was an unmistakeable Fauve influence in Innes' work from that time.

His colour became brighter and less naturalistic, and the paint was applied in a vigorous, almost primitive manner. Landscape was his favourite subject, either
46 panoramic views of sea or mountains or, occasionally, small studies of plants such as *Aloes* or *Ranunculus*. His attempts to integrate figures into his landscapes — prompted by John's obvious success with this device — were usually disastrous, for he had none of John's brilliant and sometimes facile draughtsmanship.

Innes' forte, and his passion, was for mountains, and he painted many views of Canigou, an impressive peak in the Pyrenees, visible from Collioure. But his favourite mountain was Arenig Fawr, in Merioneth, and in 1911 he persuaded Augustus John to accompany him on a painting expedition to north Wales. He had been there alone the
47 previous year, and he was eager to introduce the older man to his beloved mountain. John was suitably impressed and, fired by Innes' enthusiasm and still tuned to landscape painting from his Provençal studies, he produced some of his finest landscapes. The most
48 notable of these is Llyn Tryweryn, at that time a remote lake in the mountains between Bala and Ffestiniog.

This episode in north Wales, with its artistic, social and amorous complications, is affectionately described by John in his autobiography *Chiaroscuro.* What is also implicit in the account is the reciprocal influence that both artists gained from their relationship. The passion and energy that Innes displayed convinced John that his native heath was just as fruitful a painting location as was the more exotic landscape of Provence. Innes in turn benefited from John's experience of landscape painting in the South of France, in Normandy and in Ireland, and adapted John's painterly technique in his own
49 transpositions of topographical landscape.

Three years after this season in Merioneth, Innes was dead from tuberculosis. He was 27 years of age and, though little is known of his personal life, he had a fair measure of success in his professional career. In his younger days, he had painted along the coast of south Wales, at Chepstow and Llanelli, and then in Monmouthshire and the Brecon Beacons. But the works he produced then were immature and his style was unformed. It was after his contact with Post-Impressionism that he began to attract attention, and it was Augustus John who was influential in arousing that interest.

It was John who brought his work to the attention of John Quinn, an eccentric but rich and influential American lawyer. Quinn became an enthusiastic patron of John, who in turn introduced Quinn to the work of Innes and Gwen John. It was through Quinn's influence that the three Welsh artists were represented in the celebrated Armory Show, held in New York in 1913. It was through John's recommendation to Quinn that another
50 of his painter friends, Derwent Lees, was also included in the exhibition. The Armory Show has now become a legend in the history of American art, for it thrust before the public a vast selection of progressive European art, including the *succès de scandale*, Duchamp's *Nude Descending a Staircase.*

It has always been stated that Redon was the artist most generously represented, with 40 works, while John was second with 38. This number, however, omits the six works ex-catalogue that John exhibited in Boston, which gave him the distinction of being the individual artist with the greatest number of works on show. At this time Augustus John was regarded by the Americans as a symbolist painter, and as such he was warmly admired by the exhibition committee's chairman, Arthur B. Davies, himself a painter and the son of a Welsh preacher at Utica, NY. But credit must also go to Quinn, legal adviser to the exhibition, who generously supported John during his poorer years, and who also bought many paintings from Augustus' sister, Gwen.

Gwen John parted with her paintings only reluctantly, for she was possessive about her work and indifferent to the success that her brother so ardently sought. Two years older than Augustus, she followed him to the Slade in 1896. For a while they shared accommodation in London, poor but cheap, and they had many friends in common. But though they remained close for several years, involved in each other's personal problems, interested in each other's work, Gwen gradually grew apart. She was determined to avoid her brother's overpowering personality and to establish her own pattern of living and working.

And this she did with remarkable success, though it involved courage and effort and
51 the renunciation of many things that would have given her a normal life. She never married, never strove for worldly success, willingly accepted conditions of austerity, and always remained committed to her painting. Through this obsession with her work and the patient development of her style, she became one of the most individual painters of her day. It was an achievement that Augustus was among the first to recognise, and one that he came to envy.

Gwen John was born in Haverfordwest and her first paintings were of her family and the scenes of her childhood around Tenby. An early painting of the town (now in a private collection in America) shows figures promenading in front of the beach and the harbour wall. It is a charming picture but untypical of her mature work for it shows the influence of late Pre-Raphaelitism. After she left Tenby for the Slade, she rarely visited Wales and never painted there.

In 1903 she went to France and, for the rest of her life, lived alone in a succession of
53 studios in Paris and Meudon. Unlike her brother, Gwen John avoided superficial and random influences and took from other artists only what she needed to refine her own vision of the world. A short period at Whistler's *Académie Carmen* in Paris consolidated her predilection for a personal version of Intimism: a single figure dominating the canvas, set in a simple interior and composed with elements such as a picture on the wall or a piece of furniture. Whistler remained the one important influence on her work, for she adopted not only his motif of a single figure in an interior but his dogma of tonal values. She
52 developed the theme into a completely personal image, refining the composition and evolving a methodical system of tonal relationships, often based on a cryptic series of notes and numbers.

Another important influence on Gwen John — though less on her work than on her attitude towards it — was that of Rodin. To keep herself in Paris she worked as a life model in the studios of various artists, and it was Augustus who advised her to pose for Rodin. At the time Rodin was 63 and regarded as the greatest living sculptor; he had
54 many commissions and needed many models, and he readily employed Gwen John. Through this encounter she became his mistress, and she remained deeply attached to

him, though he had a wife and had many similar affairs. It was the greatest emotional experience of her life, and it caused her intense joy as well as deep distress. But the affair also reinforced in her the conviction that hard work was as important as inspiration for an artist. It was Rodin's abiding creed, and it was a lesson she took to heart. He encouraged here with her work and, like Augustus, urged her to take better care of herself.

By the time Rodin died, in 1917, Gwen John had become a Catholic and had settled in Meudon, between Paris and Versailles. She lived alone with her cats, gradually withdrew from her family and friends, and sublimated her passionate nature into a love for God and an obsession with her work. She produced innumerable paintings, drawings and gouaches: of nuns, women, children, flower studies, small landscapes and a repetitive series of drawings taken from photographs. Though virtually none of these was concerned with Wales, the greatest single body of her work is now in the permanent collection of the National Museum of Wales. There is evidence of a period of great activity during her earlier years in Meudon but, either through ill-health or failing powers, her output declined towards the end of her life. Very little work survives from her later years, and she died in Dieppe, on a visit to the seaside, in 1939.

Although her exile was prompted mainly by personal factors, in its professional aspect it exemplified the problems and anomalies of Welsh-born artists of her period. For the greater part of her life she lived in and around Paris, which at that time was the centre of Western art. Yet the experience of living through the greatest period of change in the history of European art had little effect on her work. This, however, was not through ignorance. She was well aware of the new ideas that were being explored in Paris and she knew the work of the new masters.

Whatever the reasons for this detachment might be, it resembles the attitude of other Welsh artists, who chose to work apart from the mainstream of modern art, to take from it only what they needed and to find some form of isolation — either psychological or geographical — in which to work. Even Augustus John fits the description, for though he was the most celebrated British artist of his generation, he never embraced modernism, and tried all his life to resolve the dichotomy in his character and to find some physical refuge from the modern world.

But in this time of artistic upheaval it was often enough simply to remain in Wales in order to find isolation. Even Cardiff was sufficiently remote from any revolutionary fervour, pre-occupied as it was with its grandiose and traditional monuments to civic glory. There were many artists working in Wales, but they all practised as individuals, with no collective identity, and they left no legacy of ideas or style to make a mark on history. There were, for example, John Francis, Christopher Williams, Margaret Lindsay Williams and Edgar Thomas — the last an artist from Llanddewi in Pembrokeshire, who studied in London, Antwerp and Paris before returning to Cardiff and retiring into obscurity as a landscape painter. There was also the brief and enigmatic appearance of Henri Gaudier, who was eventually to find fame among the international *avant-garde*. Towards the end of 1908, Gaudier, later to meet and take the surname of Sophie Brzeska, took up residence in Claude Road, Cardiff. He worked as a clerk for a firm of coal contractors and spent all his spare time drawing: at the docks, the museum and in

Victoria Park. But there is no record of him making any contact with other artists and, in April 1909, he left Cardiff and went to Nuremburg and Munich, en route for Paris.

One artist who was deeply concerned about the identity and coherence of Welsh art
was Christopher Williams. He believed that Welsh art had special characteristics which
distinguished it from that of other countries, and in much of his work he tried to distil its
56 uniqueness. Ironically, Williams had to work in London to survive as an artist, though
there is no doubt that he promoted his belief with conviction and practised it with
diligence. But like other searchers for this particular Welsh ideal, he could come up with
little beyond the notion of Welsh subject-matter. He was fired with enthusiasm for the
Mabinogion, the *Black Book of Carmarthen*, Charlotte Guest's *Red Book* and all the ritual of the
Eisteddfodau, and he used them as material for his paintings. Yet, apart from a fixed
intensity of anguish about his figures, there is little to distinguish his work from that of
other academic British artists of the period.

Perhaps Williams was too cosmopolitan to be tuned into the Welsh ethos. He was
born in Maesteg and after studying art at Neath, he went to London, to the Royal College
of Art and the Royal Academy schools. He travelled in Italy, France, Spain and Morocco,
57 he spent some time in Paris and visited the Western Front in 1916 as a war artist. He
admired Corot, Carrière, Manet and Rodin, and was influenced by Leighton, Watts and
Augustus John. Except for his small landscapes and some of his portraits, his painting
never reached towards twentieth-century modernism but remained fixed in a poetic form
of late nineteenth-century academism. Even his work from the First World War showed
all the virtues of conventional heroics and none of the despair that was becoming part of
the modern spirit.

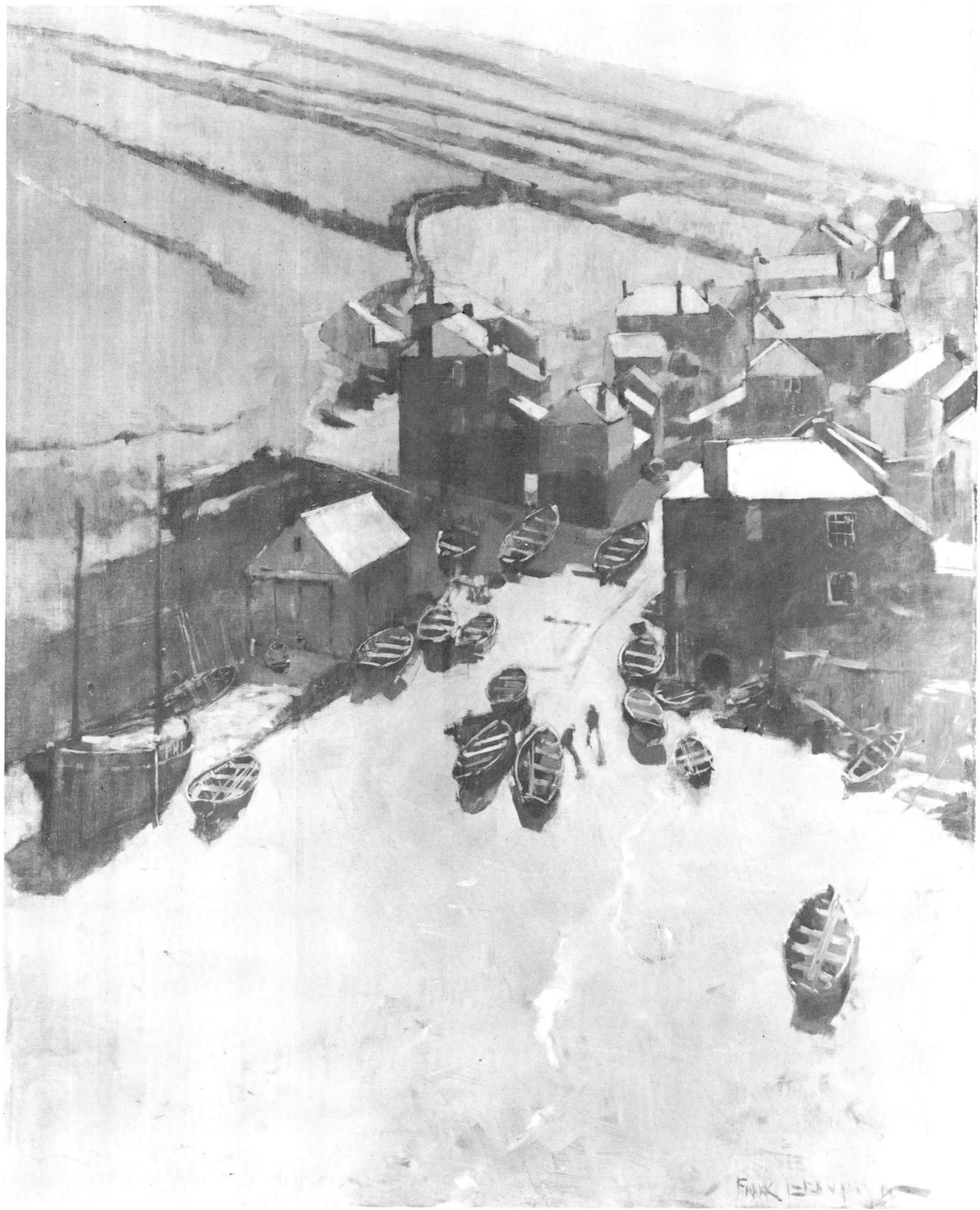
FRANK

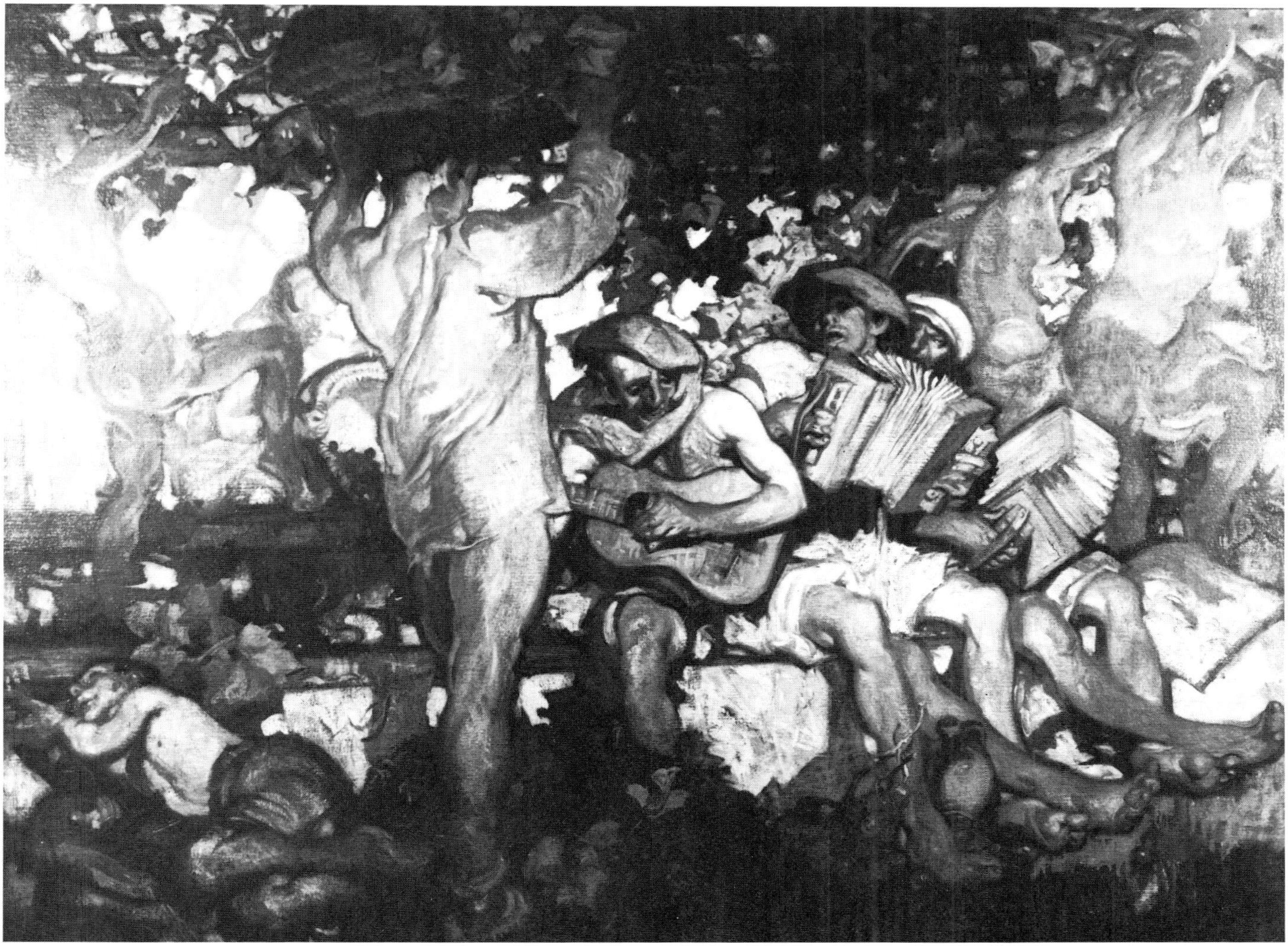

36. Frank Brangwyn
Sunday (1887) Oil on canvas 91.5 x 71 cm
Private Collection

Painted during his first trip to Cornwall, this picture is rare in Brangwyn's work in that it is a straightforward topographical landscape. The place is Mevagissey, seen from a high viewpoint, where Brangwyn went to paint after encouragement and financial help from Mr Mills, a colourman and friend of young artists. Although most of Brangwyn's Cornish paintings have affinities with the work of the Newlyn School, this one shows some influence of Impressionism. One early biographer (Walter Shaw-Sparrow) described this brief Impressionist period as the time when Brangwyn sowed his 'wild oats'.

37. Frank Brangwyn
The Wine Press (1946) Oil on canvas 117 x 155cm
Dudley Art Gallery

Despite a long painting career, spanning more than sixty years, Brangwyn remained surprisingly loyal to his chosen style and subject-matter. As a young man he had travelled widely in Africa, Europe and the Near East, and his fondness for exotic studies of working people - often sentimentalised - persisted throughout his working life. This painting, for example, is close in content and treatment to works that he had produced half a century earlier. This consistency is all the more remarkable, considering the tremendous changes that had overtaken European art in that period.

38. Augustus John 1878 - 1961
French Fisherboy (1907) Oil on canvas 218.5 x 90 cm
National Museum of Wales

While he was living in Paris in 1907, John was visited in his studio by Maurice Cremnitz, who brought along a young Spanish painter, Pablo Picasso. John later reciprocated with a visit to Picasso's studio, where he saw some early Cubist works. They were not to John's taste but he did admire Picasso's earlier paintings of the 'Blue' period, particularly those of children, and their influence is evident in a few of John's paintings of the time, such as this one. John reported, 'Picasso is a wonder'. Some time later Picasso described John as 'the best bad painter in England'.

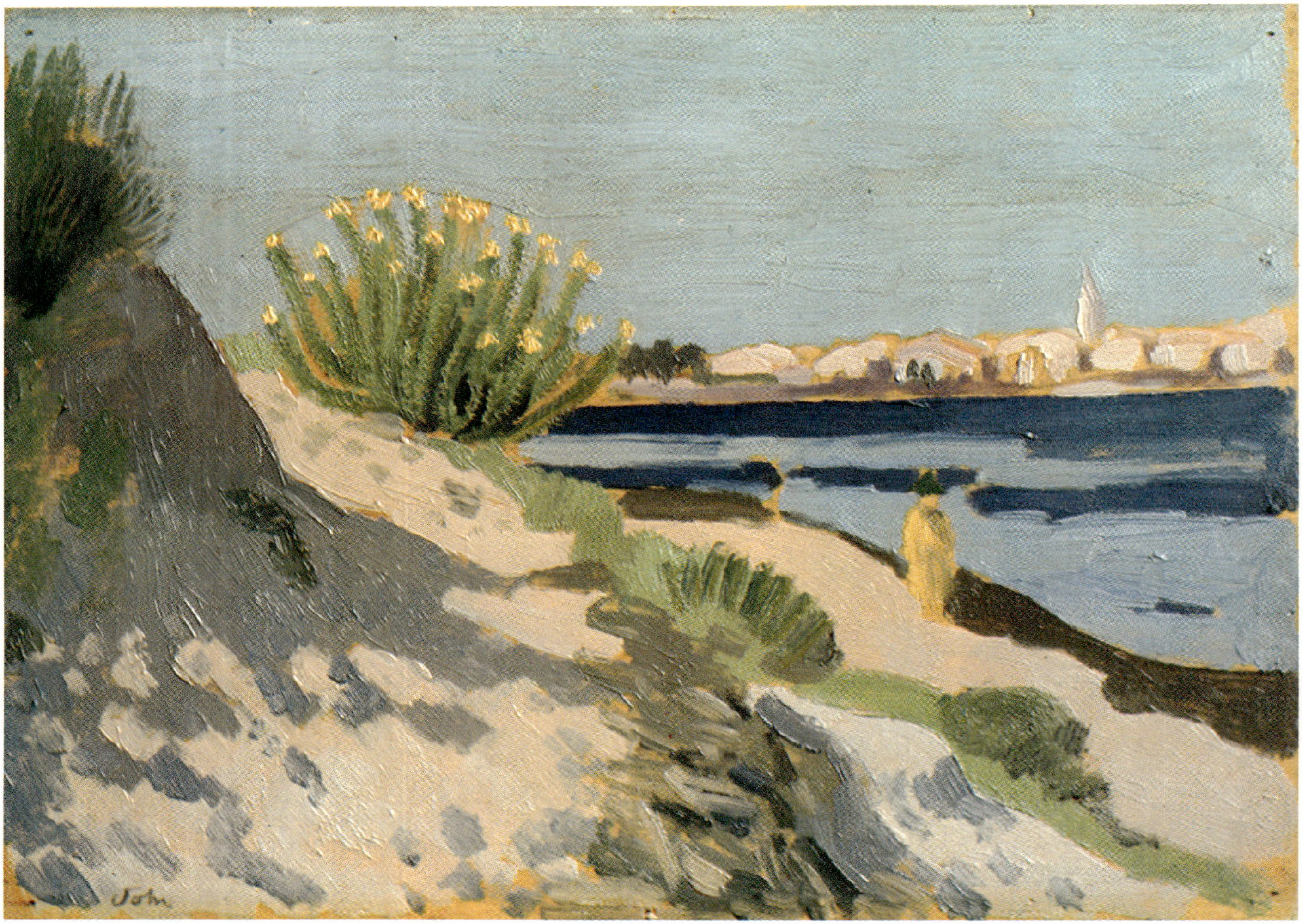

39. Augustus John
View of Martigues (1910) Oil on panel
24 x 33 cm
Private Collection

All his life Augustus John sought a refuge from modern civilisation. One escape route was to 'the classic lands' of the Mediterranean countries, and in Provence he decided he had 'found an anchorage at last'. Based in Martigues, a fishing port on the great lagoon, the Etang de Berre, John painted a series of small, brilliant pictures which represent his closest approach to abstraction and an individual form of Post-Impressionism. This one shows a view of the town across the lagoon. Outside Martigues, John rented the Villa Ste. Anne for his family as a bolt hole from the modern world. But the refuge was transient and the modern world caught up with them. The villa is now a luxury hotel, in front of which passes the main highway to Marseille.

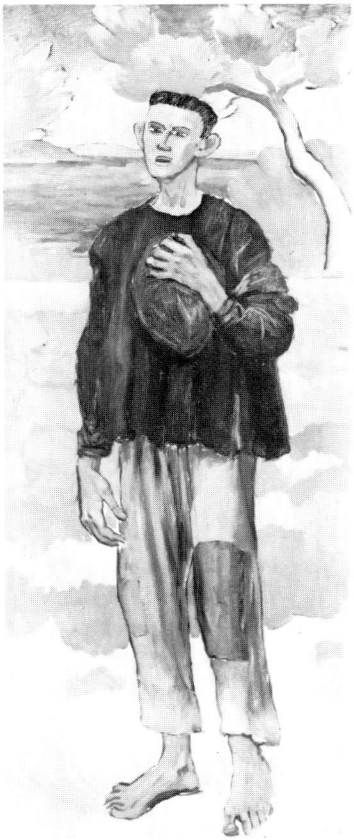

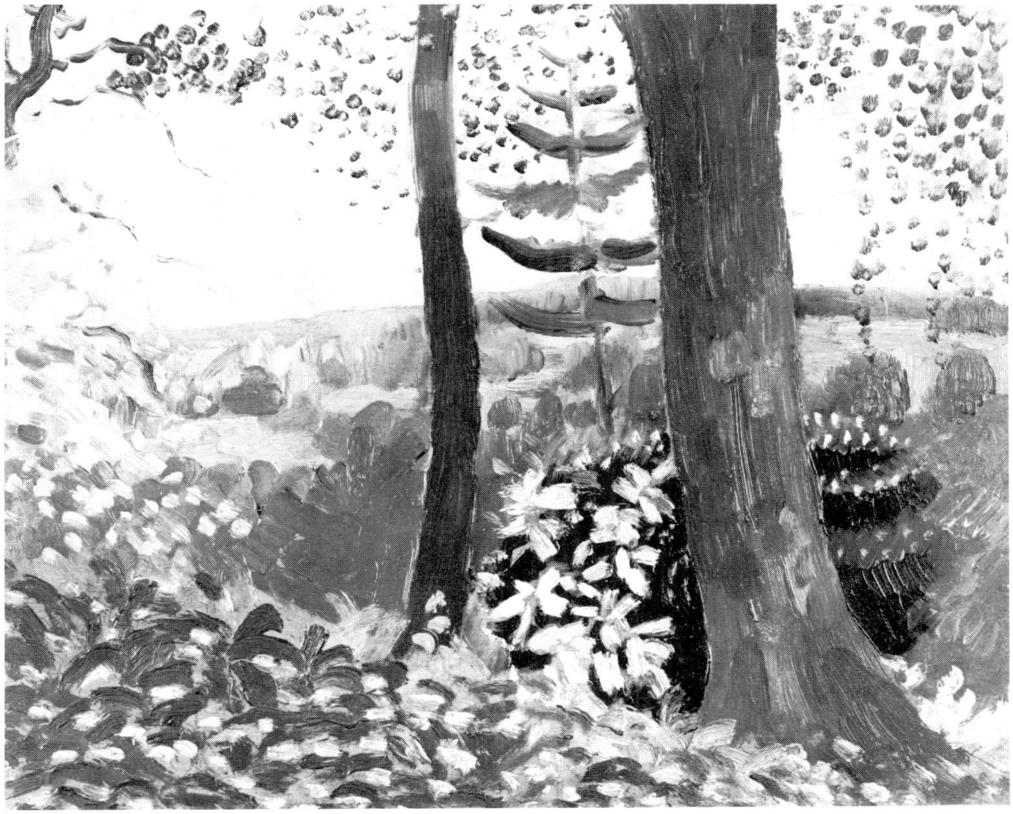

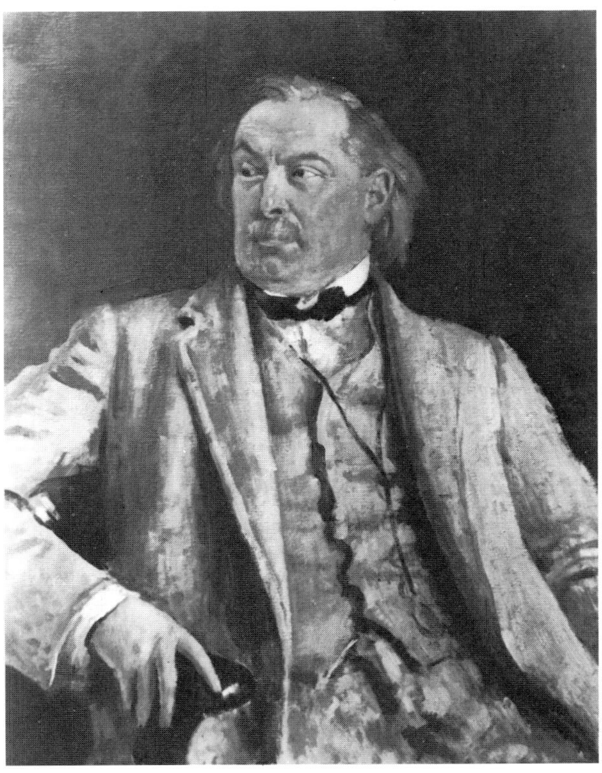

40. Augustus John
Landscape at Chirk (c.1912) Oil on panel 33 x 40.6 cm
Temple Newsham House, Leeds

After his series of Provençal scenes, John painted the landscape of north Wales, often in the company of J.D. Innes (Nos. 46, 47, 48). During this period, John was commissioned to paint the portrait of Lady Howard de Walden, and promptly installed himself at Chirk Castle. The ménage there was more to his taste - he mentions finding Lord de Walden seated at breakfast one morning reading 'The Times' while clad from head to toe in a suit of armour. There was also a constant flow of writers, composers and artists - including Derwent Lees (No.50) and Wilson Steer (c. 1916) who pronounced himself disgusted by John's portrait of Her Ladyship. For the portrait was a disaster and John was happier painting the country around Chirk. This painting is one of a series of studies he made for a decorative scheme he devised for the music room at Chirk - a large chamber containing an organ which had 6,000 pipes in a loft beyond the chapel. The Chirk decorations were in hand at the same time as those for Hugh Lane (No.43) and suffered the same fate, for they never materialised. On the reverse of this panel is another painting 'Cottage near Arenig'.

41. Augustus John
The Rt. Hon. David Lloyd George (1916) Oil on canvas 91.5 x 71 cm
Aberdeen Art Gallery

In order to support his style of living, John was obliged to paint portraits throughout his life - often of sitters with whom he was not in sympathy. This portrait of Lloyd George was commissioned by Sir James Murray, who no doubt expected that the two Welshmen would get on famously. They did not. In a letter to John Quinn, Augustus complained that Lloyd George 'was a rotten sitter - as you say a "hot-arse who can't sit still and be patient"'. In fairness to Lloyd George, it must be remembered that this was painted during the middle of the war, at the height of the Serbian crisis and while he was suffering from toothache.

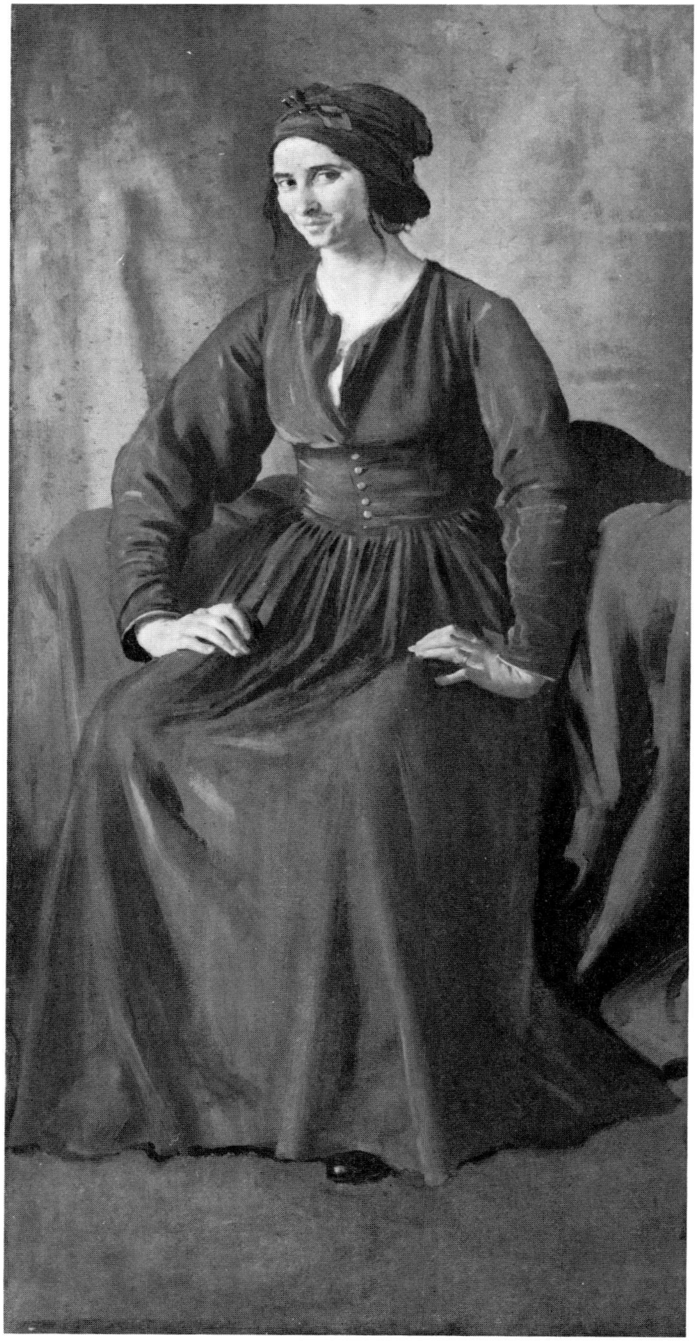

43. Augustus John
Lyric Fantasy (1911 - 15) Oil on canvas 249 x 470 cm
Tate Gallery
Though unfinished, this figure composition is one of John's most successful large-scale compositions, and it shows the influence of Puvis de Chavannes. The precise nature of the fantasy is obscure, though there is a strong personal element in it. The children are portraits of the artist's sons, the central figure is Dorelia, and the woman on the right is his wife Ida - who had been dead for more than four years when the picture was painted. The background is a synthesis of some of John's favourite locations: mainly the Blue Pool in Dorset, with touches of north Wales and Provence added. John never finished this painting - it was commissioned by Sir Hugh Lane who was drowned in the Lusitania - and it was discovered years later, rolled up and neglected in his studio.

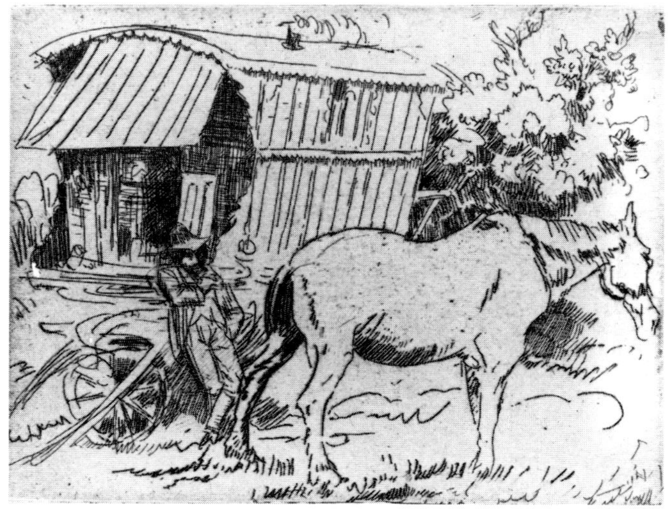

44. Augustus John
Caravan with Horse (1909) Etching 10.16 x 13 cm
Another of John's escape routes from civilisation was into the world of the gypsies. While teaching at Liverpool University art school (1901-1902) John came to know the celebrated authority on gypsies, John Sampson, who was the University Librarian. Sampson, a diligent and active enthusiast, took John to the gypsy encampments around Liverpool, the Wirral and north Wales; and around Bala they found the few survivors who still spoke the ancient Romani. John learned the language and acquired a deep and lasting love of the gypsies and gypsy lore - though it appears only rarely in his art. But he did acquire a couple of caravans, and for a while (c.1905-1909) he travelled the roads of England in them with his women and children. The caravans and their reluctant occupants figure in several of his paintings, drawings and etchings of those years. John first took up etching around 1901 in Liverpool, inspired by Rembrandt and Whistler, and prompted by his friend from the Slade, a fellow-Welshman, Benjamin Evans.

42. Augustus John
The Smiling Woman (1909) Oil on canvas 195.5 x 96.5 cm
Tate Gallery
The portraits that John genuinely enjoyed painting were of people close to him: his wife, children, mistresses and friends. Here the sitter is Dorothy McNeill, known as 'Dorelia', who lived with John for nearly sixty years and who appears in many of his finest paintings and drawings. This portrait was a great success when it appeared in the International Society's exhibition 'Fair Women' at the New Gallery, London in 1909. To a large extent, it founded John's reputation as a portraitist, though it is a traditional work, for John was chiefly influenced by the old masters, and it is Hals who has emerged here.

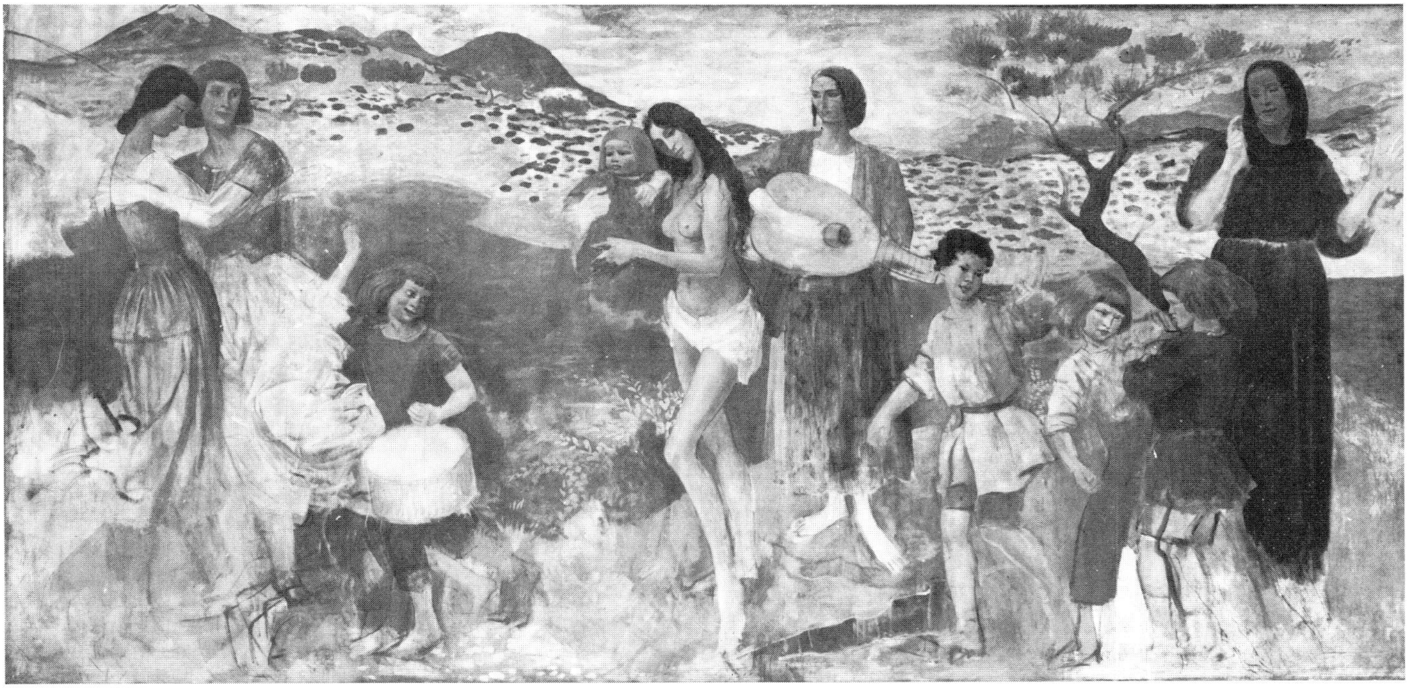

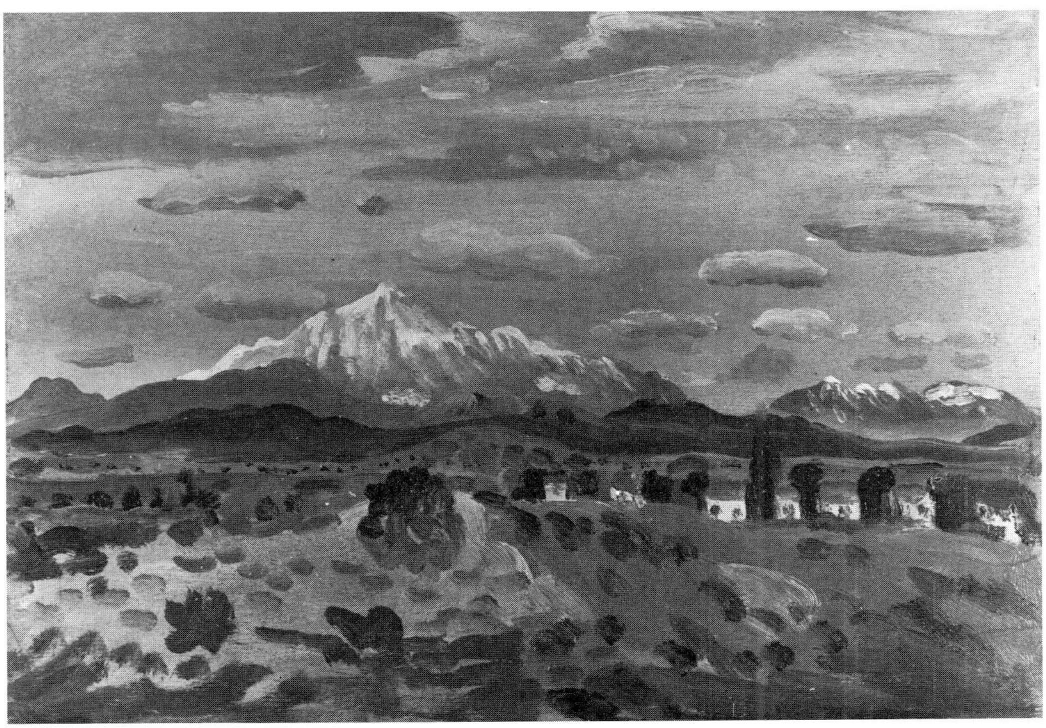

45. James Dickson Innes 1887 - 1914
Canigou in Snow (1911) Oil on panel 23 x 32.5 cm
National Museum of Wales

Mont Canigou, the highest peak in the Pyrenees, can be seen due west from Collioure, a picturesque fishing port on the Mediterranean coast. Innes visited Collioure several times (in 1908, 1910, 1911 and 1912) during the period when Matisse and Derain were working there. Though there is no evidence that Innes ever met the French artists, his experience of light and colour in the South of France was crucial in the development of Innes' painting. This can best be demonstrated by comparing the Welsh landscapes that he painted before, with those of north Wales that were painted after his first visit to the Mediterranean. In his pictures of Mont Canigou and Mynydd Arenig, there is a distinctly Fauve colouring and freedom of handling absent in his earlier work.

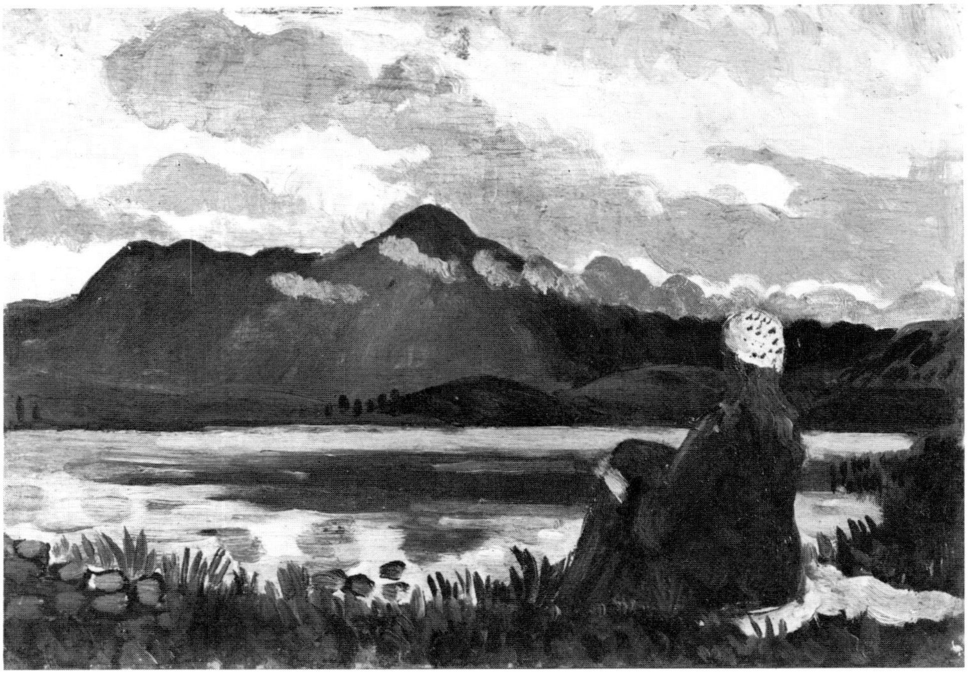

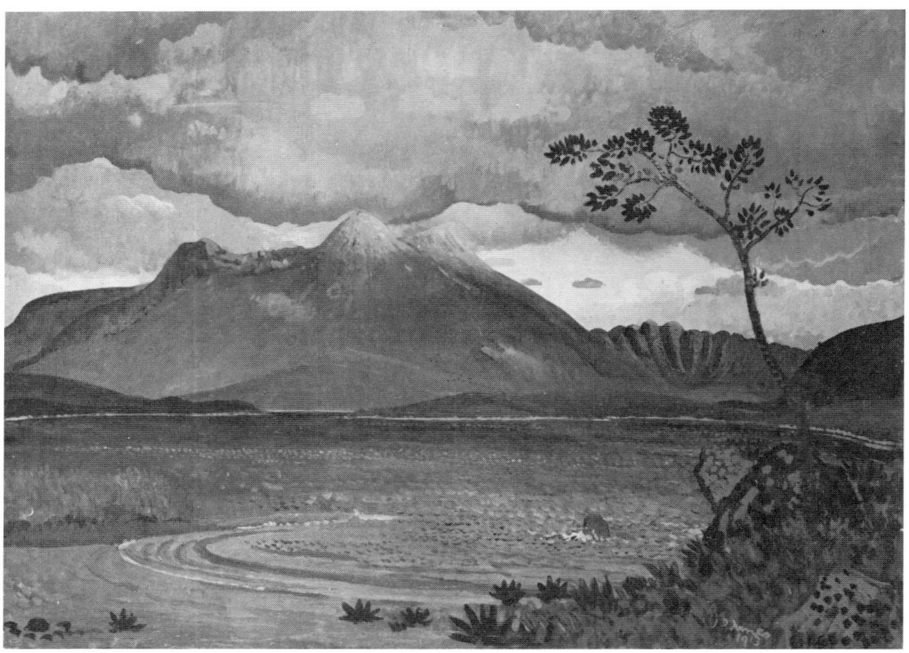

46. James Dickson Innes
Girl Seated by a lake (c.1911) Oil on panel 23 x 33 cm
Graves Gallery, Sheffield

Prompted by Augustus John's example, Innes occasionally introduced figures into his landscapes - though never successfully. The setting here is Arenig Fawr, seen across Llyn Tryweryn. The girl appears to be a gypsy, and in his autobiography John recounts his friend's hopeless infatuation for a Romany girl called Florence. In another mood of romantic despair, Innes is reputed to have buried a silver casket, probably containing love letters from Euphemia Lamb, under a cairn on the peak of Arenig. John also tells how Innes first showed him the mountain, 'experiencing, I fancy, the scruples of a lover on introducing a girl to his best friend'.

47. James Dickson Innes
Arenig (1913) Oil on panel 85.75 x 113.75 cm
Tate Gallery

Arenig Fawr, like Canigou, is a handsome mountain which is picturesque in all kinds of weather. It rises from the mooriand between Bala and Ffestiniog - an area favoured by John and Innes, who both painted many landscapes there. A later and larger painting than the preceding view of Arenig, this view is also taken from the far side of Llyn Tryweryn. The lake is adjacent to the cottage at Nant-ddu, that the two artists rented, and it is the view across the lake in the opposite direction (to the west) that was painted by John in the next illustration.

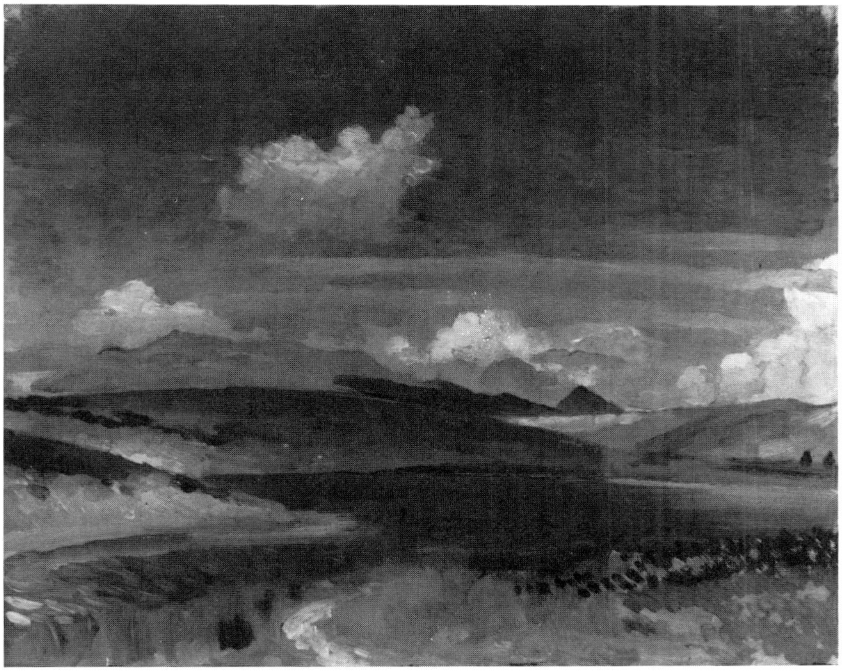

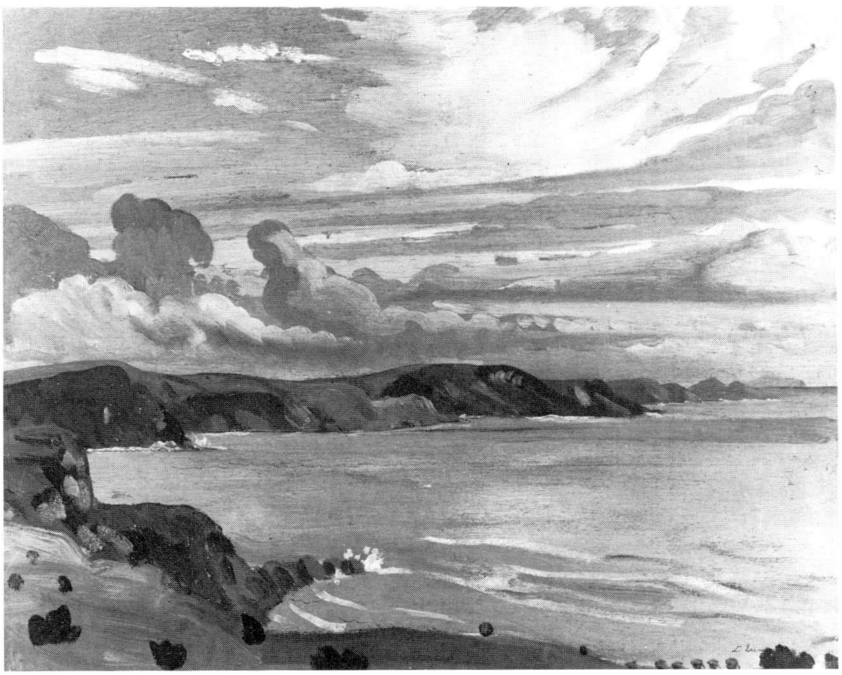

48. Augustus John 1878 - 1961
Llyn Treweryn (1911) Oil on panel 31.75 x 40.5 cm
Tate Gallery

In 1911, John and Innes stayed at the Rhyd-y-Fen Inn (now a farm) near Arenig. Later John rented a cottage by Nant-ddu Brook, a mile or so to the west. Apart from one distant pylon, the view is unchanged. A comparison of the view with the painting shows how John also remained faithful to topographical detail, while intensifying the colour. A painting of Rhyd-y-Fen by John was among those he exhibited at the Armory Show in New York in 1913.

49. James Dickson Innes 1887 - 1914
Pembroke Coast (c.1911) Oil on panel 31.75 x 38 cm
National Museum of Wales

Here it is the sky that dominates the composition, a device which Innes may have learned from Constable and from the earlier paintings of one of his favourite artists, Corot. In this painting, Innes has also applied his experience of Mediterranean light and Post-Impressionist colour to a Welsh scene, a view from Stackpole Quay, looking towards Caldey Island.

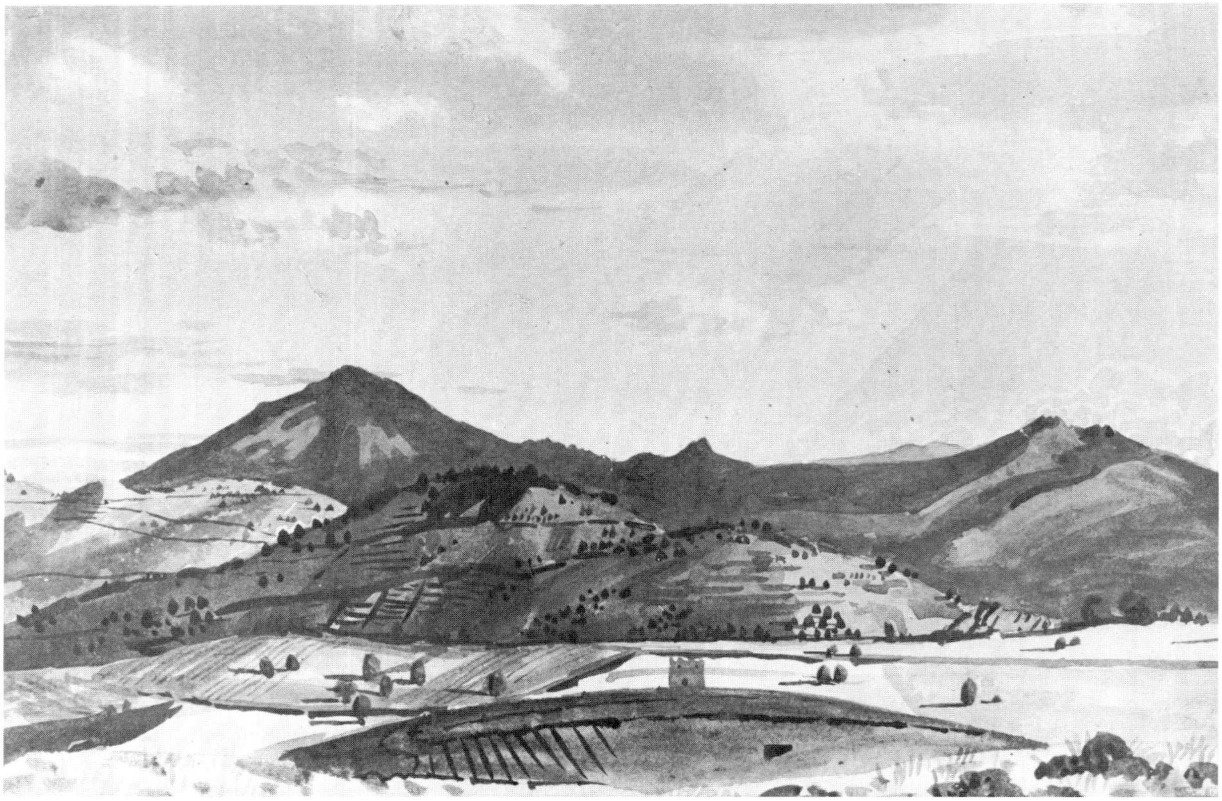

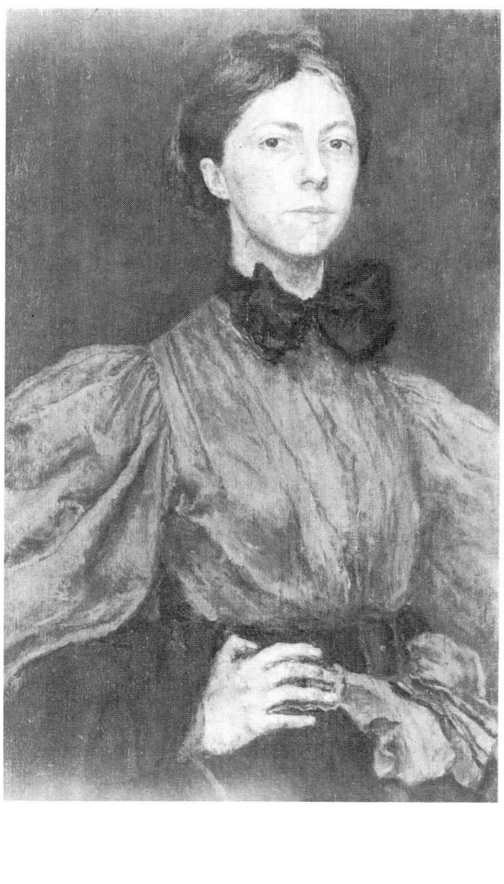

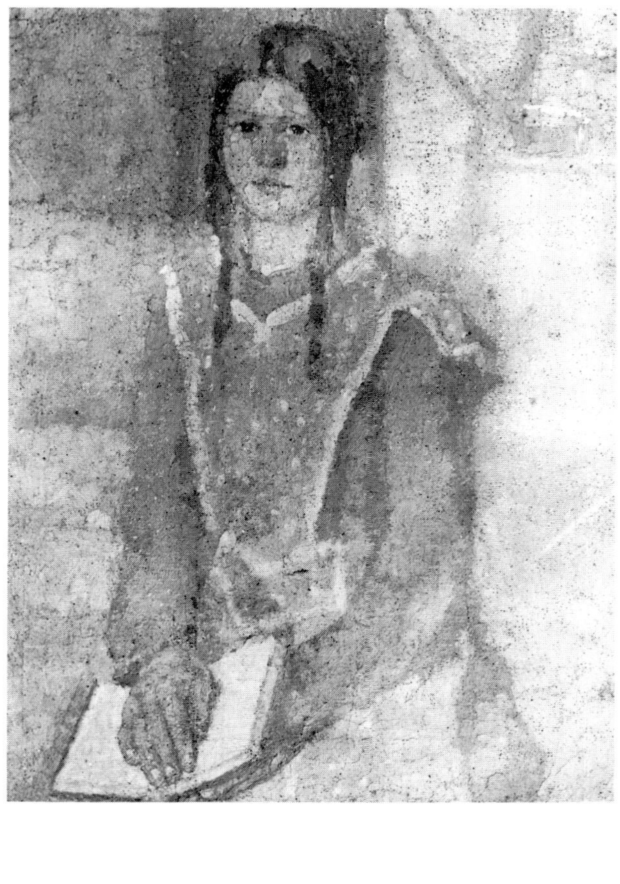

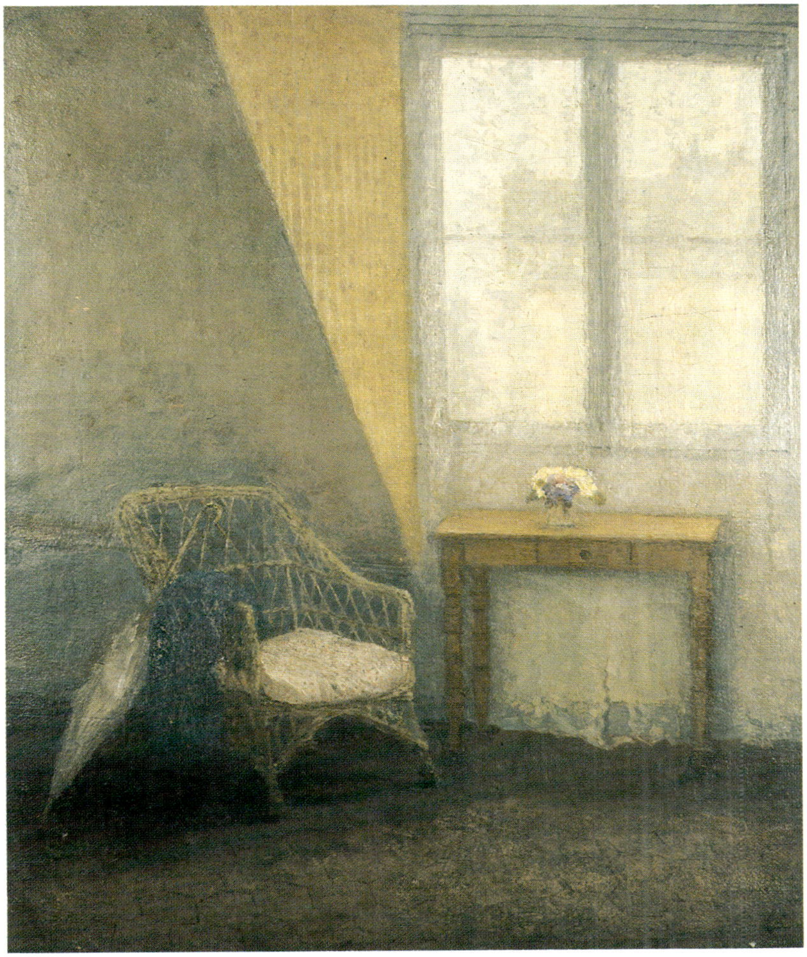

50. Derwent Lees 1885 - 1931
Evening, Wales (c.1912) Watercolour 24.8 x 36.2 cm
Temple Newsham House, Leeds
Derwent Lees was born in Brisbane, Australia, and studied in Paris before enrolling at the Slade in 1904 - a year before Innes. The two became friends and Lees was later involved in the bohemian coterie that John and Innes imported into north Wales in the years immediately preceding the First World War. Lees took a cottage near Ffestiniog, and was later taken by John to Chirk Castle, where both artists stayed as guests of Lord Howard de Walden. Lees painted many views of north Wales in the wake of John and Innes, and was profoundly influenced by both artists: his figure paintings owe an allegiance to John's, while his watercolours of landscapes - such as this one - are indebted to Innes' earlier works in this medium. This sometimes exasperated Innes, who complained 'I tire of seeing my own subjects so many times'. John, ignoring his own influence on Lees, was more tolerant: 'Lees owed much to the example of Innes... a means of release from his academic shackles'. But even during the period in north Wales, Lees was showing signs of insanity, and from 1918 until his death thirteen years later, he was confined to a mental hospital.

51. Gwen John 1876 - 1939
Self-portrait (1902) Oil on canvas 44.75 x 35 cm
Tate Gallery
Dating from the time of her middle twenties, this painting shows Gwen John as she was shortly after leaving the Slade. It was probably painted during a stay in Liverpool, while she was visiting her brother Augustus, who was teaching at the University Art School there. Although quite gregarious, she was already showing a taste for ascetic living, a characteristic that Augustus deplored and attempted to alleviate. He was constantly imploring her to look after her health and to exhibit her work.

52. Gwen John
The Convalescent (c.1920 - 4) Oil on canvas 40 x 32.5 cm
National Museum of Wales
The artist's favourite motif was a single figure seated in a simple interior. It was repeated with many variations and sometimes in several versions of one variation, as was the case with this picture of which at least nine versions are known. The influence of Whistler is evident, not only in the subject-matter but also in the careful orchestration of tones. When Augustus questioned Whistler about his sister's work, he replied that she had 'a fine sense of tone'.

53. Gwen John
A corner of the Artist's Room (c.1907) Oil on canvas 32 x 27 cm
Graves Gallery, Sheffield
Unlike Augustus, Gwen John painted few landscapes and never attempted large or imaginative figure compositions. Much more objective, she painted the commonplace things around her: her furniture, her cats, flowers, friends and several interiors, taken from her studio, and remarkable for their air of quietude. This interior was painted in one of her studios in Paris, an attic room at 12 rue du Cherche Midi in Montparnasse.

54. Auguste Rodin 1840 - 1917
Study for the Whistler Memorial (c.1906) Bronze
Musée Rodin, Paris

After Whistler's death, Rodin was commissioned by the Royal Society of Engravers to produce a memorial monument. Rodin's design was rejected by the Society and all that now remains are several heads and nude studies, for which the model was Gwen John, then about 29 years of age. According to Augustus, Rodin told him that his sister had 'un corps admirable'.

55. Gwen John 1876 - 1939
Studio Interior (c.1920 - 4) Oil on canvas 22 x 27 cm
City Art Gallery, Manchester

When Rodin moved to a studio in Meudon, just outside Paris, Gwen followed and found this studio nearby in the rue Terre Neuve. Like her others, this was sparsely furnished but neat and tidy. After Rodin's death, she remained in Meudon and later bought a piece of land on which stood a shed, in which she lived and worked. She stayed there until her death, in growing seclusion, alone with her cats, and seeing only a few friends, her nephew Edwin, and the nuns in the nearby convent.

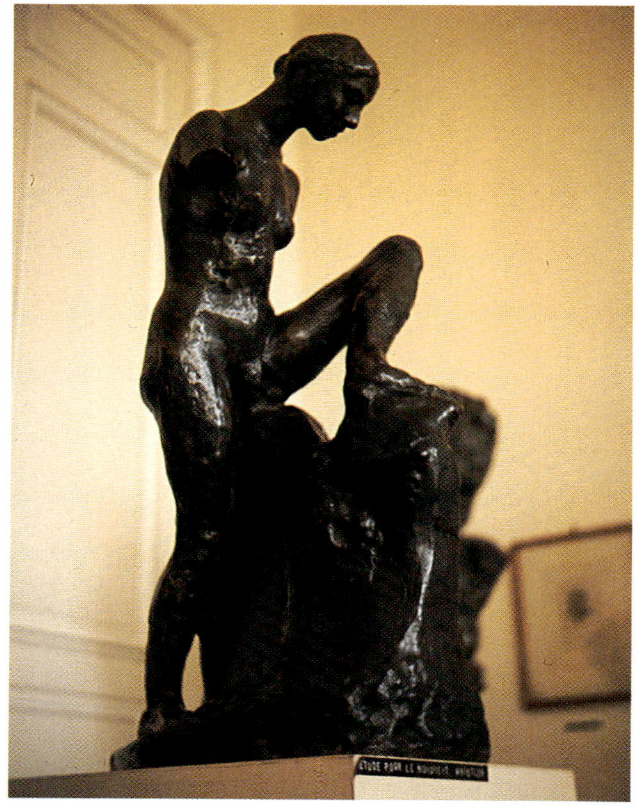

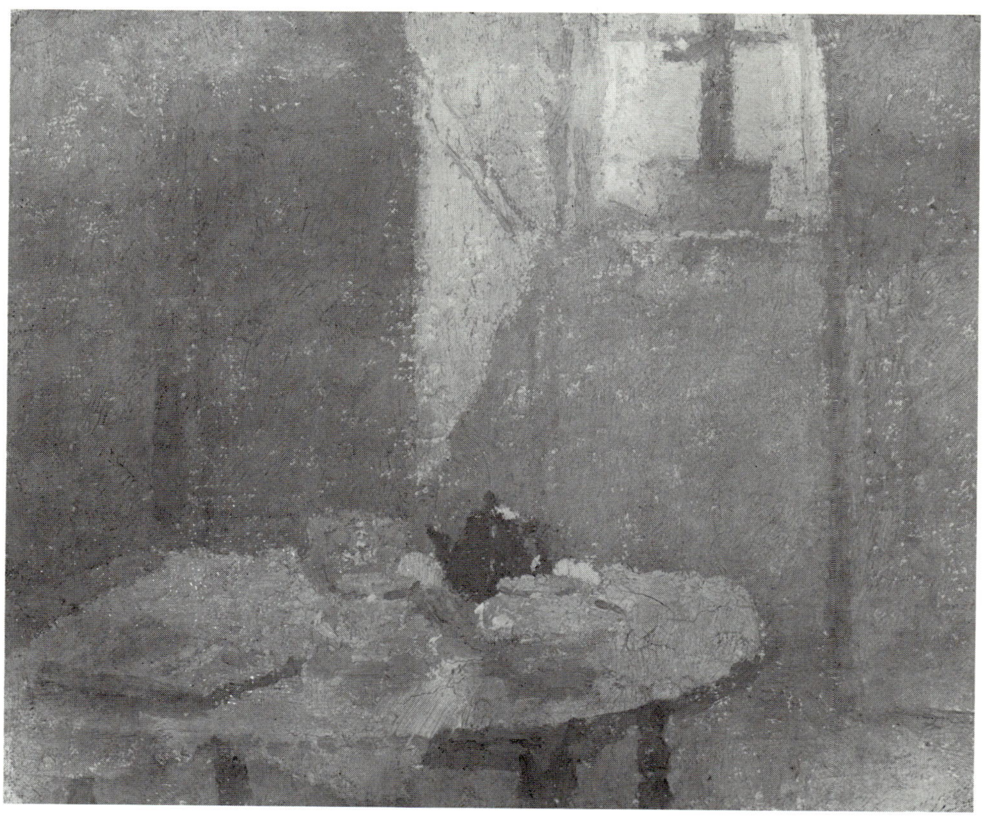

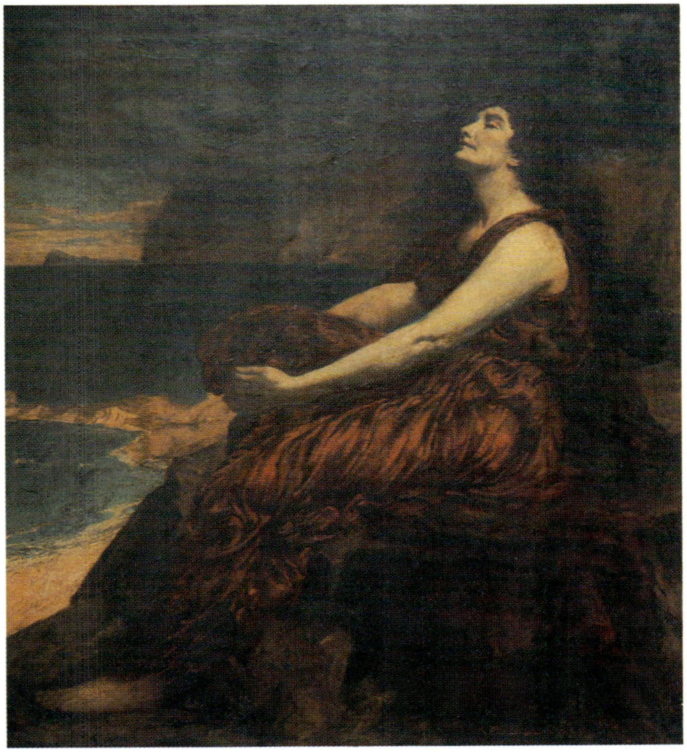

56. Christopher Williams 1873 - 1934
Branwen (1915) Oil on canvas 148.5 x 135.25 cm
Glynn Vivian Art Gallery, Swansea

The subject is taken from the Mabinogion and represents Branwen, sister of the British king, and wife of his enemy the King of Ireland. The anguished division of loyalties suggested in this painting is an expression of Williams's belief that 'the highest form of art is that which portrays the deep problems and aspirations of human life and sets people thinking'.

57. Christopher Williams
The Charge of the Welsh Division at Mametz Wood 11 July 1916 (1916) Oil on canvas 172.75 x 274.25 cm
National Museum of Wales

The episode is taken from the Battle of the Somme, and was painted at the request of Lloyd George, then Minister for War. This painting is concerned more with the theatrical effects of war than with its 'deep problems of human life'. Such problems were expressed more subtly by David Jones when, in the pages of 'In Parenthesis', he described his first-hand experiences of the Battle of the Somme. Lloyd George was a friend and patron of Williams, who had previously painted Lloyd George's portrait as Chancellor of the Exchequer (1912) and later as Prime Minister (1917).

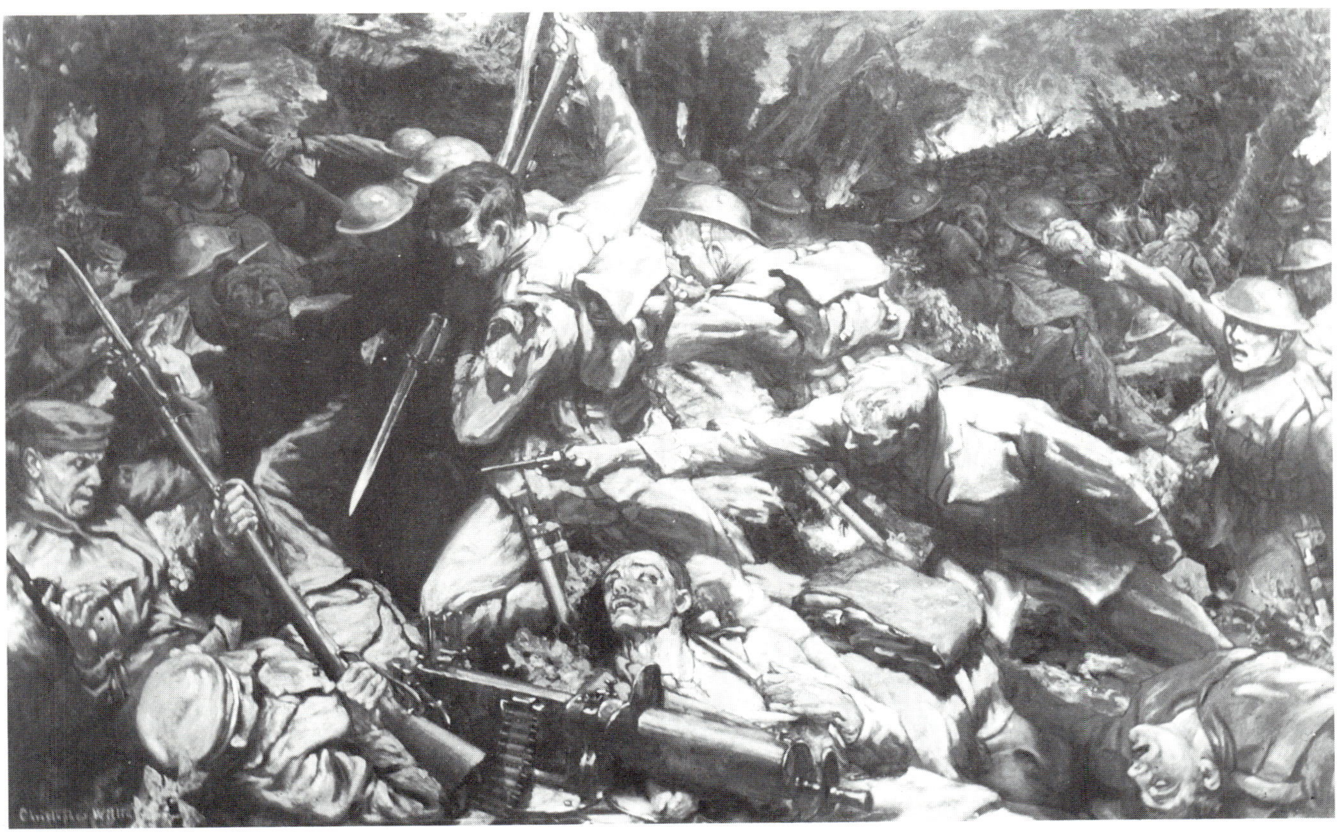

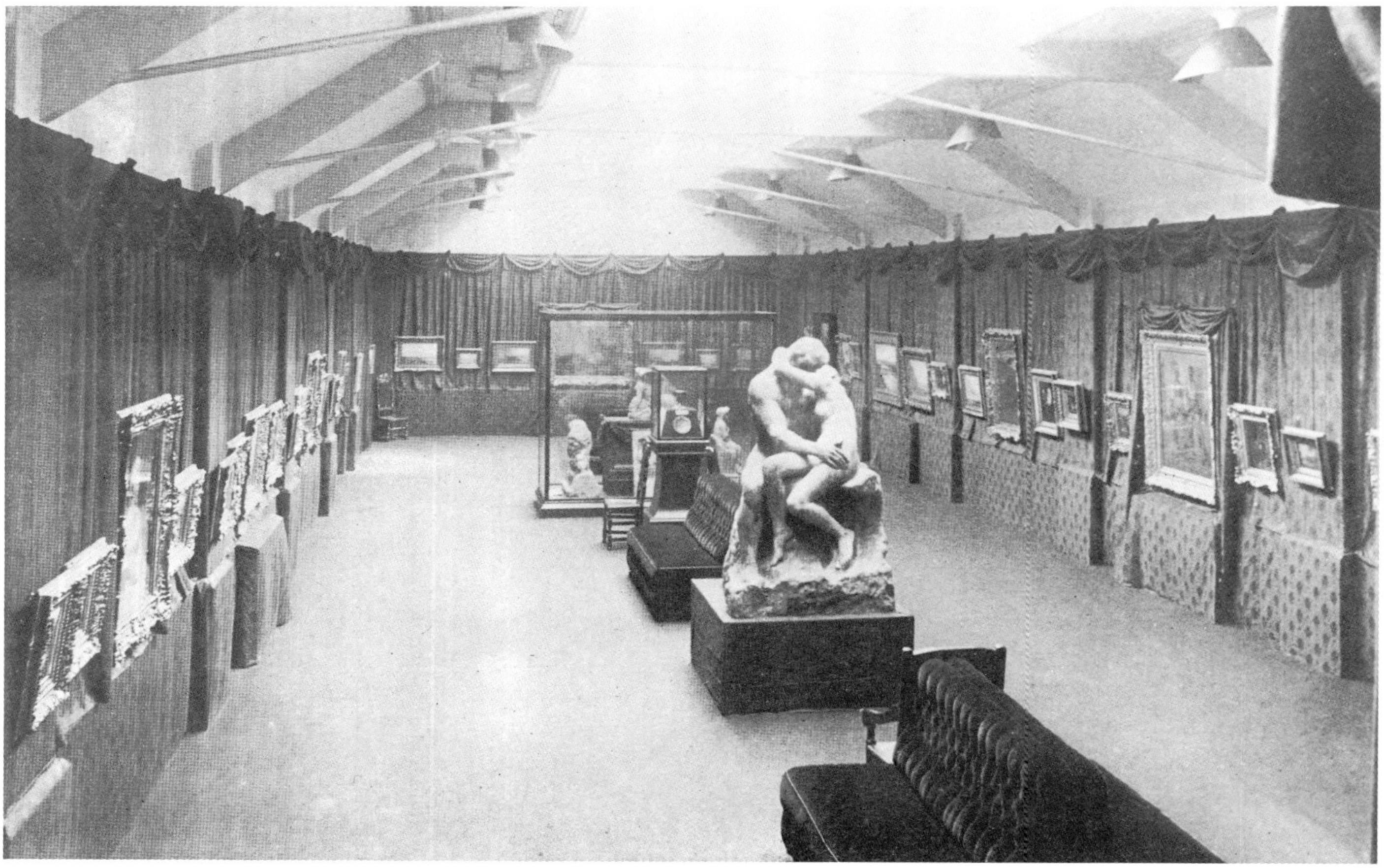

'THE LONG-DELAYED REVIVAL'

Chapter Four

Just as the First World War shattered the old social order, so the Modern Movement in art demolished the cultural complacency of the bourgeoisie in Europe and America. Having just come to terms with Impressionism, such new horrors as Fauvism, Cubism, Expressionism, and Futurism strained its tolerance too far. In 1913, in London, Picasso was condemned as 'the Public Enemy of art'. In New York, the *bête noire* was Marcel Duchamp, notorious for his recent painting *Nude Descending a Staircase*, the sensation of the Armory Show. In Cardiff, in the same year, it was Impressionism, and particularly a 43-year old painting by Manet, that roused the indignation of some visitors to *A Loan Exhibition*. Nevertheless, by the end of this inter-war period, Wales had again asserted its potent appeal; this time to the artists of the New Romanticism. As a result, Welsh subjects and Welsh artists were in the forefront of British art.

58. A Loan Exhibition, Installation View, City Hall, Cardiff February 1913

The gallery in the old City Hall was specially decorated for this exhibition, being tastefully draped with brown velvet. The dominant work was 'The Kiss', a large bronze by Rodin, dating from 1888 and now in the National Museum of Wales. Hugh Blaker, the curator of The Holborne Museum in Bath and one of the exhibition organisers, in a letter to the 'Western Mail' (12 February 1913) expressed his belief that 'from this historic exhibition may start a movement which should place the Welsh nation, temperamentally fitted for artistic expression, among the leading art producers of the world'.

In the period between the two World Wars, the progress of the visual arts in Wales
began to gather momentum. In retrospect, this seems to have been the result of tentative
efforts by public bodies and private individuals, uncoordinated in their respective
activities, but adding up gradually to a growing confidence and a sense of national
58 purpose. The National Museum of Wales, though not formally opened until 1927, began
to organise exhibitions well before then. Among the first of these was *A Loan Exhibition*,
which opened in Cardiff's old City Hall in February 1913; a month after the closing of
Roger Fry's second exhibition of Post-Impressionism in London, and exactly concurrent
with the Armory Show in New York.

When compared with these two, the Cardiff exhibition appears an uncontentious
affair. With 59 works on show, there were only a few that could be described as modern,
and none that would have caused a spasm among conservative critics in either London or
New York. The bulk of the exhibition consisted of works by established masters such as
59 Turner, Constable, Millet, Burne-Jones and Monticelli; going back as far as Wilson and
going forward no further than Whistler. The most modern ideas were represented by the
Impressionists: Monet and Manet.

But though the battle for Impressionism had already been fought and won in other
places, it still drew some withering fire from the *Western Mail*. Writing of Monet, its critic
J.M. Staniforth declared: 'the artist endeavours to hide, by a plentitude [sic] of gaudy
60 colours, his ignorance of some of the other branches of knowledge which go to the making
of a work of art'. He was equally scathing about Manet, and even condemned Corot for
his 'spotty, dirty, colourless landscapes'.

The exhibition, however, had its champions. Writing in the *Daily Telegraph*, Sir Claude Phillips said that 'London ... has much reason to envy Cardiff' while Hugh Blaker, in a reply to the *Western Mail*'s criticism, stoutly maintained that the exhibition was '... the greatest artistic event in the history of Wales'. On the whole, informed opinion was in favour of the exhibition, and the public appeared to agree. Over 26,000 people visited the exhibition in Cardiff — an impressive total considering the time and place — and a series of supporting lectures was well-attended.

What the controversy did reveal was a common agreement about the state of art and art education in the Principality at that time. In the same article, Staniforth quoted 'one of our most respected townsmen' as saying that 'few cities in the United Kingdom of the same magnitude, and none at all on the continent have been, or are doing less to educate its population in the love of art'. Staniforth also deplored the standards of Cardiff's art school 'controlled from its inception by a corporation whose distinguishing characteristic has been a porcine indifference to art'. Blaker was equally critical about the visual arts, but more positive in his hopes, declaring that the loan exhibition would 'give a stimulus to the long-delayed revival in Welsh art'.

These quotations sum up the range of responsible opinion about the visual arts in Wales around the time of the First World War; that they were neglected by the responsible authorities, and that this neglect was hindering an inevitable but overdue renaissance. It is a matter of contention, however, as to whether Blaker might have been more accurate in discerning not a revival, but a long-delayed arrival.

61 However, *A Loan Exhibition* of 1913 was heralded by those who cared about Welsh art as the faint glimmer of a new dawn — and on the whole they were right. But what was equally significant about the exhibition was that it was virtually a private enterprise, in that all the works were lent by private collectors. Thirty-eight works, well over half the total exhibited, had been lent anonymously; it only later emerged that the lenders were two sisters, Gwendoline and Margaret Davies, who had also paid the expenses for the exhibition.

The Davies sisters were the grand-daughters of David Davies of Llandinam, an industrial pioneer who had founded a fortune on coal and railway enterprises in South Wales in the middle of the nineteenth century. His grand-daughters were wealthy
62 spinsters, cultured and enlightened about art, who lived at Plas Dinam at Llandinam in Montgomeryshire. In 1908, advised by Hugh Blaker, the brother of their governess, they began to build up a collection of art, gradually acquiring the confidence to make their own purchases. In this, they were surprisingly progressive, and their tastes were often in advance of those of the public galleries in Britain. By 1924, they had gathered together about 200 works, half of which formed an important selection of nineteenth-century French art, and the other half consisting of old masters, as well as some modern British masters such as Whistler and Augustus John.

The Misses Davies were equally enterprising in promoting art. In 1920 they bought Gregynog Hall, near Newtown, and in the centre of rural Wales. It was their intention to establish an arts centre at Gregynog, with studios, pottery workshops, a printing press and facilities for the recitals of music. It was a private endeavour to create the ever-elusive
63 Welsh Academy and, as such, it was remarkably ambitious. But like any such enterprise, private or public, it was at the mercy of wider pressures. The industrial unrest and the financial depression of the 1920s and 1930s undermined the financial stability of the sisters, and curtailed the complete development of the scheme. The Davies sisters themselves moved into Gregynog in 1924 and, though there were several impressive performances of music, the only important manifestation of the visual arts was the printing press.

The declared aim of the Gregynog Press, '... to help cultivate a love of beautiful things in the people of Wales by means of the practice of ... printing, binding, illustration ...', takes it into the area of crafts and the applied arts. However, the extremely high standards of the press, the rare, exquisite volumes it produced, and the fact that it employed artists such as David Jones, Blair Hughes Stanton, Gertrude Hermes and Agnes Miller Parker as illustrators, meant that the press was making a distinguished contribution, along parallel lines, to the growing recognition of Welsh art. The wide and high reputation of the Gregynog Press helped to support the aspirations and the confidence of those who believed that Welsh art had its own destiny. This general advance was supported in a palpable manner by the Davies sisters; not only through their enterprise in founding the Gregynog Press, but by their generosity in donating their collections of art to the National Museum of Wales.

Another venture into private patronage — less deliberate but certainly more diverse — was happening concurrently in north Wales. In 1911, Thomas Evelyn, the eighth

Baron Howard de Walden, took a lease on Chirk Castle; originally for twenty years,
64 though he and his family remained there until 1946. Lord Howard de Walden was a generous, even impetuous patron of painters, writers and composers; indeed, he functioned as a one-man, self-appointed Arts Council. Among his earliest protégés at Chirk was the unruly, Bohemian trio: Augustus John, J.D. Innes and Derwent Lees, whom he had probably met at their London home from home, the Café Royal. In May 1912, Lord Howard went with Innes on a painting trip to Ronda in southern Spain; in September of that year he commissioned John to paint Lady Howard de Walden's portrait, and allowed John to install himself at Chirk Castle as resident artist with a grandiose scheme of decorations for the Music Room. John found other creative people at the Castle, notably Sidney Sime the painter, and Josef Holbrooke the composer. Together with Sime, Holbrooke and John, Lord Howard rented a ramshackle bungalow Llwynythyl, up the mountain behind Tan-y-grisiau, near Blaenau Ffestiniog, where John imported a model to pose for him, and Holbrooke transported a grand piano, on which he and Lord Howard were to compose operas.

They collaborated on several operas: the trilogies *Druids and Heroes* and *The Children of the Don*, as well as the one-part *Dylan*, and there was talk of a ballet. As well as financing Holbrooke — and humouring his notions of genius — Lord Howard also supported Thomas Beecham and his fledgling orchestra and sent them on a concert tour of the 'distressed' areas of south Wales. He gave prizes for Welsh woodwind players — because, since the Welsh invariably 'sang and fiddled', they therefore neglected the wind instruments. In the field of literature and drama, the Howard de Waldens gave prizes for the best plays in Welsh and English by Welsh writers, commissioned a Welsh translation of Ibsen's play *The Pretenders*, and, around 1918, founded at Chirk the Welsh National Repertory Theatre. This was intended as a touring company and it began with a magnificent opening night in Cardiff when the guests of honour were Lloyd George and John Lewis (of Oxford Street fame). Individual writers who were financially helped by Lord Howard — some of whom were frequently to be found at Chirk — included Hilaire Belloc, John Masefield, Rudyard Kipling, George Moore, Laurence Binyon and G.K. Chesterton, whose political magazine *The New Witness*, beleaguered at Beaconsfield, was periodically rescued from the bailiffs by a cheque from Chirk.

Among the visual artists who were given refuge and hospitality at Chirk Castle was Derwent Lees, whom Augustus John retrieved from his cottage at Ffestiniog and deposited with Lady Howard de Walden with the words 'he needs a bit of a rest cure and feeding up: I hope you don't mind'. As it happened Lees was in a stage of incipient madness; he was terrified of Chirk Castle and its occupants and thought he had been committed to an expensive lunatic asylum. Other, saner artists at Chirk included Wilson Steer who, in 1916, painted dozens of watercolour sketches of the countryside around Chirk and a portrait of Lady Howard de Walden; Jacob Epstein who worked on a portrait head at the Castle; Eric Gill who made the war memorial in the town; and Sir John Lavery, who, having painted the Plymouth family on the terrace at St. Fagans, also portrayed the Howard de Waldens in the Saloon at Chirk.

One interesting feature that Chirk Castle had in common with Gregynog Hall and

Plas Dinam is that they were all situated in a rural environment, remote from the major towns in Wales, and far removed from the metropolitan centres of England. Perhaps this factor was indicative of the mood of the times, for in the same year that the Davies sisters moved into Gregynog, another artistic community was founded in rural Wales.

65 On 14 August 1924, Eric Gill, with his family and friends, arrived at Capel-y-ffin, four miles north of Llanthony Abbey in the Honddu valley in Breconshire. After the disappointments of a similar enterprise at Ditchling, it was to be a new start in a new place for Gill's ideal of a self-sufficient community. (By a curious coincidence, it was in 1924, the year the Gills left, that Frank Brangwyn moved to Ditchling where he was to remain, in growing seclusion, for the rest of his life.) At Ditchling in Sussex, Gill had been a founder of the Guild of St Joseph and St Dominic, 'a religious fraternity for those who make things with their hands'. But the fraternity had been beset by the usual problems of such ventures — of personality conflicts and finance — and by 1924 Gill was searching for another place.

At first he thought of Caldey Island, off the coast of Pembrokeshire, attracted by the idea of a ready-made Catholic community of artists and craftsmen. For among the Benedictines there was an artist Gill particularly admired, Dom Theodore Baily, a painter who had worked in Paris with Maurice Denis. But, quite apart from Caldey's evident financial problems, Gill was mainly deterred by 'the artistic slush in which Caldey now wallows', and by the 'arty, ornamental and garden cityish' standards which he found there. Besides this, Capel-y-ffin was in remote and beautiful country and, being deserted and neglected, it offered a challenge to his creative and pioneering instincts. And, as a final bonus, there were the remains of an earlier Anglo-Catholic enterprise, the abandoned monastery of Father Ignatius.

66 Gill was remarkable for his energy and enthusiasm, his personal charisma, and his passionate belief in the supreme values of art and the Holy Catholic Church. With his wife and daughters, with his friends the Hagreens and the Attwaters, and with his disciple David Jones, he set about establishing Capel-y-ffin as a self-sufficient community, unsullied by the principles of capitalism and dedicated to the furthering of the high ideals of creativity and Christianity. It was a goal that Gill was capable of reaching, for not only was he an intellectual Catholic, he was also an eminently practical man.

67 At Capel-y-ffin there was daily mass and weekly confession, earnest moral discussions and, for light relief, community singing or reading to each other from uplifting books such as Malory's *Morte d'Arthur*. There was also an immense amount of work to be done; repairing and restoring the buildings, providing for the bodily needs of the community, as well as the means to support all this, Gill's work as an artist. Conditions for creating art were just as primitive as were the working conditions. Nevertheless, Gill managed to produce a considerable amount of work during his period in Wales, including carving, engraving and lettering.

68 Among the stone carvings he made were *The Deposition*, *The Sleeping Christ*, *Mankind*, and the simple font, banded with lettering, for the church on Caldey Island. In wood, he carved *Caryatid*, and the monumental war memorial that served as an altar-piece for Russell School. In his lettering, for which he is now perhaps best-known, he designed the

Perpetua and *Felicity* typefaces, the *Caslon* script and, at the end of his stay in Wales, the beginnings of the *Sans Serif* alphabet which now bears his name.

The titles and the subjects of the books that Gill illustrated are a peculiar but characteristic contrast of erotic and ascetic subjects: *The Passion of Our Lord Jesus Christ*; the treatise on Hindu love, *Ananga-Ranga*; G.K. Chesterton's *Gloria in Profundis*; and the *Song of Songs*. In addition, there was also Virgil, Chaucer's *Troilus and Criseyde*, Boccaccio, his sister's *Sonnets and Verses*, his own *Id quod visum placet* and E. Powys Mather's dubious masterpiece *Procreant Hymn*.

It was a fertile period for Gill and he produced an impressive body of work during his four years in Wales. Unfortunately, the very success of his work demanded frequent absences from the community and he discovered, once again — though from different causes — that idealistic ambitions are not always compatible with realistic circumstances. And apart from the inconvenience of the Black Mountains as a base for an artist with compelling metropolitan contacts, it was a nightmare for the women who had to stay and keep the place functioning. Although they went on a pilgrimage to Rome, and paid several visits to Salies de Béarn in the Pyrenees, this discontent with Capel-y-ffin could not be buried forever, and in October 1928 Gill and his family moved to Piggotts, near High Wycombe in Buckinghamshire.

But Eric Gill did not turn his back on Wales; his daughter Betty continued to live at Capel-y-ffin and he paid frequent visits there throughout the 1930s. It was there that, during a bout of illness, he began to write his autobiography in the spring of 1940. It was his last creative work for he died in the November of that year.

Gill's venture in Wales is important historically because it was virtually the first of such creative communities, deriving from the Arts and Crafts Movement, and it was certainly the most impressive. There have been, and still are, many similar craft co-operatives in Wales, but they are by no means as high-powered or as professional as was Gill's. What is also significant about the four years at Capel-y-ffin is that, in spite of
his prolific output, Gill left behind little permanent work dating from that period. The
69 font at Caldey is an austere work, and his best known work in Wales, the War Memorial
at Chirk, was executed by Gill in 1919, five years before he went into Wales.

The only works that were executed at Capel-y-ffin, and have remained *in situ* there, are two paintings by David Jones. On the wall of what Father Ignatius called 'The Bible Cloister' (which is now a games room), Jones painted a crucifixion. It is a strong painting,
free from superfluous detail; a monumental icon in a faintly Byzantine style that Jones
70 had probably assimilated on his visit to Caldey. But Jones's painting is free of the flaccid
71 piety that permeated much of the Caldey style, it is much more intense, full of feeling, and
72 now all the more poignant because it shows the effects of time and decay. For, whatever
technique Jones used on this painting, it has not been robust enough to withstand the cold and damp of fifty winters in the Honddu Valley. Even his other painting at Capel-y-ffin shows the ravages of time, for it was painted on iron which has begun to rust through the paint. A small, emblematic picture showing the Lamb and the Cross, it is painted on the door of the tabernacle which stands above the altar of the simple chapel designed by Gill in the attic of the old monastery.

Jones first met Gill in 1921, when, during his second period as an art student, he paid
a brief visit to the Ditchling community. What he discovered there gave some focus to his
73 complicated notions of relating art to life and to religion, and in Gill, Jones found a
mentor who had faced and resolved similar ideas. During the latter part of his war service
on the Western Front, Jones had considered the idea of becoming a Catholic, and in
September 1921, nine months after his first meeting with Gill, he was received into the
Roman Catholic Church. It was a decision that had a profound effect on his later work for
it established a pattern for his ideas and feelings; a pattern which was to find an obvious
expression in his Capel-y-ffin crucifixion, and was to co-ordinate the subtle allegories of
his later work.

74 The multifarious nature of David Jones's inspiration is too involved to be analysed
briefly, for it came from a variety of sources: his love of landscape and the sea, his
experience as a private in the First World War, his obsession with religion and myth, and
his passion for the history and legends of Wales.

Although he was born in Brockley, Kent, his father was a Welshman from Holywell
and, as a child, Jones was moved by his father's Welsh songs and by his visits to his
grandfather at Rhos. It was these and other emotive experiences that caused the
germination of his fervent love of all things Welsh. Jones's longest period in Wales was
spent at Capel-y-ffin, and it was a time that saw his mature development as an artist. It
was then that he developed his skill as an engraver, in both wood and copper, producing
75 the illustrations for *Gullivers Travels*, *The Book of Jonah*, *Llyfr y Pregethwr* and *The Chester Play of
the Deluge*.

It was also the time when he began to explore his extraordinary and highly personal vision of landscape, and to experiment with watercolour painting. His early pictures of Welsh subjects such as *Hill Pastures - Capel-y-ffin, Tenby from Caldey Island* and *Tîr y Blaenau* show a stylisation derived from the limitations of the engraver's art. But as his experience grew, so did his freedom of expression. Throughout the 1930s and 1940s, using mainly pencil and watercolour — with only rare excursions into oils — he evolved his individual form of figurative art. It shows little direct influence from other artists, but is analogous to several other artists that he most admired: Breughel, Blake, Rousseau and the English watercolourists.

76 It is a serene form of Romanticism, searching for the mysterious life behind the
superficial appearance of the world. The sea — that prime symbol of Romantic art — is
a frequent motif. Sometimes it is seen with a landscape, sometimes through a window —
another device that Jones used to compound the symbolism of the inner and outer being.
The immaterial life of living things: people, animals, plants and flowers is suggested by
the broken strokes of colour and the disconnected line, which also flux the objects
depicted with the space they occupy.

The period dating from Capel-y-ffin to the middle 1930s was the most fruitful of
David Jones's life, when he was again living with his parents in Brockley and producing
many paintings, drawings and engravings. After a collapse of his health, he turned to
77 writing and produced *In Parenthesis*, a poetic interpretation of his experiences of war, that
search (as he described it) for the 'formal goodness in a life singularly inimical, hateful,

to us'. Published in 1937, *In Parenthesis* had been written some four years earlier and, after its completion, there was a shift of emphasis in the iconography of Jones's work.

From that time on there appears a growing interest in the legends of the *Mabinogion*
78 and Malory's *Morte d'Arthur*; related themes and both with strong Welsh currents running through them. But Jones was not concerned simply with sentimental medievalism of the kind that had engrossed the Victorians. He regarded the Arthurian legends as commentaries analogous to the Christian epic; two complementary manifestations of the human urge to order complex thoughts and feelings, aspirations and ideals, 'all things visible and invisible', into a coherent whole. Throughout the rest of his life it was his epic intent to formulate this ideal, not only in his major writings, *In Parenthesis* and *The*
79 *Anathemata*, but in his paintings and drawings and, to a lesser degree, in his calligraphy.

David Jones was a highly individual artist, following a lonely road in search of an elusive destination, and ending up as a recluse. In this, he was not unlike Gwen John — who also found order and solace in Catholicism — just as in his dual fluency in both painting and literature he was in the British tradition of artists such as Blake, Rossetti and Wyndham Lewis. But until his illness in 1933, he was regarded as a contributor to the mainstream of modern art in Britain. In 1928 Ben Nicholson recruited Jones into the Seven and Five Society, and he exhibited with them until 1933. After that, he went his own way into a world of myth, faith and legend, detached from contemporary theories of art and with no place for pure 'abstraction' in his vision of the world.

But though he was detached from abstract art, Jones was by no means indifferent to it. Nor was he the simple-minded visionary that some of his admirers have claimed him to be. In a letter to *The Listener*, dated 3 August, 1950, he summed up his interpretation of abstract art and its place in his work: 'Those of us whose work no one, I imagine would call "abstract" , know, nevertheless, that it is an abstract quality, however hidden or devious, which determines the real worth of any work. This is true of Botticelli's *Primavera*, of the White Horse of Uffington, of the music of Monteverdi, of *Finnegan's Wake*, of the "Alfred Jewel", of the glass goblet I am now trying to draw, of the shape of a liturgy, of the shape of a teacup. The one common factor implicit in all the arts of man resides in a certain juxtaposing of forms.

'In theory "abstract art" is no more than a conscious assertion of this truth. It is then the assertion, in isolation, of a real, and indeed a first, principle. The least "abstract" work (in the contemporary sense) could not be made apart from this principle, for without it a "thing" having integration and a life of its own, could not be. Therefore without it the arts could not be. With this clearly understood we may then be in a better position to consider what possible aridities or impoverishments may or may not attend, or be latent in, the practice of what is called "pure abstraction" among us today. That is a real and interesting issue and a totally impersonal one.

'Like much else, it is best considered in its historical setting, e.g. why has a certain preoccupation with the "Abstract" marked much of the painting of our day? It is certainly no accident. It is a complex matter, but this we can say, that whatever vacuities and banalities have accompanied this preoccupation, it has also been directly responsible for works of real creativity, and indirectly has influenced to this or that degree most of the more vital work of our time.'

It is worth quoting at some length from this letter, for in it, Jones not only asserts his own opinion, he also describes the principles that governed much of English art and most of Welsh art, not only of the 1950s but also of the pre-war decade of the 1930s. It applies in general to all the important artists who were connected with Wales, and it applies in particular to another Welsh artist who appeared among the contemporary *avant-garde* at the same time that Jones departed.

At the Zwemmer Gallery in London, in 1933, Ceri Richards was represented in an exhibition called *Objective Abstraction*, in the company of Ivon Hitchens and several other artists who worked in a painterly form of abstraction. This was not quite the appropriate context for Richards, and two years later he was grouped with the abstract-constructivists, who included Henry Moore, Ben Nicholson, Barbara Hepworth and John Piper among their ranks. The philosophy of the group was propagated through its
80 magazine *Axis*, edited by a Welshwoman, Myfanwy Evans, the first issue of which contained an illustration of one of Richards's abstract reliefs.

But though the ideas expressed through the medium of *Axis* were flexible and in no way doctrinaire, Richards was still somewhat out of place. There was a poetic element even in his abstract constructions that did not accord with the purer formalism dominant at that time in the work of Hepworth, Piper and Nicholson. Perhaps, like many other outstanding Welsh artists, his was a strong individual vision which could not conform easily to collective ideas. However, in that hectic period for the British *avant-garde*, there were alternative ideologies to be considered and, because of the imaginative strain in his work, Richards gravitated towards the Surrealists. Indeed, he had already felt the influence of Max Ernst when, in 1936, he exhibited at the London Gallery with the Surrealist Group.

Throughout the 1930s, Ceri Richards gained a growing reputation and gathered into
81 his work those influences from the modern masters — such as Ernst, Picasso and Matisse — which have led to charges of eclecticism. But this was, in practice, more a process of collecting material, from whatever source that might excite his imagination, which he was to fuse into his more mature work. Richards's maturity, and the peak of his fame, belongs to the period after the Second World War; the years when he won many public commissions and was represented in several important international exhibitions.

Nevertheless, in the decade before the war, during a time of relative obscurity, Richards's work had a freshness and an inventiveness that was a symptom of the infectious enthusiasm that had gripped British artists. His numerous reliefs and studies
82 for reliefs from the middle 1930s have a purity and directness that are absent from his later constructions. It was also a time when he had stronger ties with Wales. Born in 1903, at Dunvant, near Swansea, he attended Swansea Art School from 1920 to 1924, during its heyday under the direction of Grant Murray. William Grant Murray, a Scot, was principal at Swansea from 1910 to 1943, and under his enlightened leadership it became the most vigorous art school in Wales. Among the generations of talented and professionally-
83 minded students that he trained were Alfred Janes, Will Evans, Evan Walters and Kenneth Hancock — who succeeded Murray as principal in 1943.

Of them all, Richards became the most eminent as an artist, though most of the others merit a place in history for furthering 'the long- delayed revival' in Wales during a difficult and repressed period. Indeed, there is an imponderable hanging over the careers of those artists who, divided between native loyalties and professional ambitions, made the difficult decision to remain and work in Wales. Evan Walters, for example, who studied in London and spent some years in America, chose to paint the people of Wales and the landscapes around Llangyfelach,. Yet with his creative energy and his interest in the theories of optics, there is no telling what direction his art might have taken had it been fostered in a more intense and metropolitan milieu.

As it happened, Swansea provided the nearest approach to such conditions in Wales
84 in the period between the wars. It was Grant Murray, for example, who helped Will Evans, an artist who began his working life as a tin-plate printing apprentice, but who was encouraged to study art at Swansea School of Art. Among all the towns in Wales, it was Swansea that was most enterprising in promoting the visual arts, and its most important contributions to the Principality were the Glynn Vivian Art Gallery — the largest municipal gallery in the country — and the School of Art.

Even so, Swansea could only provide a pliable springboard to launch young artists on to higher levels of training. There were no post-graduate art courses in the whole of Wales, and so, with the exception of Will Evans, all the artists mentioned above went on to London to complete their training. Richards attended the Royal College of Art, while Janes, Hancock, and Walters all continued their studies at the Royal Academy Schools.
85 This was also the case with Morland Lewis, a painter from Ferryside, Carmarthenshire, who, after training at Carmarthen School of Art and the Royal Academy Schools, remained in London to attend Sickert's private art school, which opened in 1927.

The relative success of Swansea, among the art schools of Wales, was one more of the unco-ordinated factors that contributed to a growing awareness of the visual arts in Wales during the years between the wars. Another was the growth of the various art societies which, operating principally at an amateur level, helped to foster an appreciation of modern art. Organisations such as the South Wales Art Group, simply by providing regular exhibition facilities, provided professional artists with some outlet for their work in Wales, and created an unusual but democratic situation where amateur and professional artists could work together. The struggle of the professionals was given a further lift by the founding, in 1937, of the Contemporary Art Society for Wales. Under the chairmanship of Lord Howard de Walden and the patronage of Augustus John, it was modelled on the lines of the Contemporary Art Society in England, which encouraged its
86 younger sister-society by donating the first picture to its collection: a portrait of Eric Gill's daughter Petra, by David Jones. From its modest beginnings, and with limited funds, the society gave a valuable impetus to the visual arts in Wales; for the practice of buying individual works and presenting them to public bodies not only helped the artists materially, it also strengthened their tenuous status as professionals.

For the years of economic depression were difficult ones for artists in all countries, and particularly in Wales, which at that time had few wealthy collectors and little public patronage of the kind that the Arts Council was later to provide. Artists working in Wales must have looked with envy at the achievements of fellow Welshmen such as Ceri Richards, who was becoming established in the London art world, or marvelled at the fame of expatriates such as Augustus John, who had become rich by plunging into the international world of art.

By the 1930s, Augustus John's fame and notoriety were at their zenith. The aging playboy of British art was recognised as an international celebrity, who painted the portraits of the rich and famous, and who thereby earned enough to maintain a manor house in Hampshire, a cottage in Provence and a studio in London. John made no claim
to be included among the new *avant-garde*; his work was still firmly fixed in the bravura
87 style of the New English Art Club. But, even so, discerning critics insisted that his work
had suffered a decline in standards; that facility had replaced invention, and that his best work had been the earlier figure studies and the landscapes of twenty years before. There was considerable truth in this, and no one was more aware of it than John himself. The demands of his large family and his many other commitments compelled him to produce work that was often without enthusiasm or inspiration. Depressed by this insight, he felt a greater longing for Wales, and, as he grew older, he voiced the regret that he had ever left his native country and had never learnt its language. He visited Wales on several occasions: to receive the Freedom of Tenby, to see friends and to search for a house; but he never again painted the scenes that had inspired him as a young man.

But other artists came to Wales, attracted by those scenes, and the visits of John
88 Piper, Graham Sutherland, John Nash, Kenneth Rowntree and Edward Bawden heralded
a reawakening of the fascination of the Welsh landscape. Of all these artists, none of them Welsh, it was Sutherland and Piper who produced the largest number of works and who gained the greatest rewards from their experiences in Wales. Piper first became acquainted with the landscape of south-west Wales in 1937, the year he married Myfanwy Evans, the editor of *Axis*, and the daughter of a Pembrokeshire minister. Until that time, Piper had been working in an idiom of pure abstraction; a style that was akin to, but distinct from, that of Ben Nicholson, and which seems to have been a progression from the ideas of synthetic cubism.

89 After his encounter with the Welsh landscape, there was a move in Piper's work
towards an earlier cubist medium: the use of descriptive collage. On the beaches at Aberaeron and St David's Bay, often working on the spot, he cut and pasted fragments of coloured or printed papers to form witty simplifications of the scene. In terms of ideas this was not a move from fashionable abstraction to fashionable surrealism, but more of a revival of Romantic and picturesque notions. This has always been a persistent strain in British art and the topography of Wales has often inspired it. And it was in Wales that Piper found the material by which he is best known today. At the same time that he made
his collages of beach scenes, he also became fascinated by the architecture of Wales; its
90 homely chapels, its picturesque ruins and buildings such as Hafod and Castell Coch. It
was a radical shift from the principles of intellectual, formalised abstraction towards their
polarities of melancholy, decay and mystery. From these works of the late 1930s stemmed
91 92 most of his later work: churches, chapels and ruined buildings, with textured walls and
deep shadows cast by strong, dramatic lighting. Perhaps it was a presentiment of war, for

by the experience gained in his depiction of the ruins in Wales, Piper was well-equipped for the series of bomb-damaged buildings that he was to produce in the next decade.

As with Piper, it could be said that Graham Sutherland's experiences in Wales were the mainspring for much of his subsequent work. 'It was in this country that I began to
93 learn painting', he wrote in *Horizon* in 1942. He was referring to Pembrokeshire, where he was overcome by what struck him as the magical quality of light and the mysterious presence of the landscape, with its bare hills, empty beaches, stunted trees and curious rock formations. From his first visit in 1934 he was deeply moved by what he saw there: '...the clear, yet intricate construction of the landscape of the Welsh experience, coupled with the emotional feeling of being on the brink of some drama, taught me a lesson and had an unmistakable message that has influenced me profoundly'.

Because it deals with a single consistent theme, the Welsh series — stretching for over forty years from 1934 until his death in 1980 — shows more clearly than any other body of Sutherland's work his attitudes to landscape and his methods of creation. In his descriptions of south-west Wales he wrote about 'an explosion of light' in 'an exuberant landscape' with its 'element of disquiet' and 'its exultant strangeness'; and he responded to the Pembrokeshire scene in a manner not unlike that of an eighteenth-century traveller in search of the sublime.

Sutherland's drawings of Wales convey more of this spirit than do the paintings derived from them. He acknowledged that there were no ready-made subjects and, though at first he tried to paint directly in front of the motif, he soon abandoned this process. He found that the only way he could capture the essence of the location was by storing in his mind, and in drawings, the impressions he received, and paraphrasing them later in his studio.

Through this process of contemplative synthesis, he transformed the magic of the place into the mystery of the object. The *genius loci* of Pembrokeshire was transmuted into enigmatic still-lifes, displaced from their places of origin, and weighted with surrealistic meanings. This detachment of the image from its source is particularly evident in the later pictures that Sutherland produced in his Welsh series, for the landscape of south Wales was paraphrased in the South of France, in the artist's studio in Menton.

94 But these were to come later, in the years after the Second World War. In the interim, during the war, Sutherland continued to visit Wales, though often for other, more malevolent attractions than the peaceful coastline of Pembrokeshire. For two years, from 1940 to 1942, in his studies for the War Artists Committee, he found a new form of
95 inspiration in the devastation left after the bombing of Swansea.

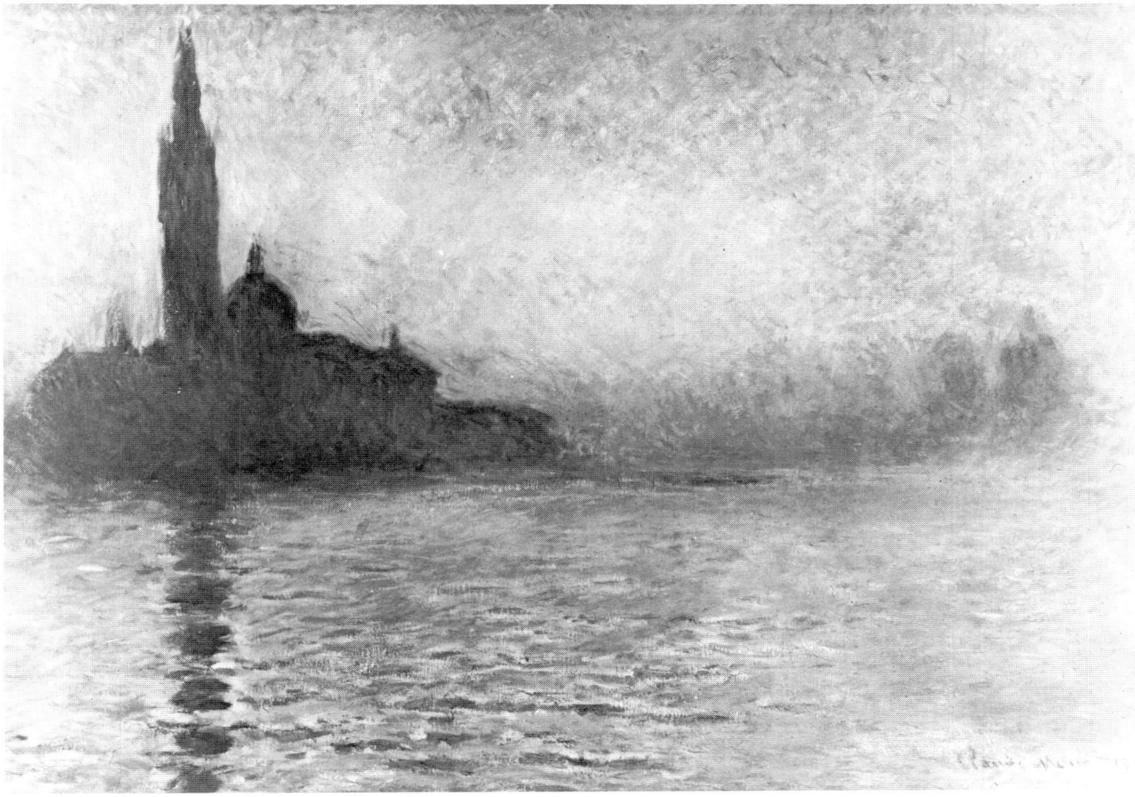

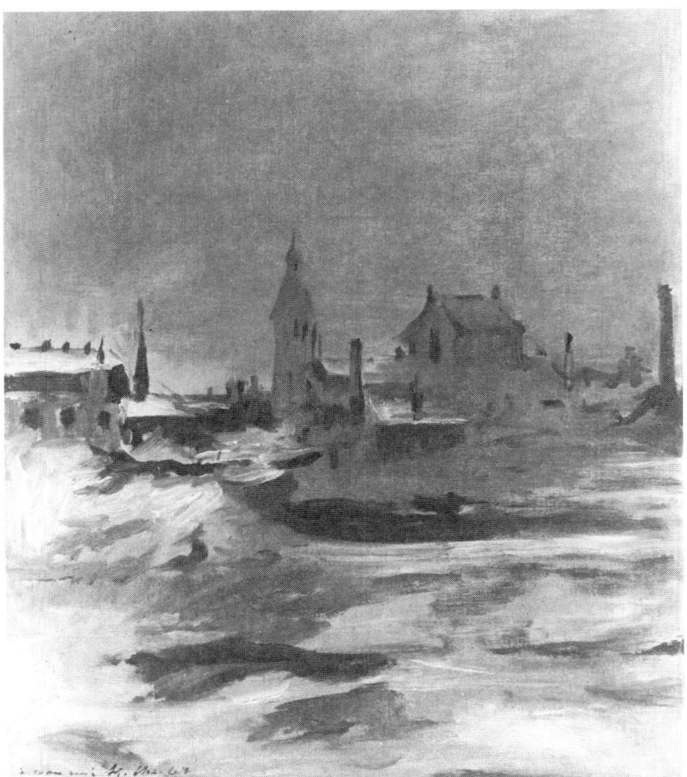

59. Claude Monet 1840 - 1926
Crépuscule, Venice (1908) Oil on canvas 63.5 x 89 cm
National Museum of Wales

Although the lenders to 'A Loan Exhibition' were officially anonymous, it soon transpired that the owners of the greatest number of works were two wealthy spinsters, the Davies sisters of Llandinam. By 1912, Gwendoline and Margaret Davies had already established the foundation of a collection of modern art that was equalled in Britain only by that of Hugh Lane. In the autumn of that year they instructed Hugh Blaker to purchase for them some paintings by Monet. In Paris he bought three Venetian scenes, one of which was this painting, exhibited the following year in the Loan Exhibition in Cardiff.

60. Edouard Manet 1832 - 83
L'Eglise du Petit-Montrouge (1870) Oil on canvas 59.75 x 49.5 cm
National Museum of Wales

This painting had also been bought by Hugh Blaker on behalf of the Davies sisters. Although it was Post-Impressionism which had caused a furore in London the year before, Impressionism still had the power to incense the critics in Cardiff. In the 'Western Mail' of 6 February 1913, its art critic described this painting by Manet as 'merely a slapdash impression, it is of more use to its author than anyone else, and ought never to have been framed, let alone exhibited'.

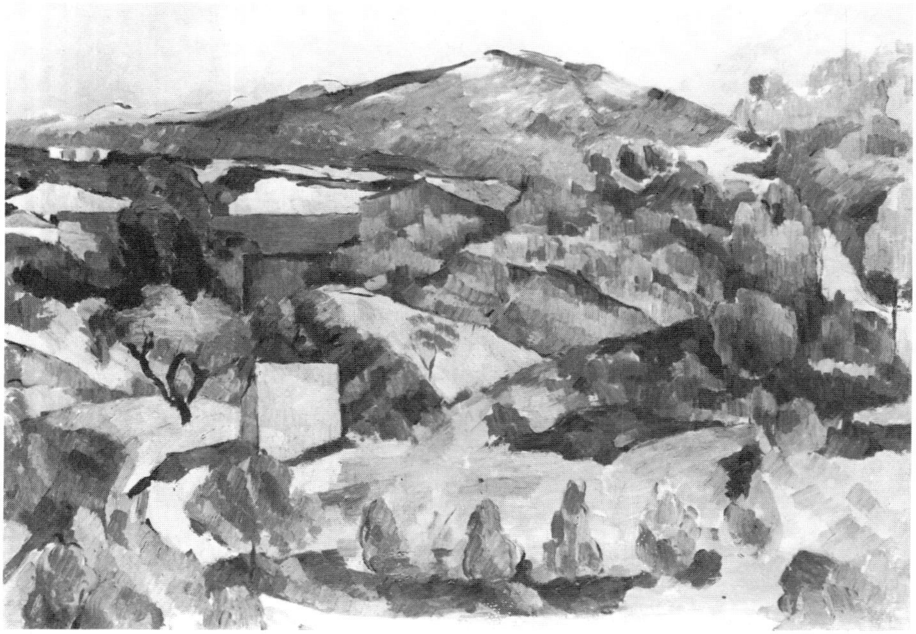

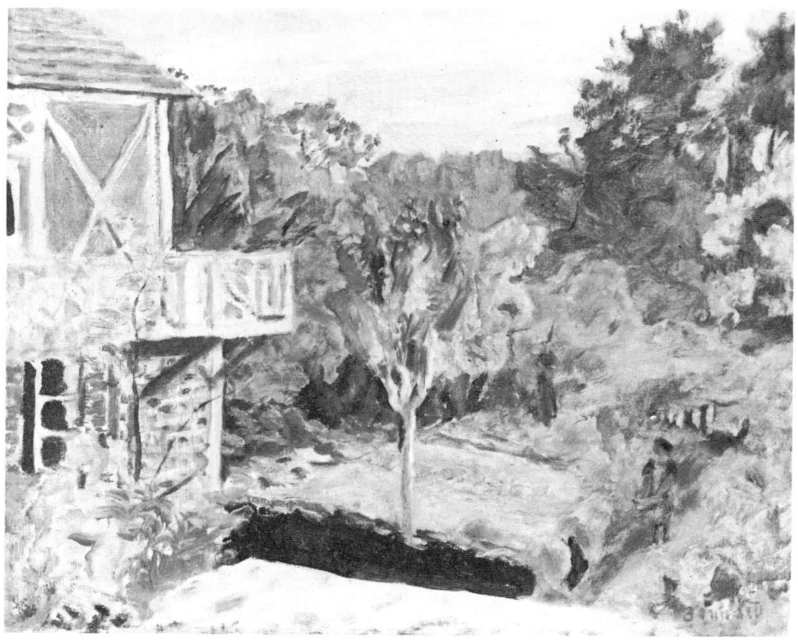

61. Paul Cézanne 1839 - 1906
Montagnes, L'Estaque (1878 - 80) Oil on canvas 53.25 x 72.5 cm
National Museum of Wales

The most advanced of all the works acquired by the Davies sisters were the paintings by Cézanne. This landscape, one of two Provençal scenes, was bought by Gwendoline Davies in 1918, and offered by her in 1921 as a loan to the Tate Gallery. The Trustees at first declined to accept the loan, though after much public debate accepted the picture in 1922. The painting had originally been bought from Cézanne by Gauguin (in 1882), and he later made a copy of it on a paper fan. Roger Fry, the tireless champion of Cézanne in Britain, described it as 'one of the greatest of all Cézanne's landscapes'.

62. Pierre Bonnard 1867 - 1947
Soleil à Vernon (c.1920) Oil on canvas 47 x 54.25 cm
National Museum of Wales

It was not until 1924 that the Davies sisters acquired work by twentieth-century artists. By then styles in art had progressed, though the sisters' taste had remained relatively static and their preference was for the less controversial forms of modern art. This fine painting by Bonnard was bought by Margaret Davies in 1960, along with works by Marquet, Sisley and Utrillo. In 1952 and 1963, Gwendoline and Margaret Davies made their generous and spectacular bequests of paintings, drawings and sculpture to the National Museum of Wales. By this simple process, the museum acquired an outstanding collection of modern art that is now its most single important section in the visual arts.

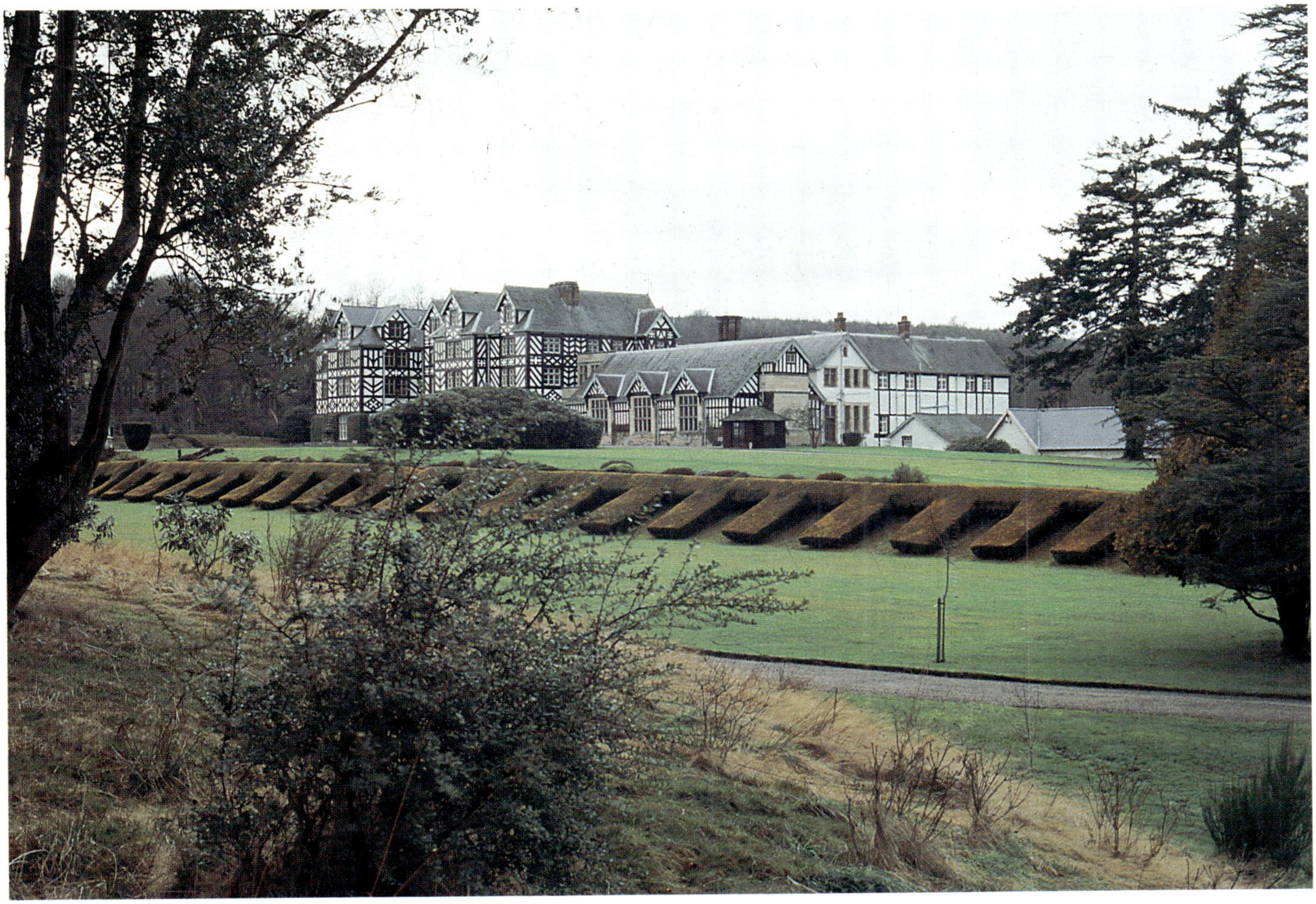

63. Gregynog Hall, Powys
Gregynog Hall is a mock-Tudor mansion, set in the middle of an extensive estate and situated in the middle of rural Wales. It was bequeathed by Margaret Davies to the University of Wales, and is now used as a conference and a study centre. There is also an extensive library and a collection of art at the Hall, and, after many years of disuse, the press began to produce fine books again in 1976.

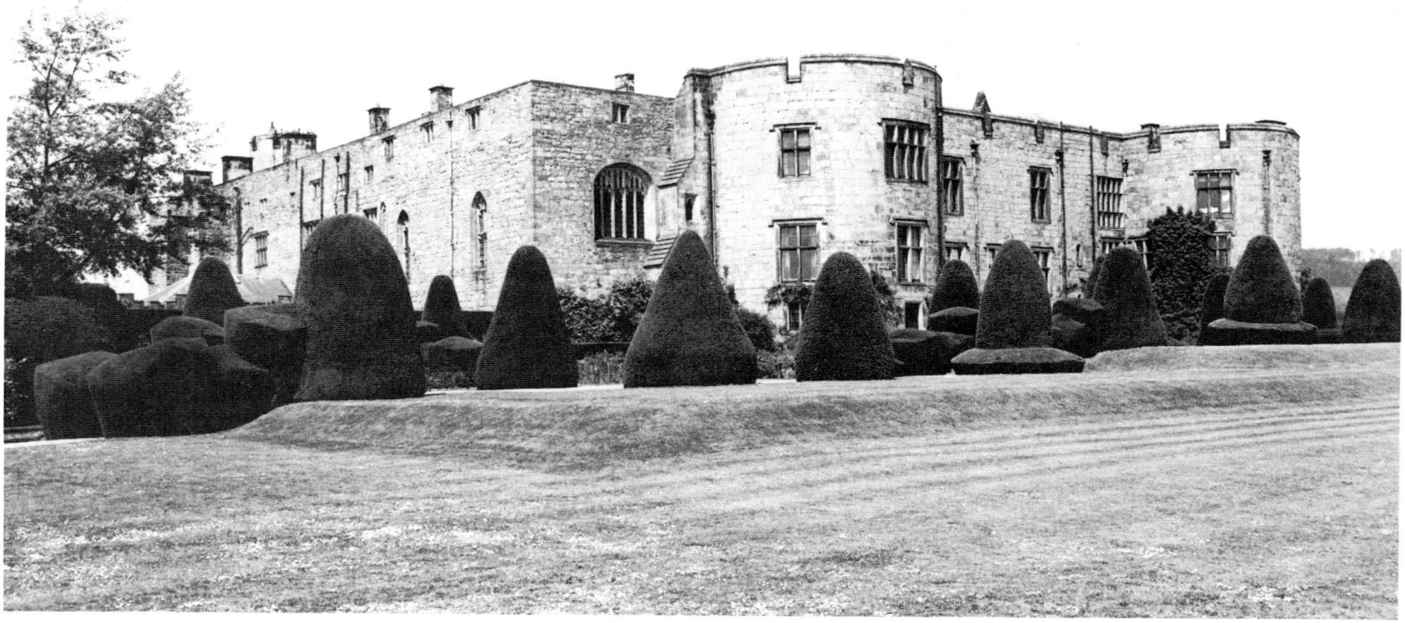

64. Chirk Castle, Clwyd

Completed in 1310, and from some viewpoints a gaunt, forbidding place, the state rooms of Chirk Castle had been modernised in the sixteenth, seventeenth and eighteenth centuries, with nineteenth-century additions by Pugin. In the twentieth century, Augustus John proposed a scheme of decorations for the Music Room, though these were never realised (No.40). The castle was leased by the Myddleton family to Lord Howard de Walden in 1911, originally for twenty years, though the lease was extended until 1946. Chirk Castle provided a refuge for many writers, musicians and artists during the Howard de Waldens' tenancy: Hilaire Belloc was a frequent visitor and wrote 'I miss Chirk very much'; Lionel Tertis came with two string quartets, to play at Chirk; Derwent Lees, partly insane, was tended by Lady Howard de Walden '... every day I took him for a walk but he would only come if I wore white gloves. So white gloves I wore over hills and dales'. Augustus John found the castle a convenient, and free base, and a welcome change from his more primitive ménage with Innes at Nant-ddu (Nos. 47, 48) - among the entertainments John enjoyed at Chirk was stalking deer through the park with bows and arrows. Chirk Castle now belongs to the National Trust.

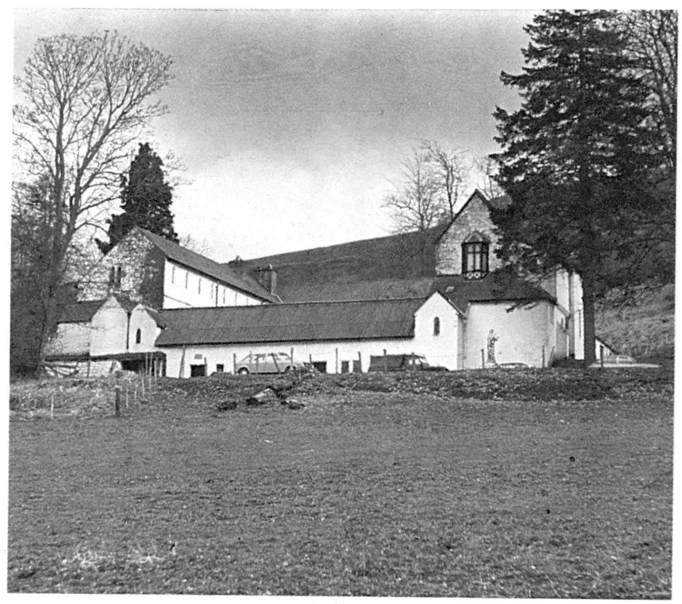

65. The Monastery
Capel-y-ffin, Powys

On 16 March 1924, Eric Gill wrote to Father Joseph O'Connor, 'I was in South Wales last week looking at a farm. We may buy it ! ... Capel-y-ffin's the name and just describes it. 2,000 feet of mountain wall on both sides and to the north of it - no outlet but to the south. Benedictine monastery 400 yards away - Bd Sacrament and Daily Mass. Good land - fair price - nice little house and 107 acres with some timber and two rushing streams. Sheep run on mountains and stone galore, both for carving and building, no extra charge'. Gill and his community remained there for four years. Now, 60 years later, Capel-y-ffin remains virtually unchanged, except that the church built by Father Ignatius has fallen into ruin.

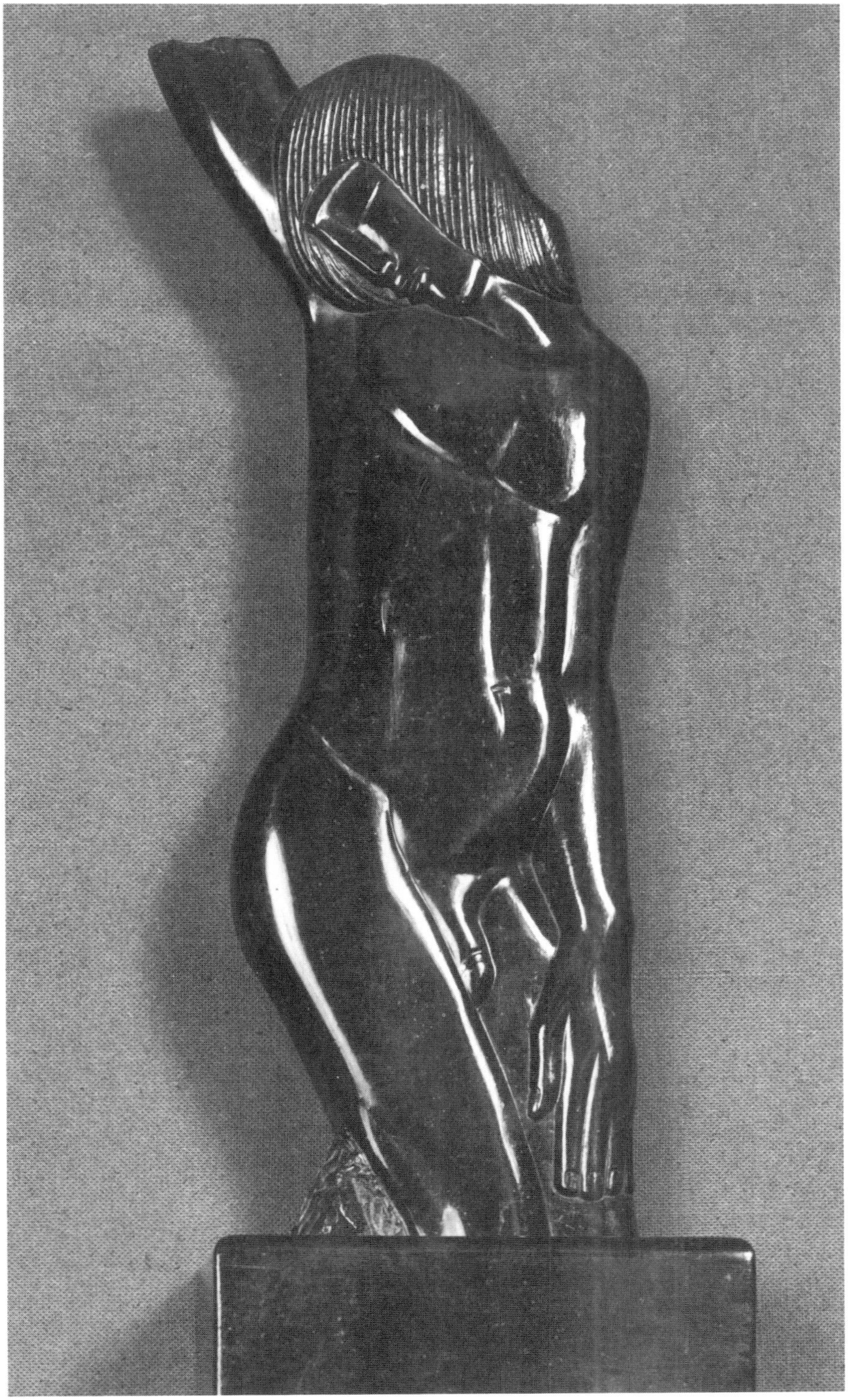

66. Eric Gill 1882 - 1940
Deposition (1924) Hoptonwood Marble height of figure 76 cm
King's School, Canterbury
This was one of the first works completed by Gill during his period in Wales. It was begun at Ditchling but remained unfinished until Gill set to work under difficult conditions, finally working in a damp cellar beneath the cloisters. Of all his sculptures it was the one he liked best, perhaps because it strikes a delicate balance between piety and sensuousness. It was exhibited at the Goupil Gallery, London, in 1924, from where it was bought by Hugh Walpole who presented it to his old school.

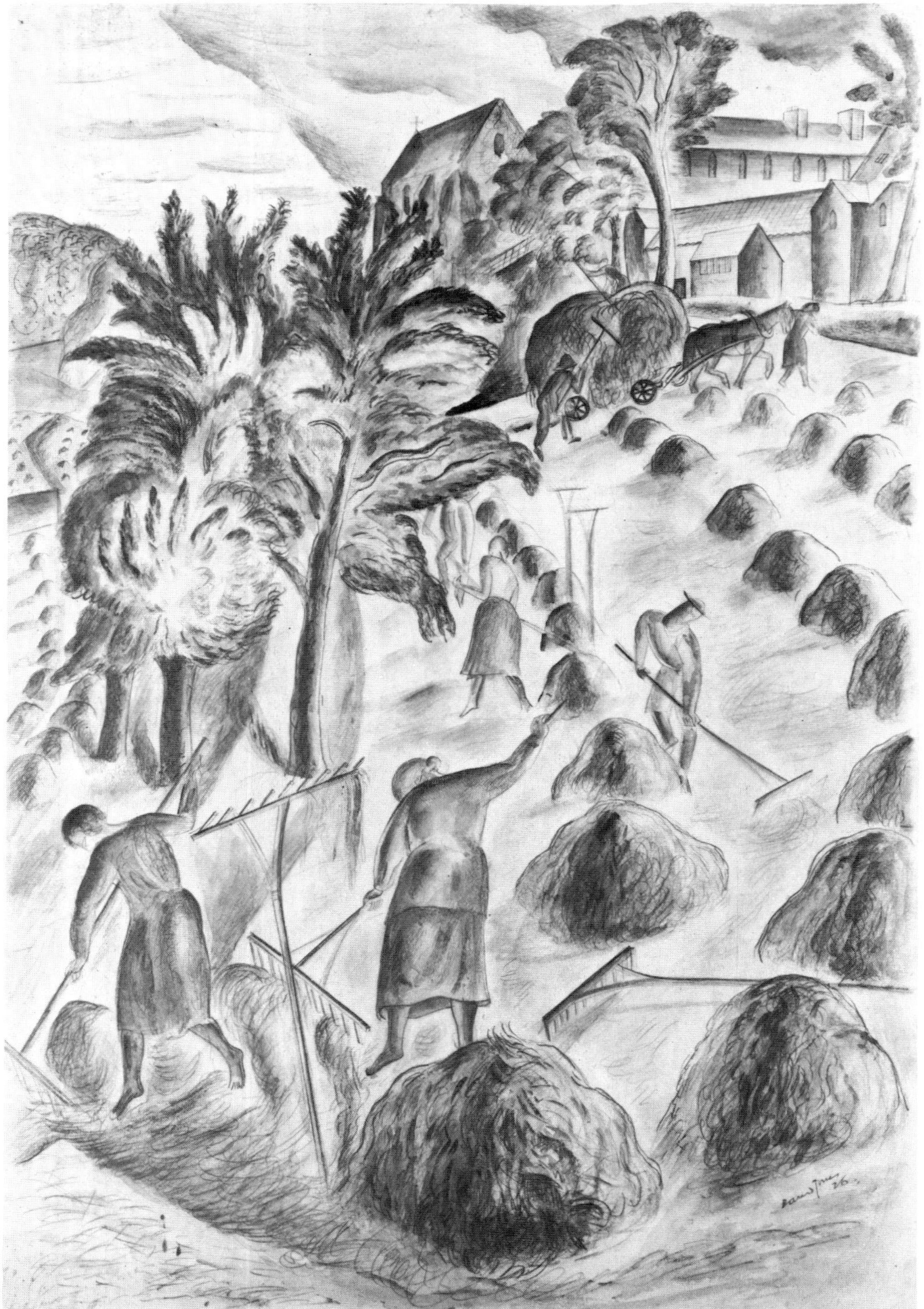

67. David Jones 1895 - 1974
Mr. Gill's Hay Harvest (1926) Pencil and watercolour
28 x 38 cm
T.L. Taylor Esq.

At Capel-y-ffin, Gill and his family and their friends tried to live as a self-sufficient community. After their unhappy experience at Ditchling, 'community' was a word they shunned; but though it was never organised in the quasi-monastic style of the earlier fraternity, the enterprise at Capel-y-ffin was, in effect, a community in the sense that the word is applied to similar projects throughout Wales today. Gill and his fellow-workers had a cow, pigs, chickens, ducks, turkeys, goats, ponies and 25 acres of land, from which they intended to provide their own food and clothing. And, as this light-hearted picture by David Jones makes clear, they were all expected to share in the work.

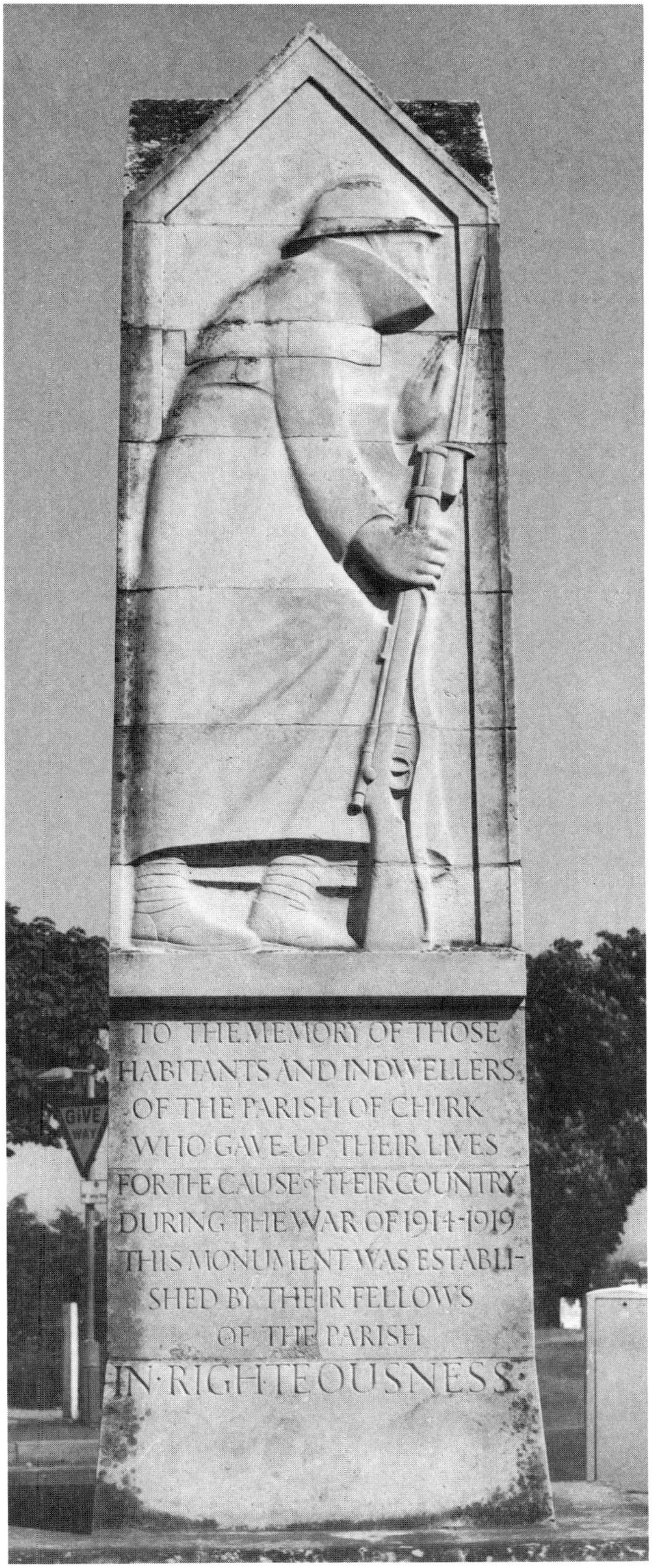

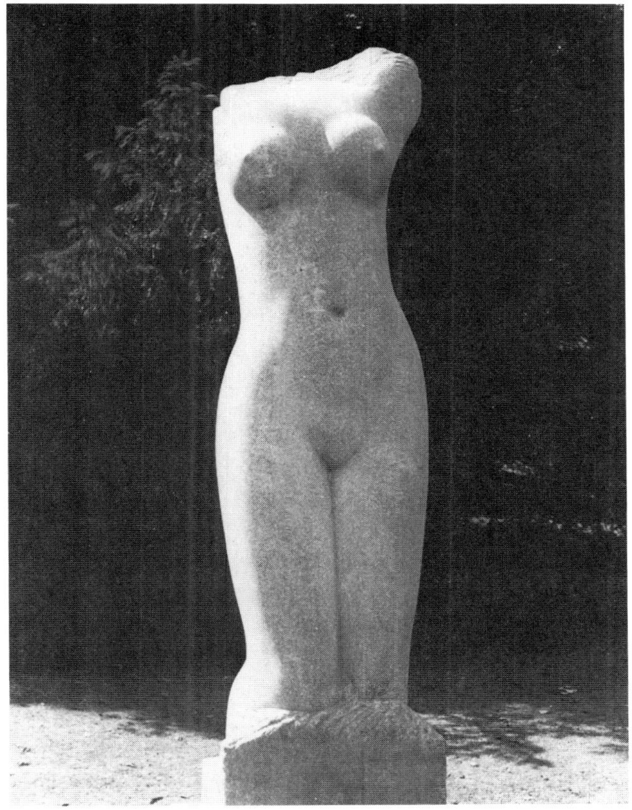

68. Eric Gill 1882 - 1940
Mankind (1927 - 8) Hoptonwood Marble 241 x 61 x 46 cm
Tate Gallery
This large sculpture was one of the last works executed by Gill during his period at Capel-y-ffin. Along with fourteen other sculptures of his, it was exhibited at the Goupil Gallery, London, in March 1928. Simplistically allegorical, it was generally well-received, and Gill was compared with Phidias, Mestrovic and Malliol. At the other end of the size scale, Gill made many small wood-engravings at Capel-y-ffin, perhaps because it was a convenient and portable medium, and they had a discernable influence on the work of David Jones, who was also developing his technique in the same medium at the same time.

69. Eric Gill
War Memorial, Chirk, Clwyd (1919) Stone approx. 4.5m high
Eric Gill's only piece of public sculpture in Wales was completed five years before he established his community in the Black Mountains. It stands at a junction in the main street of Chirk and has a large bas-relief on one face. Around the base are carved seventy names, in English and Welsh, of the 'habitants and indwellers of Chirk' who gave their lives in the Great War. The monument was commissioned by Lord Howard de Walden, and Gill explained to him that the carving represented 'a soldier on the look-out - the most typical attitude representing the war of entrenchment'.

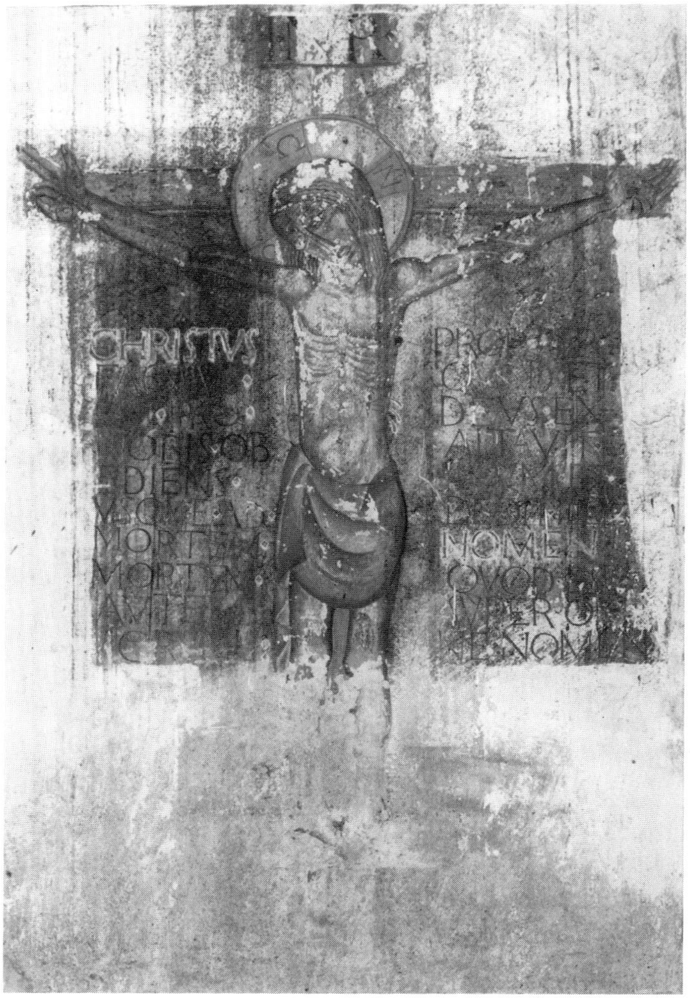

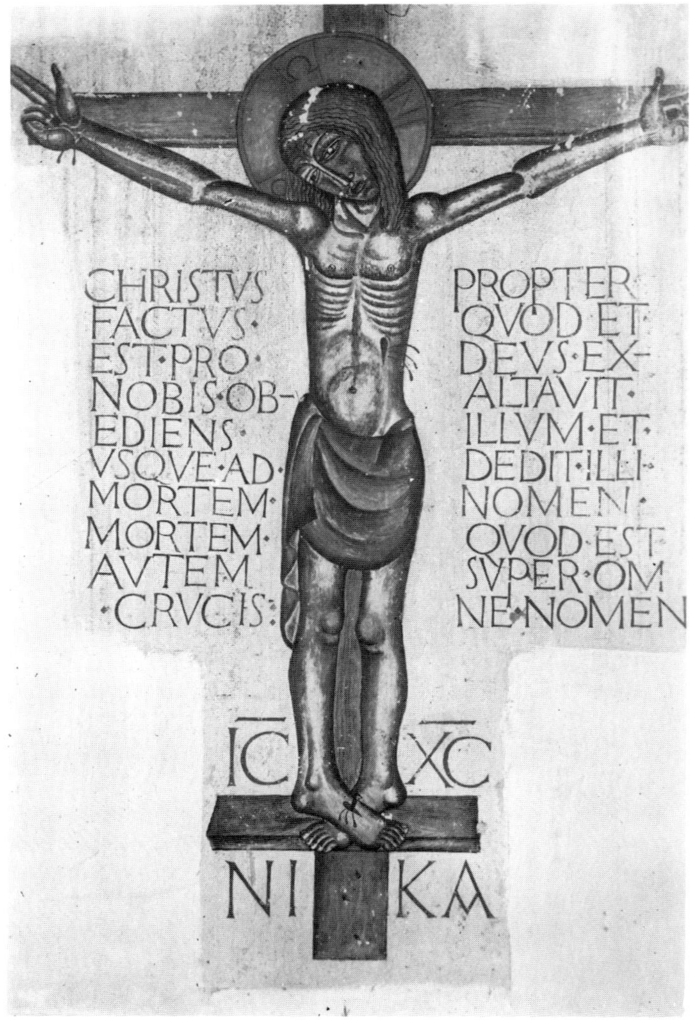

70. David Jones 1895 - 1974
Crucifixion (c.1925) Oil on plaster(?)
The Grange, Capel-y-ffin

This mural was painted by Jones soon after his arrival at Capel-y-ffin in December 1924. Although it has a novel feature in the blond hair of Christ, it is in a neo-Byzantine style - perhaps derived from the artistic influence of Dom Theodore Baily of Caldey, a place that Jones visited on several occasions around the time that he was at Capel-y-ffin. The painting has been beautiful but, because of the fragile and unidentified medium used, the surface is soft and powdery and nearly half the image has decayed. On either side of the figure are the remains of a Latin inscription which once read: 'Christus factus est pro nobis obediens usque ad mortem - mortem autem crucis propter quod et Deus exaltavit illum et dedit illi nomen quod est super omne nomen'.

71. Photograph of David Jones's *Crucifixion*, at Capel-y-Ffin, taken in 1948 by Edgar Holloway

This photograph, though cropped in the taking, shows Jones's mural some 23 years after it was painted - the previous illustration shows it after 57 years. Eric Gill's daughter Betty, told Edgar Holloway that Jones used her watercolours mixed with egg medium. Jones himself (letter to Winifrede Wilson, 30 April 1966) wrote: '... it was painted in ordinary oil paint on to a (whitewashed?) plaster wall & was pretty certain, especially in that dampish atmosphere, to scale off and fade. I understand that the people consulted about the matter [restoring and preserving the mural] were doubtful if anything could be done ... I said that I did not feel it was all that important (it's not a Giotto or a Piero della Francesca after all!) ... I did not make it with any particular thought of permanency - I just used what was to hand ... The inscription, which I rather liked ... I think is some part of that text from the Epistle to the Phillipians, used as the gradual for the Maundy Thursday mass (& elsewhere) ... but I may be wrong.'

72. David Jones
Sanctus Christus de Capel-y-Ffin (1925) Gouache on paper
19 x 13.3 cm
Edgar Holloway, Esq.

A small version - on paper and in a better state of preservation - of the theme of No.70. Perhaps because of its size - more suitable to Jones's art - it conveys more of the feeling of intense piety that was a characteristic feature of life at the monastery.

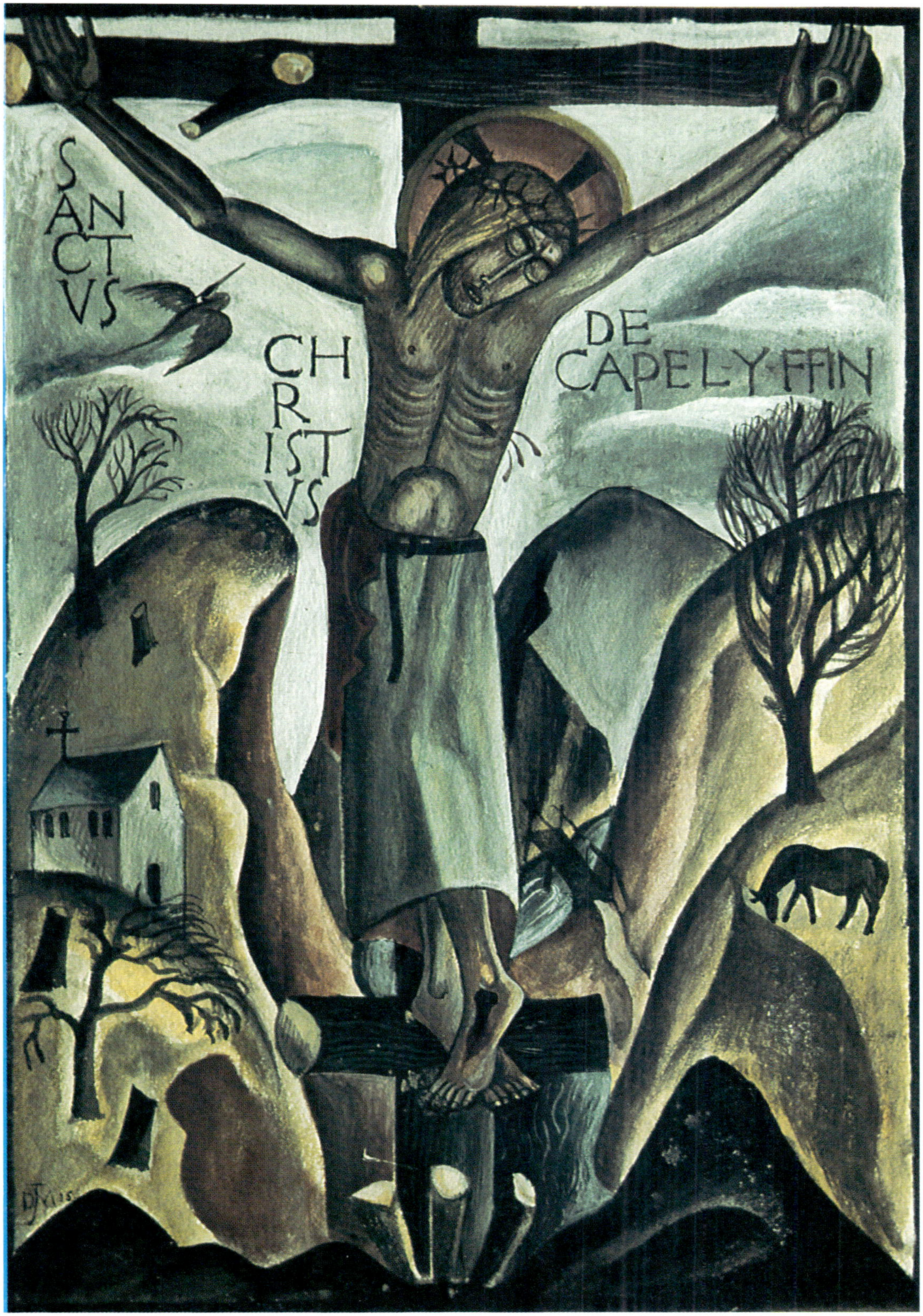
SANCTVS
CHRISTVS
DE CAPEL-Y-FFIN

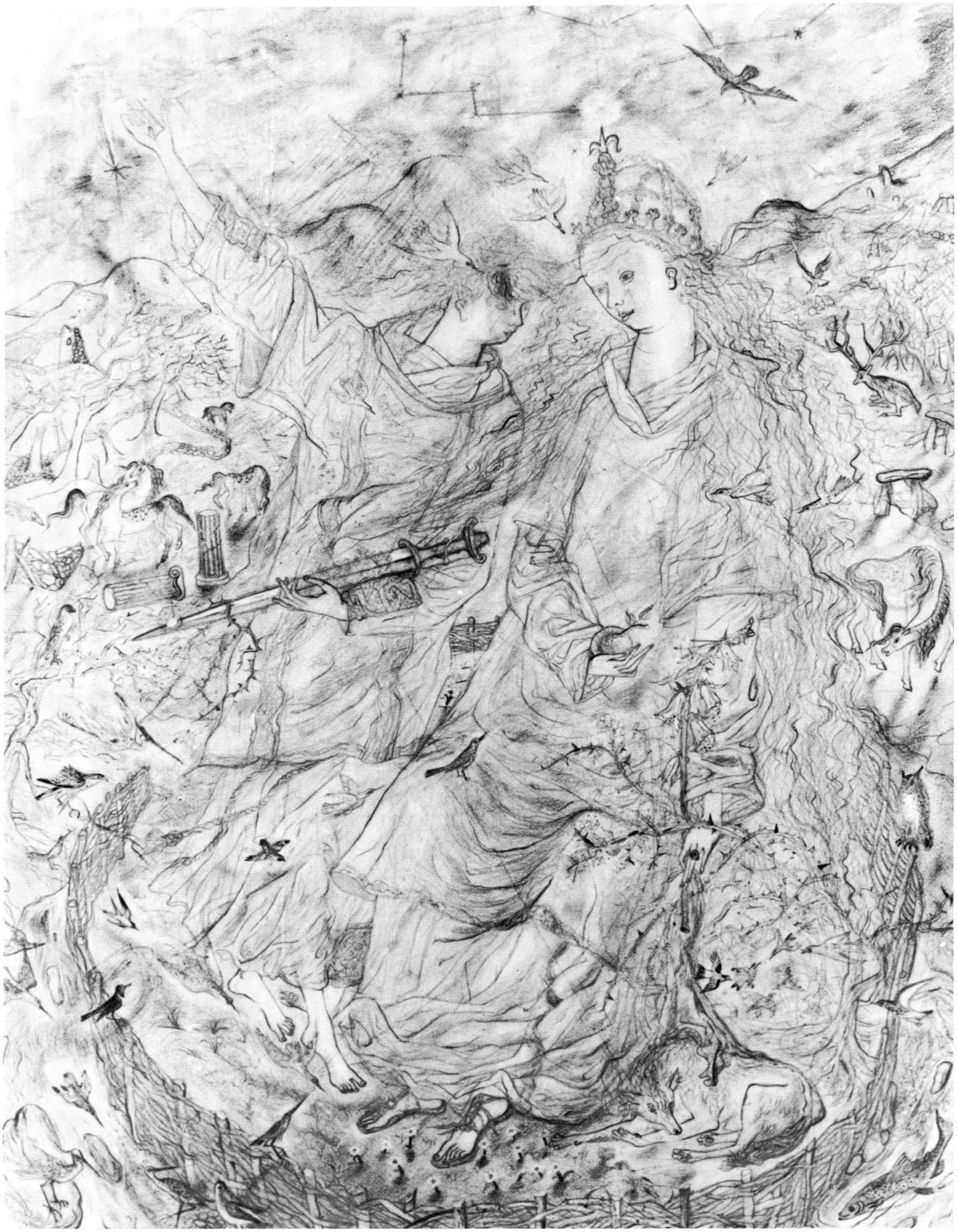

73. David Jones
The Annunciation in a Welsh Hill Setting (1963) Pencil, crayon and watercolour 77.5 x 57.75 cm
National Museum of Wales
Painted nearly forty years after the crucifixion in the previous illustration, this picture shows a return to traditional subject-matter, treated in a relatively direct manner. Like the artists of the Middle Ages and the Renaissance, Jones has set a biblical subject in his own country and in a modern context. Such explicit Christian themes were strong and persistent in Jones's work and continued throughout his life. In this later work, Jones's mastery of his medium allows him to express a more complex interpretation of his subject.

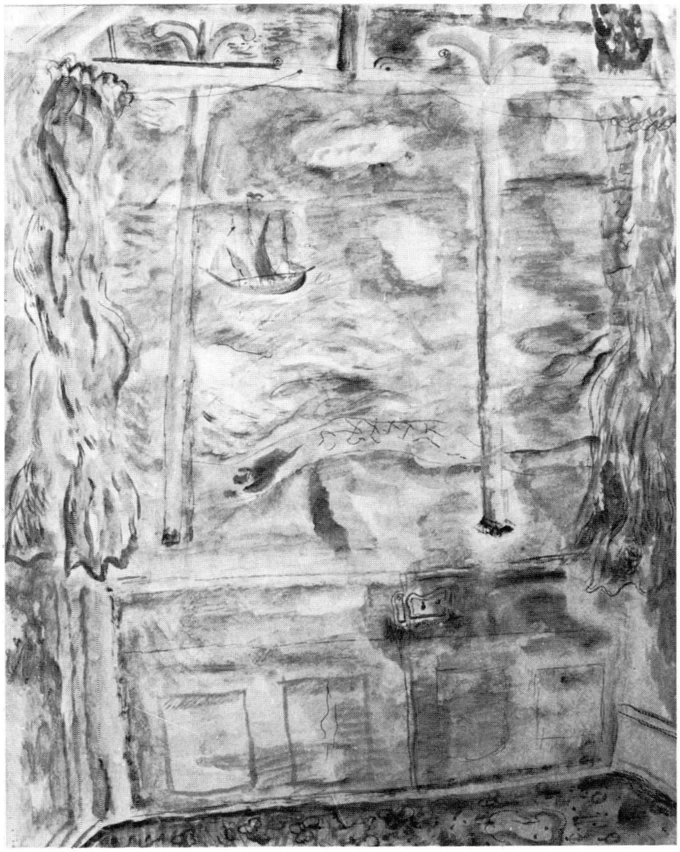

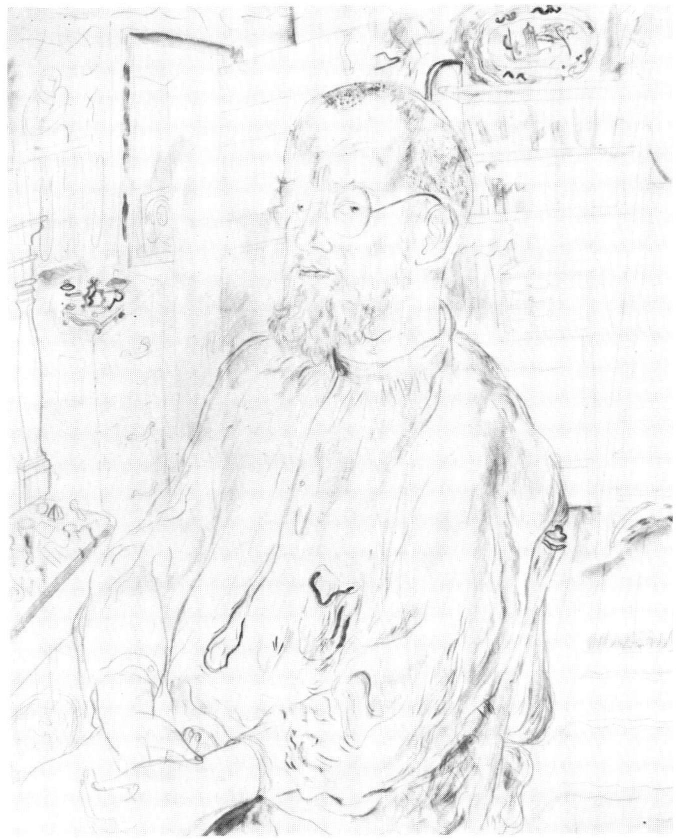

74. David Jones
Manawydan's Glass Door (1931) Watercolour drawing 63.5 x 49.25 cm
Arthur Giardelli, Esq.

This painting shows another side of Jones's complex iconography. The conjunction of the inner and the outer world is represented and symbolised by the sea viewed through the window. This can be taken not only as symbolic of general spiritual conflict but also of the specific example contained in the title. The reference is to the 'Mabinogion', and the story of Branwen; Manawydan's door is similar in effect to Pandora's box; once it is opened all remembrance of past sorrows returns to those living happily within. Jones used the same idea - of someone yearning towards the sea from a balcony - in another painting of 1931, 'Eisteddfa Calupso'.

75. David Jones
Eric Gill (1930) Pencil, watercolour and gouache 61 x 48.25 cm
National Museum of Wales

As with his still-life subjects - and particularly flower studies - Jones could invest his portraits with dimensions beyond physical appearance. There is about this drawing a suggestion of Gill's nervous energy, indicated by the short, broken lines and the rapid calligraphy. At the time this portrait was made, Gill had left Capel-y-ffin and was living at Piggotts in Buckinghamshire. Jones had known Gill for about nine years and had been considerably influenced by the older man.

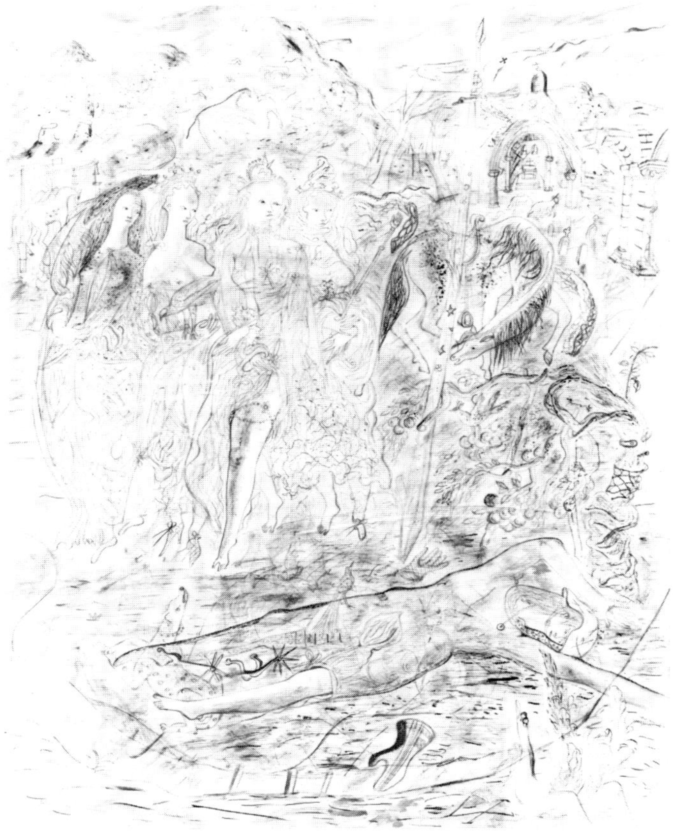

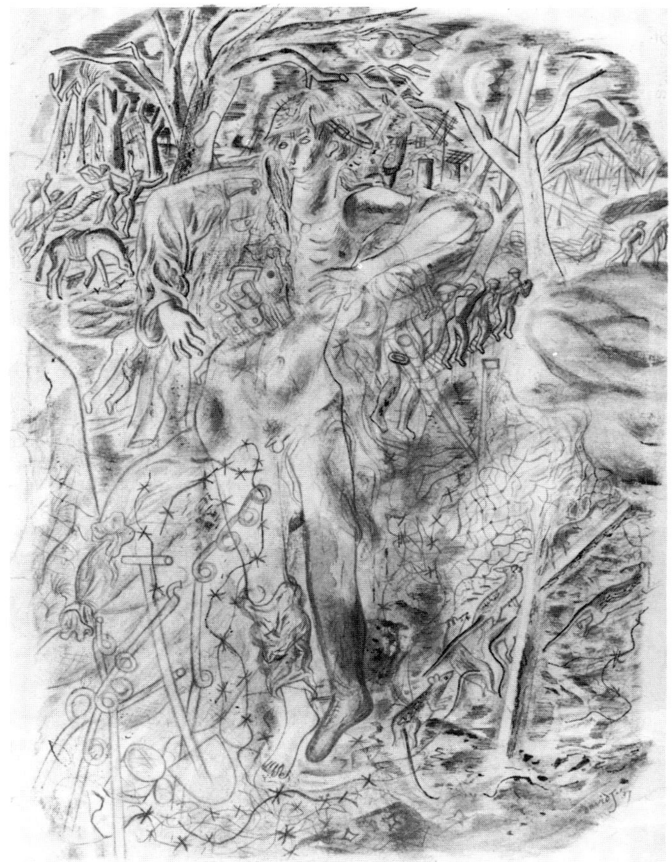

76. David Jones
The Four Queens Find Lancelot Sleeping (1941) Drawing and watercolour 63 x 49.5 cm
Tate Gallery
Around the time of the late 1930s Jones's interest in the Arthurian Legends grew stronger, and themes from Malory and the 'Mabinogion' appeared more frequently. In this picture the theme is taken from Malory's 'Morte d'Arthur', where Lancelot falls asleep under an apple tree and is visited by four queens. The one in advance of the others is Morgan Le Fay, sister to King Arthur, and a sorceress. She shows her desire for Lancelot by her seductive pose, and she is casting a spell over the sleeping knight. He, however, remains faithful to Guinevere, who is symbolised by the swan at his side.

77. David Jones
Frontispiece for *In Parenthesis* (1937) Pencil, watercolour and ink 36 x 28 cm
National Museum of Wales
Both of David Jones's long literary works bear many references and allusions to Malory's 'Morte d'Arthur'. 'In Parenthesis' particularly, has many parallels with the Arthurian legend, but the ostensible theme was the subject of war, and the artist's response to war. The long poem was begun in 1927 but was not published until ten years later. Jones intended the designs to be executed as engravings for the first edition, but in the event they were reproduced as drawings.

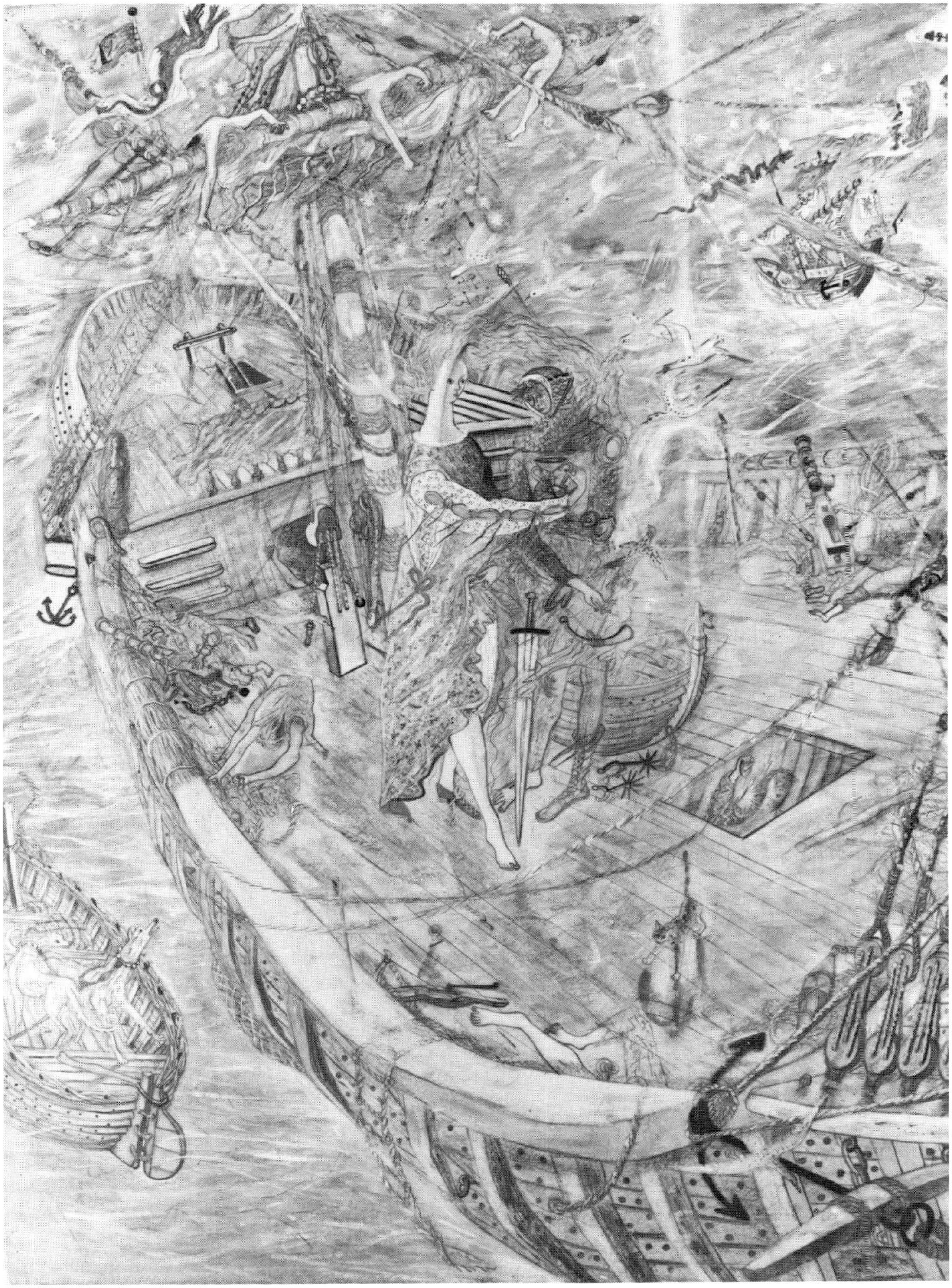

78. David Jones
Tristan ac Essyllt (1962) Pencil, watercolour and gouache
77.5 x 57 cm
National Museum of Wales
In this late, unfinished picture, the artist combines two of his favourite motifs: the sea and the Arthurian legend. The picture is crowded with detail and tells a complicated story in a very succinct, visual manner. The scene shows Tristan bringing Essyllt from Ireland to Cornwall as a bride for King Mark. On board ship they unwittingly drink a love potion, watched in dismay from below by the maid, Brangwain. In the midst of this disaster the ordinary life of the ship goes on; sailors are furling the sails, the hawk flies away, and the ship ploughs on towards the lovers' destiny.

79. David Jones
Beird Byt Barnant (1958) Gouache on Chinese white
59.75 x 38.75 cm
National Library of Wales

Although David Jones could not speak Welsh, and could only pick out occasional words, he liked the visual, incantatory quality of the language. In his calligraphy - an area where his painting and poetry sometimes merge - he uses Welsh, together with Latin and old English, almost for their abstract qualities. This inscription, intended as a frontispiece to his book 'Epoch and Artist', is taken partly from Ecclesiastes and partly from the early Welsh poem 'Y Gododdin'. In modern Welsh the full title would read: 'Beirdd byd barnant wŷr o galon'.

80. Ceri Richards 1903 - 71
Nude (1932) Oil on canvas 89 x 106.5 cm
Mrs Frances Richards

At the same time (1933/4) that illness and inclination persuaded David Jones to retreat into seclusion, Ceri Richards first exhibited in London. He appeared in the exhibition 'Objective Abstraction', held at the Zwemmer Gallery in 1934, which was organised by Robert Wellington and included Rodrigo Moyniham, Graham Bell, Victor Pasmore and Ivon Hitchins. This painting by Richards was also included in the exhibition, and it gives some indication of the tolerance allowed to categories of art at that time that this nude was allowed in a show of abstract art.

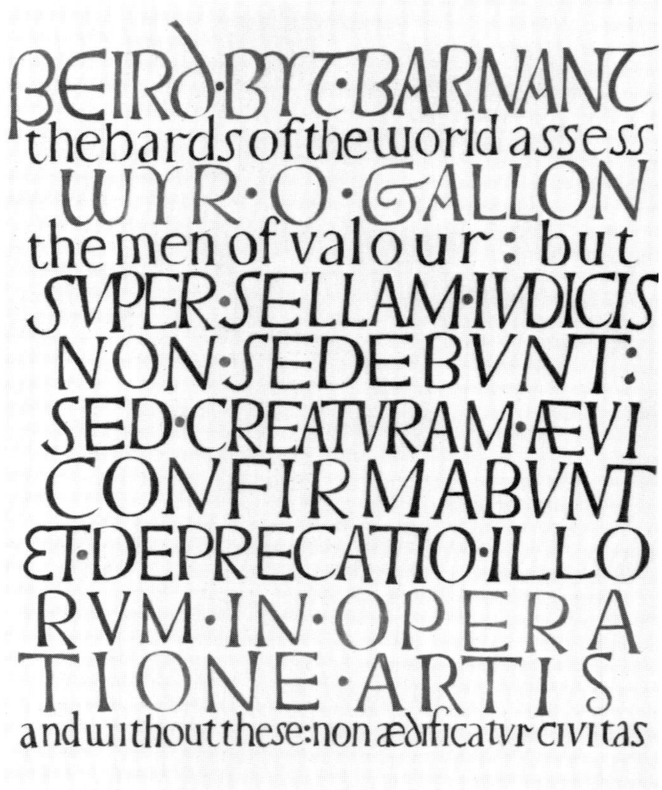

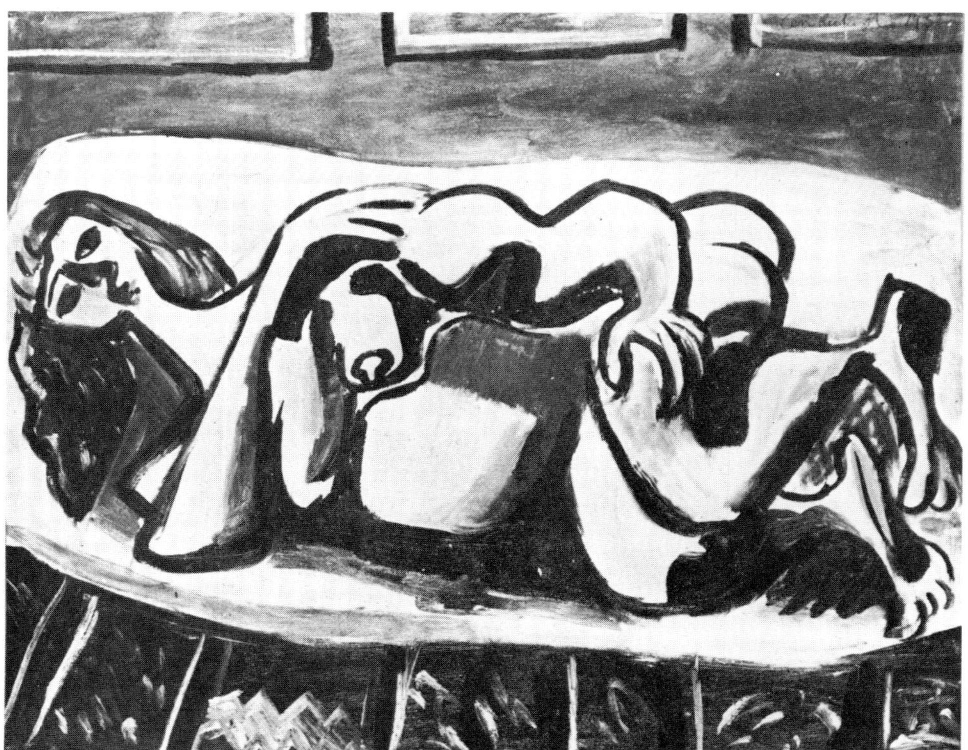

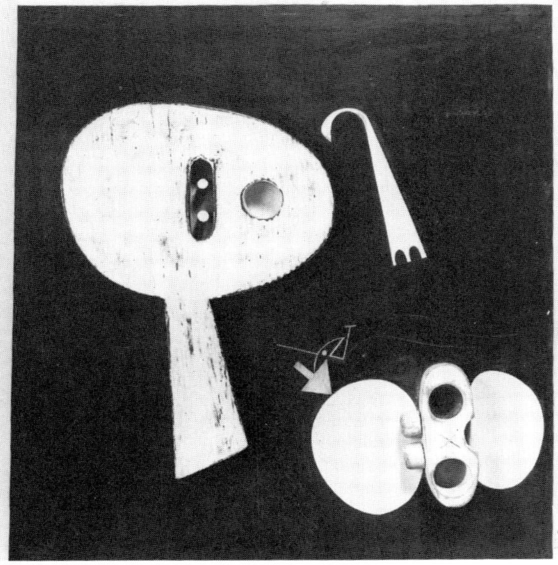

81. Ceri Richards
White and Dark (1936) Wooden Construction 50 x 54 cm
National Museum of Wales

By the time that Richards began to make his name among the progressive artists in London, the tide of British art had turned from lyrical figuration to geometric abstraction - exemplified in its purest form by Ben Nicholson's white reliefs. Like that of other artists of his generation, Richards's work had also undergone a change, though like much of theirs it still preserved some of the earlier lyricism, and owed a debt to the influence of Arp and Hélion

82. Ceri Richards
The Variable Costerwoman (1938) Construction: wood, string, metal etc. 83.75 x 81.25 cm
City of Manchester Art Galleries

At the time when he was making his constructions, and when he was closer to Surrealism than to any of the other movements, Richards became fascinated by the figures of the London costers - the pearly kings and queens. The costerwomen in particular became to him 'a sort of flower symbol, something like a marvellous bouquet', and the poetic associations of their image liberated his imagination. In this way he was able to lift the somewhat hackneyed medium of construction up to new heights of expressiveness.

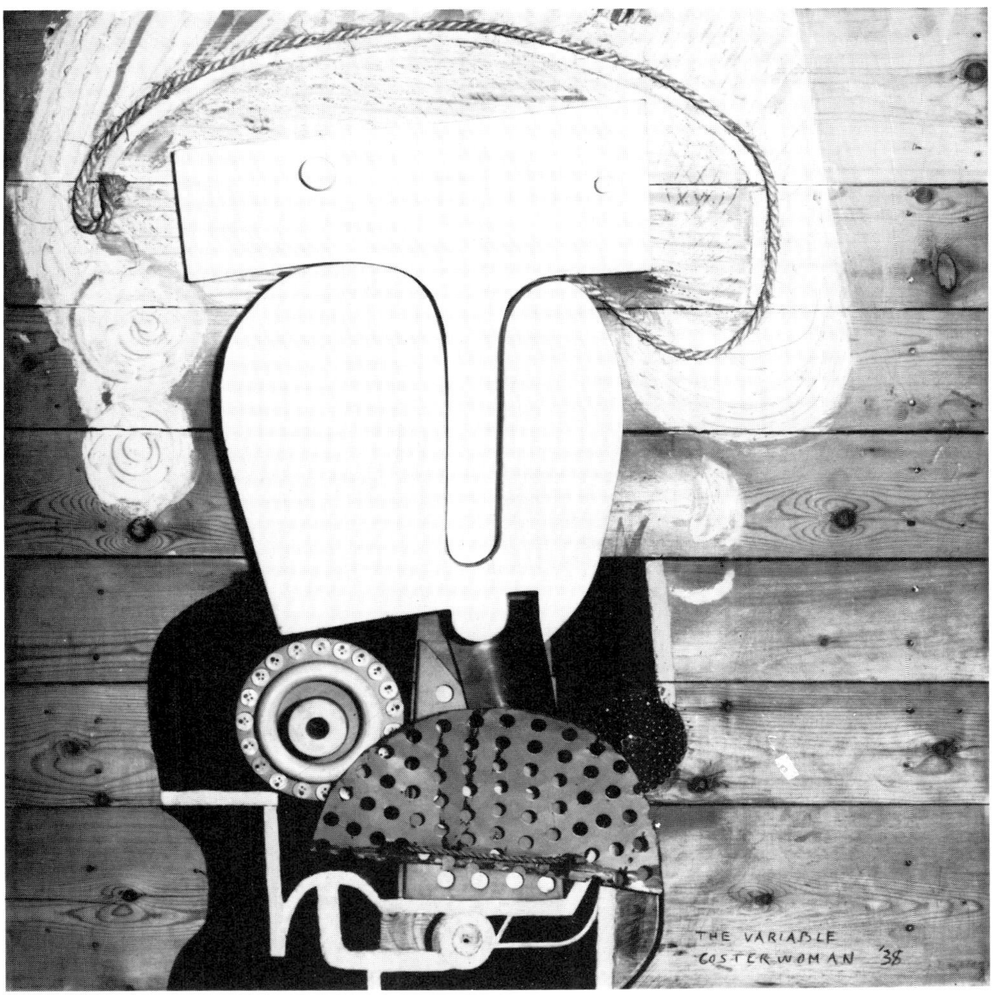

83. Alfed Janes b. 1911
Salome (1938) Oil on canvas 76 x 61 cm
Merthyr Tydfil Corporation

Janes has worked in so many distinct styles, that it is not easy to select a typical example of his work, or to place him neatly in any movement or period. Perhaps this painting is indicative of his many-sided, nonconformist talent for, considering its date, it is an eccentric work with many apparently incompatible strands knitted together. There are hints of Surrealism blended with Cubism; a touch of Pre-Raphaelitism in the figure(s), the colouring and the incised details of the fabric; and a suggestion of Symbolism in the choice of subject-matter and the general atmosphere of enigma.

84. Cedric Morris 1889 - 1982
Llanthony (1938) Oil on canvas 61 x 76 cm
Arthur Giardelli, Esq.

Cedric Morris was something of an anomaly in the history of Welsh Art. Born in Sketty, Swansea, he travelled widely in Europe and overseas, painting in Cornwall, East Anglia, London, Mexico and many other exotic places. Along with David Jones, he became a member of the 'Seven and Five Society', and later principal of the East Anglian School of Painting and Drawing. His chief contact with his native country was during the Depression of the 1930s, when he spent a considerable amount of time in south Wales. As well as organising exhibitions of contemporary art in Cardiff, Swansea and Aberystwyth, he became a trustee of the Gwerddlynn Foundation at Dowlais, and helped to run it. During that period, he painted several views of south Wales, of which this is one, some showing the influence of J.D. Innes. At about the same time he acquired some land in England which tempted him to give more time to his other enthusiasm, horticulture.

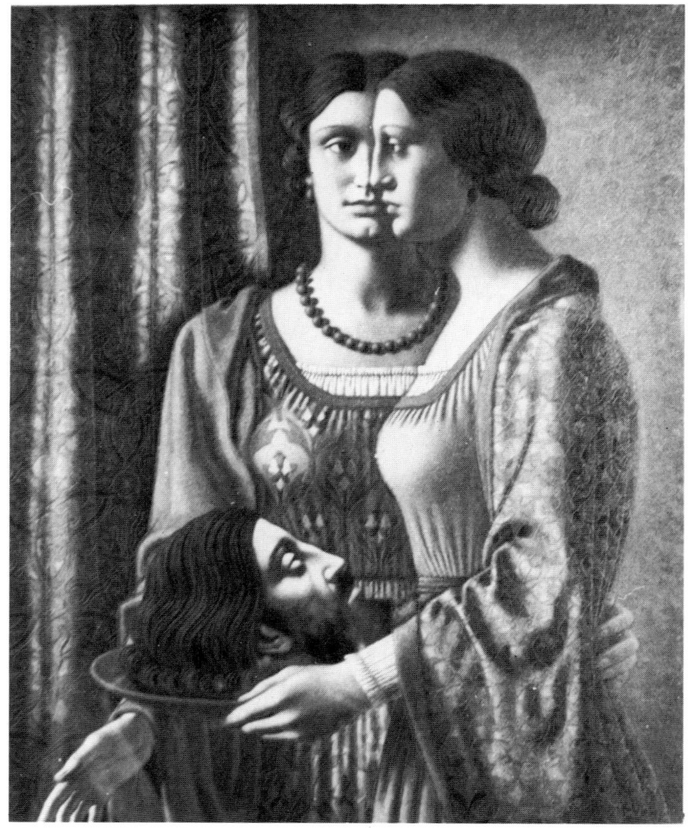

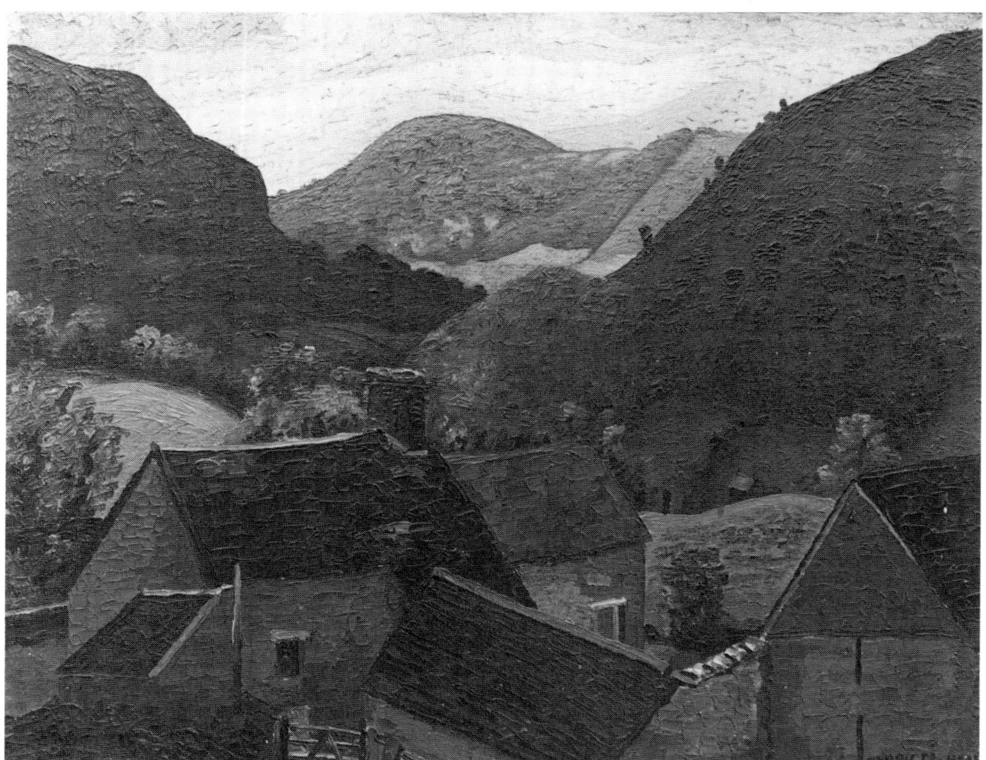

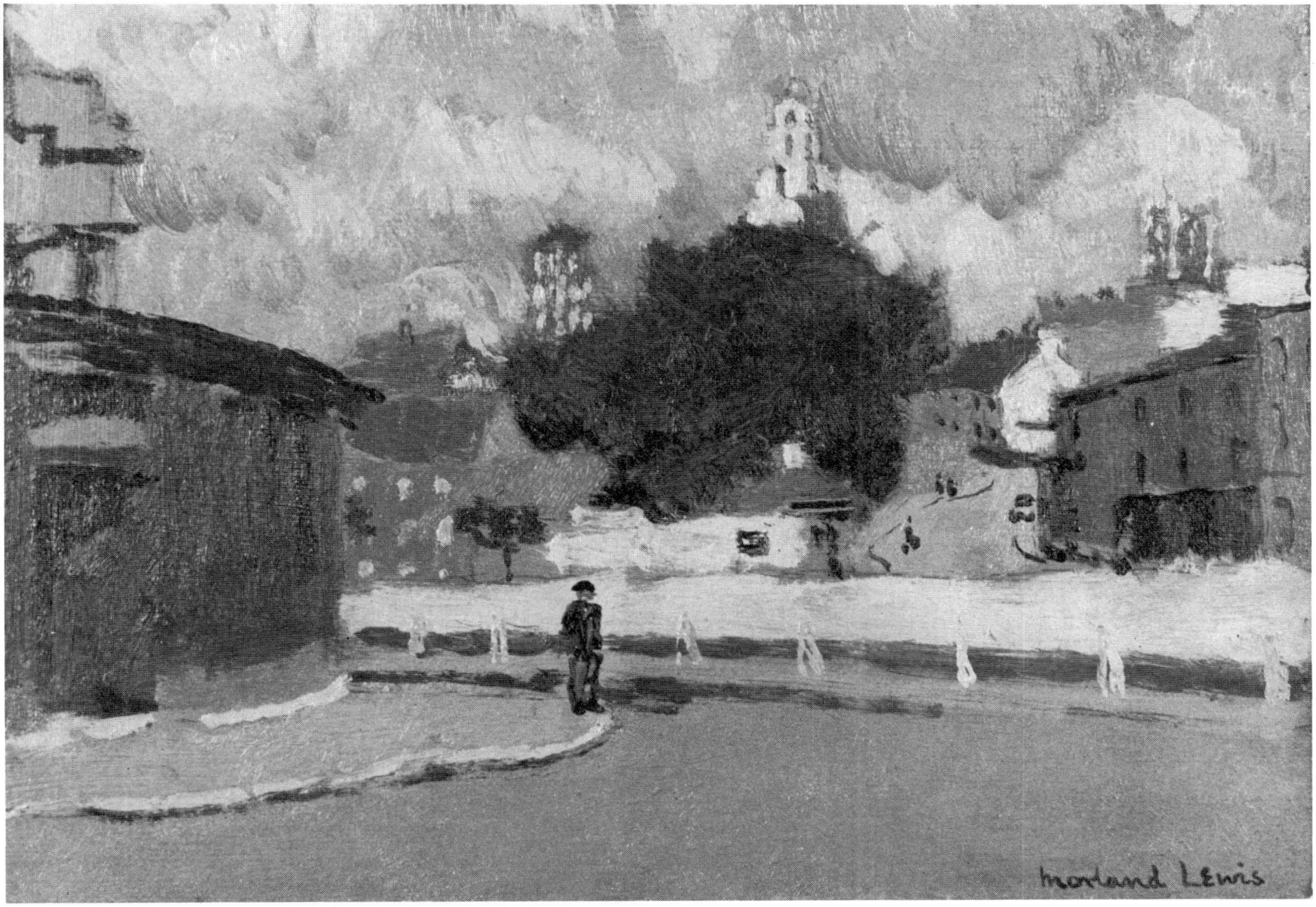

85. Edward Morland Lewis 1903 - 43
Shendon Church (c. 1938) Oil on canvas 39.25 x 47 cm
Glynn Vivian Art Gallery, Swansea

Morland Lewis painted mainly around his birthplace, Ferryside, in west Wales, and in Ireland. He was preoccupied with tone values, and it was probably this interest that led him to enrol in Sickert's private art school (his sixth) which opened in London in 1927. The curriculum consisted chiefly of drawing out of doors or from squared-up photographs of the 'Daily Mirror', though Lewis also helped in the underpainting of some of Sickert's paintings. The school was never very large or very successful and ended, according to Sickert, by 'a process of evaporation'. After that, Lewis painted many landscapes, though before his talent had matured he was killed in North Africa in 1943 during the war.

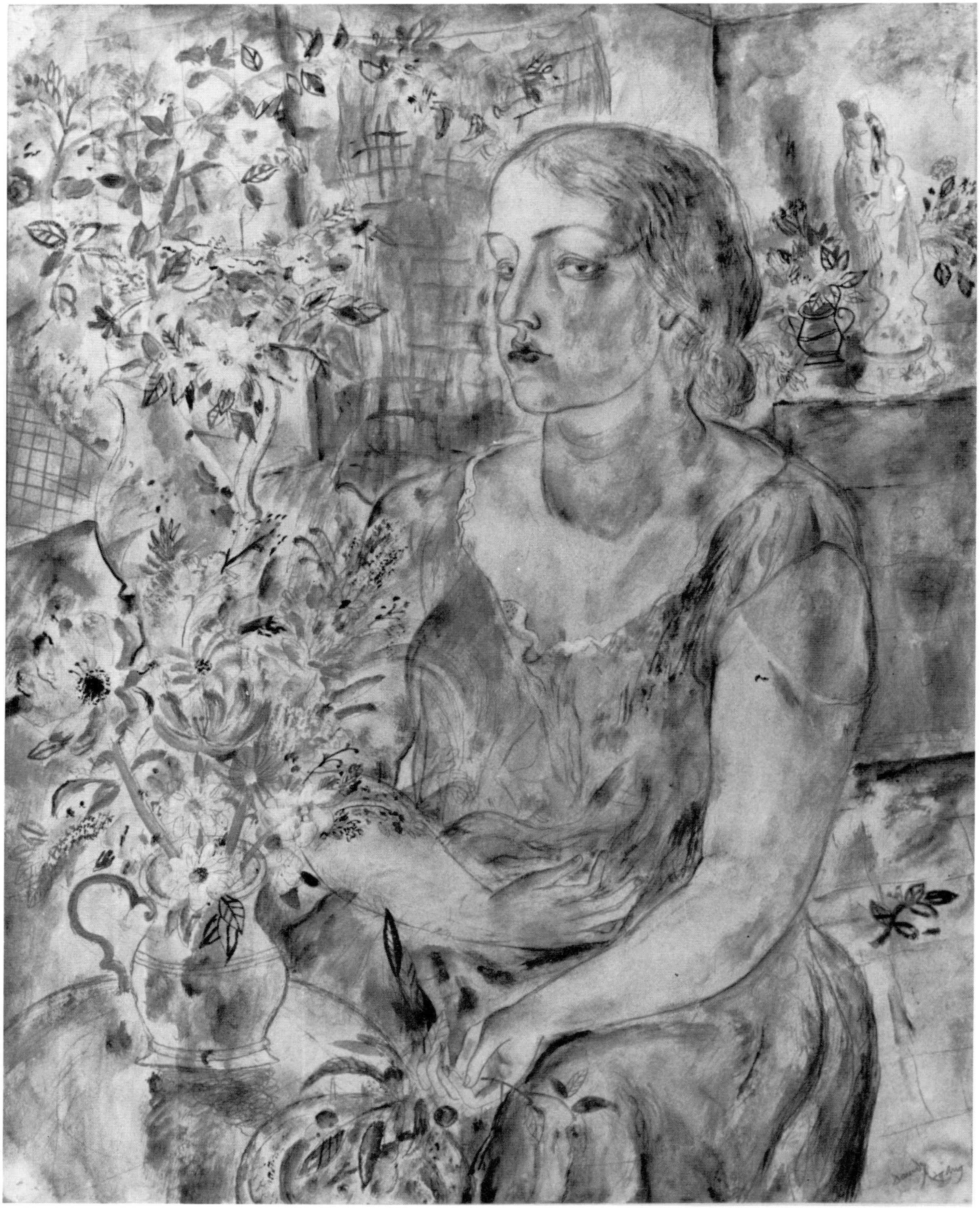

86. David Jones 1895 - 1974
Petra (1932) Watercolour 77.5 x 64.75 cm
Glynn Vivian Gallery, Swansea
This painting, a gift from the Contemporary Art Society, was the first work acquired by its Welsh counterpart the Contemporary Art Society for Wales - which in turn donated it to the Glynn Vivian Gallery. Petra was one of Eric Gill's daughters to whom Jones was at the time engaged. But it does not appear as a sentimental portrait, which is due to Jones's objectivity or to the fact that the engagement had by then been broken off.

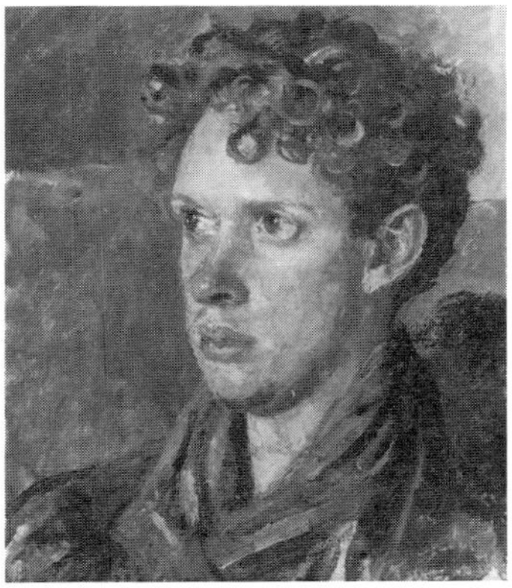

87. Augustus John 1878 - 1961
Portrait of Dylan Thomas (c.1936) Oil on canvas
40.75 x 34.25 cm
National Museum of Wales

Augustus John was introduced to his fellow countryman, appropriately, in a pub, the Fitzroy Tavern in London. In this portrait Thomas is still the fresh-faced young writer of promise (about 22 years of age), and John's verbal description of him is an accurate paraphrase of this portrait: 'Dylan's face was round and his nose snub. His rather prominent eyes were a little veiled and his curly hair was red, or auburn rather. A pleasant and slightly sardonic smile registered amusement and, I think, satisfaction'. Their relationship was both affectionate and aggressive; Thomas thought John should give up painting for poetry; John thought that Thomas's flair for shove ha'penny was superior to 'Under Milk Wood'. What this portrait shows is that, however much his other work might have deteriorated at this period, John could still capture a vivid and revealing likeness of those who were near or dear to him. *(See frontispiece)*

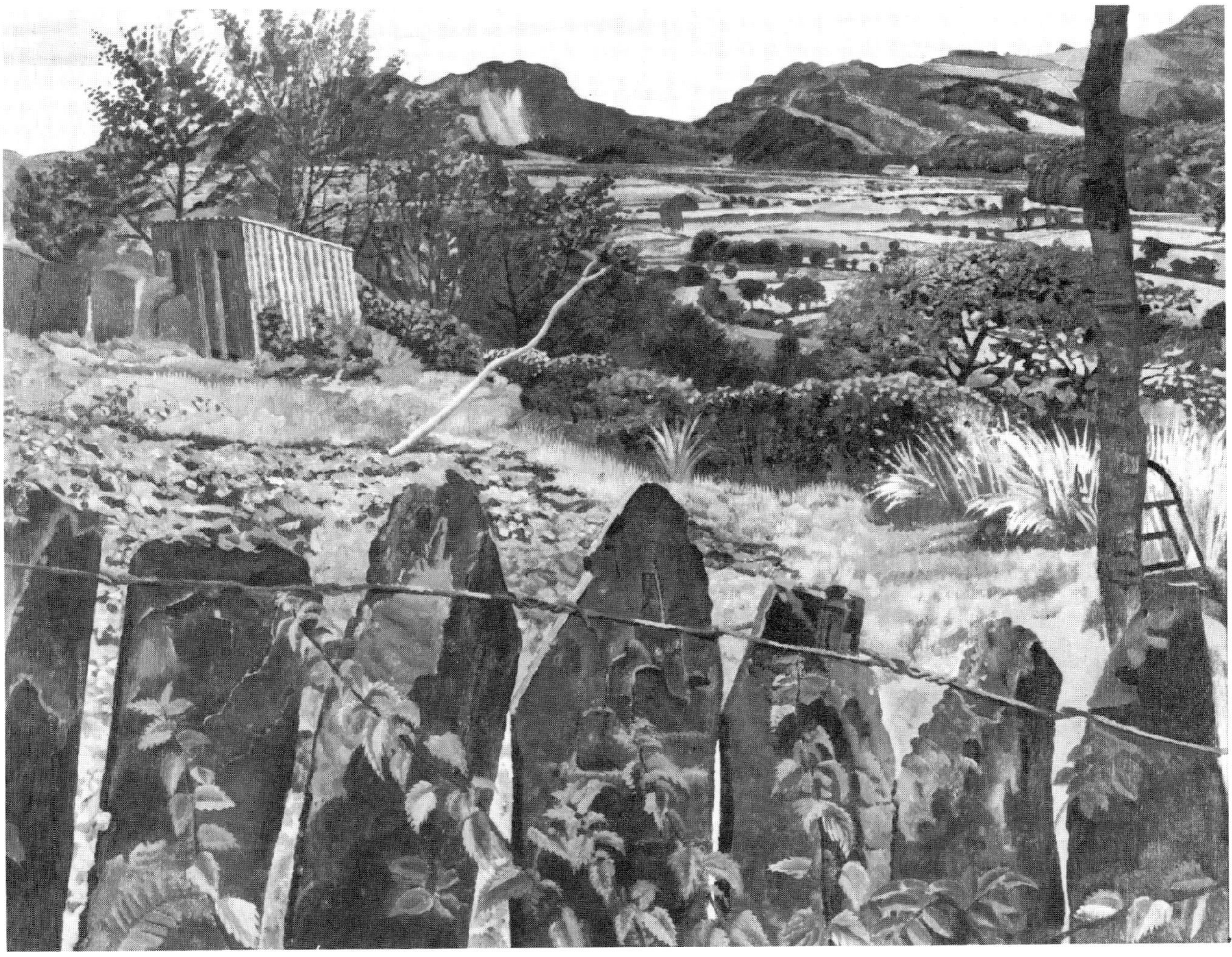

88. Stanley Spencer 1891 - 1959
Landscape in North Wales (1938) Oil on canvas 56 x 71 cm
Fitzwilliam Museum, Cambridge

Spencer always preferred working on his imaginative figure compositions and never painted landscapes from choice. However, to support his second wife Patricia and his ex-wife Hilda, he was obliged to turn to landscape painting to earn money. In September 1938, he was staying with Hilda and her mother near Snowdon, when he painted this picture and another, 'Snowdon from Llanfrothen', now in the National Museum of Wales. In spite of his disinclination, Spencer always made a competent, sometimes brilliant job of his landscapes. In this one he maintains two factors that were important to him in his imaginative work: the picture starts in the spectator's immediate foreground, while the artist's sense of relative values ensures that the privies are given equal emphasis with the mountains. A later (1952) and promising commission for a picture by Spencer to go in Llandaff Cathedral never materialised.

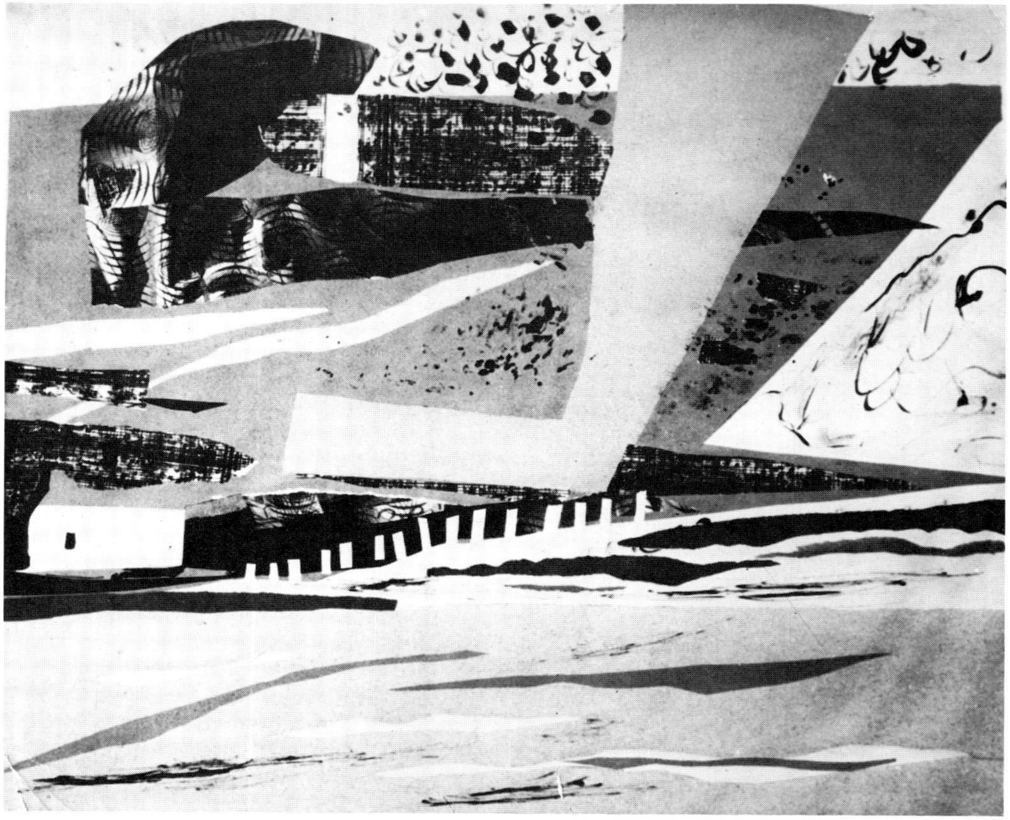

89. John Piper b. 1903
Welsh Beach, Aberayron (1938) Collage 40.5 x 51 cm
The Artist
Unlike Spencer, Piper's experience of the Welsh landscape had far-reaching effects on his work, for it coincided with a shift in ideas and provided him with a convenient subject for those ideas. The collages of this period, however, are not in the true Cubist tradition, for they are built on conventional space perspective, and the superimposed drawing, though schematic, is also descriptive of textures and objects in the landscape.

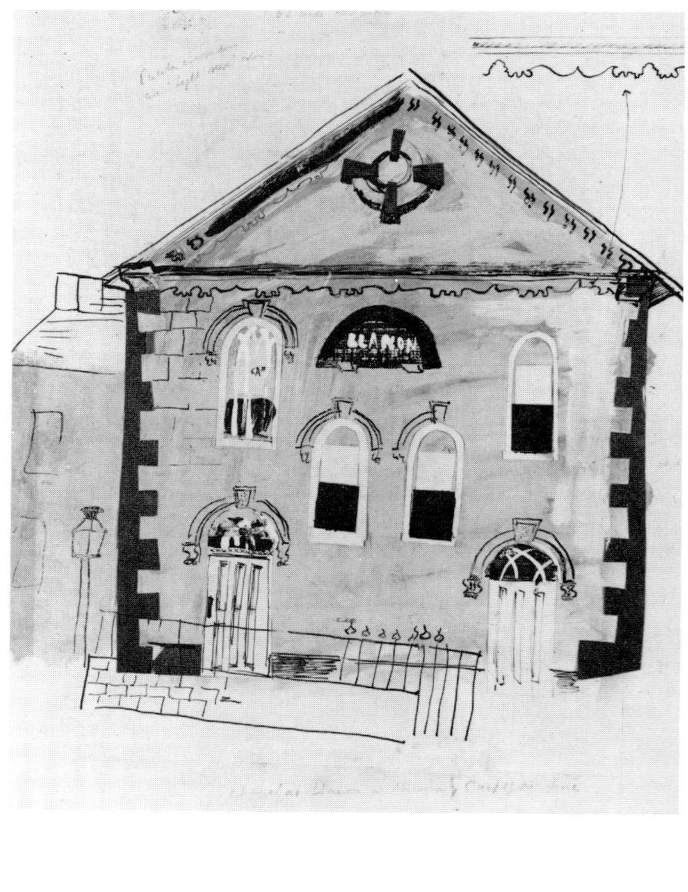

90. John Piper
Welsh Nonconformist Chapels (1937) Five drawings with collage, mount 91.5 x 61 cm
National Museum of Wales
These drawings were made only two years after Piper had been working in an idiom of geometrical abstraction. This change was described by Piper in his essay 'Lost, a Valuable Object', which appeared in 1936 in 'The Painter's Object', edited by his wife Myfanwy. His attitude was part of a general shift in sensibility, sometimes known as Neo-Romanticism; in part, a re-appraisal of landscape through the eyes of Surrealism. Like the earlier Romantics, these new ones of the 1930s looked to Wales for inspiration; both Piper and Graham Sutherland found the stimulus for their new ideas in the Welsh landscape.

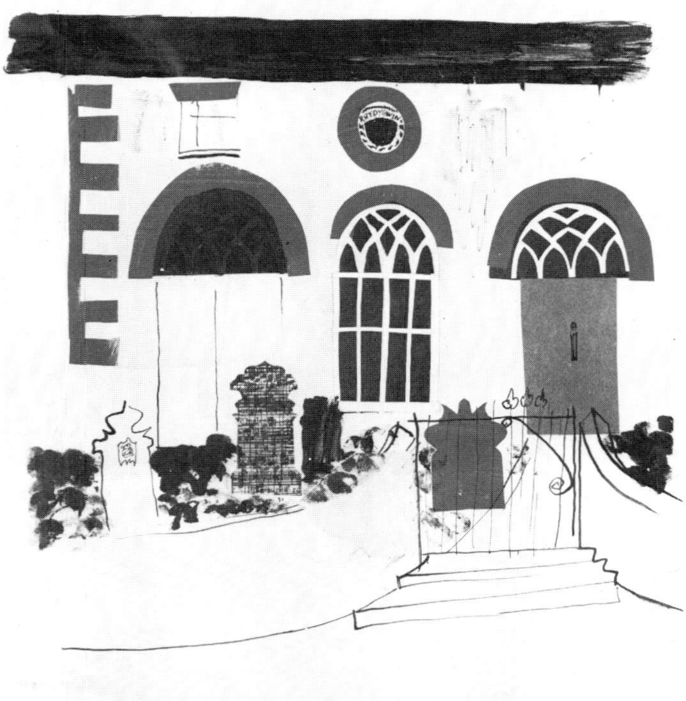

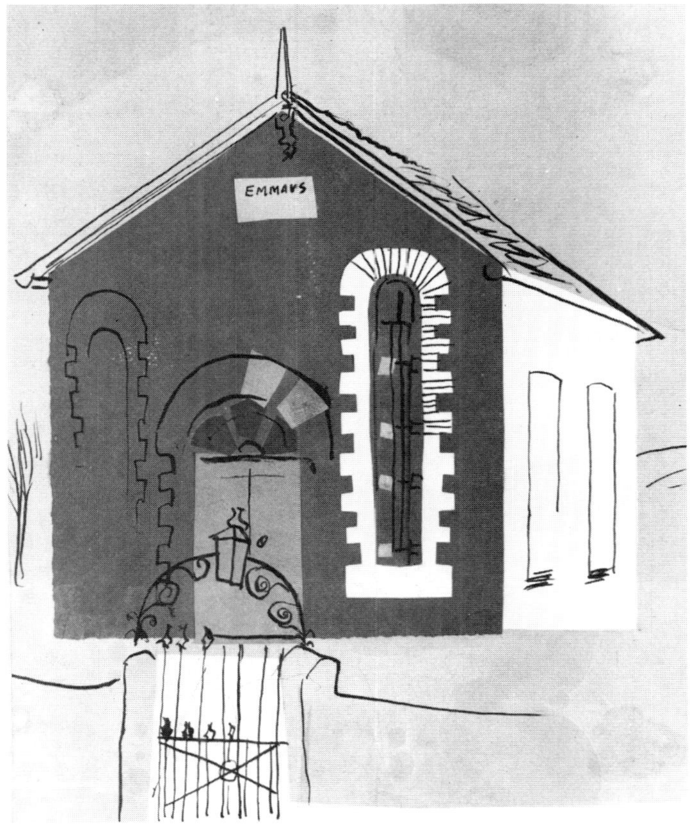
EMMAVS

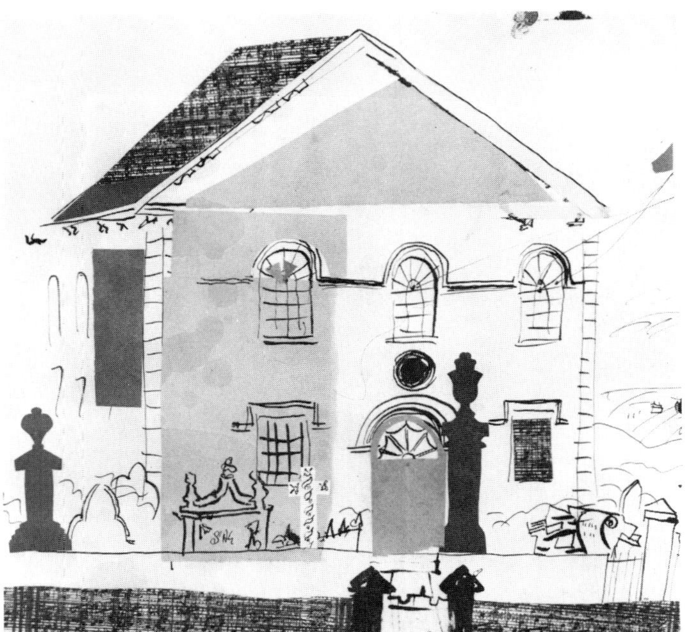
Typhos. Nr Kilgerran

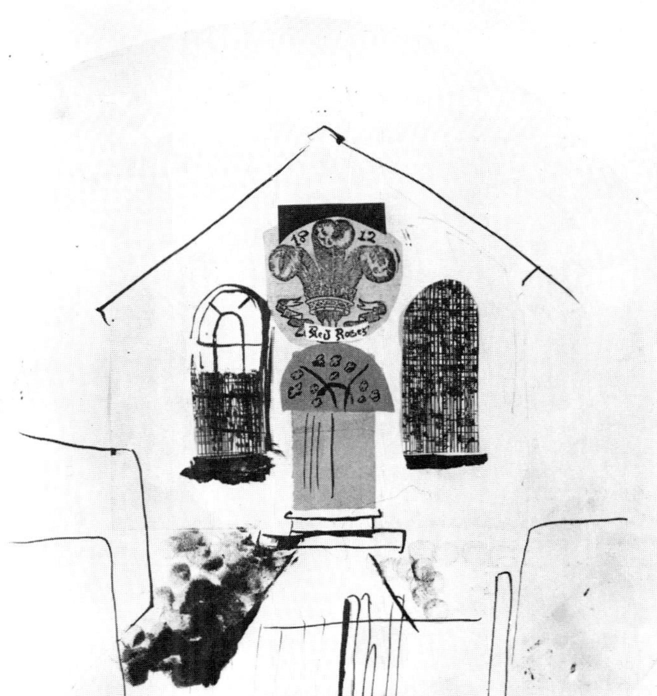
1812
Red Roses

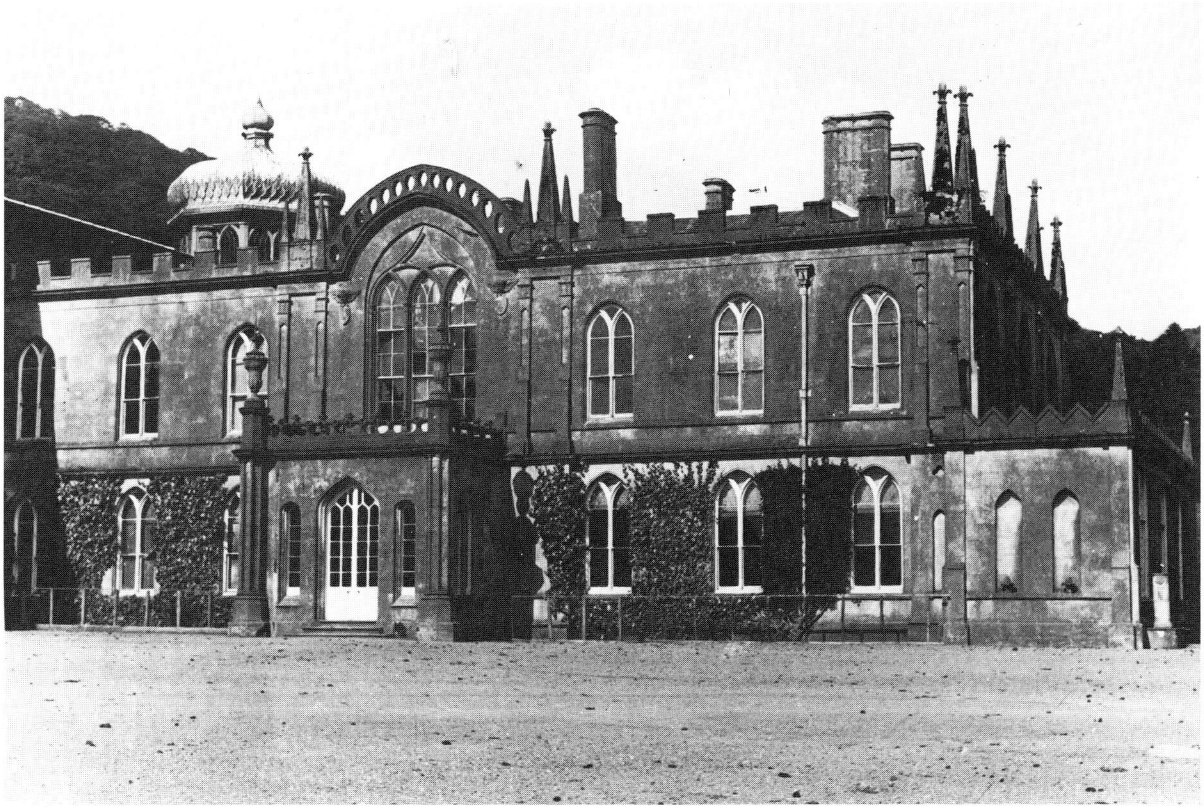

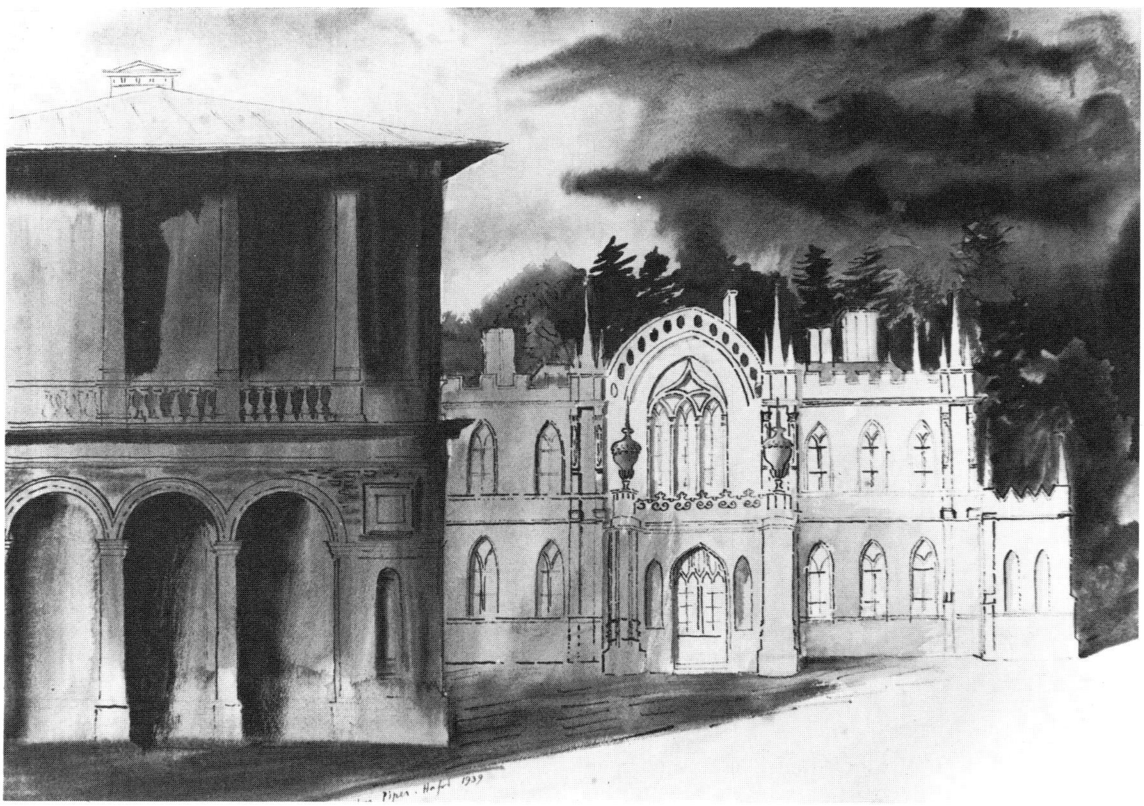
Piper · Hafod 1939

91. John Piper
Hafod (1939) Photograph

92. John Piper
Hafod (1939) Oil on canvas 63.5 x 76 cm
Lady Betjeman

Piper's taste for the quaint and picturesque also took a turn towards nostalgia; to the topographical delights of Regency architecture, Victorian pubs, Welsh chapels and the splendours of such places as Stourhead, Hafod and Castell Coch. It was Hafod, near Aberystwyth, that particularly appealed to him, for it was not only picturesque but also a ruin. In its prime, Hafod had been a favourite subject with many painters, among them Turner. Piper, however, caught it in its last stages of melancholy decay, for the ruins were demolished by dynamite in 1958.

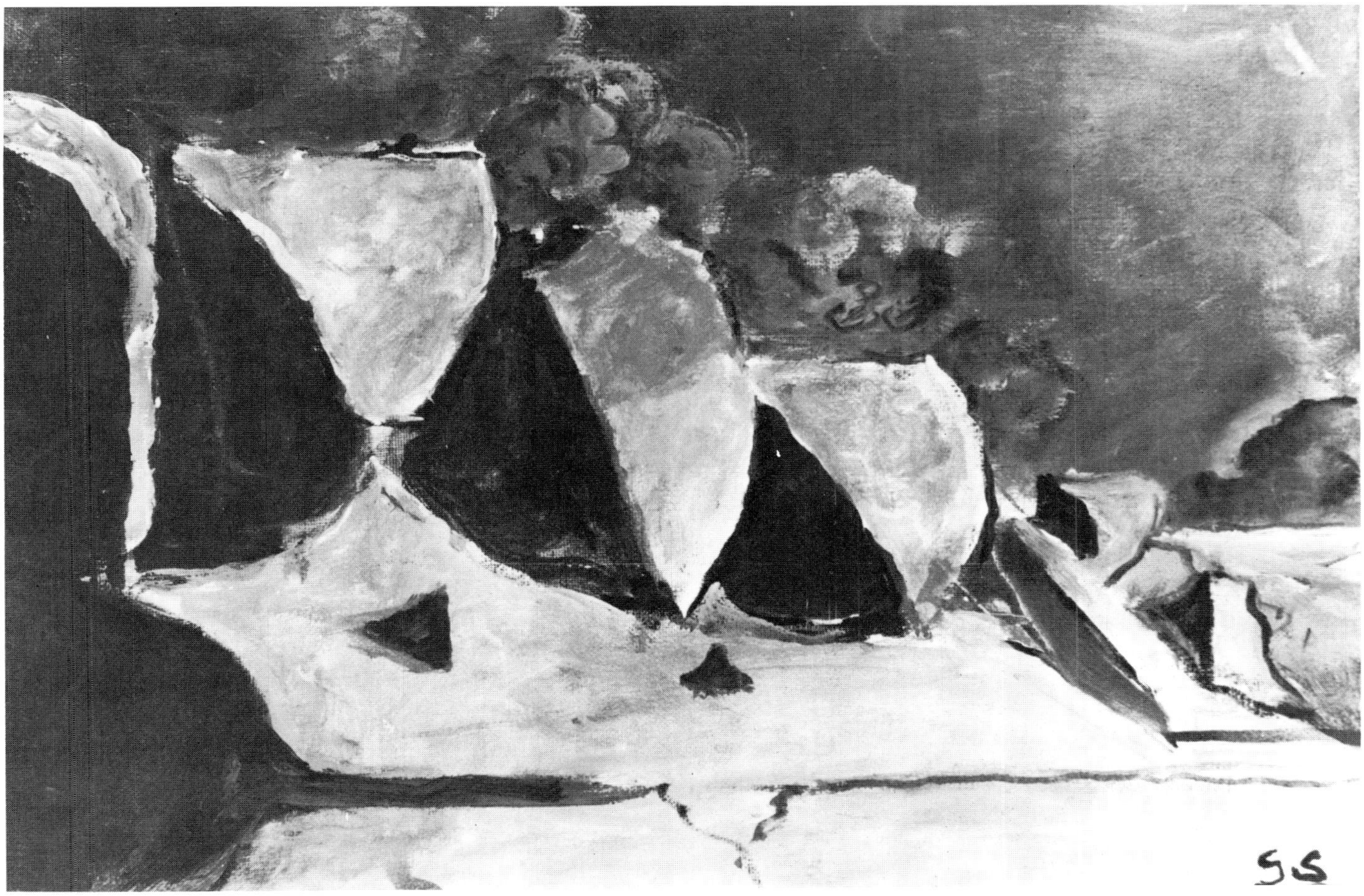

93. Graham Sutherland 1903 - 80
Estuary with Rocks (Sandy Haven) (1937 - 8) Oil on canvas 27 x 41.25 cm
Picton Castle Trust

'It was in 1934 that I first visited Pembrokeshire' wrote Sutherland. 'I was visiting a country, part of which, at least, spoke a foreign tongue, and it certainly seemed very foreign to me, though sufficiently accessible to feel I could claim it as my own!' In his 'Welsh Sketchbook', published in 'Horizon' in April 1942, Sutherland described in eloquent detail his first encounter with what was to become a major influence in his work. He was particularly impressed with St. Bride's Bay, with its topography, its tree forms and rocks and his response to these commonplace objects was almost mystical. The result was a series of paintings and drawings that made Sutherland the chief exponent of the so-called Neo-Romanticism. His 'paraphrases' of the Pembrokeshire landscape, painted away from the location, were derived from drawings made on the spot, often from two or three separate motifs. At the conclusion of his 'Welsh Sketchbook' he wrote '... it was in this area that I learned that landscape was not necessarily scenic, but that its parts have an individual figurative detachment'.

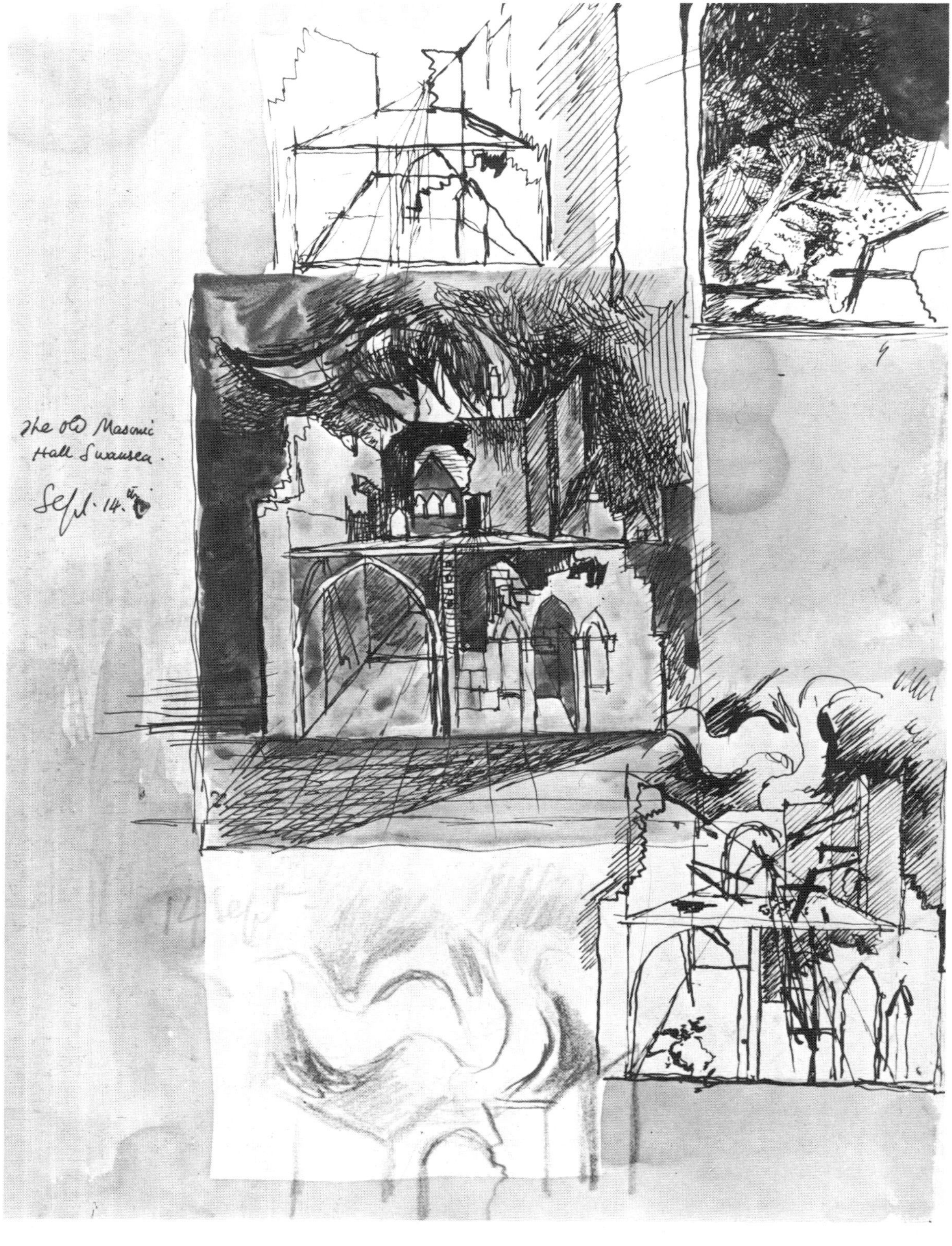

94. Graham Sutherland
Study for Masonic Hall, Swansea (1941) Watercolour, pen and ink 26.5 x 21.25 cm
Picton Castle Trust

When he was appointed an Official War Artist in 1940, Sutherland continued to visit Wales. He chose as his subjects the devastation of the bombing in Swansea, and the steel works in Cardiff. He also made more landscape studies, both in Pembrokeshire and along the Gower peninsula.

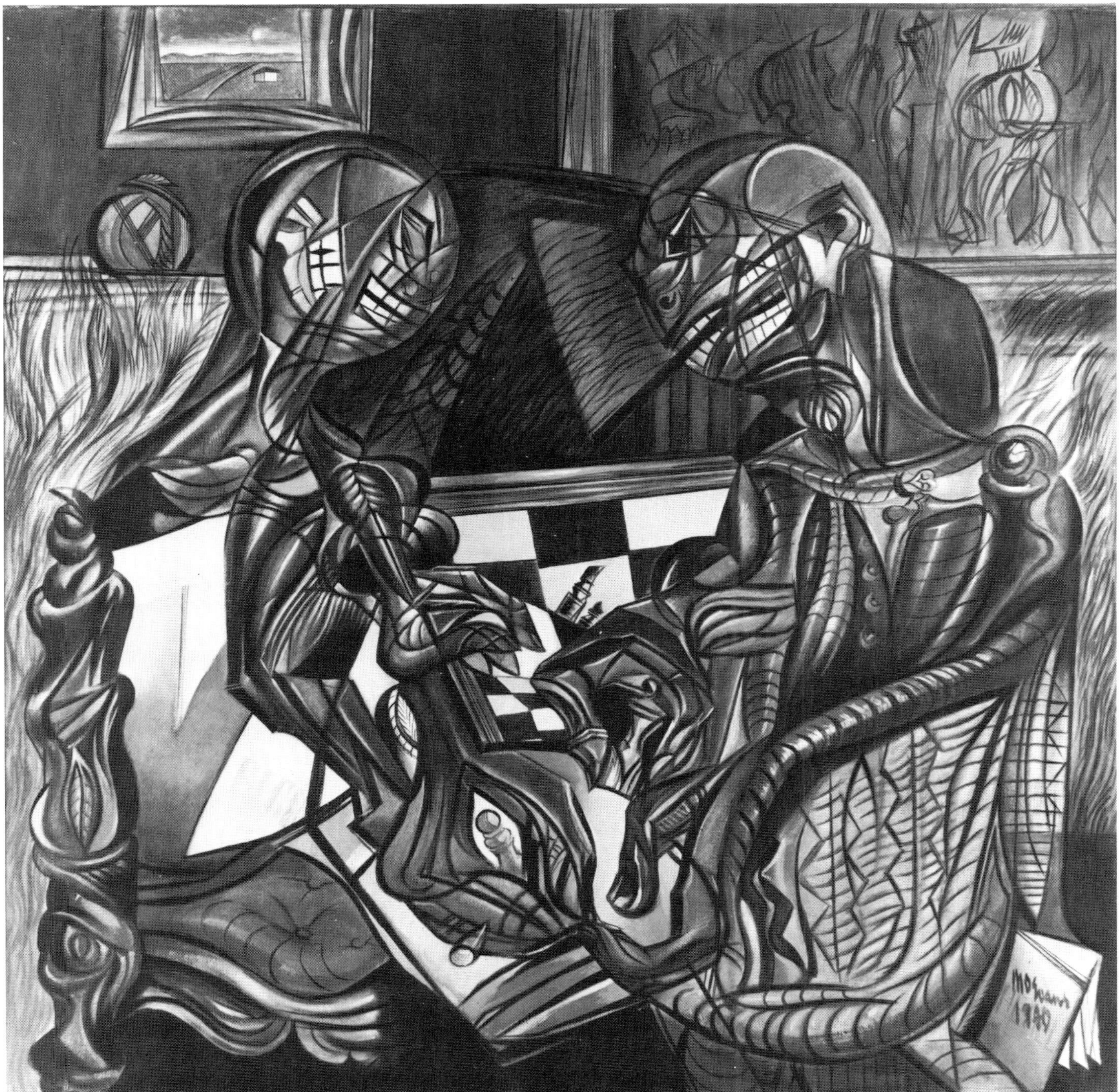

95. Merlyn Evans 1910 - 73
The Chess Players (1940) Oil on canvas 101.5 x 101.5 cm
Eldred Evans

Merlyn Evans was born in Llandaff, though his family moved to Scotland when he was 3 years old. He never worked or lived in Wales after that, though he was awarded a gold medal at the Royal National Eisteddfod at Aberaeron in 1966. Some commentators, however, have seen in his work a Celtic quality which found expression in both figurative and abstract paintings. Evans's sensibilities emerged most emphatically when, as in the late 1930s, he was deeply concerned with the problems of human suffering. More committed and compassionate in his work than either Piper or Sutherland, Evans used his own version of Surrealism to illuminate wider issues, as in this painting of two chess players, who symbolise Hitler and Stalin signing the infamous Nazi-Soviet pact.

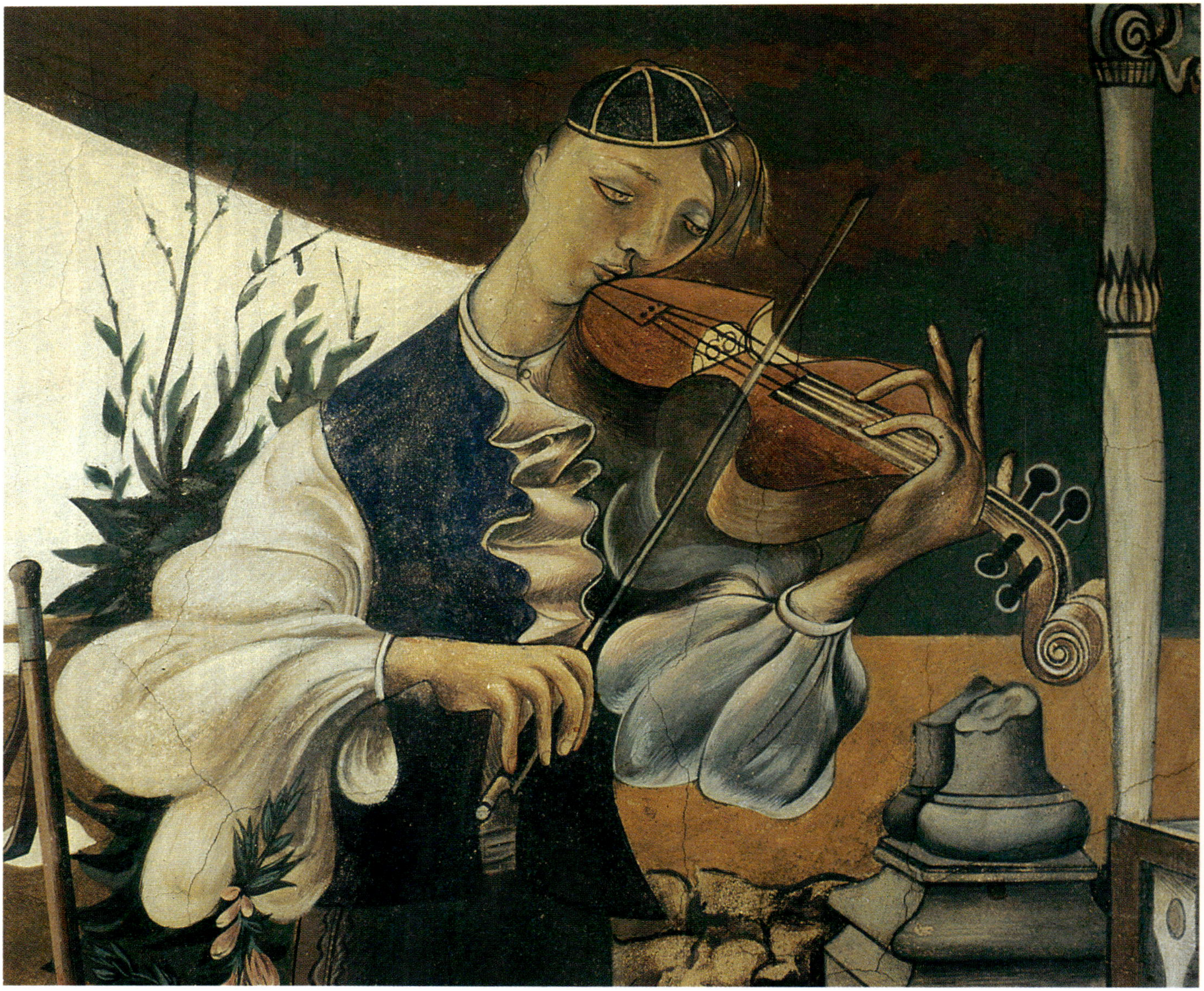

AFTER 1945

Chapter Five

The quest for that elusive chimera, an identifiable Welshness in the visual arts, seemed to be nearing fulfilment with the emergence of an autonomous Welsh Arts Council. Yet in the very period when the Council was evolving (1946-67) the visual arts became both more diverse and more de-nationalised. In addition, the centre of western art had shifted again; this time to New York, which was more remote than Paris. However, the second tidal wave of Modernism that swept over Europe and America after 1945 also lapped the shores of Wales. Now the new quest was to float Welsh art out into the main current of ideas. But it was not simple; privately and publicly, individually and collectively, artists and organisations tried to resolve the dilemma: was it to be art in Wales, art for Wales, art from Wales, or a combination of them all?

96. (a) Ceri Richards 1903 - 71
Mural Paintings (1944) Tempera on plaster 3.5 x 9.2 m
County Hall, Swansea (part-restoration)

During the Second World War, Ceri Richards was living and working in Cardiff. As well as teaching at the College of Art there, he was commissioned by the Ministry of Information to make a series of drawings based on the tin-plate works of his home town, Swansea. In the following year (1944) he was also commissioned by the Norwegian Government-in-Exile to produce this mural decoration for the British Council Offices in Cardiff. The murals were a gift to the Council in recognition of its achievements in war-time Britain, and were on the theme of Norwegian myth and history. In 1981, by an ingenious and successful method, the fragile murals were lifted from the walls of the old British Council offices, in premises due to be developed. The preserved murals are now partly in store and partly re-located in the West Glamorgan County Council buildings.

During the years of the Second World War, the gradual revival of the visual arts in Wales suffered a setback. Artists were conscripted — some, like Morland Lewis, were killed in action — connections were broken, information was scarce, funds were short, and exhibition facilities, never wholly adequate, were curtailed. This, of course, was the case with all the countries of the Western world — combatant or not — and it had a
96 similar effect on their art. But in Wales the effect of the war on the visual arts was more
97 crucial because their condition was more precarious.

In the years immediately after the war, art in Wales was in a confused state and the impetus of the previous decade had been halted. By international standards, the quality was not high and the indigenous artists neither formed a cohesive school nor made any significant contribution to the mainstream of contemporary European art. And to a different degree, the same criticism applies to the whole period from the end of the war
98 to the present day. It is a story not of influential movements or challenging theories, but of many individual artists diligently pursuing their own lines of enquiry with little more than coincidence to connect them in any aesthetic concern.

But from another point of view, the history of the period is one of steady progress and success in the quality and quantity of art produced in Wales. There are now much higher standards, many more artists, and infinitely better conditions than was the case in the late 1940s. At that time, the community of Welsh artists consisted of several unrelated categories. There was a generation of older artists still pursuing the lines of enquiry laid down at the beginning of the century by some of the movements of early Modernism: Cubism, Expressionism and Surrealism. The achievements of this generation were enriched, and at the same time challenged, by the presence of a small body of *émigrés*, who were grafting first-hand experience of those styles onto a Welsh genre. There was also the return of those visiting artists who had found inspiration in Wales before the war, and who now returned to revitalise it. And there was, at the same time, emerging a younger generation of artists striving to understand, assimilate and propagate the new aesthetics that were current in the artistic centres of Europe and America.

For, in spite of the upheaval of the war years and the artistic isolation of many countries, there was discerned a curious consistency of style and ideas. What is more, the
99 dominant style was a new one — a form of abstraction that depended not on geometry or predetermined theories of form, but on the response of the individual's sensibility to the world about him, the world within him, and the materials before him.

In France, England, Germany, Italy and the northern countries of Europe, there was an unexpected similarity in the painting and sculpture of the *avant-garde*. What was equally surprising to the European artists was the emergence of the United States as an important influence in western art, and the fact that, in America too, there was a style similar to that prevailing in Europe. So that, by 1950, it was generally recognised by the international art community that the most dynamic new visual art form was Abstract Expressionism, and that its most vigorous manifestation was to be found in America.

At the time, art in Wales was almost entirely isolated from this phenomenon, for
100 there was virtually no abstract painting or sculpture being produced. From one point of view this is surprising for the tenets of spontaneity and intuition that formed the roots of

Abstract Expressionism were the very qualities often regarded as being typically Welsh. On the other hand, there were few galleries in Wales prepared to show the new work from outside, and it was much more difficult for young Welsh artists to travel to New York than it had been for their predecessors to visit Paris. So that whatever influences did filter through to Wales usually came by way of London.

But the main handicap was a lack of cohesion among the artists themselves, of some force of authority that could form like-minded artists in Wales into an autonomous group, with some common agreement on ideas and styles. But no such flux appeared, neither in the shape of active patronage nor in the person of a respected leader. The one individual artist who had sufficient reputation and personal esteem was Ceri Richards, and he had already left Wales and returned to the challenging arena of the London art world. But without doubt, he was the outstanding Welsh artist of this or any subsequent period. Though his ideas had been largely formed before the war, his style continued to develop,
101 and by 1950 he was acknowledged as one of the foremost British painters and, as such, he was acquiring an international reputation. In the 1950s Richards was producing some of his most accomplished and confident works; paintings that represented his nearest approach to the prevailing form of abstraction.

102 The later stages of his series: *Cycle of Nature*, *The Beekeeper*, *La Cathédrale Engloutie*, and such works as *Blue Vortex in the Primaries*, all bear a generic likeness to contemporary French and Italian paintings of the period, and are often quoted in that context. This was more likely to have been a case of history catching up with Richards, rather than of his absorbing yet another influence. He had always believed in transposing his responses to people, poetry, music and nature into painterly metaphors, and it so happened that this was the current European aesthetic. Out of the profusion of symbolic images that
103 crowded his earlier canvases, Richards began to construct a more serene, personal vision of the world. It was a liberation from his attachment to Surrealism, which had by then run its full course.

By1960, his energy and inventiveness were at their peak; in the preceding decade he had produced innumerable drawings, watercolours and prints, as well as many paintings on themes relating to music, to poetry, and to one of his most deeply felt themes, *The*
104 *Return of the Patient*. It came from his own experience in hospital and it resulted in a new emphasis on the human figure; the figure not subordinate or simplified but dominant and expressive. The distortions of limbs and faces denoted a new humanist element in his
105 work which appeared in many of his finest late works, overwhelming even interests as enduring as music, as in his fine painting of 1970, *Music Room with the Head of Beethoven*.

When he died in 1971, Ceri Richards was not only regarded as an important painter of international status, he was at the same time and by the same standards known to be the greatest individual Welsh artist in the history of modern art. It is a position he still holds, even posthumously, and is likely to hold for some time to come. His achievements are too well-known to need further elaboration here, though it must be remembered that he spent the period of his greatest fame living outside Wales. These were the years when he was exhibiting at Pittsburgh, Sao Paolo, Moscow, Leningrad, New York, Dallas, San Francisco, Hamburg, Zurich, Basle, Milan and London; winning awards at Lugano,

Lublijana, Delhi, the Venice Biennale (1962), the John Moores Liverpool Exhibition (1959) and the Royal National Eisteddfod of Wales (1961). He was also producing commissions for stage and opera décor, and for ecclesiastical locations at Oxford, Derby and Liverpool.

It is one of the misfortunes of history that Ceri Richards was never given a commission for any large-scale public work in Wales. Apart from the wartime mural at the British Council Offices in Cardiff, there is no work specifically designed for a public place anywhere in Wales. And yet there was at least one opportunity for such a commission. When Llandaff Cathedral was being restored after the bomb damage it suffered during the war, there were two commissions on offer: one for sculpture and one for painting. The architect, and the Dean and Chapter, clearly wanted figurative work for
106 they commissioned the sculpture from Jacob Epstein and the painting from Stanley Spencer. Epstein produced the huge figure of Christ in Majesty, which now dominates the nave of the cathedral, but the arrangements with Spencer raised many problems. The Dean, Glyn Simon, wrote to the artist in October 1952, and asked him to '...help in our work of restoring our cathedral here ...'. Spencer visited the cathedral and expressed a wish to paint a *Last Judgement*, a subject that had been on his mind for some years, and for which he had already done some preparatory work. He stipulated, however, that 'I myself could only do oil painting', and was surprised when, the following summer, he was asked to produce a mosaic. He offered to make 'a cartoon from which a mosaic could be done', but nothing came of it, and the rather querulous discussion, involving money as well as materials, continued until it appears that the project sank from its own inertia.

Epstein's *Majestas*, however, provoked enough controversy to obscure the loss of a Spencer painting, and it is still a matter of contention as to whether the great metal figure fits convincingly into the nave of the cathedral. For, though he was an old man of seventy-five when he completed the work, and had only four more years to live, Epstein's public commissions continued to be sources of dispute. The stained glass window by John Piper, situated above the high altar, has always been generally admired, though from a central view along the nave it is obscured by the organ loft which bears the *Majestas*.
107 Piper's window is much smaller in scale than Epstein's statue, and the subject is not easily identifiable. Depicting *The Supper at Emmaus*, it appears that the iconography has been subordinated to the decorative qualities of the medium. But there is little doubt that the window conforms more gracefully than the sculpture to both the nineteenth and
108 twentieth-century reconstructions.

After the war, John Piper preserved his connections with Wales and, in 1949, with his wife Myfanwy, he took a cottage in the Nant Ffrancon Valley near Snowdon. In the
109 following years he drew and painted many views of the mountains, often based on his own photographs; dark and brooding and unrelieved by human presence. This period coincided with Piper's growing reputation in the wider world, with the increasing demands for his work in stage designs for opera and ballet and for public commissions. The Pipers left their house in Snowdonia and did not make any lengthy stay in Wales until 1963 when they acquired another house, this time at Strumble Head in Pembrokeshire. Here, Piper revived his interest in beach scenes, executed in a painterly form of collage.

In their subject-matter and medium, these works of the 1960s hark back to his early enthusiasms for Pembrokeshire, dating from 1937. But they are without the wit and freshness of his earliest Welsh work, and deficient in the dramatic power that characterised his mountain scenes. There is nothing in them that is indebted to the specifically Welsh location, and they could almost have been derived from any beach in any country.

To Graham Sutherland, however, the same area of Wales exerted a constant attraction. His loyalty to Pembrokeshire never flagged and, until his death, he continued to make an annual visit to the scenes around the south coast of the county that first dazzled him in 1934. Indeed, so great was his indebtedness to this area for the
110 development of all his subsequent work that in 1976 he gave 15 paintings, nearly 100 drawings and watercolours, and 69 prints to form a gallery at Picton Castle near Haverfordwest. It was a gesture unparalleled in modern art, and it allows us to compare the means and the end of his creative process. This process was not altered greatly during the forty or more years of Sutherland's connections with Wales. In 1976, the artist gave a lengthy interview with John Ormond, for the latter's perceptive television documentary, *Sutherland in Wales*. In this interview, and in his introduction to the catalogue of the Picton Castle Gallery, Sutherland reaffirmed the nature of his inspiration and his working process. He made notes,'following the first *frisson* of an encounter', usually in the form of rapid drawings, sometimes by photographs, and then worked on the 'paraphrases' at his studio at Menton in the South of France. There, 'one remembers: one's encounters become redefined, paraphrased and changed into something new and different from that of the first encounter - yet the same'.

This practice, of gathering material in Wales, and of working on it in a studio far away, meant that Sutherland had little or no direct effect on artists working in Wales. The same was true of another artist, David Jones, who gained his inspiration from Welsh subjects but who worked on it in a place as remote — in spirit — as Sutherland's Riviera studio. But, though both these artists were at the height of their fame, their ideas had been formed before the war, and their work had little relevance to a younger generation in the post-war era.

The external success of such individual artists as Jones and Sutherland, Piper and Richards, did cast some reflected prestige onto the visual arts in Wales. And though extraneous it was valuable, for by the wider standards of the time, the visual arts in Wales were hermetic, even provincial. During the 1950s there was little that could be described as Abstract Expressionism, there was no assemblage art, there were certainly no signs of proto-Pop Art of the kind that was appearing in England. The most prominent Welsh
111 artists of the period, painters such as Brenda Chamberlain, Kyffin Williams, John Elwyn, Alfred Janes and Eric Malthouse, all subscribed to a figurative style owing debts of varying magnitude to a diversity of early twentieth-century ideas. All shared a common interest in simplified and stylised forms, though they never seemed to have attempted to formulate a common aesthetic.

It seems, in retrospect, as if this individualism and the isolation from current international ideas came not so much from a lack of contact with those ideas as from a

deliberate detachment, a withdrawal from theories that could serve no purpose in the ideology of Welsh artists. They were prepared to select and utilise established styles in order to shape the images of their individual vision, but not to adopt them for their own sake as a means of keeping in fashion. Brenda Chamberlain is a particularly apposite example of this attitude. Indeed, in her life as much as in her art, she demonstrated the principle of detachment, of a deliberate retreat from fashions in art and the centres of
112 fashion. An early attachment for the work of Gauguin — with its simplified form and its preference for remote, primitive subjects — coloured much of her later work. In her self-imposed isolation in Bardsey, Snowdonia and the Greek island of Hydra, she tried to distil her feelings, recollected in tranquillity, into her paintings and poems. Her pictures of children — calm, dignified, statuesque and detached — symbolise her personal confrontation with the world.

The drama of isolation also forms the dominant theme of Kyffin Williams's work.
113 Though he lived and taught in London for many years, and is now a Royal Academician with a reputation for rugged portraiture, he is best known for his landscapes of Wales. He is a native of Anglesey and the scenery of north Wales has held a long and obsessive interest for him. In spite of his periodic separations from Wales, Williams has become a prolific painter of its landscapes, producing pictures with a fluency and rapidity that occasionally lapse into a repetitive formula; an unvarying, heavy technique that makes no distinction between contrasting textures or atmospheric effects. Nevertheless, in his many successful paintings of the landscape of north Wales there appears a feeling of romantic detachment of the kind that is sometimes evident in Innes' paintings of distant mountains. Williams, however, ignores modern theories of art; his canvases are dedicated chiefly to high menacing mountains, remote farms, dark and empty; bleak skies heavy with grey clouds; all suggesting a sense of melancholy and a yearning for retreat and escape.

It might have been these same qualities that led some European *émigré* artists to forsake London and the larger cities, and to seek refuge in the quieter parts of Wales. Certainly it must have been compelling enough to keep some of them there after the dangers of war had passed. Once there, they enlivened and disturbed the artistic life of the post-war years, for they brought a direct European influence to their adoptive country, challenging the Welsh synthesis of modern styles and exerting a strong influence on some of the younger artists.

Mostly of an Expressionist persuasion, painters such as Frederick Konekamp, Heinz Koppel and Josef Herman either settled or made prolonged stays in Wales. Others, among them Fred Uhlman, Martin Bloch and George Mayer-Marton, paid shorter visits, mainly in search of subject-matter. Whatever their reasons, and however long their stay, they all contributed in varying degrees to the growth of the visual arts in Wales. Herman is the outstanding artist of this *émigré* group, and his work and influence are probably the
114 most familiar, because the most powerful and most easily recognised.

Herman's early life is a classic saga of our time. Born into a Jewish family in Warsaw, he was a printer's apprentice until illness, brought on by a practical joke, obliged him to become an art student. In 1938, growing anti-semitism in Poland forced him to flee to

Belgium, where he remained until the German invasion of 1940 drove him on once more. This time he went to Bordeaux, where, almost by chance he caught a boat to Glasgow. In Scotland he learned to speak English, acquired friends and patrons, and stayed for three years, painting portraits and nostalgic evocations of his early life in Poland.

His style showed a mixture of influences, notably Permeke — whom he had known in Belgium — and Chagall, whose work represented all the rich poetry of Jewish life. But Herman's complete individuality as an artist came to him, not in Scotland, but in Wales. Some time in 1944, the wandering painter left Glasgow and appeared in Ystradgynlais, a mining village in the hills north of Swansea. It may have been a random choice, but what he found in the industrial part of Wales was just as thrilling and revolutionary to him as the unspoilt coast of Pembrokeshire had been to Graham Sutherland ten years before.

115 In an eloquent description of his experience in Ystradgynlais, he tells how, one summer's day in 1944, on a hot afternoon, he became intensely aware of the quiet of the scene; of the colour and the light and the shadow; of how some miners suddenly appeared on the bridge against the sun. And he acknowledges that 'the image of the miners on the bridge against this glowing sky had a feeling which mystified me for years, with its mixture of sadness and grandeur, and it became the source of my work for the rest of my life'.

Whatever picturesque or romantic notions other artists may have derived from the industrial landscape of Wales, for Herman it had a more elevated appeal. For him it
116 symbolised the dignity of labour, man's struggle for survival, and the close affinity that exists between a man and the environment in which he works. Patiently and systematically, Herman developed his technique, his sense of colour and a refinement of imagery, until he had acquired the means to convey his sense of the mystery of Ystradgynlais. Through this discipline he was later able to find the same mystery in the working people of Spain, France, Mexico, Italy and Israel.

There is a metaphysical element underlying all Herman's pictures, whatever the specific subject, that is absent in the work of his Welsh followers. But with his positive, deeply-held opinions and his robust technique, and with the authority of European experience behind him, it was not surprising that he should have a considerable influence on the younger Welsh painters around him. Himself influenced by Rembrandt, Grünewald, Brueghel, Munch and Van Gogh, Herman passed on, to artists such as George Fairley and Will Roberts, his personal distillation of Expressionism.

117 Of them all, Roberts was the most obviously influenced, because he was the most vulnerable to positive ideas. His only training in art was part-time and, after the war, he met Herman, who invited him to become his pupil. Working in the same studio he soon adapted his ideas to Herman's style, using large, lumpish figures in crepuscular settings and painted in dark, glowing colours. But Roberts became more than a mere imitator; though he could never achieve Herman's dark luminosity of colour, his paintings have a more sinuous quality about them and, once again, it is possible to detect an apocryphal Welsh element, with less angst and more poetry.

Another *émigré* artist with an equally positive attitude, and a persuasive influence,
118 was Heinz Koppel. Like Herman, he was obliged to adapt to whatever geographical

location he found himself in and he too could transform what he saw, wherever he saw it, into his own imagery. Working around Merthyr Tydfil, Koppel changed the grim industrial scene into a world of colour and fantasy, and showed how the most unpromising environment could be transformed by the workings of the imagination. It was this latter ability, as much as any stylistic features, which excited the younger Welsh painters, and through Koppel's example, a small, ephemeral, but lively group of artists joined together to form *The Rhondda Group*. These painters: Ernest Zobole, Charles Burton, Glyn Morgan, Nigel Flower and C. Mainwaring, began to see their native environment through the filter of a kind of magic realism, tinted with the ideas of Chagall as transmitted by Koppel. Perspective was flattened, proportions distorted, objects
119 simplified, multiple viewpoints used and a child-like, map-like, almost naive vision of life in the industrial valleys of south Wales was the result.

At its worst, this school of painting lapsed into sentimentality and spurious marvel-making; at its best it showed the wonders that the artist can detect beneath the drab, commonplace world of the industrial scene. And though this school of painting was short-lived, it is of greater historical interest than its products perhaps deserve, for it is a rare example of a movement in Welsh art. Though no manifesto appears to exist, or indeed to have been formulated, there was a collective aesthetic with a recognisable style. It may be that Koppel's influence was responsible for this, for he was an artist who declined to comment on his work, and preferred the work to speak for itself. On the other hand, it is a reasonable generalisation to say that native Welsh artists tend to be individualistic in their work and self-conscious about the use of words to describe their ideas, and they certainly avoid any form of collective theorising.

This is perhaps the reason why outsiders find it difficult to define a particular formal quality about Welsh art, and why they try to identify a common denominator in terms of content or sentiment. For, though the members of *The Rhondda Group* moved on to develop in individual and different ways, their kind of work became conveniently identified as the style and subject-matter that was expected from Wales.

Such an emphasis on content helped to shape the public view of modern Welsh art in the immediate post-war period. It established a self-perpetuating canon, whereby only the kind of art that conformed to the canon was recognised as Welsh. It was an extra burden on the shoulders of those artists who were attempting to bring the art of Wales into line with developments in England, Europe and America. But though the stress on content was irksome to the more progressive painters, it was a severe handicap for sculptors.

Compared with painting, sculpture lays more emphasis on form than on content; it is less flexible in its narrative potential and it is, therefore, less capable of conveying Welsh subject-matter. The principal subjects of figurative art in Wales, pastoral or industrial landscapes, could not at that time be adequately represented within the formal limitations of sculpture.

120 Another reason for the relative scarcity of sculptors in Wales during the 1940s was that sculpture had been deprived of stimulus in the formative period between the wars; the years that followed the burst of Edwardian ostentation at Cardiff's Civic Centre.

That was the time of the Depression, when there was little public money available for municipal commissions, and consequently little encouragement for sculptors. War memorials or some church adornments were the chief manifestations of sculpture during the difficult period before the Second World War. The practice of studio sculpture, work produced solely for exhibition and sale, was almost non-existent. Eric Gill in his cellar at Capel-y-Ffin was the outstanding exception, and most of his output went straight to galleries in London. Another factor is that sculptors are less mobile than painters, and the counterparts of Piper and Sutherland, sculptors such as Hepworth and Moore, did not work in Wales.

With these handicaps it is not surprising that painting should have been the
121 predominant activity during the first half of the twentieth century. After the war several sculptors, Jonah Jones and Frank Roper among them, began to produce studio sculpture and to revive some measure of patronage for it. But it was not for some years, until the 1960s, that sculpture in Wales reached the prominence that had already been attained by Welsh painting.

So that if the 'long-delayed revival' prophesised by Hugh Blaker started before the First World War, it did not begin to gather momentum until after the Second World War. In fact the visual arts in Wales have made such remarkable progress during this second period that 'revival' is hardly the appropriate word. In all the history of art in Wales there has been nothing to compare with the period from 1945 to the present day, which has seen an unprecedented burst of activity. Consequently there is no precedent with which to compare it and thus deem it a renaissance. This is to refer to the quantity of art produced, and to defer, for the moment, any discussion of the quality. Though with the very increase in activity there should inevitably be some improvement in standards.

Without question, the most important single factor contributing to the expansion of the visual arts in the second half of this century has been the growth of the Welsh Arts Council. From modest beginnings during the war as a regional branch of CEMA (Committee for the Encouragement of Music and the Arts), the Council then became a regional office of the Arts Council in 1946. Under the firm guidance and control of David Bell — painter, poet, historian of art and curator of the Glynn Vivian Gallery — it continued with this status until it became the Welsh Committee of the Arts Council of Great Britain in 1953. In 1967 there was a final metamorphosis, and it emerged as the Welsh Arts Council; a fully-fledged, autonomous body financed by central government but with complete independence in the manner in which it disbursed its funds. This meant the creation of an influential, independent, relatively affluent agency for patronage of the arts, managed by both laymen and practitioners, and dedicated to the furtherance of Welsh art, art in Wales, and art for Wales. These distinctions are worth noting for the Welsh Arts Council has always seemed unencumbered by a rigid, theoretical policy. Not caring to discriminate between Welsh-born artists and other artists working in Wales, or between art going from Wales and art coming to Wales, the Council happily steers a pragmatic course between promotion and edification, and thereby seems to satisfy the greater number of people concerned.

Nor is the Council's function entirely a passive, supportive one. By various means it seeks to promote a policy of unobtrusive enlightenment; careful not to seem too didactic but anxious to foster an understanding of all forms of art. One way in which it attempts this is by publications, another is by exhibitions; some modest and conventional, others more radical in their concepts. Among the Council's innovations has been the poster scheme of 1968, as well as the ambitious series of large exhibitions on the theme of art and society. Sparked off in 1968 by a suggestion from Gordon Redfern, then the chief architect at Cwmbran New Town, the first exhibition was held at the Glyn Vivian Gallery in Swansea in 1969. Its subject and its title was *War*, and during the next few years it was followed by *Work, Worship* and *Marriage.* In spite of their cryptic titles, these exhibitions were immensely complex and diverse. By gathering together a variegated mass of objects connected with the subject they attempted to point out new categories, to establish new relationships, and to widen the definition of what constitutes an art object. The declared aim was '...to try to explain the relationship between art and life' which was a grandiose aim, and though the dialectic was sometimes obscure, the exhibitions were unquestionably thought-provoking.

These, though, are some of the Welsh Arts Council's more controversial activities. Since its inception it has steadily supported the arts in Wales in more conventional ways. Although in the beginning its budget was small, it deployed its resources judiciously and democratically: helping societies, galleries and individuals, promotion exhibitions, and making purchases of art works to a degree that at first equalled and then eventually outstripped the patronage of the Contemporary Art Society for Wales. At first there was a danger that the introduction of mandatory patronage of the arts might diminish the capacity for self-help that has helped to shape the history of art in Wales. The threat does not seem to have materialised except for the new custom whereby any group or individual beginning in the spirit of self-help or rebellion, eventually asks for an Arts Council grant to help sustain its independence.

In spite of the growing influence of the Arts Council, the Contemporary Art Society for Wales has continued to flourish and to add to its purchases. These are made by the simple but effective system of appointing each year an individual buyer who has a completely free hand in selecting works of his own choice. This method ensures a diversity of selection, and also demonstrates the principles of both individual and collective self-help for the visual arts in Wales. The same sense of obligation towards the arts has also been apparent in the efforts of individuals who, acting either independently or in concert with some public organisation, have made several distinguished contributions in the post-war period.

Leslie Moore was an outstanding example of this principle. As art adviser to the county of Glamorgan, his achievements at the grass roots of art education were self-evident; but with his own painting and in his voluntary involvement with all forms of adult art activity, he helped along the cause of Welsh art. And nowhere was the effect more far-reaching than in his organising of the Barry Summer School. Characteristically, Moore never sought any credit for the success of this annual venture, but it was through his imaginative approach, his contacts with the wider world of art, and the respect in which he was generally held, that the Summer School at Barry became an international event. Not only did it bring students from all over the world to spend a summer fortnight at what was then the Training College, it also attracted a varied and talented group of artists. This, in turn, enabled Welsh artists and teachers to widen their horizons, and in some cases added to their number when visiting artists were encouraged to make a longer or permanent stay in Wales.

122 Another resident artist who encouraged outsiders to make a more permanent contribution to Welsh art was Eric Malthouse, though his efforts were perhaps less organised, and a little more idiosyncratic. Born in Birmingham, Malthouse went to Cardiff after war service, to teach in the College of Art. From 1952 his paintings were concerned with the theme of pigeons: *A Flight of Pigeons, A Flurry of Pigeons* and *Flying Pigeons* are typical titles of the period, which lasted until about 1958. All these were concerned with the transformation of movement into static formal qualities of painting, and this factor, combined with another indicated in the title *Pigeon's View*, led to a further series of paintings. This was on the theme of rock pools, and started in 1955, overlapping the pigeon series by some three years. Both were concerned with movement, and the rock
123 pool paintings were seen from a bird's eye view. These paintings of rock pools, the sea and the activities of fishermen, were inspired by the visits Malthouse paid to St Ives during those years . It was in the heyday of St Ives as an artists' colony, and Malthouse was one of the few artists from Wales who kept regular contact with their fellow-artists in Cornwall.

His concern for a wider perspective among Welsh artists also led Malthouse to venture into what might be called the politics of art. For some years there had been rumblings of discontent among progressive artists who believed, rightly or wrongly, that the 'official' view of Welsh painting and sculpture was sentimentalised and atrophied; that it favoured the kind of art that had a discernable 'Welsh' character. It was also maintained that this art — mainly landscape and genre — was perpetuated by official patronage, at that time centred in London. No one seems to have attempted a precise definition of 'official' and so now, twenty-eight years later, it is not easy to assess the truth of this belief – but it has undoubtedly passed into legend.

In 1956, it was a firm conviction — with Malthouse, at least. He joined two other malcontents, David Tinker and Michael Edmonds, and together they devised a plan to form a pressure group of artists sympathetic to their ideas, and whose work was sufficiently progressive and, presumably, neglected. As a gesture of radical art politics it was in the heroic tradition of European art, and unique in the history of art in Wales. So the three instigators approached ten other potential recruits among the artists working
124 throughout Wales, and, to their surprise and delight, nine of them accepted the notion with enthusiasm. And though much of their work could only be seen as progressive in a Welsh context, these nine: Trevor Bates, Hubert Dalwood, George Fairley, Arthur Giardelli, Robert Hunter, Heinz Koppel, Will Roberts, John Wright, and Ernest Zobole, were highly professional artists. Choosing an appropriate but neutral title, the twelve insurgents dubbed themselves the *56 Group* , and prepared themselves for action.

Once again, in the tradition of European art, they were ignored by the people they challenged; partly because, this time in the Welsh tradition, they were orderly and civilized in their rebellion. There was none of the aggressive gestures or verbal fireworks

that had distinguished the revolt in England by Wyndham Lewis (whose only Welsh
125 attribute seems to have been his name) some forty years before. Nevertheless, the *56 Group* made some modest headway, though in Wales they were initially regarded with indifference or, at best, suspicion. Their lack of influence in the official quarters that they denigrated led them to exhibit for the first time in a place where they did have some slight influence — Worcester.

Happily, the group's first exhibition in Wales confirmed their revolutionary posture, for much of their work was ridiculed, and some was vandalised. From this promising beginning, with a combination of energetic campaigning and adroit public relations, they consolidated their position, gained a grant from the Gulbenkian Foundation, and were eventually recognised and helped financially by the Welsh Arts Council.

So sustained have been their efforts that, a quarter of a century after its formation, the *56 Group*' s position in the establishment remains unchallenged. This could be the result of any of a number of possible factors: the group's finesse at maintaining its position; its readiness to recruit new members; the continued progressiveness of the members' work; apathy or lack of organisation on the part of other artists; a dearth of competitive talent; or an ironic respect for age and past achievement (the group is known by some of the younger generation of artists as 'Dad's Army'). Probably, the answer is a combination of all these, though the absence of any new rebellion over a period of twenty-eight years is somewhat dispiriting. Perhaps there is now such a relative abundance of official patronage that any revolutionary manifestation is immediately and gratefully rewarded.

But, whatever the criticisms that are levelled against the *56 Group Wales* (as it is now called), no one can deny its propagandist zeal. During its existence, the group has mounted exhibitions of contemporary art from Wales in London, Amsterdam, Dublin, Belfast, Edinburgh, Ludwigshafen, Nantes and Bologna, in many cities throughout Britain, and (equally important) in small towns and obscure locations throughout Wales. From all these exhibitions — well over a hundred in twenty-five years — it is evident that in no way does *56 Group Wales* constitute a movement or school of art. There are no collective ideas or common aesthetic doctrines and, consequently, no '56 Group' style. Any similarity between the work of artist-members is coincidental, and there is no tradition of theoretical debate. New members are recruited not because they subscribe to a predetermined philosophy, but because their work is recommended (by an existing member) as being excellent in itself. There are now about twenty members, all working in Wales, though not all of them Welsh. Even so, there must be some factor in the Welsh cultural milieu that is inimical to intellectual discussion, for in no field of creative endeavour is there any evidence of collective theoretical effort. Without some such debate, *56 Group Wales* remains simply a political organisation, existing almost exclusively for the opportunities of mixed exhibitions. Consequently, those exhibitions now appear as anthologies — often uneven in quality — of the art of about twenty individuals who happen to work in Wales.

Although the group can only claim to represent a proportion (and now a dwindling proportion) of the professional artists in Wales, it has, in its time, included several of outstanding ability, who have also helped along the general cause of Welsh art. Most prominent among these is Arthur Giardelli, the chairman of the group, a founder-member and its most active agent. Born in London, he took an MA in languages at Oxford, before attending the Ruskin School of Art there, and until recently was an art historian at the Extra-Mural Department of the University College of Wales, Aberystwyth. But Giardelli is primarily an artist, working in both landscape painting and in the area of abstract reliefs. The landscape paintings mark a continuing loyalty to his early admiration for the works of Girtin and Turner; Giardelli derives considerable satisfaction from the activity and sees no reason to relinquish it because it might not be fashionable.

His constructions, however, are in a direct line of European Modernism. After seeing Mondrian's works in their original state during a visit to Holland some twenty years ago,
126 Giardelli adjusted his attitude to the representation of nature. He began to express the essence of things seen through the associations of abstract values: either formal or in the innate quality of materials. Gradually, the interest in materials became more important, and he found that it was futile to try to imitate the colours and textures of natural objects like wood, metal, cork, slate, fabric, etc., when the materials themselves were intrinsically so rich. So, in his studio at Castlemartin, in a remote part of Dyfed, he began to explore the innate visual qualities of 'found' materials, and set in train a long series of collage reliefs that is still in process and which he has brought to a point of sombre refinement.

Apart from the inescapable problems of experimenting in an unusual idiom, Giardelli has had to face the handicap of geographical isolation. For Dyfed is separated from the metropolitan nucleus of south-east Wales which, in turn, is distant enough from London. With faster travel, more touring exhibitions, television, and an abundance of art magazines, the actual isolation is not as serious as it once was; but the feeling of relative isolation remains and it inhibits some of the artists living in the remoter parts of Wales. Some accept this condition, some gladly choose it, seeing it not as a handicap but as an advantage. Others, such as Kyffin Williams — until he retired from teaching in London — have tried to make the best of both worlds, though their hearts have always been in the hinterland. At its best, their work is committed, with a genuine feeling for a specific place, at its worst it becomes provincial and superficial.

Two other artists who, during a period of inadequate communications, coped with the problems of maintaining contact with the mainstream ideas while being relatively isolated, were Robert Hunter and David Tinker. Hunter is an artist whose personal development is inseparable from the fact that it has occurred largely in Wales. There is no saying how his painting might have appeared after thirty years working in another environment, but it would certainly be different. From his first experience of the landscape of Carmarthenshire in 1952, he has responded to the characteristic features of Welsh culture, evolving a language that had universal significance. Hunter arrived in Carmarthen from Liverpool, and was immediately struck by the contrast between the
127 two. And who would not? But Hunter turned the dramatic impact of west Wales to advantage, producing a series of paintings emphasising its openness and emptiness. Throughout the following years, as he became more attuned, and therefore more

responsive to his adopted environment, he depicted its unique subtleties: the qualities of old stone walls, groups of buildings clustered inside a vast landscape and, most fruitful of all, the runic marks on ancient stones. These have provided the mainspring of his work since at least 1964, when, as he declared in a recent statement, he came to believe '...that the pictorial sign or symbol is capable of the most variable means and modes of communication and possesses the necessary degree of wonder'.

David Tinker is another Englishman who has made his home in Wales. Since 1949
he has lived and worked first in Cardiff, then in Aberystwyth. By contrast with Hunter,
128 Tinker is less obviously inspired by his physical environment, but has a wider focus to his
notions, and he appears as a more complex, less resolved artist. He takes his ideas both
from the outside world and from what he once called 'moments of vision'. His attempt to
reconcile external and internal stimuli has caused his style to fluctuate between the two
dominant modes of twentieth-century abstraction: an intuitive, aformal, painterly idiom
and a cerebral, geometric, hard-edged kind of painting. His period of 'Abstract
Expressionism, "contaminated" with periods of Surrealism', was followed around 1964
by a long series of paintings committed to the ideas of perceptual abstraction; large, cool,
precisely painted canvases, exploring the potential of 'space-bending, light-creating and
129 optical effects'. His subsequent period showed a return to the up-dated principles of
Abstract Expressionism; small paintings 'swiftly executed and seen as a response to a
particular idea'. It seems that Tinker is not prepared to confine himself to one particular
idiom – an heretical attitude in these times of identifiable individual styles – but to search
for a personal solution among the contrasting options of contemporary painting.

Whatever the intrinsic merits of the work of these artists, its historical importance to the arts in Wales is beyond question. Regardless of the status to which posterity may consign them, these few artists were among the first to show the art-conscious public of Wales something of the new ideas that had been born beyond the confines of their own country. The momentous exhibitions of modern American art — so new and so powerful, and therefore so influential — which were shown in London and other European capitals during the late 1950s never appeared in Wales. There was no place large enough to hold them, for Wales had always lacked a large exhibition gallery; and even if there had been, there would probably have been insufficient funds or few people in authority with much interest. So it was left to the individual artists to travel abroad and to bring back to Wales their interpretation of Abstract Expressionism, Assemblage Art, Post-Painterly Abstraction and the other movements that were established or evolving. It is also to the credit of this small band of artists that, by their example and positive encouragement, they promoted the work of younger, native Welsh artists who began working with new ideas.

Artists such as Jeffrey Steele, Anthony Stevens and John Selway were already exhibiting and independently gaining recognition when, in 1963, they were invited to join the *56 Group*. By accepting this offer they did not create a Welsh style but they increased the diversity of organised art in Wales and, by giving their work a Welsh context, they reinforced the growing opinion that there was a body of artists in Wales that could claim to be contemporary and international in outlook. The practice of mutually sympathetic artists exhibiting together helped to establish Wales as a small but viable source of contemporary art. So much so that, in 1965, it was possible to mount an exhibition of modern art from Wales at the Jefferson Place Gallery in Washington DC. It was the first small step in a new direction: no longer was Wales regarded simply as a storehouse of subject-matter for artists; it was beginning to be acknowledged as a country which had its own artistic community.

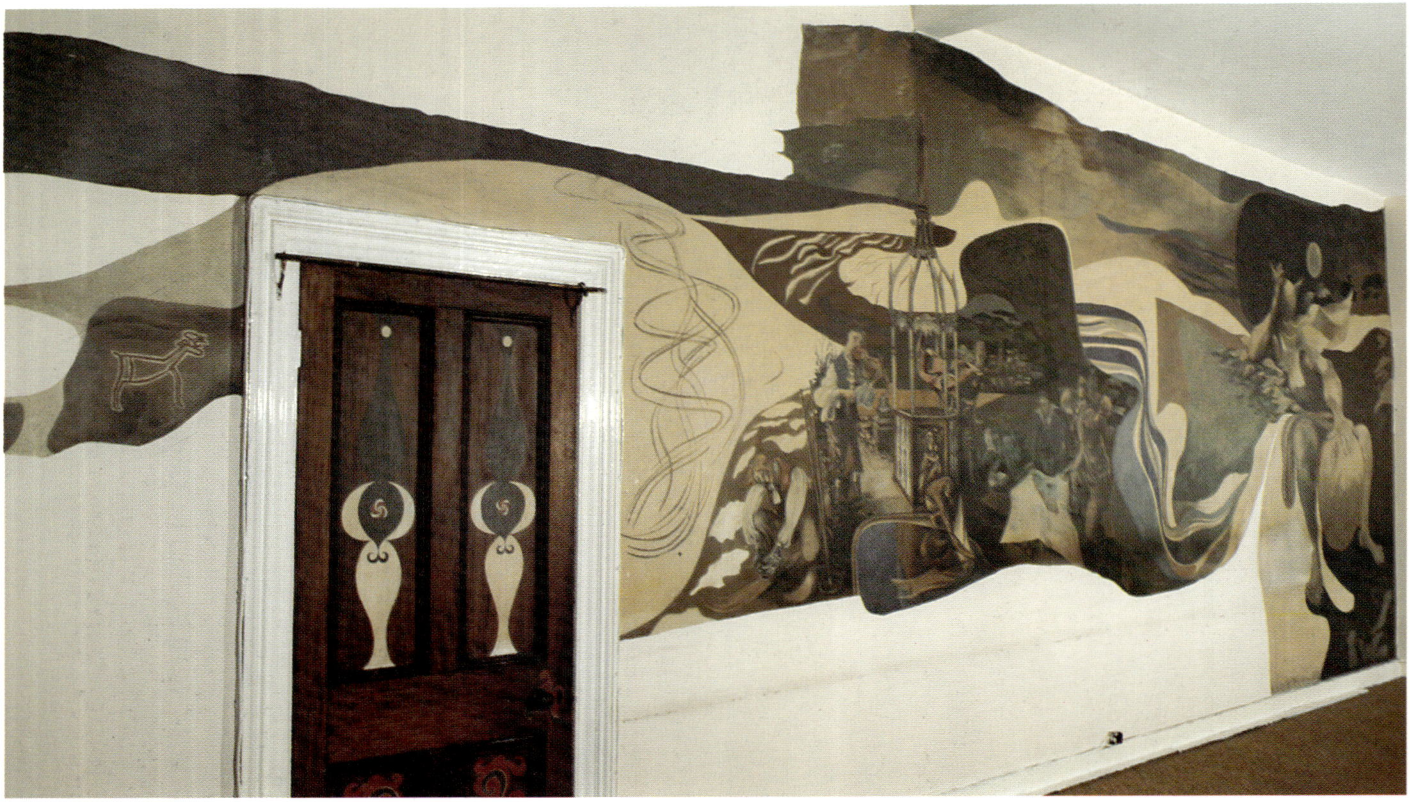

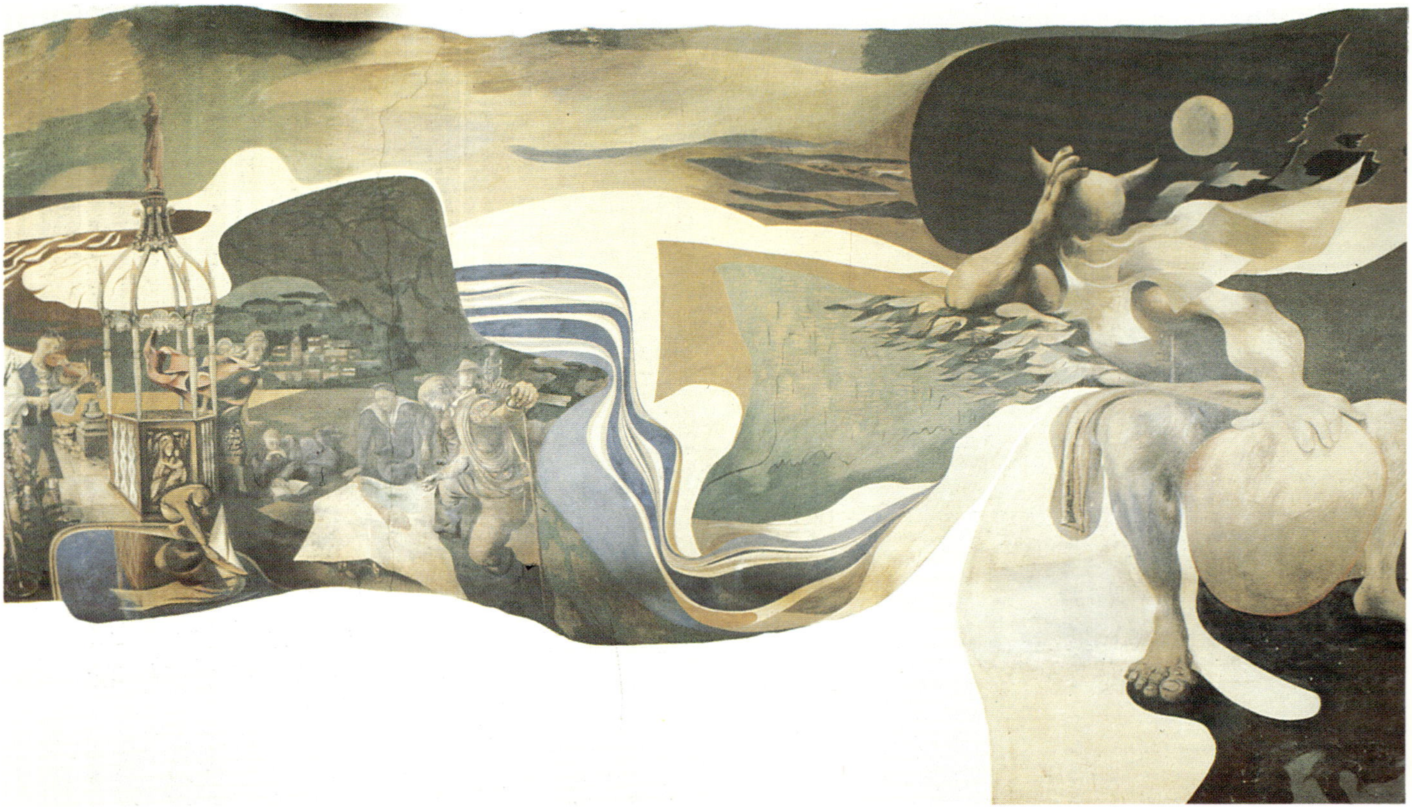

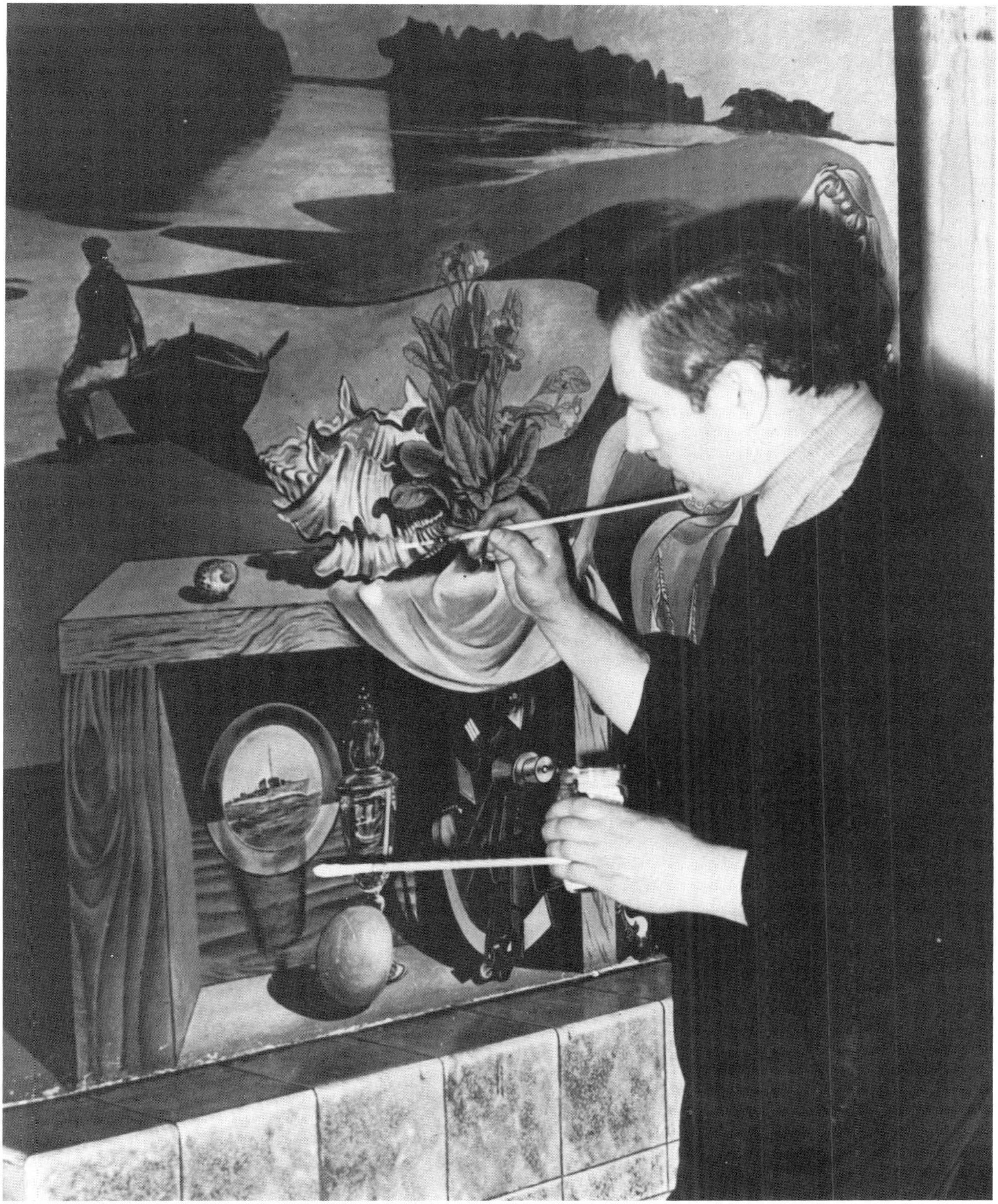

96.(b) Details of 'Norwegian' murals

97. Ceri Richards retouching the 'Norwegian' murals at the British Council Offices, 46, Caroline Street, Cardiff (March 1955). Copied from a *Western Mail & Echo* photograph.

99. Ceri Richards
Blue Vortex in the Primaries (1952 - 3) Oil on canvas
101.5 x 127 cm
British Council

In the 1950s, Richards was producing some of his finest paintings, and some that represent his nearest approach to the kind of aformal abstraction that was the dominant idiom in contemporary western art of the period. His status, on this account, was acknowledged by many exhibition organisers and, by this painting alone, Richards was represented in mixed exhibitions such as the Sao Paolo Bienal of 1953, the Tokyo 3rd International Art Exhibition (1955-6), a Mediterranean Tour of British Contemporary Painting (1965), and at Il Fiorino in Florence (1967).

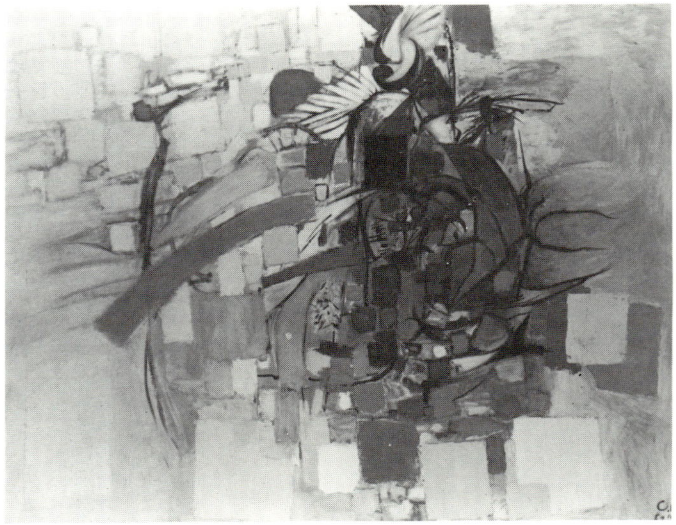

98. Ceri Richards
The Force That Through the Green Fuse Drives the Flower (1965 - 6) Lithograph 127 x 127 cm

If there were hesitancies in Richards's interpretation of Norse mythology, there were none in his work based on Welsh poetry. This picture, the outcome of another commission - from 'Poetry London' - was part of a series of pictures based on Dylan Thomas's poems that occupied Richards periodically from 1945 until at least 1969. In them, the painter manifests his understanding of the poet's ideas, though there was little similarity of temperament, and it is believed that they had only one brief meeting. Another Welsh poet in whose work Richards found inspiration, and with whom he had close personal ties, was Vernon Watkins.

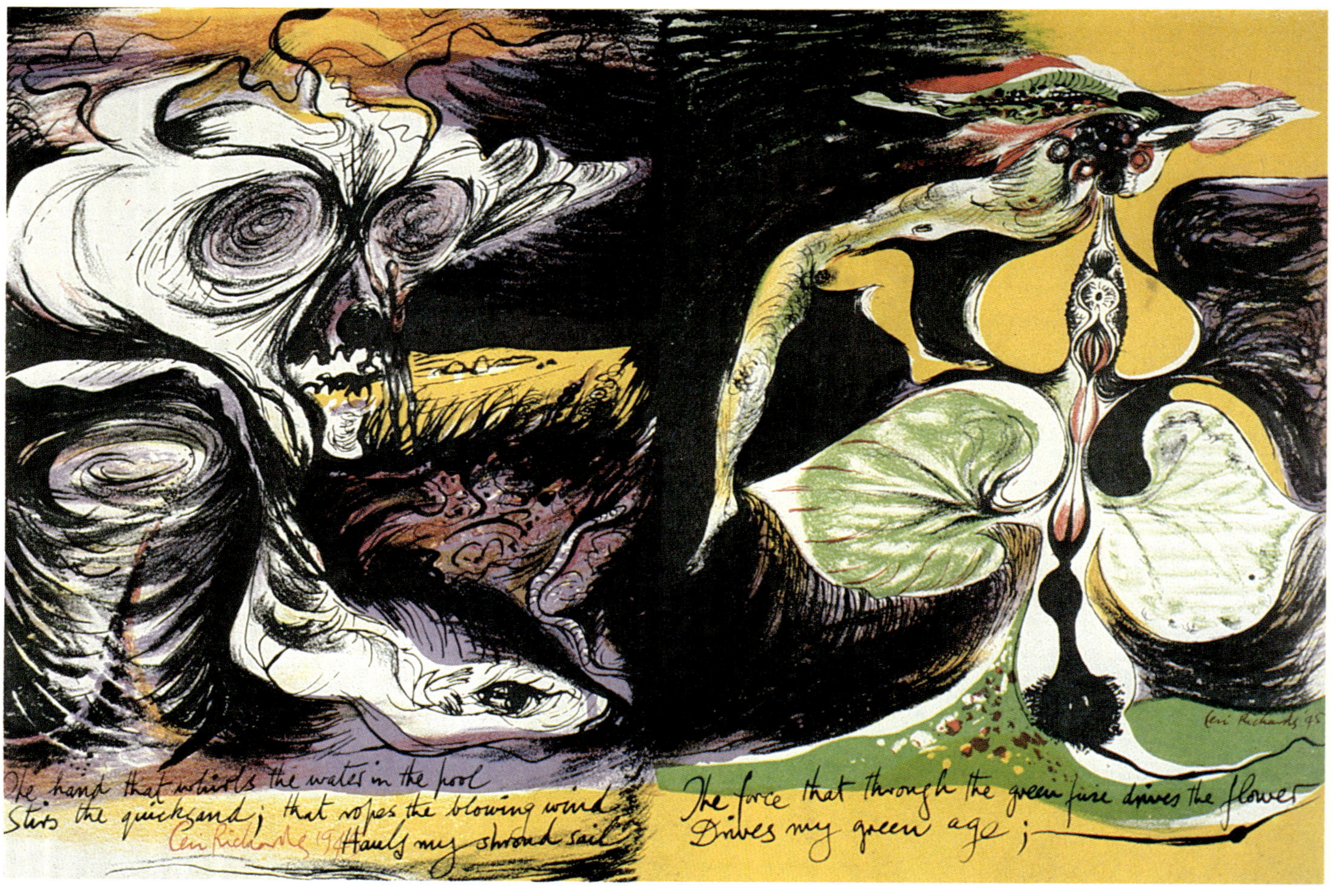

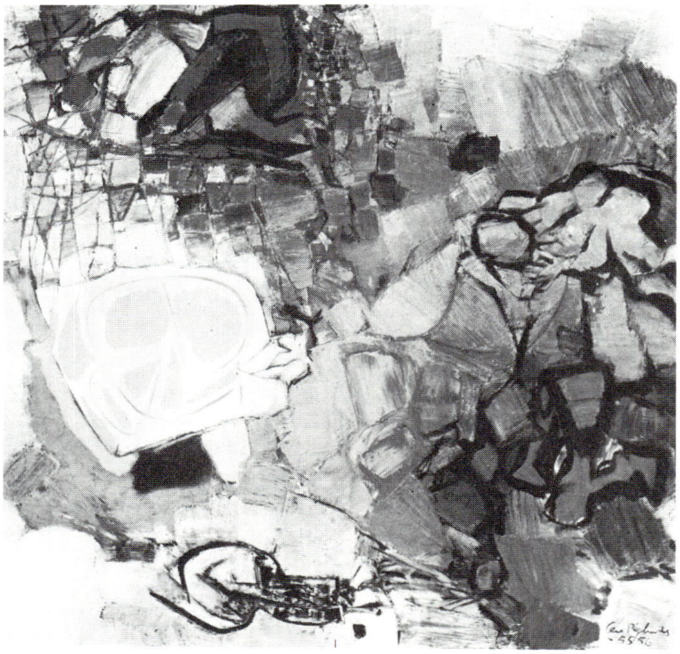

100. Ceri Richards
Cycle of Nature (1955 - 6) Oil on canvas 101.5 x 101.5 cm
F.E. McWilliams, Esq.

This is another painting from the period when Richards was at the peak of his international reputation. It has been quoted and reproduced as an example of the British contribution to the international style of art in the decade after the war. As such, it is interesting to compare it with earlier paintings from the 'Cycle of Nature' series - which grew from 'The Force that through the Green Fuse' series (No.98) - where the images have a more obviously symbolic, surrealistic quality to them.

101. Ceri Richards
Trafalgar Square (1950) Oil on canvas 150 x 244 cm
Tate Gallery

Another motivation for the work of Richards's mature period came from public commissions. One such came during the Festival of Britain in 1951, when he was asked to contribute a work to the Festival Exhibition. Richards chose the theme of Trafalgar Square, and with characteristic inventiveness used it as the basis for a series of paintings, of which this is the largest. It is not one of his most successful pictures, for the movement of people, pigeons and water combines uneasily with the schematic space of the square. Also, the dominant colour chord of blue and yellow is not the most appropriate for the subject (see Richards's comment, quoted in the caption to No.103).

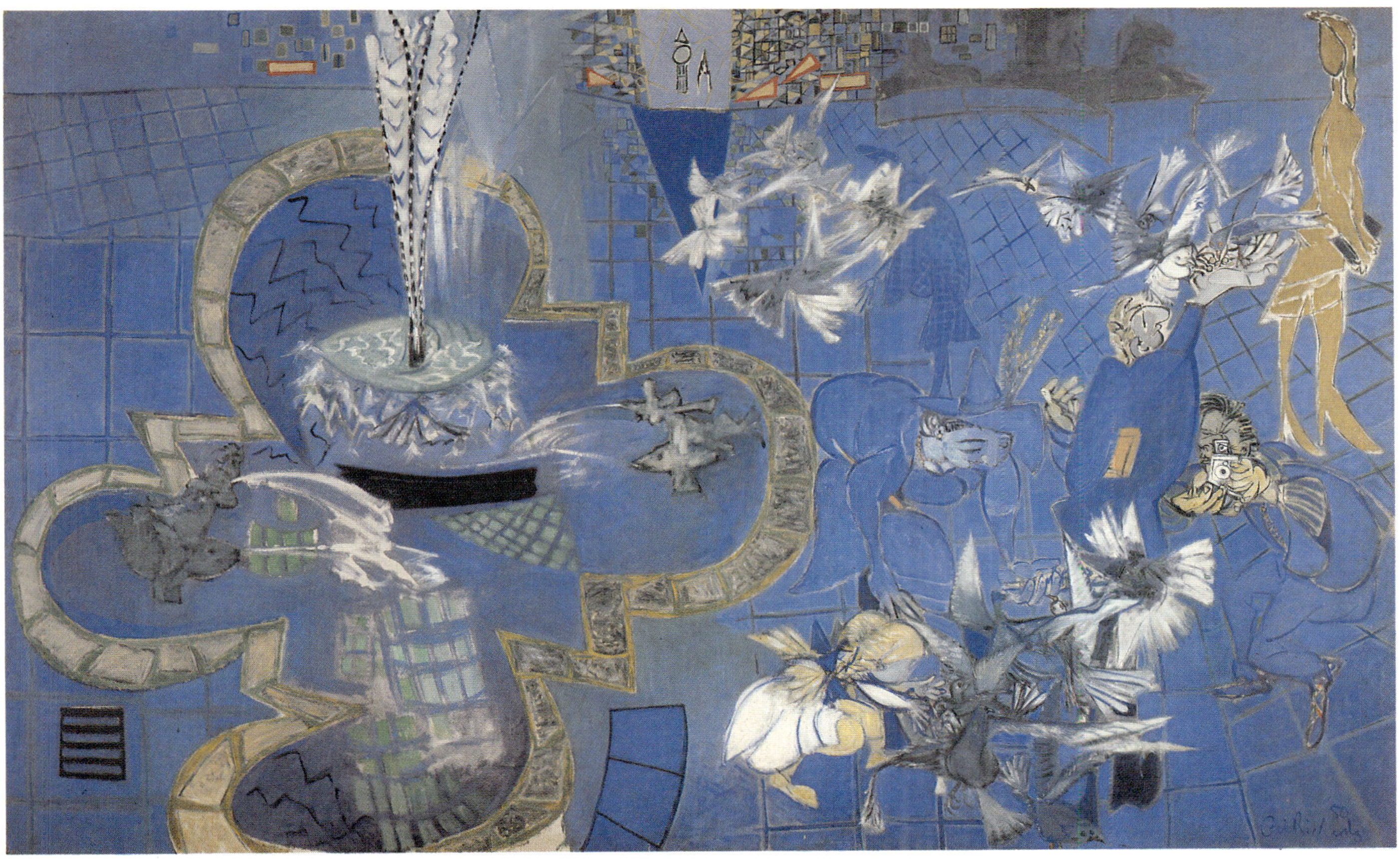

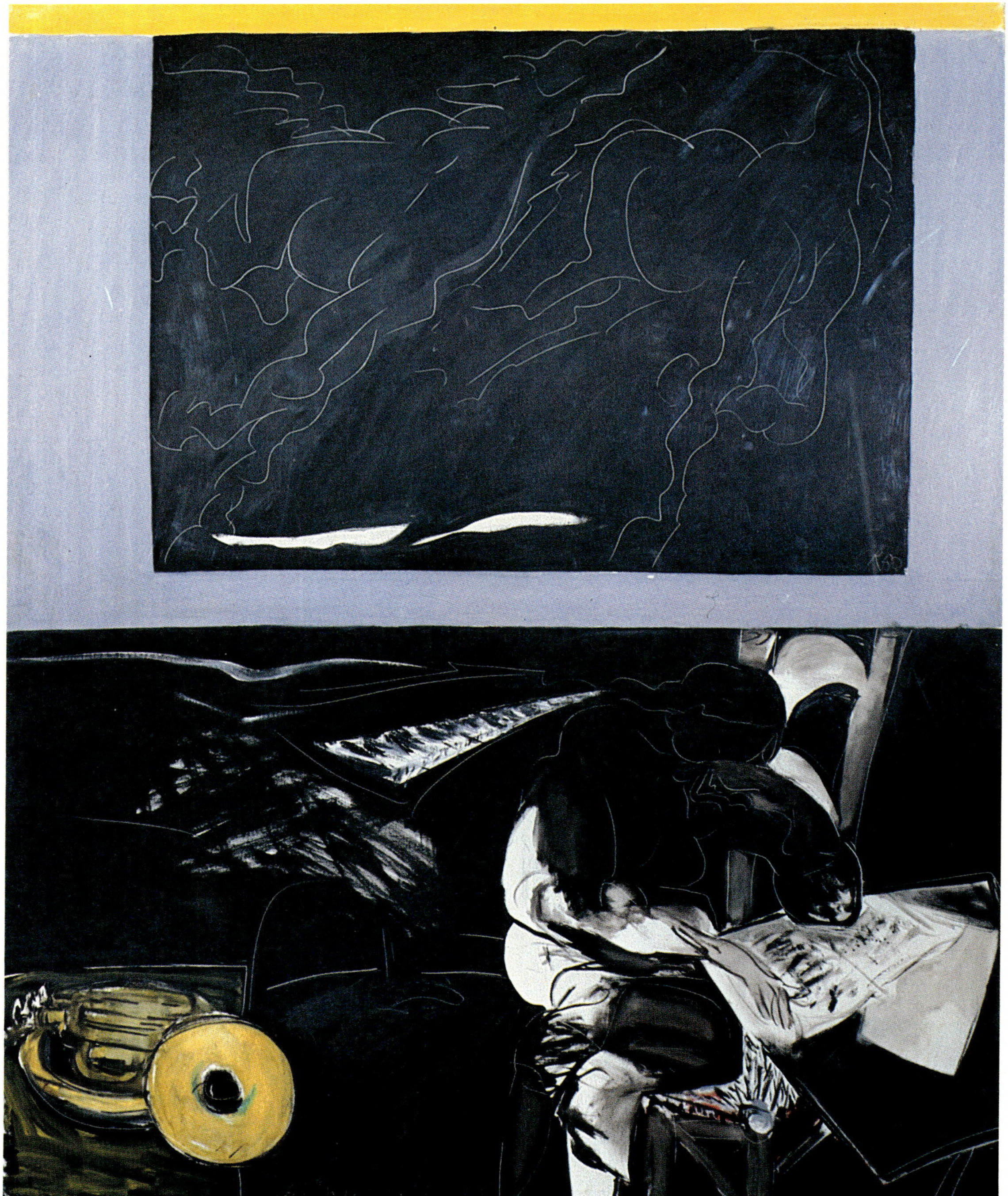

102. Ceri Richards
Homage to Beethoven (1953) Oil on canvas 127 x 101.5 cm
National Museum of Wales
Even more than poetry, Ceri Richards found music to be one of the richest sources of ideas. Musical instruments, performers, music rooms and musical scores are featured in many of his works in the post-war period. His homage to Dylan Thomas had its counterpart in paintings such as this, and in the 'Hammerklavier' suite. His most sustained interest in the work of a composer appeared in the late 1950s when he began the long series of works based on Debussy's piano work 'La Cathédrale Engloutie'. Richards himself was an accomplished pianist, with a family background rich in music; his father, for example, had been conductor of three choirs in Dunvant.

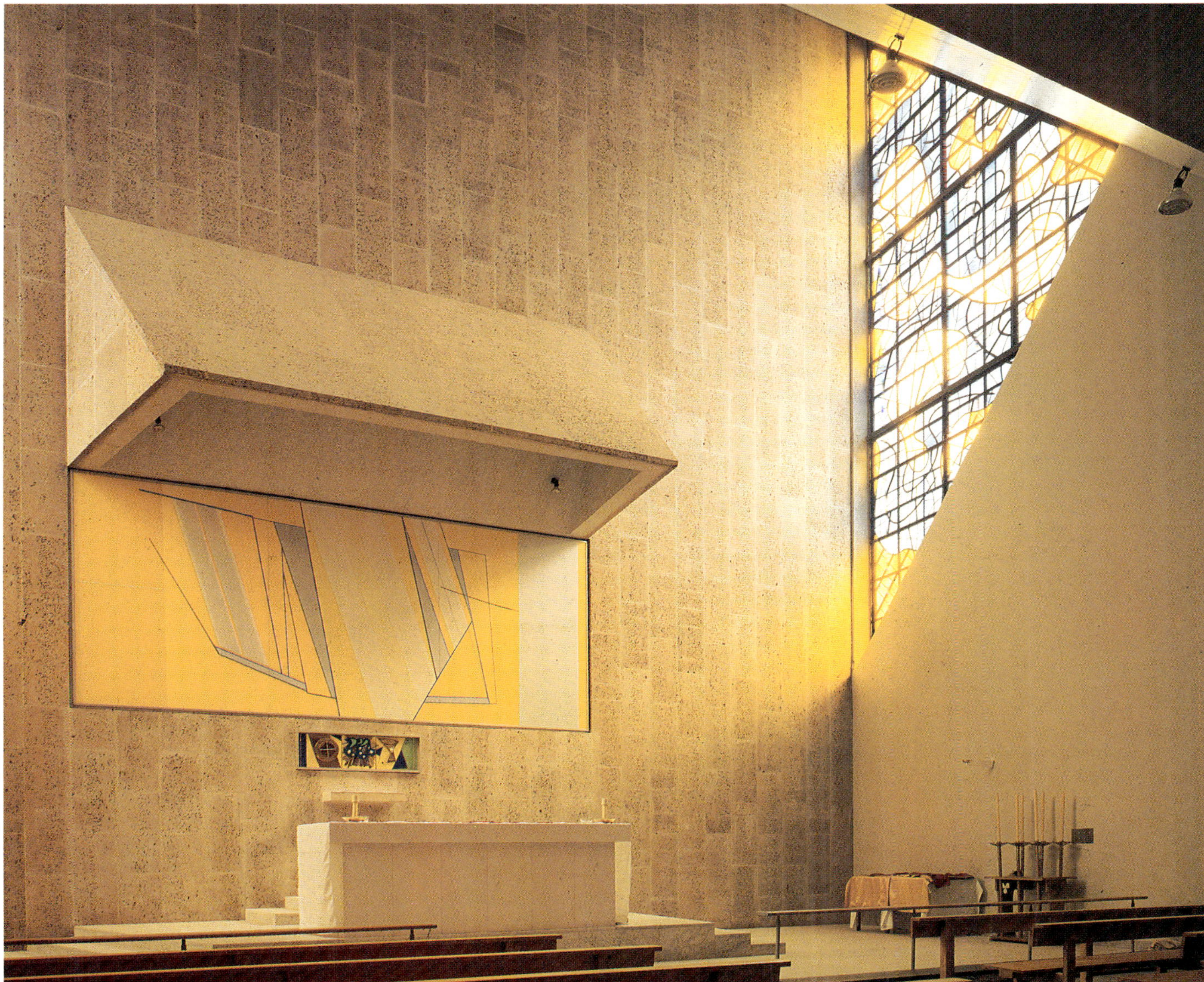

103. Ceri Richards
Blessed Sacrament Chapel (1965 - 7) Reredos: oil on wood, 259 x 609 cm. Window: 10.6 x 4.8m. Tabernacle: silver, bronze, brass, enamels, coloured glass and ivory, 45.75 x 152.5 cm. Metropolitan Cathedral, Liverpool

The last and most important of Richards's public commissions was for the decoration of the Chapel of the Blessed Sacrament in Liverpool's new Roman Catholic Cathedral. Although not a Catholic himself, the artist was entrusted with the art for the most sacred place in the whole building. The colour scheme for the reredos and its two flanking windows is Richards's favourite harmony; 'blue to signify thought and Heaven, yellow for light and the Divine Spirit'. The geometrical abstraction is rare, if not unique, in Richards's work. He had originally designed a more symbolic theme, but Archbishop Beck believed this would be too sensuous for its purpose, and he persuaded the artist to substitute a completely abstract, more contemplative design.

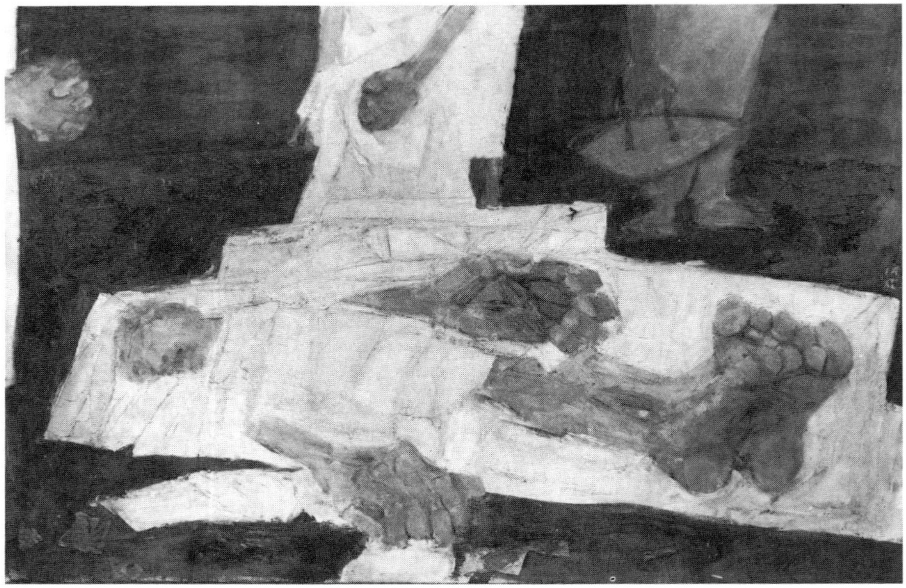

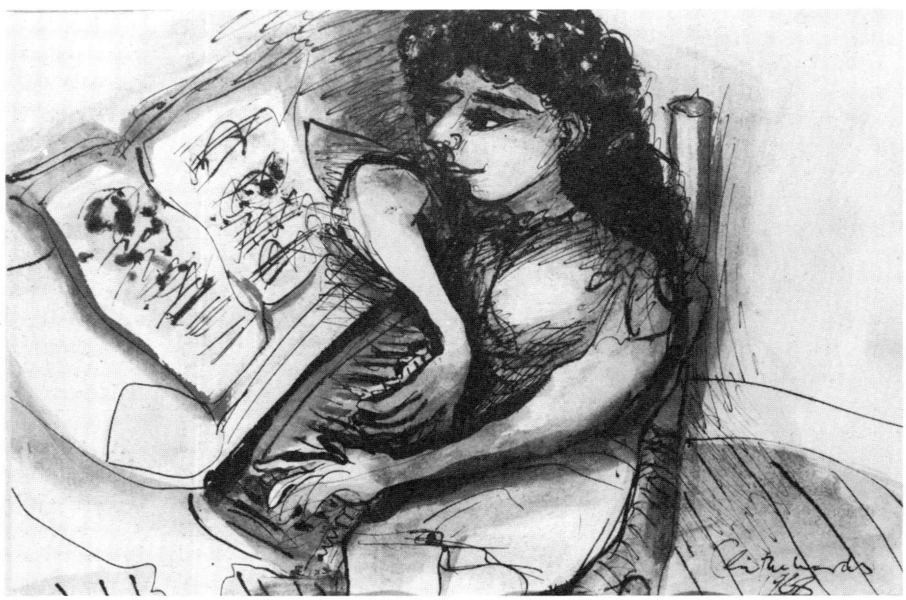

104. Ceri Richards
The Deposition (1958) Oil on canvas 152.5 x 183 cm
St. Mary's Church, Swansea
The inventiveness which Richards showed in all his work was nowhere more evident than in his series where one initial idea would go through many transformations to apparent exhaustion, before being revived and extended even further. This was true of his 'Cycle of Nature' series, 'The Beekeeper', and 'La Cathédrale Engloutie', and it also applies to his theme of the 'Return of the Patient'. This subject, like all his successful ones , was derived from an intense personal experience, when he was confined to hospital in the early 1950s. It prompted many fine paintings, provided the imagery for his canvas 'Do not go gentle into that good night', and culminated in this poignant version of 'The Deposition', which was later acquired by St. Mary's Church in Swansea.

105. Ceri Richards
Pianist (1968) Pen, ink and watercolour on paper
36.8 x 54 cm
Mel and Rhiannon Gooding
Left to his own devices, Richards abandoned the geometric style imposed on him by the Liverpool commission, and for the last few years of his life returned to his favourite, more familiar romantic mood. Such deviations, prompted by necessity and his own versatility, sometimes led to charges of inconsistency or eclecticism - which Richards resented. In a conversation quoted by his dealer, Harry Fischer, Richards once said, 'they accuse me of imitating; they all misunderstand me and don't try to see me in my true spirit. Everybody must have a father and a mother ... I'm haunted by Picasso ... But I try all the time to enrich and supplement my early visual and intellectual experiences. I'm a Welshman, a Celt, and what I find lacking in so many artists whose work I nevertheless love, is the romantic spirit'.

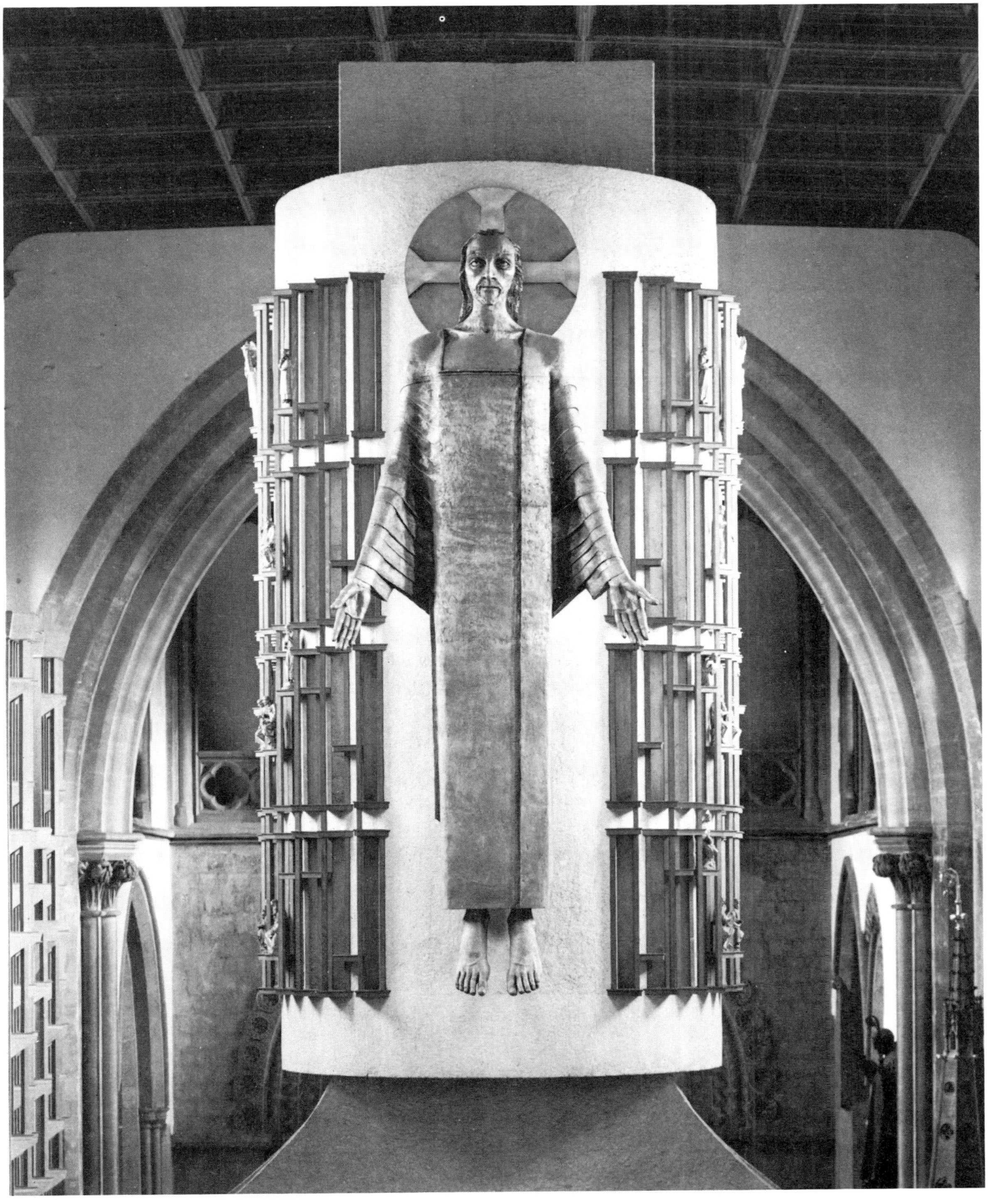

106. Jacob Epstein 1880 - 1959
Christ in Majesty (1955) Cast aluminium height 5.55m
Llandaff Cathedral

Llandaff Cathedral was bombed in 1941, and in 1953 the architect in charge of the restoration (George Pace) brought to Llandaff Epstein, John Piper and Stanley Spencer, who were to provide the new works of art. Spencer's painting never materialised, and the most important commission was this 'Majestas' by Epstein. He was paid £2,000 for the statue, which was initially intended to be of gilded plaster. At his own expense (£500) Epstein cast it in aluminium, working on the cast in his studio and assembling it in the Royal College of Art. It is pseudo-Byzantine in style; the gown is straight and smooth and only the sleeves have folds. The face was taken from an earlier work of Epstein's, 'Seraph' of 1923, which was a portrait of Marie Collins

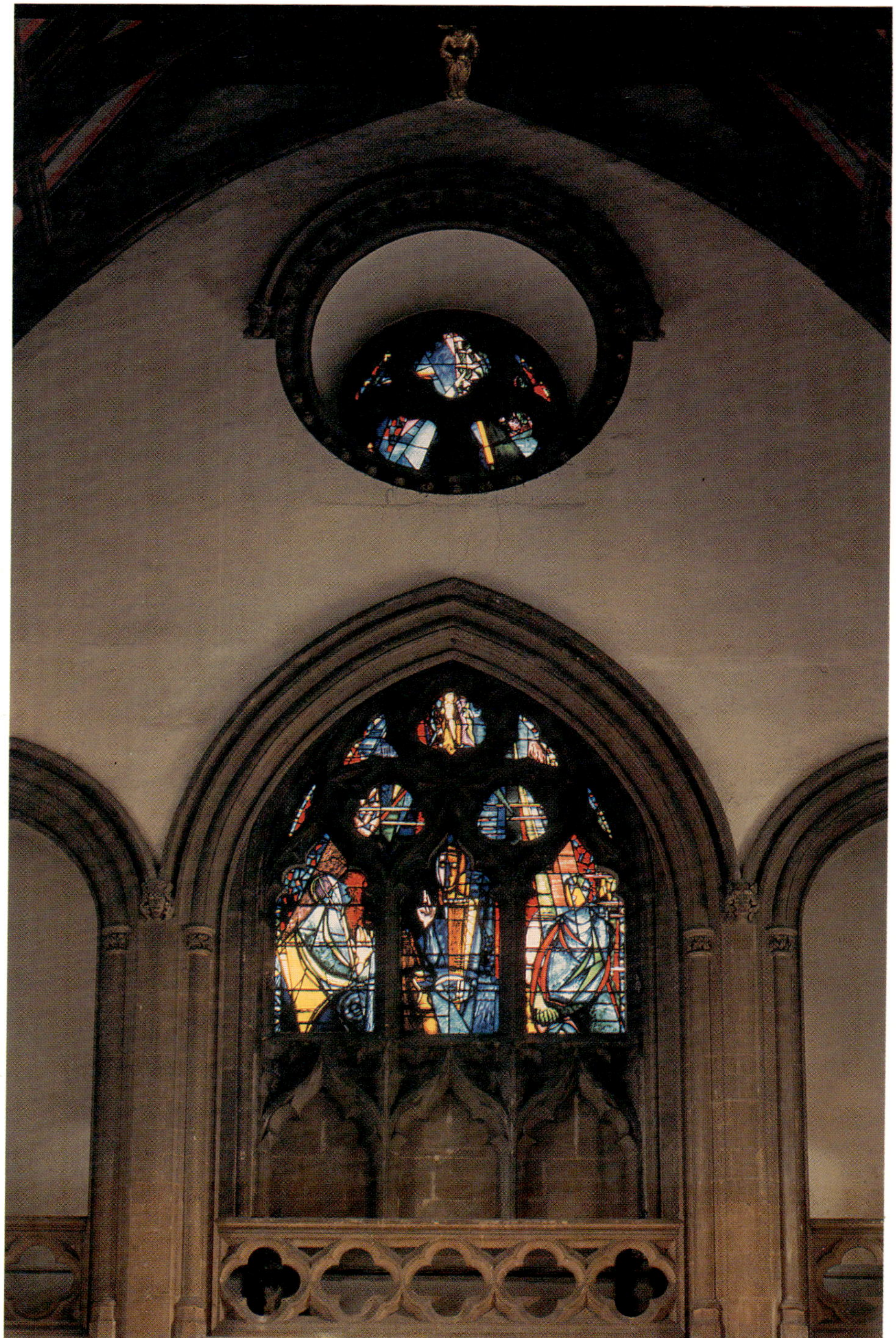

107. John Piper b. 1903
The Supper at Emmaus (1955) Stained glass Llandaff Cathedral
Smaller than the windows he designed for other, modern cathedrals at Coventry and Liverpool, this one is notionally representational. The subject is the breaking of bread at Emmaus, though the narrative details are not at first readily interpreted. The window, however, makes a fine decorative feature in the nave of the cathedral; it was designed by Piper and made by Reyntiëns.

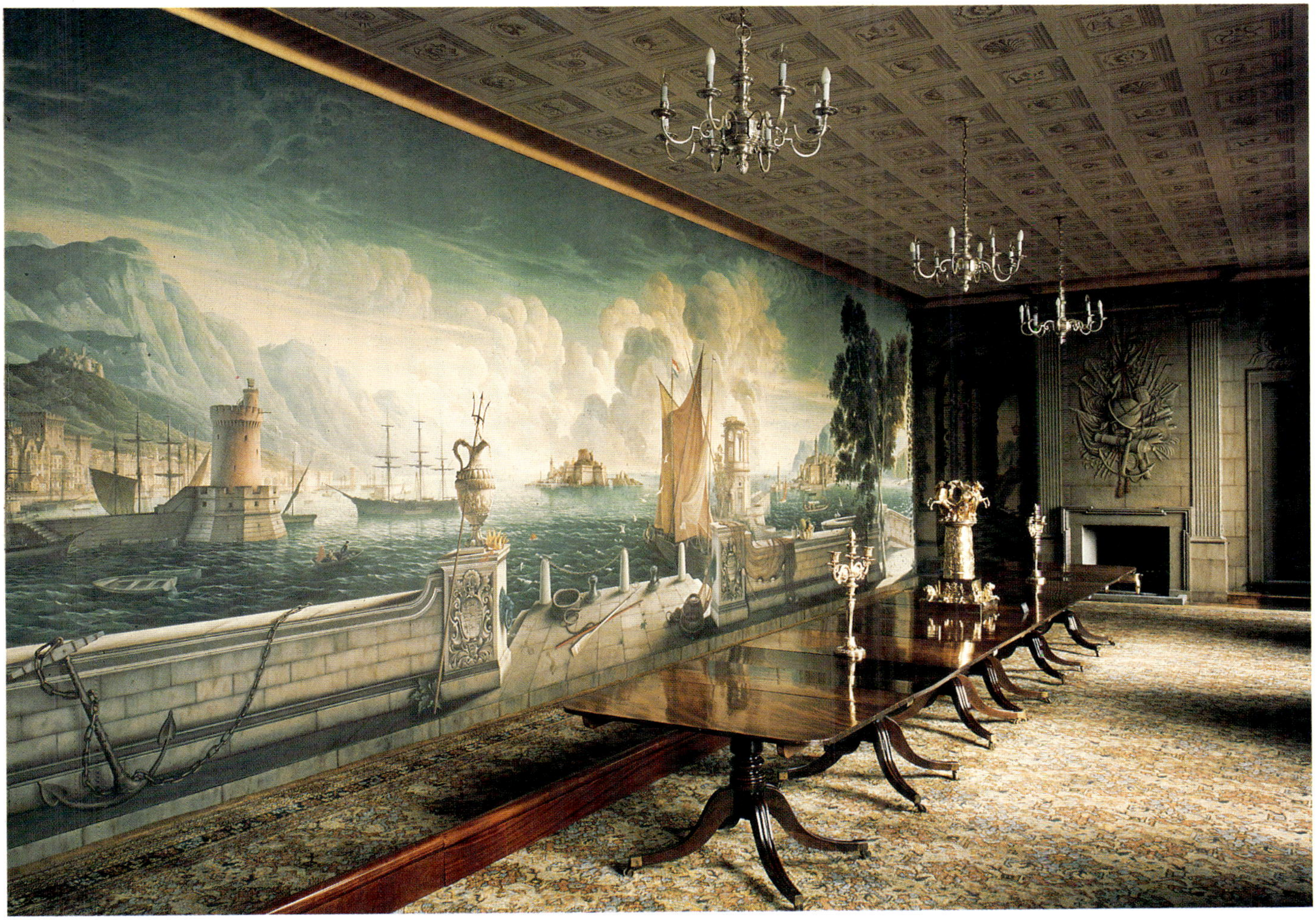

108. Rex Whistler 1905 - 44
Harbour Scene (main section) (1936 - 40) Mural 3.96 x 17.37 m (overall)
National Trust, Plas Newydd, Anglesey

One of the largest mural decorations executed in Wales during the modern period, this was originally painted for the home of a private patron. Commissioned by the 6th Marquess of Anglesey for the dining room of his house, Plas Newydd, it is the work of Rex Whistler, who also painted the murals in the restaurant at the Tate Gallery, and those at Nottisfont Abbey in Hampshire. Considering the taste of the period, the subject and style are eccentric, though the mural is perfectly in character with the house, which has Gothic additions by Wyatt. The painting is in the fashion of a 'Capriccio', showing an invented and improbable harbour scene, surrounded by classical buildings, and suffused with a mood that is serene, melancholy and romantic. A figure sweeping leaves in the colonnade (out of photograph, left) is a self-portrait of Whistler, who was killed when serving with his regiment, the Welsh Guards, in the Normandy landings. Plas Newydd and the mural now belong to the National Trust.

109. John Piper b. 1903
Rock Face Under Tryfan (1950) Watercolour 53.3. x 69 cm
The Artist

During the war Piper had continued to visit many parts of Wales, painting near Llantony, Ffestiniog, Snowdon, Cader Idris and also, as a war artist, at Cardiff docks. In 1945, immediately after the war, the artist and his family again visited Wales. They went by train to Denbigh and then cycled around the mountains and lakes of mid-Wales. Later, Piper took a cottage in the Nant Ffrancon Valley in Snowdonia, and later a farmhouse, Bodesi, by Ogwen Lake. This house looked across to Tryfan, a view that he captured in a photograph from which this watercolour is derived. After an absence of about five years, Piper acquired another cottage in Wales, this time in Pembrokeshire, near Strumble Head.

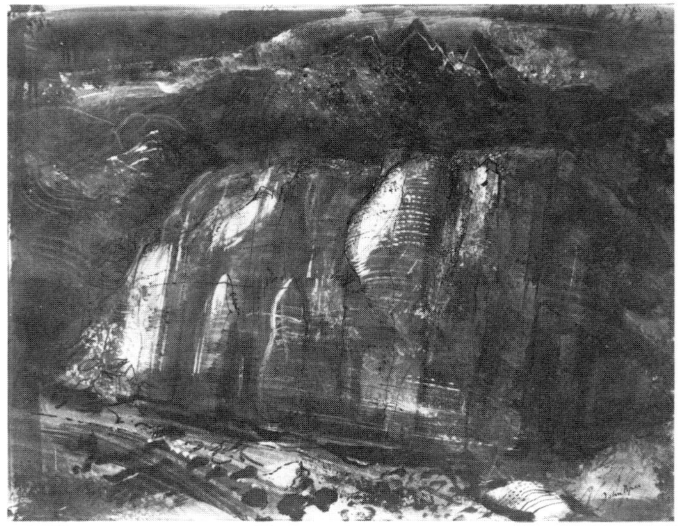

110. Graham Sutherland 1903 - 80
Road at Porthclais with Setting Sun (1975) Oil on canvas 52 x 49.5 cm
Picton Castle Trust

Sutherland's favourite description of his working process was 'paraphrasing'. This is perhaps more evident in his work of the 1970s than in the paintings of forty years before (No.93). In the later paintings, Sutherland often gathered the elements of the scene into a tightly organised form, which rests in the centre of the canvas on a flat, horizontal surface, giving the effect of a surrealistic still-life set upon a table. More rarely, a recognisable topographical element appears. In this painting, the yellow disc of the sun resting on the dark bar of trees and skyline, the orange lane that winds in and out of the blue-tinged landscape, all convey so expressively the haunting quality that the artist discovered on his first visit to Pembrokeshire forty years earlier. There is a drawing of this scene, also at Picton Castle, similar in almost every detail, that the artist made in 1935.

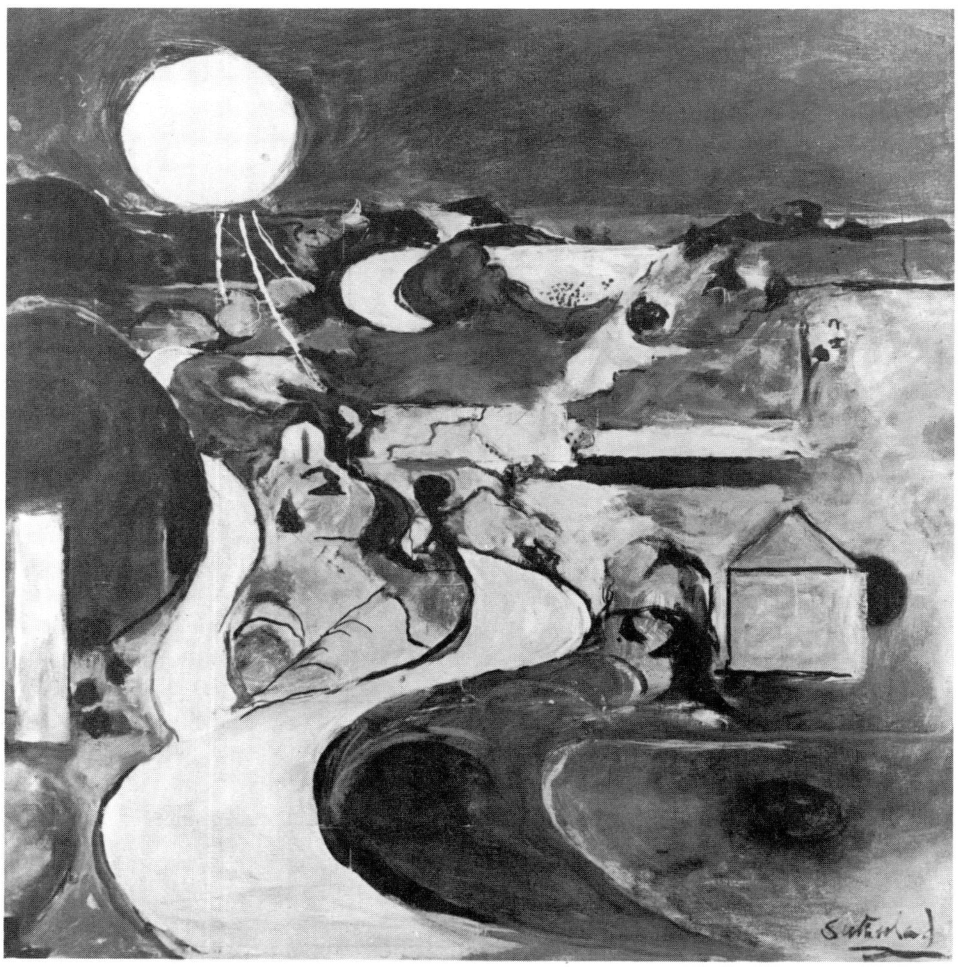

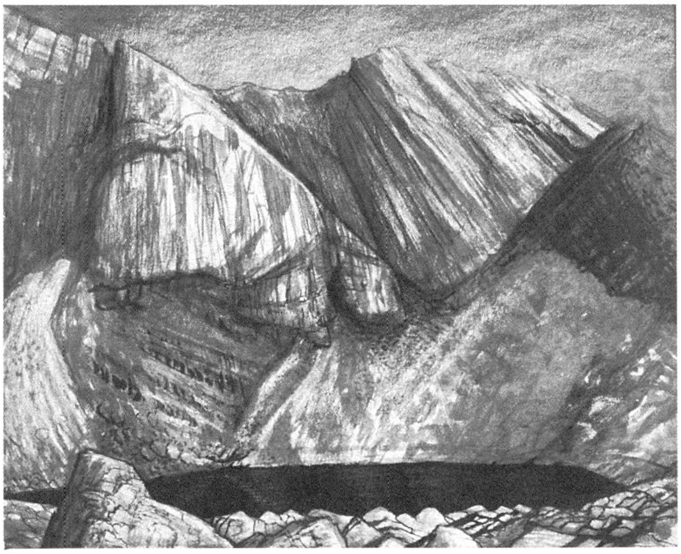

111. John Petts b. 1914
Clogwyn du'r Arddu Eryri (1956) Ink and watercolour
50.75 x 61 cm
Welsh Arts Council

John Petts is one of the artists who, in a difficult period, kept the visual arts in Wales alive without making any wide reputation for themselves. A Londoner by birth, Petts first came to Wales in 1935 and settled in a cottage above Llanllechid, in Snowdonia. As well as producing paintings and wood engravings, he started the Caseg Press there, re-opening it after the war at Llanystumdwy. In 1956, after five years as Art Officer with the Welsh Committee of the Arts Council of Great Britain, he went to live at Llanstepnan, where he added mosaic and stained glass to his other creative activities.

112. Brenda Chamberlain 1912 - 71
Children on the Sea Shore (1950) Oil on canvas 91.5 x 104 cm
Merthyr Tydfil Corporation

Brenda Chamberlain was born, and died, in Bangor, and many of her chosen habitations were near the sea. From the 1940s on, her work had close connections with the sea, often combined with the images of children, fishermen, boats and the paraphernalia of the sea shore. This preference for the imagery of the littoral was combined with a style formed at the Royal Academy Schools in London, and developed through her enthusiasm for several French painters - notably Gauguin. Brenda Chamberlain was also a poet, and her gift for words won her an Arts Council Poetry Award in 1956.

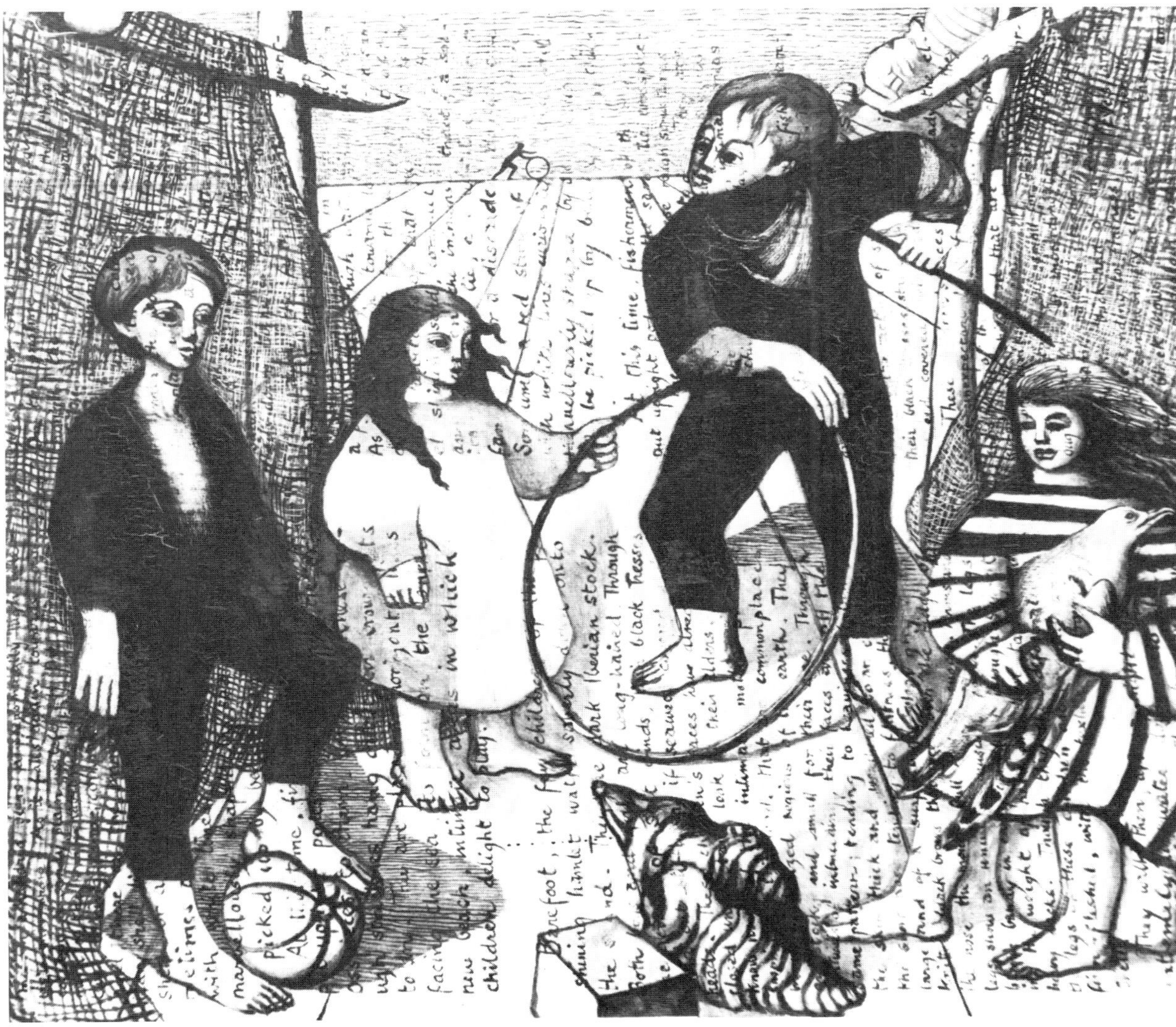

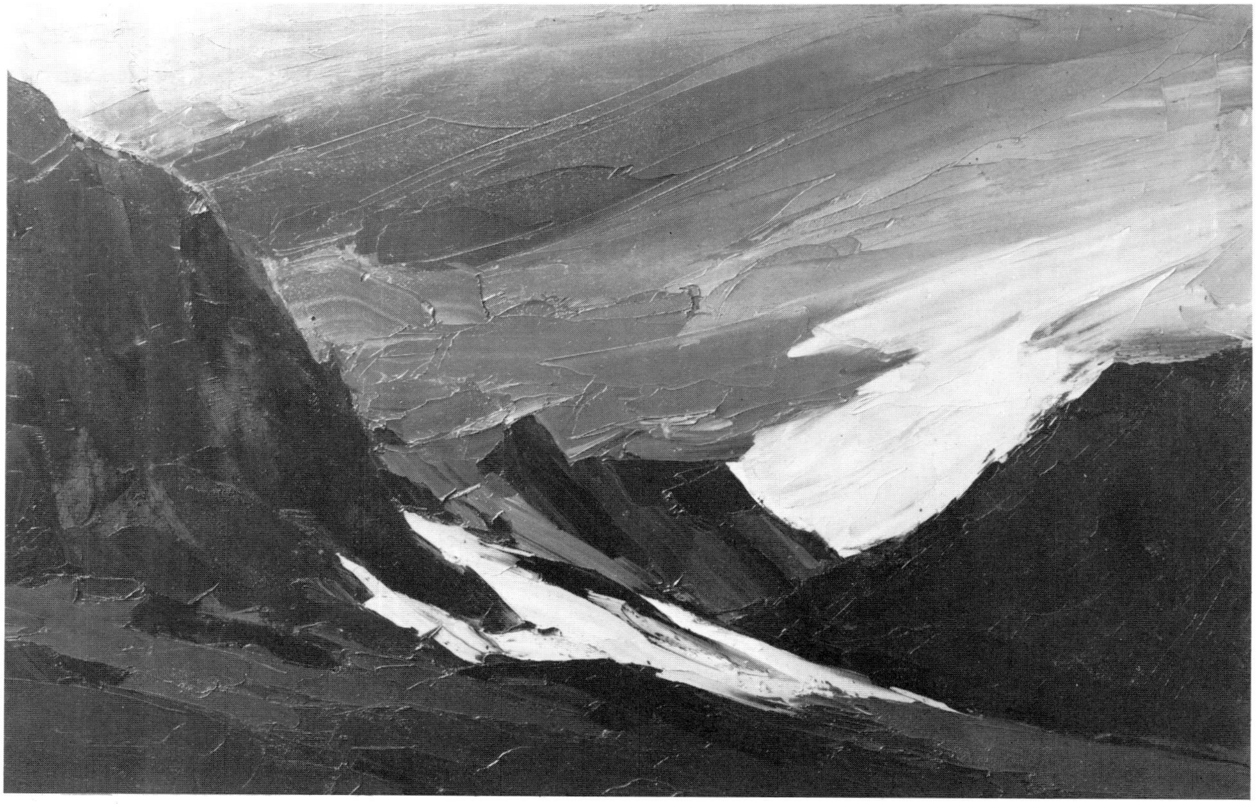

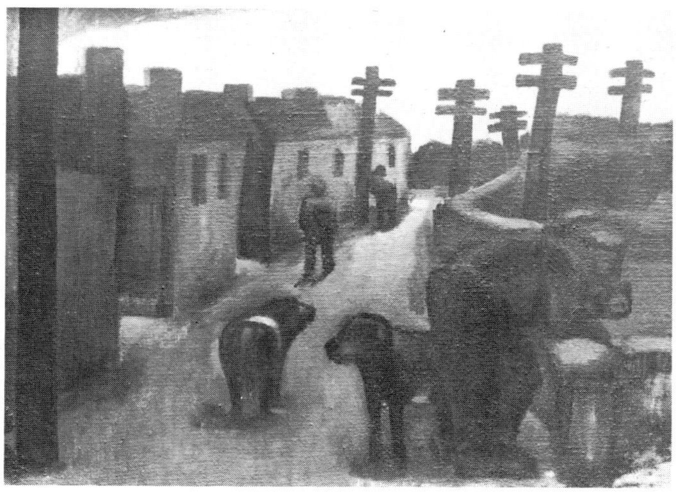

113. Kyffin Williams b. 1918
Ogwen (1966) Oil on canvas 76 x 117 cm
His Honour Judge Bertrand Richards

Williams once listed the artists who were most important to him, and they included: Piero della Fancesca, Botticelli, Crivelli, Memlinc, Titian, Tintoretto, Rembrandt, Courbet, Van Gogh, Modigliani, Soutine, Rouault and Braque. From this motley collection of influences it is the expressionist strain which has emerged dominant in this painting. There is something of Soutine and perhaps of Courbet in its treatment, though the final synthesis emerges unmistakably as Williams's own style. The mountains in the distance are Y Garn and Foel Goch, above Nant Ffrancon. The snow, always late in clearing the high grassy slopes, is seen by the artist as an integral part of the landscape.

114. Josef Herman b.1911
Evenfall, Ystradgynlais (1948) Oil on canvas 76 x 101.5 cm
Leicestershire Museums, Arts Galleries and Record Service

After suffering the vicissitudes of being a Jew in Nazi-dominated Europe, Herman arrived in Glasgow in 1940. After three years there, he descended on Ystradgynlais in 1943, staying for a holiday at the Penybont Inn. He was captivated by the place and its unique quality of mystery, and returned in 1944, acquiring and converting a local 'pop' factory for a studio, and remaining in Ystradgynlais for the next ten years.

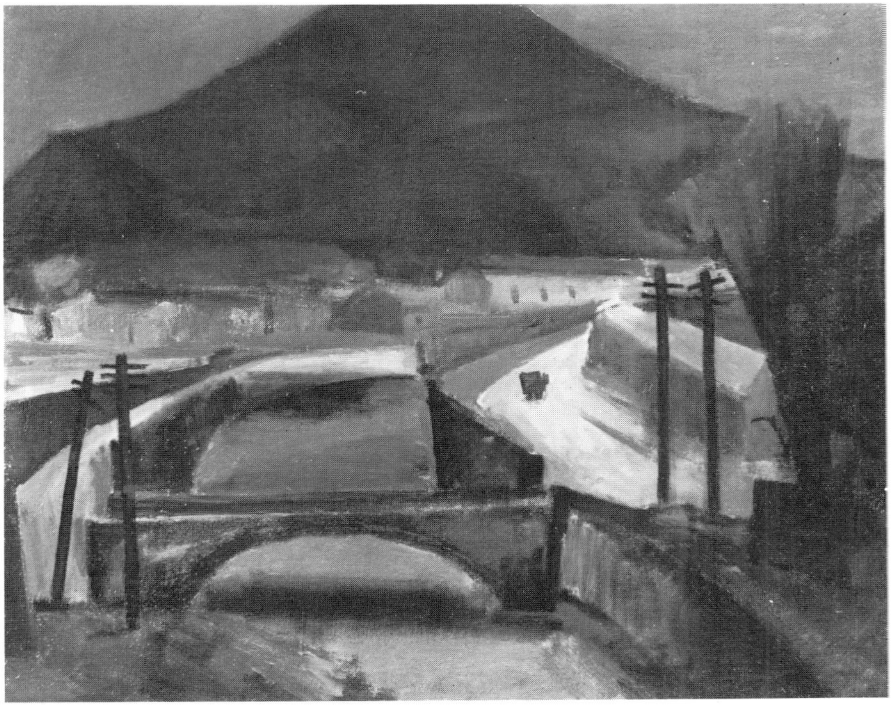

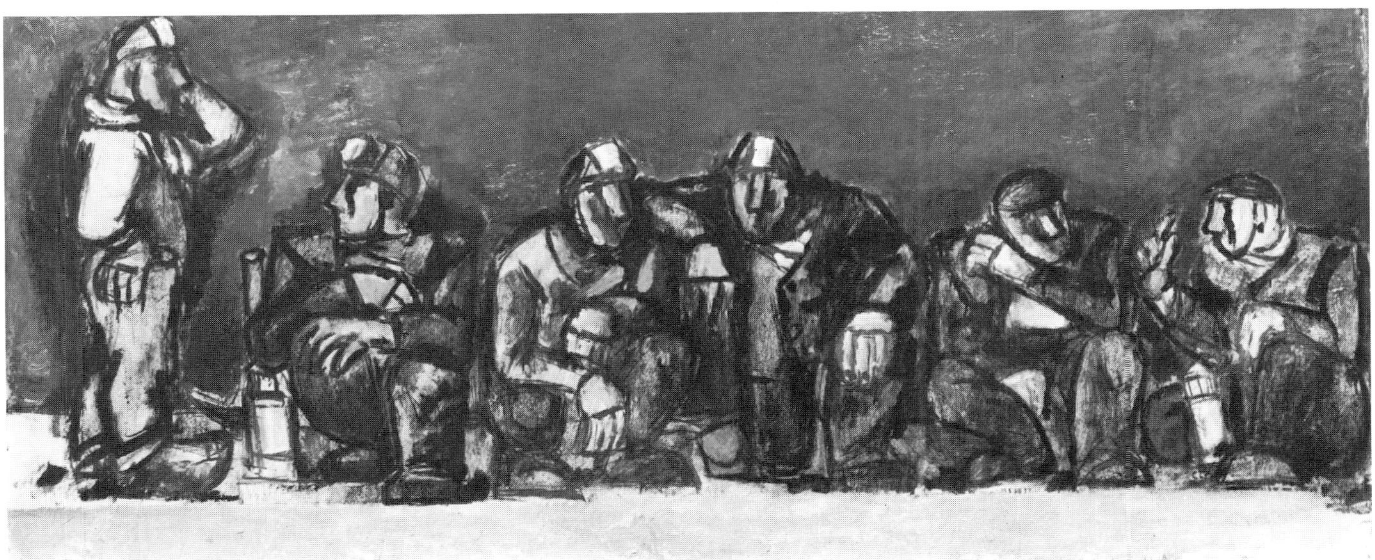

115. Josef Herman
The Bridge at Ystradgynlais (1948) Tempera and oil on canvas 63.5 x 76 cm
Southampton Art Gallery

It was on the bridge at Ystradgynlais, one summer afternoon in 1944, that Herman first experienced the almost mystical sensation of 'sadness and grandeur'. This was not a sudden, magical awareness, but a dramatic climax to years of searching for the right synthesis of humanity and aesthetics. With the miners on this bridge, Herman found the solution, and it 'became the source of my work for the rest of my life'.

116. Josef Herman
Miners (1951) Oil on paper laid on board 53.25 x 120 cm
Scottish National Gallery of Modern Art

Like Ceri Richards, Herman was one of the 60 artists who were commissioned to produce paintings for the Festival of Britain Exhibition in 1951. Unlike Richards, who chose a London theme (No.101), Herman painted a 12-foot long picture called 'South Wales'. He also painted a much larger mural for the South Bank called 'Miners Crouching' - for which this painting is a study. Herman made many paintings and drawings of the miners of South Wales; though it was not until about 1951 that his drawing became 'more sculptural' and he escaped from '... under the shadow of Rembrandt's pictorial ways'. Herman was also awarded the Gold Medal at the Royal National Eisteddfod of 1962, the year after it was won by Ceri Richards.

117. Will Roberts b. 1910
Farm at Cimla (1961) Oil on canvas 76 x 101.5 cm
National Museum of Wales

Born in Ruabon, Denbighshire, Roberts attended Swansea School of Art as a part-time student, and also learned to play the violin. After war service he met Josef Herman who invited him to work in his studio. Allowing for Herman's forceful personality, and his role as mentor, it is remarkable how Roberts succeeded in creating his own form of Welsh Expressionism. After Herman left Wales, Roberts continued to work in Glamorgan, in the Vale of Neath, endeavouring to give his painting 'mood, expressive form, emotional content'.

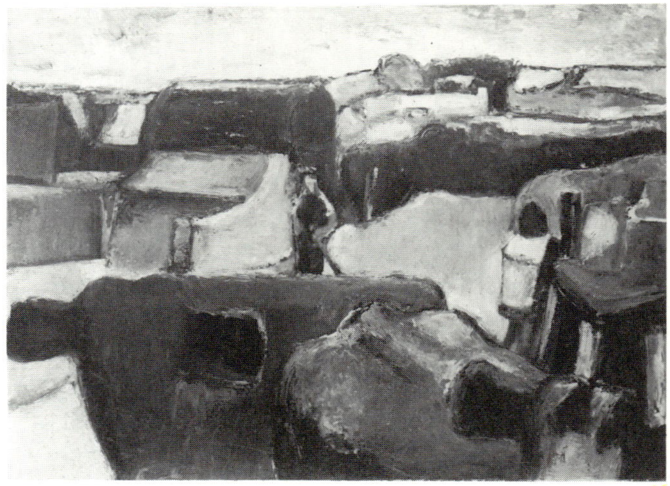

118. Heinz Koppel 1919 - 80
Lover's Lane (1955) Oil on canvas 60.3 x 101 cm
Welsh Arts Council

Born in Berlin, Koppel studied in Germany, Czechoslovakia, Italy and Belgium, before the upheaval of war brought him to Britain. In South Wales, through the interest and influence of other artists such as Cedric Morris and Esther Grainger, he settled in Merthyr Tydfil, began to teach at the Dowlais Art Centre, and became one of the founders of the Merthyr Art Centre. Koppel, an artist not disposed to verbalise about his work, had exhibited with Schwitters in London; but in the industrial valleys of South Wales, his influence and example proved of inestimable value to a community hitherto neglected by the wider world of art. In the later years of his life, Koppel lived and worked near Aberystwyth.

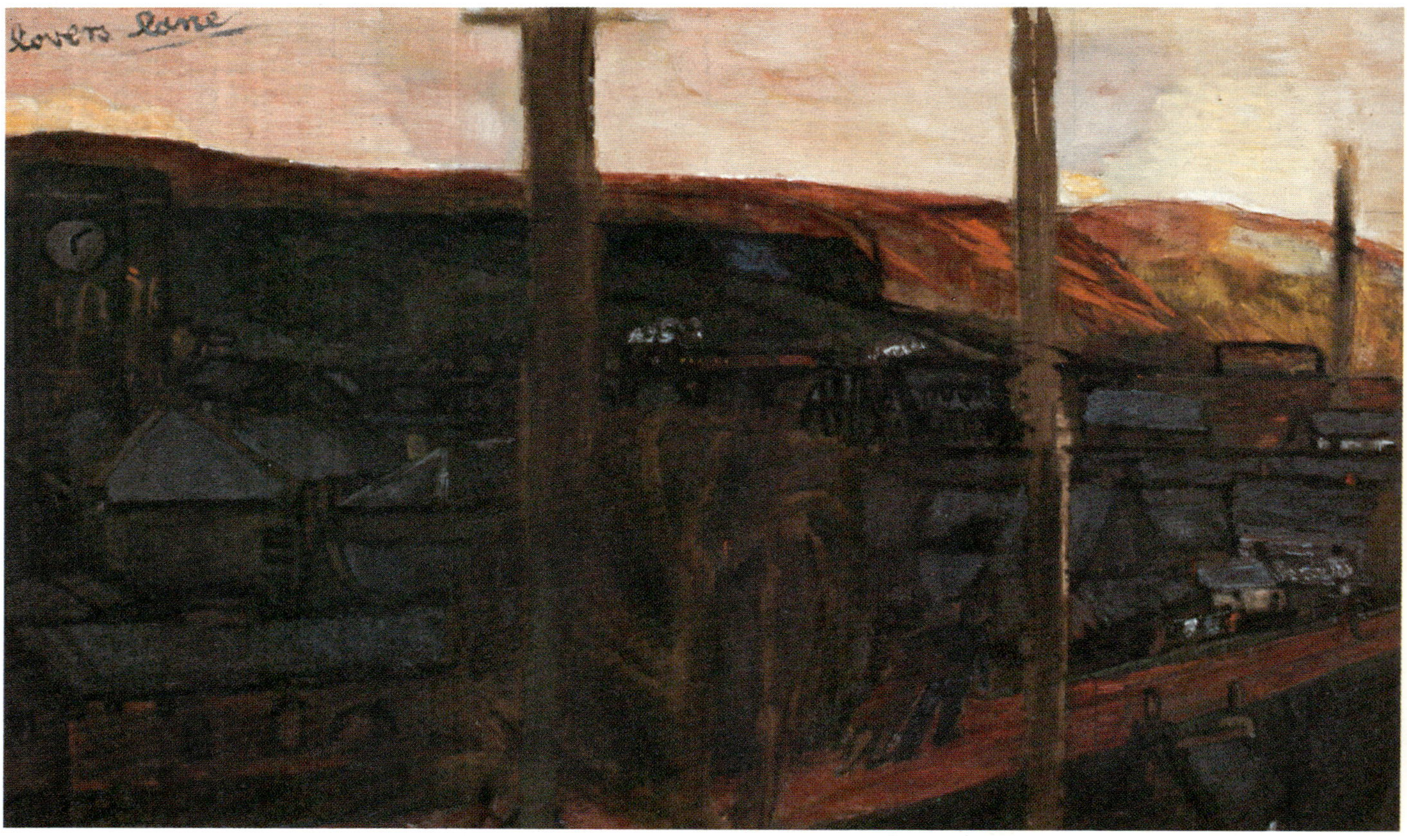

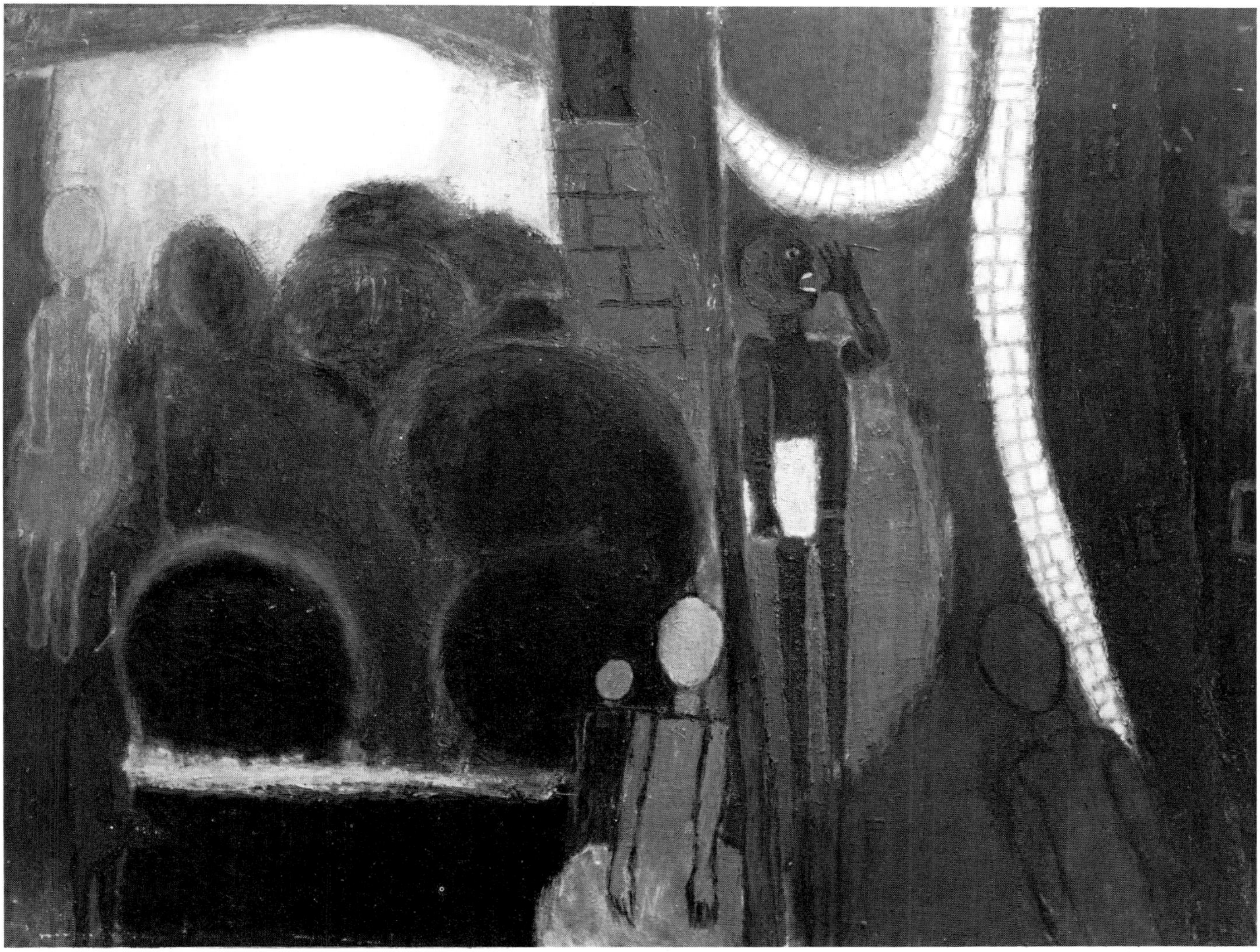

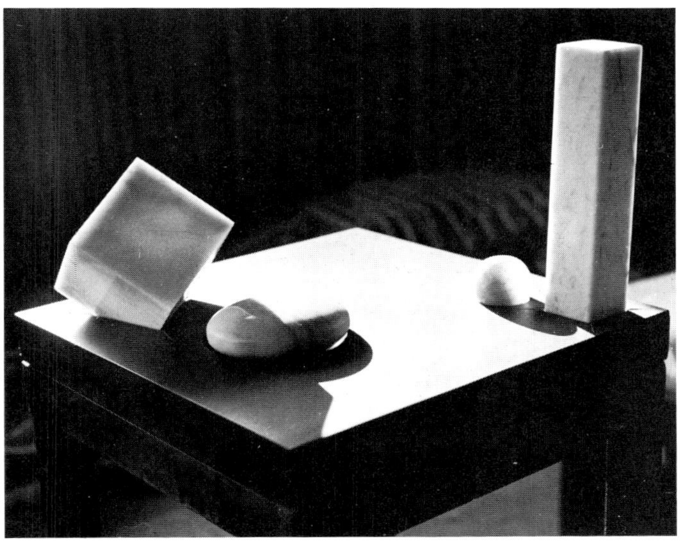

119. Ernest Zobole b. 1927
Ystrad and People No. 1 (1960) Oil on canvas 152.5 x 117 cm
Glynn Vivian Art Gallery, Swansea

Zobole was born in the Rhondda, and, impressed by Koppel's teaching and example, began to discover there a rich source of imagery. To this he added the influence of Chagall, which accounts for the high viewpoint and complex perspective often seen in his earlier paintings. The Rhondda has remained a powerful force in Zobole's work and he has continued to develop and refine the attitude towards figurative imagery that it first produced.

120. Jonah Jones b. 1919
Still Life With Table (1973) Slate and Marble
height 75 x 40 x 40 cm
Professor David Sherlock

Jonah Jones is one of the few sculptors who, in the underprivileged, pioneering period of the 1950s and 1960s, managed to survive by the full-time practice of their art in Wales. Jones was awarded some valuable commissions - for Mold Law Courts, Bangor Cathedral and Coleg Harlech among others - but had to supplement them by less prestigious work such as lettering and inscriptions. Although not a native Welshman, he has always preferred to live and work in North Wales.

121. Frank Roper b. 1914
13th Station of the Cross (1960) Cast Aluminium
height approx. 76 cm
St. Martin's Church, Cardiff

Another of the sculptors who continued to work in Wales during the 1950s, Roper's subsequent career has been remarkable for two conflicting factors: he has been almost entirely unrecognised by the art establishment of Wales, and yet he is the only sculptor in Wales who now supports himself by the sale of his work. Whatever may be the significance of these facts there is no doubt that much of Roper's success is due to his highly developed and individual technique, and his independent professionalism in finding and fulfilling commissions - many of them, such as this, coming from church authorities.

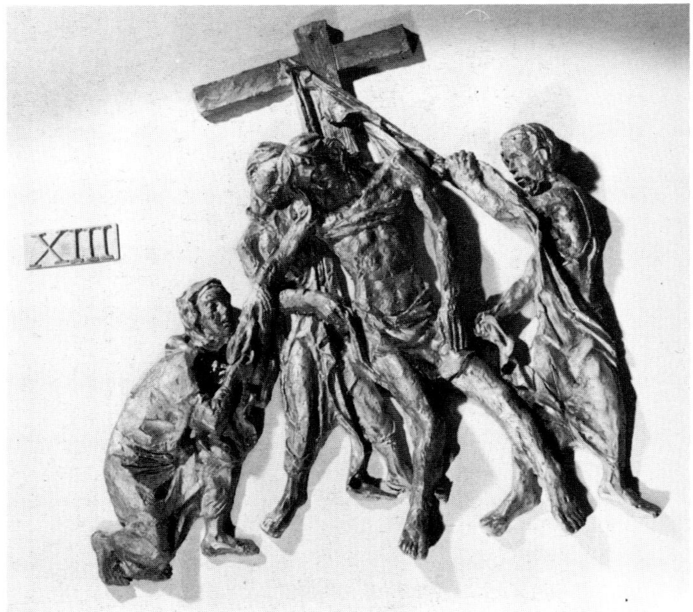

122. Eric Malthouse b. 1914
A Flurry of Pigeons (1954) Oil on board 122 x 152.5 cm
Cyfarthfa Castle Museum, Merthyr Tydfil

After a period which he described as a 'naive realism', Malthouse began his series of Pigeon paintings in 1952. It was a fertile theme and it engrossed him for at least six years. Considering the date, and the subject, and the high viewpoint which characterised many of these paintings, it is difficult to avoid pointing to the influence of Ceri Richards and his series of paintings of Trafalgar Square (No. 101). But just as Richards developed the influence of other artists in an individual manner, so Malthouse did with this detail. He developed the idea into compositions containing clusters of details that led naturally to the abstraction of his later paintings.

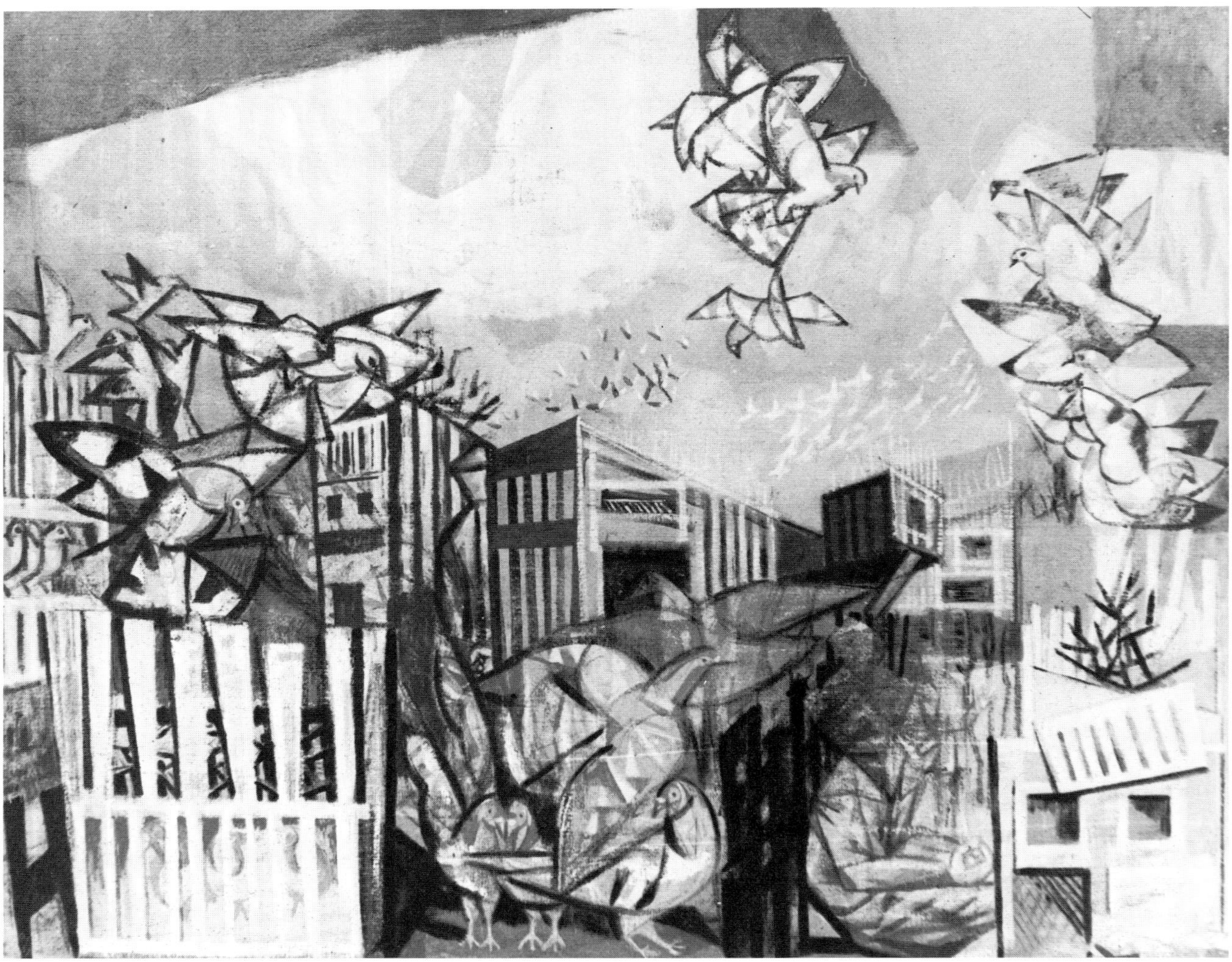

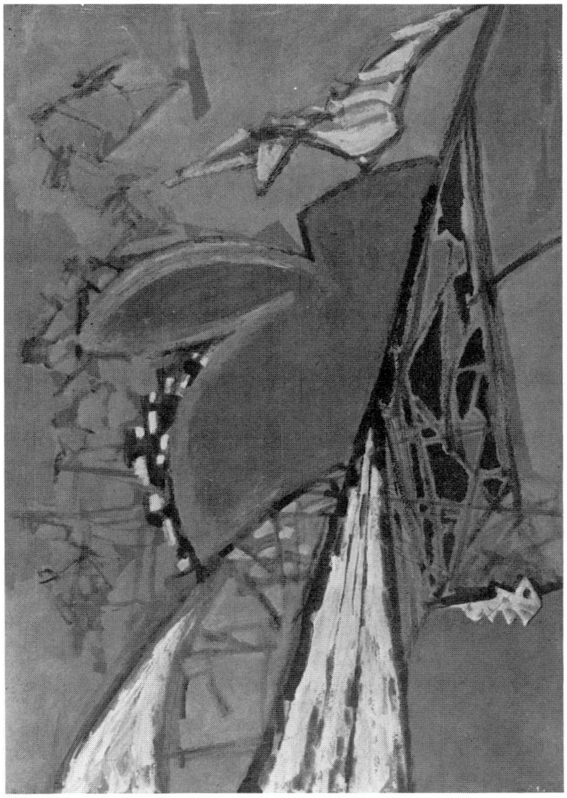

123. Eric Malthouse
Rockpool VIII; Twisted Wicker (1956) Oil on board
122 x 81.25m
(Destroyed in 1979)

During the middle 1950s, Malthouse paid many visits to St. Ives, and was one of the main contacts between Cornwall and Wales. It was the period when the postwar St. Ives school was in its heyday, and Malthouse assimilated the notion of painting large, expressionistic 'abstractions' from nature. In his paintings taken from rockpools he discovered new forms by restricting his viewpoint to the vertical and by limiting the area of the motif to a few square feet. Even then, it is evident from this painting that he could not quite eliminate the pigeon image, or the pigeon's eye view.

124. John Wright b. 1930
Cothi Pool (1956) Oil on canvas 76 x 101.5 cm
Lord Reilly

Like the previous two illustrations, this painting was completed in 1956, the year that marked the forming of the 56 Group. Wright was one of the founder-members of the group, and the youngest. But he was by no means the most advanced artist, for there was always in his work a figurative element, which was often derived from the Welsh landscape, and which resulted in a style that was more in the established European tradition than in the new American style.

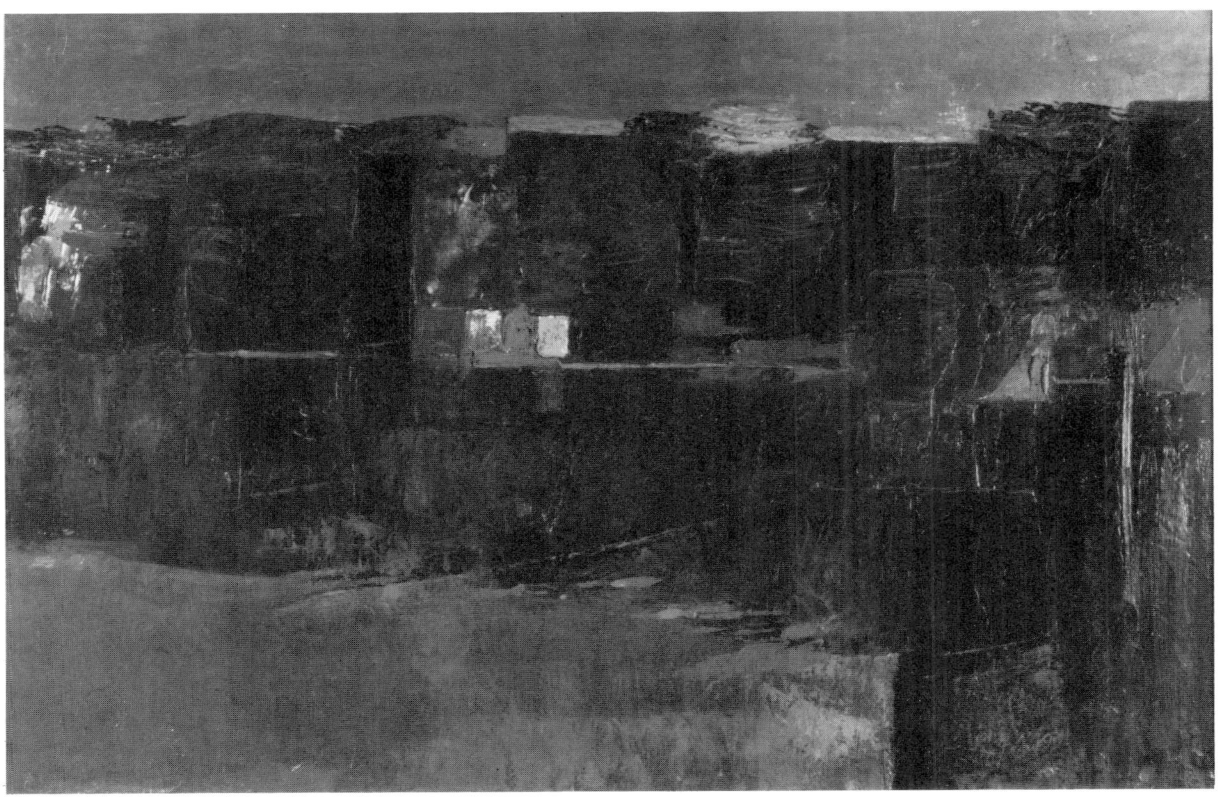

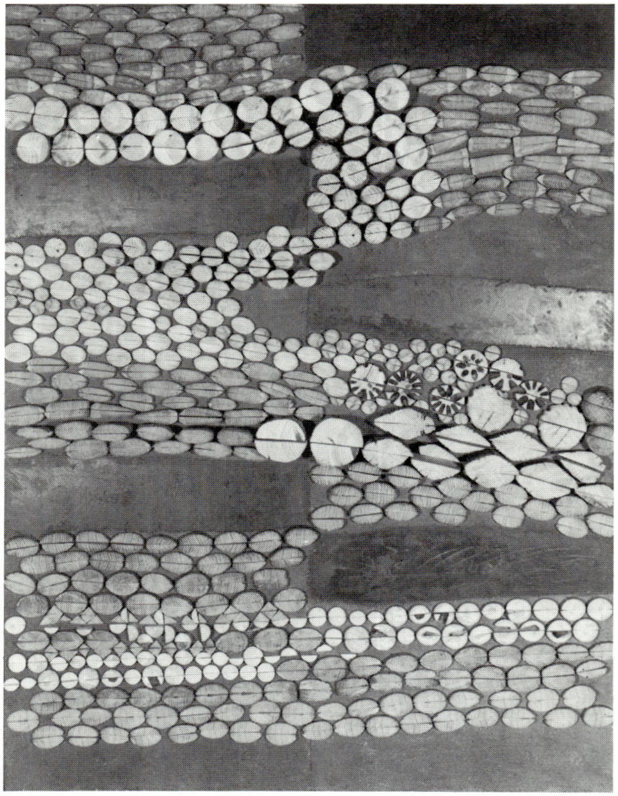

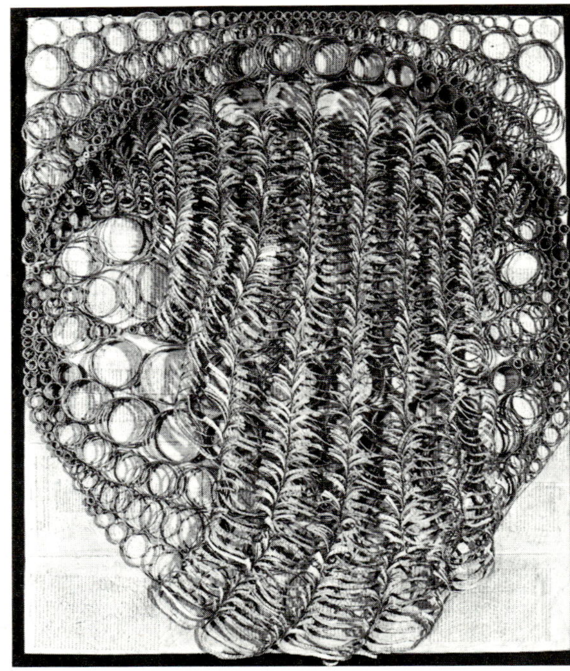

125. Arthur Giardelli b. 1911
Coedwig Sal (1963) Wood and sacking 122 x 91.5 cm
Arts Council of Great Britain

Giardelli was also a founder member of the 56 Group, and for many years has been its Chairman, under its new title, 56 Group Wales. Of his two working styles it is the abstract constructions that place him in the mainstream of modern European art, for they have an affinity with the work of other continental artists such as Burri and Kemeny. Like them, he would often use cheap or cast-off materials: hessian, wood, furniture mouldings, clock parts etc., which, deprived of their functional value, would convey new, poetic or symbolic meanings to the spectator.

126. Arthur Giardelli
The Veil (1976 - 7) Relief construction in paper and pencil 77 x 64 cm
The Artist

Giardelli's later constructions have become more fragile, more delicate and literally more literary. With the true romantic's affection for the melancholy of decay and the discarded object, he now uses old books as the material for his reliefs. Whatever the content of the books, the paper is generally superb and it has a formal potential that Giardelli has been quick to grasp. The result has been a series of sombre works, utilising the tensile quality of the paper, and evoking in a visual form the poetic associations of its original function.

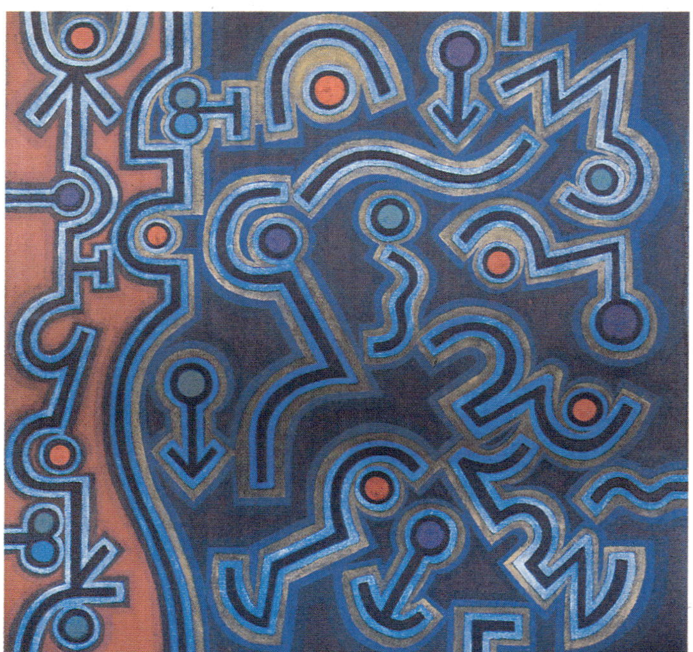

127. Robert Hunter b. 1920
Banner for Pwyll and Rhiannon (1974) Acrylic on canvas 122 x 122 cm
Welsh Arts Council

The Celtic Crosses in the National Museum of Wales, Hunter once declared, 'are the most contemporary things in the whole place'. The runes and marks on the stones, though unintelligible to the modern mind, provided for him an abstract language capable of infinite expression. Influenced to some degree by the work of Paul Klee, working both as signs and symbols, his paintings are intended as formal solutions to the problem of activating the surface of the canvas, and as self-contained icons with a universal, if non-specific message.

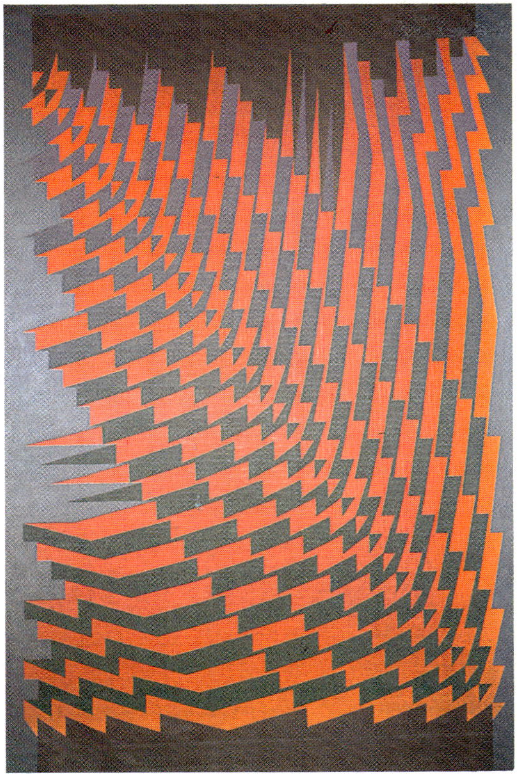

128. David Tinker b. 1924
MJQ (1971) Acrylic on suspended canvas
193 x 138.5 cm
The Artist

Throughout the 1950s, Tinker's style developed from a romantic figuration based on city scenes through to a personal form of symbolic abstraction. This was similar in concept to the later forms of American Surrealism, where the artists searched for the individual expression of a personal mythology. Later, in the 1960s, Tinker moved on to a type of geometrical abstraction where the latent symbolism was subordinated to the 'optical' qualities of the work, as in this painting, where 'MJQ' presumably stands for 'Modern Jazz Quartet'.

129. David Tinker
Relief Mural (1966 - 70) Cast aluminium
3 x 21.3 m (approx.)
Great Hall, University College of Wales, Aberystwyth

Tinker has completed several sculptural commissions in west Wales, among them an external wall relief for Haverfordwest County Library (1969), and this relief for the University College of Wales, Aberystwyth. It occurred during the period of the artist's interest in numbers, serialism, and the harmonies of proportion. This interest had to be reconciled with the demands of the location: the function of the building, the materials, the integrity of the long, low wall surface, and the symbolism of the university concept. The result is a surprisingly cohesive work, which is strong without being aggressive. The central panel is based on the harmony of numbers, the one on the right is derived from the classical Greek 'key' pattern, which is contrasted and complemented by the ancient Celtic forms which provide the basis for the panel on the left.

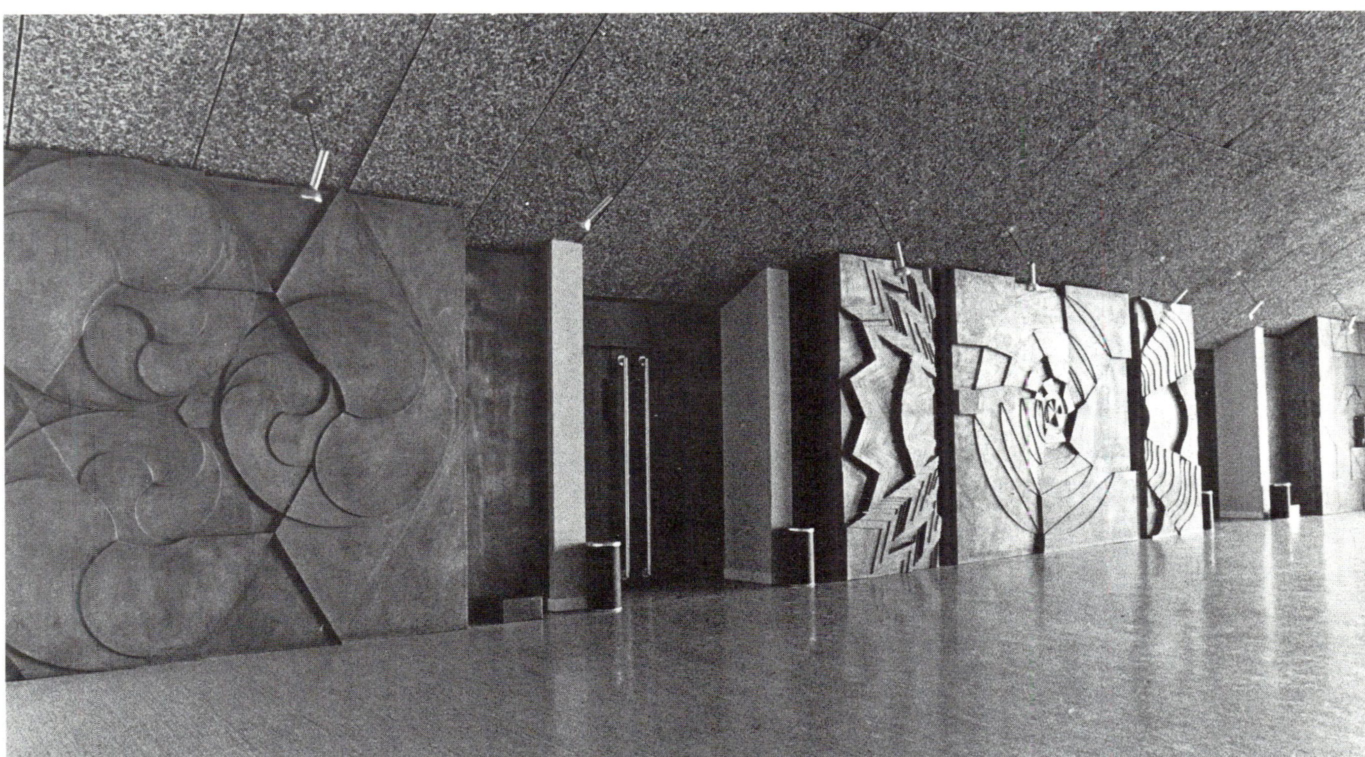

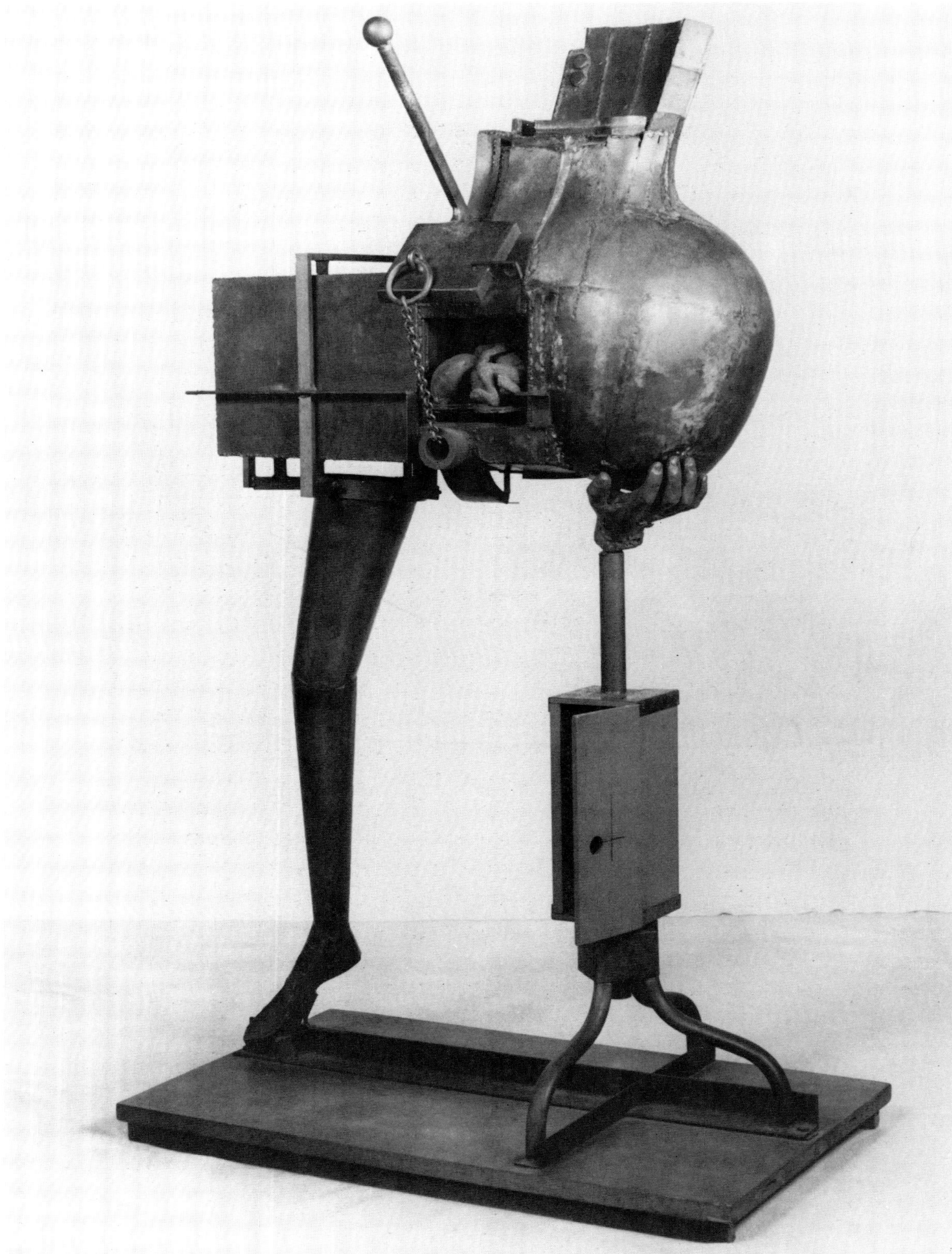

CONTEMPORARY ART IN WALES

Chapter Six

The heyday of the New Modernism, in the 1960s and 1970s, saw new modes, new materials, a raised status, and a wider public for the visual arts. The news media discovered their appeal and they became part of the instant tradition of 'sixties' culture. The visual arts in Wales also shared in the euphoria and achievements of the period; there were more artists, more galleries, more exhibitions, more individuals and organisations willing to purchase or commission works of art. But, by one of the commonplace ironies of history, just as all this activity seemed to reach its optimum, the arts ran out of steam. The late 1970s and early 1980s saw the emergence of Post-Modernism, one of the terms invented by critics and purveyors of art to convince themselves that a new movement was at hand. It was, in fact, a re-working of old discoveries, which disguised a slump in ideas; one of the periodic recessions in the world of art that are analogous to those in the world of commerce. The question for Wales is whether (in the cant of the period) the infrastructure of the arts will survive until the next reflation of ideas comes along.

130. Laurence Burt b. 1925
'Machine AD '65: Function: the Depopulation of the World and the Degradation of Man' (1965) Steel and bronze
Welsh Arts Council
Self-taught as an artist, and without academic qualifications, Burt became one of the most influential teachers and sculptors during the years he spent in Wales. He was trained as a metalworker; a skill that he utilised to great effect in his work. His earlier work was influenced by Henry Moore, and resulted in a series of helmet heads, one of which is now in the Tate Gallery. During his Welsh period, Burt gave full rein to his taste for the fantastic, the bizarre, and the surreal. This ominous metal structure has moving parts; when the handle is pulled, chains and hinges clank, and the bronze cast of a foetus appears from inside.

About the time of the middle 1960s, several factors accelerated the progress of the visual arts in Wales. One was the transformation of the Welsh Committee of the Arts Council into the autonomous Welsh Arts Council, a simple procedure which was to have far-reaching material and psychological effects. Not only did the new council acquire control over its own finances, it had new premises and a new gallery entirely at its disposal. Another factor, less imposing but equally indicative of that buoyant period, was the success of two private art galleries, modest but enterprising, and devoting a fair share of their programmes to new work from Wales. These two, the Howard Roberts Gallery in Cardiff, and the Dillwyn Gallery in Swansea, flourished in what appeared to be a boom time for modern art. Through their energetic, private enterprise, they bolstered the confidence of artists in Wales by showing and selling their work.

A factor of equal importance — indirect though nonetheless effective — also occurred in the middle of the decade, when the whole system of higher art education in England and Wales was overhauled. The old National Diploma in Design was allowed to expire and was replaced with a new qualification, the Diploma in Art and Design, a diploma of degree equivalent subsequently promoted to an Honours BA. To qualify for the granting of this new diploma, all the art schools awarding the old diploma were subjected to a rigorous test of standards, staff, equipment, budget and premises. Among the Welsh art schools, only one, Newport, passed the stringent examination of its facilities. The other two large art schools, at Swansea and Cardiff, were both refused recognition. After intense activity and expansion, Cardiff was granted limited recognition the following year, though Swansea never gained recognition.

One immediate effect of this new status was that it demanded large increases in staff
130 at both Cardiff and Newport Colleges of Art. As a result, more artists were recruited to
teach in the colleges, most of them coming from beyond Wales, and a high proportion of
them being sculptors. This sudden increase in the number of artists working in
contemporary styles not only brought greater variety into the visual arts in Wales, it also
131 lifted the morale of those pioneers who had been struggling against difficulties for many
years. Another, incidental gain to Welsh art was the appearance in the colleges of art theorists: historians of art, sociologists of art, psychologists of art, aestheticians and their like. They were something of a novelty to the cultural life of Wales, for none of the university colleges had a department of art history, and only the few museums could claim to have art historians on their staffs.

One further, less fortunate aspect of all this activity in art patronage and art education, was its concentration in the south-east corner of Wales. This was an area
already considered by the rest of the country as being over-privileged and exerting an
132 undemocratic supremacy in too many spheres of public life. But it was another link in the
chain of historical circumstances, and at least Wales was beginning to develop something like a cultural focus — even if that focus was way off centre. The middle 1960s also
witnessed one of those periodic climaxes in Western art when new movements such as
133 Pop Art, Op Art, Funk Art, Happenings, Minimal Art, Hard-Edge Painting and
Chromatic Sculpture all made their impact on the public. Equally remarkable was the increased and more prestigious contribution made by British artists, of which the Welsh

share was correspondingly enlarged.

In terms of personalities, a considerable share of the credit for the increased
awareness amongst the public of Wales must belong to Tom Hudson. Appointed as the
134 new Director of Studies at Cardiff College of Art, Hudson was largely responsible for the
calibre and range of the new staff appointed to the college. He was also an indefatigable
lecturer and a tireless prophet of the new art, as well as holding positive, far-sighted ideas
about the nature of art education and the part practising artists should play in it. He
believed — in the tradition of the Bauhaus — that artists were more valuable than
pedagogues for the success of an art school, and he gathered around him a team of
135 painters and sculptors which included not only Malthouse, but newcomers such as Laurie
Burt, Mervyn Baldwin, Michael Tyzack, Norman Toynton, Alan Wood and Terry Setch.
Burt, Baldwin and Hudson were particularly valuable additions to the ranks of artists in
Wales, for they were sculptors, working in relief as well as three dimensions, and
experimenting with non-traditional materials like fibreglass and synthetic resins.

136 Of all the artists named above, only two, Setch and Baldwin, continue to work in
Wales. Of the others, two now work in America, two in Canada and two in England.
Hudson himself — probably the most celebrated art educationalist ever to have worked
in Wales — left in 1977 and took his ideas and his enterprise to a similar post in
Vancouver. In an interview at that time with the *South Wales Echo* he affirmed his affection
for Wales but expressed his dissatisfaction that his work had become more involved with
administration than with ideas, following the amalgamation of the college into a larger,
cumbersome Institute of Higher Education.

137 Nevertheless, the contribution made by this team of artists to the growth of modern
art in Wales has persisted. It has helped to stimulate a wider acceptance of contemporary
art, and it has brought forth a second generation of enlightened artists who had been their
students, some of whom are now working in Wales and teaching a third generation of
future artists.

The circumstances of the revival at Cardiff College of Art were dramatic enough to overshadow the less publicised but more consistent efforts being made at Newport. In the college there, the Principal, Harry Lea, instituted a progressive form of the tutorial system, and shrewdly steered his college through the hazards that were contingent on the granting of the new diploma in art. In this he was aided by Tom Rathmell, a dedicated painter who, by encouragement, also helped many students towards a brighter future through postgraduate courses in the London colleges.

138 Other teachers at Newport College of Art, such as the sculptors Hubert Dalwood and
Anthony Stevens, though more radical than Rathmell in their own work, were also
concerned with the creative development of individual students. With their more
empirical attitude they established a counterpoint to the predetermined theories that
139 underlay the teaching at Cardiff. After the retirement of Lea in 1965, a new Principal,
John Wright, was appointed at Newport. An established painter, with considerable
experience and influence in the teaching of Graphic Design, he was less pragmatic about
educational matters than Hudson, though he too subscribed to the notion that practising
artists make the best teachers.

In Newport, as in Cardiff, there was a diversity of styles being practised, reflecting
140 almost the whole spectrum of current ideas. Painters and sculptors such as Ernest Zobole,
Anthony Stevens, Jeffrey Steele, Bryan Macdonald, John Selway, Keith Richardson-Jones
and Trevor Bates, shared with their counterparts in Cardiff the labour of raising the visual
arts in Wales to a position demanding recognition and even respect from the wider world.
Contributing to this was the practice at both colleges of inviting established artists of the
141 standing of Eduardo Paolozzi, Richard Hamilton, David Hockney, Terry Frost and R.B.
Kitaj, as well as *avant-garde* composers and creators of concrete poetry (European and
American), for brief but influential stints of teaching. In this practice, the colleges of art,
together with the Welsh Arts Council and the Welsh museums, accepted what had been
142 the traditional role of the individual patrons of the eighteenth and nineteenth centuries.
Such contacts gave flavour to the quality of Welsh art and, incidentally, helped to
propagate a modest reputation for Wales in the international arena of art.

But it must not be forgotten that, at the same time, there were other artists who stood
outside the arena, content to pursue their own interests with an admirable detachment
143 from contemporary enthusiasms. Painters of the quality of Thomas Rathmell and Evan
Charlton followed their own forms of figuration and made their reputations entirely on
the intrinsic merits of their work. Charlton is a particularly interesting example of how
time and changing fashions can reward a single-minded artist. As a young painter before
the war he was in the forefront of ideas, as a quasi-Surrealist. During the war and after,
his painting was curtailed by his duties as Principal of Cardiff College of Art, and then as
an HMI. But when he retired, Charlton was able to devote all his time to painting, and he
144 continued to investigate that line of poetic fantasy which has always obsessed him even
when it was no longer topical. However, in recent years, his ideas have once again come
to be regarded as innovatory, and younger artists have expressed their admiration for his
work.

Another category of artists contains those who live and work in Wales because they would not wish to do so anywhere else. Many professional artists come and go, motivated more by their concern for art than by love for Wales. But there is a dedicated body of artists in which these priorities are reversed. They might not change the pattern of history; they might not choose to follow it; but they perpetuate traditional values and provide a comprehensible form of art that appeals to those who might be confused or wary of contemporary notions. Sometimes professionals like Arthur Miles or Esther Grainger, sometimes gifted amateurs like the members of the various art societies, they depict the essence of Welsh life with skill and affection.

The art societies in Wales have had a long and active life, and continue to breed. The Royal Cambrian Academy for professional artists, and the *South Wales Art Society* are both about a hundred years old. Their offspring include the *South Wales Art Group* (founded 1949) and the *Watercolour Society of Wales* (founded 1960). The former has now elevated itself to national status, and is called simply the Welsh Group. It is an open society which promotes annual exhibitions that are an amiable and democratic mixture of amateurs and professionals. As such the standards of their exhibitions are uneven, though they are interesting occasions, demonstrating the readiness with which the various classes of artists will intermix, and proving that loyalty to Welsh art is often more important than professional dignity.

145 One professional artist who shows conspicuous loyalty to Wales is Glyn Jones. A painter of some repute with his aspirations directed beyond the confines of Wales, he is at the same time an activist in the cause of raising the quality and the prestige of art in Wales. An active member of *56 Group Wales*, he was also influential in the founding of the Association of Artists and Designers in Wales, a young professional body that has already become a recognised and formidable pressure group.

Jones was born in the Rhondda, studied at Cardiff College of Art and the Slade School, and is now Head of the Department of Fine Art in what was Cardiff College of Art — but which now operates under the ponderous alias of the Faculty of Art, South Glamorgan Institution of Higher Education. In his painting, Jones's affection for his birthplace is just as strong as was that of the old *Rhondda Group*, though it manifests itself in a more allusive manner. Where theirs was figurative and sometimes sentimental, his is abstract and frequently cerebral. His work is not an impressionistic view of the industrial valleys, nor is it an allegorical one; it is a transformation of their visual qualities into an art form that exists in its own right.

146 A colleague and a contemporary of Jones is Terry Setch, an artist of remarkably fertile ideas. His work is constantly developing and is perhaps the most original of the conventional forms of art being produced in Wales. In the 1960s his work was akin to a form of intellectual Pop Art, where he took images from other modern artists and transmuted them into his own. In time, this method progressed to an ironic exposition of how many of those original ideas were debased by commercial design. Later still, he moved into the area of environmental art, producing large installation pieces with themes taken from nature. These were often taken from the beach at Penarth, which is particularly dear to him because it was once the subject for Sisley's paintings.

147 Setch's capacity for monumental art was tested in 1968 when, together with Malthouse, Steele and several other artists, he was commissioned by the Welsh Arts Council to design a poster for public display on the hoardings around Wales. This was an original and enterprising scheme which used posters simply as art works to adorn public places in the most egalitarian way possible. These posters carried no message, no advertisement, and had no function save that of aesthetic appeal. They appeared enigmatically on public hoardings all over Wales, side by side with the conventional commercial posters with their bland enticements and trite exhortations. In such company, the silent dignity of these monumental prints, hanging aloof in cluttered urban environments, was very effective in visual terms. And these posters not only enhanced
148 those environments, they presented contemporary art indiscriminately to the greatest number of people. The public, however, was not wholeheartedly enthusiastic; it seemed largely approving, but it was also amused, bemused, indifferent or indignant. Unfortunately, the project was short-lived (it was probably expensive), though had it been extended it might have had a more permanent effect on the public consciousness.

Among the artists who were commissioned to produce a poster was Allen Jones, an established Pop artist, known all over the world for his erotic, girlie images, both in painting and sculpture. His poster was certainly striking and was probably the most successful in terms of public response. However, the recruitment of Jones into the ranks of Welsh artists raises the old question of what qualifications are required for that distinction. Jones does not live or work in Wales, and is only Welsh by name and descent. His work, moreover, has no affinities with what are traditionally held to be Welsh qualities, and it is most popular in more sophisticated countries such as West Germany and Japan.

There has always been a temptation to extend the ranks of Welsh artists — for the
149 sake of prestige — by including those whose qualifications are minimal, but whose work is well known. Sometimes this adoption is at the wish of an individual artist, such as Tom Phillips, who is proud of his Welsh descent, though he has never lived or worked in Wales. Unlike Allen Jones, Phillips's work does show what could be defined as truly Welsh qualities (it is often literally poetic), and in at least one work he has used specifically Welsh subject-matter.

On the other hand, there are those artists whose dormant Welshness only awakens
150 when there is an opportunity for an exhibition in Wales, or when a commission or a competition requires either a Welsh pedigree or work that contains some Welsh content. Altogether, it is a complicated issue, for detectable Welsh features (even assuming that they can be defined) are rare in the work of contemporary artists in Wales. The dominant aspiration is still that which aims at the styles of the international *avant-garde*, with a language that is universal in its appeal.

151 Most of the artists who have come to Wales in the last twenty years or so, as well as the younger generation of indigenous Welsh artists, conform to one or other of the many idioms that constitute modern art in the last quarter of the twentieth century. In addition, the number of artists now practising in Wales is greater than at any time in the past. So there is no longer any need to stretch the definition of a Welsh artist in order to inflate the numbers. It need only be reaffirmed that, within the scope of this survey, Welsh art comes from three sources: artists who were born in Wales and who work in Wales; artists who
152 were born in Wales but who work elsewhere; and artists who were born elsewhere but who work in Wales. Put together, they might thus be said to constitute the School of Wales (by
153 the same tokens which characterised the School of Paris), and from them all comes such a diverse amount of work that individual and detailed description would be difficult. Most of the salient facts, however, are all contained in Kirstine Dunthorne's exhaustive
154 compendium, *Artists Exhibiting in Wales 1945–75*.

Even so, the progress of sculpture in this recent period has been so remarkable that it cannot go unrecorded. Indeed, at one point it looked as if Wales might become the focal
155 point for modern British sculpture. This was in 1966, when the Welsh Arts Council promoted the large, ambitious, highly successful, open exhibition for sculpture in Britain. Called *Structure 66*, it was the three-dimensional counterpart to the biennial *John Moores Liverpool Exhibition*, and it sought to bring together all that was new and exciting in sculpture. The exhibition had the lure of large cash prizes, and for a while, during the summer months of that year, it looked as though Cardiff had been taken over by the sculptors of the *avant-garde*. All the galleries were full of unfamiliar objects, and strange,

exotic structures sprouted in the grounds of Cardiff Castle.

Regrettably, the exhibition was never repeated, and so Cardiff and Wales were deprived of a periodic artistic stimulus similar to, perhaps even greater than that which convulses Liverpool every two years. No other organisation has been brave enough to take over the idea, and it is probable that the Welsh Arts Council found the project too expensive and too demanding on the limited resources of exhibition space. This is to say
156 nothing about the daunting practicalities that were involved in the collection, selection and exhibition of such a variegated manifestation as sculpture in the middle 1960s.

For by that time sculpture was beginning to burst through its traditional forms and concepts, not only to embrace new materials and methods, but to include within its definition new activities such as Installation and Performance Art. It can be argued (and it often is) that these so-called 'new' art forms have historical precedents, and that only the designation is modern. It could be said, for example, that the *Eisteddfodau*, seen in the abstract, are examples of Performance Art: and that Port Meirion in Gwynedd, as constructed by Clough Williams-Ellis, is not true architecture, but is the most ambitious, most permanent, most successful and most representational piece of Installation Art in Wales.

But whether they are innovators or inheritors, the fact remains that contemporary sculptors who specialise in installation or performance pieces are handicapped by the nature of their work. For it is usually ephemeral, can only be preserved (inadequately) by means of photography, and it rarely finds a permanent place in museums. David Nash,
157 whose studio is a large converted chapel in Blaenau Ffestiniog, has to cope with these
158 problems, though he also makes rough-hewn wooden sculpture that resembles, in varying
159 degrees, the furniture of rustic giants. David Shepherd has no such compensations for he works entirely in the field of Installation Sculpture. Stemming from the American roots of environmental pieces and Minimal Art, his work has gradually acquired a personal, poetic form of expression. However, any objection that his work is divorced from the formal elements of traditional sculpture is a superficial one; for, in spite of its transient nature, it too is concerned with space and volume, the qualities of materials, and the
160 relation of the piece to its setting. It is also often derived from things seen. But because his work is ephemeral, it cannot be 'acquired' by museums or bought by collectors; and so Shepherd's reputation is not as wide as it deserves to be.

Working in an idiom even more refined than Shepherd's, because it is more 'conceptual', is Keith Arnatt. After moving to Wales and teaching at Newport College of Art, Arnatt established a reputation which was wider and more respected in progressive quarters than that of any other artist then working in the country. Like Shepherd's, his work could only be preserved by photography, as was the case with his most celebrated
161 piece, the self-burial, which took place in the forest near his home in the Wye Valley. However, always alert to the advance of ideas in art, Arnatt has now moved from photographing his art, to an interest in photography as an art in its own right.

These activities point towards two other new art forms that are flourishing in Wales. One of these is photography, which is now enjoying a world-wide prestige unknown since the early years of this century. Arnatt's shift towards photography was probably

162A influenced by the prevailing enthusiasm at Newport, and in particular by the example of
162B his colleague there, David Hurn. Newport College of Art has consistently encouraged an interest in photography as an art form — though its embryonic film school proved expensive to run — and the College established the first Department of Documentary Photography in Britain. Hurn has been the guiding force behind this department, for he is an accomplished photographer, and with his series *Wales Black and White* he revealed unfamiliar and intriguing aspects of Welsh life and landscape.

163 There are other fine photographers in Wales: Julian Sheppard, John Thomas, John
164 Chantry and Sue Wells, to name only the more established. Sheppard, among his other
165 achievements and with his flair for capturing the expressive moments in human action, has recorded the more dramatic episodes in the performances of the Welsh National Opera. It is with this activity as a recording and interpreting medium that photography comes into its own as a supporting art. It is particularly valuable in the other new activity that is flourishing in Wales, Performance Art. Like Installation Art, this too is ephemeral in form, though since the artist is physically involved in the making and, therefore, the duration of the piece, he cannot take his own photographs, but must rely on the perceptiveness of his photographer. Performance Art is present in Wales partly because there are facilities in the various arts centres, and also because there was enthusiastic teaching from artists like Tom Hudson, John Gingell and Graham Pasmore.

Like installation sculptors, the creators of Performance Art are hampered by the transitory nature of their work, and by its even greater cost. And though Performance Art drifts at the furthest end of its activities into the world of experimental theatre, there have been determined efforts to keep it within the category of the fine arts. Because it cannot be purchased, the cost of producing performance works has to be met from paying audiences or some direct form of subsidy. As is so often the case with almost all contemporary art activities in Wales, this branch of art receives its own share of financial
166 support from the Welsh Arts Council. Indeed, the main art event at the Royal National Eisteddfod of 1977, held at Wrexham, was an international programme of Performance Art, which was financed by the Council, and which included several contributions from Wales.

Public patronage in Wales has become much more widespread in recent years; the principal benefactor being the Welsh Arts Council. In fact, there has been a decided — and apparently permanent — shift in conventional patronage since the 1960s. Some private art galleries continue to function; for example, the Albany Gallery in Cardiff, the Attic Gallery in Swansea and the Tegfryn Gallery at Menai Bridge. But the standard of their exhibitions is uneven, and the two outstanding private galleries in Wales, the Howard Roberts in Cardiff and the Dillwyn Gallery in Swansea, have failed and vanished. On the other hand, in Cardiff alone, no less than six other galleries have taken on the role of presenting contemporary art by means of temporary exhibitions. What is significant about this encouraging increase is that all these galleries are supported by public bodies. Oriel, The Photographic Gallery (Welsh Arts Council), Chapter Arts Centre (local authorities and Welsh Arts Council), Sherman Gallery (University College), the Faculty of Art and Design (local authority) and University College Hall are all financed, through some channel or other, by the taxpayer. This is to say nothing of similar establishments at Mold, Aberystwyth and Wrexham, or the temporary exhibitions that are held in the various museums and art galleries throughout Wales. The one large, influential and ambitious gallery to exist outside the public sphere is the Mostyn Art Gallery in Llandudno and even the Mostyn receives support from public funds.

Support of this nature, from public funds, means that these places are more secure than private galleries, and are less hindered by the profit motive. In addition, the system
167 of awarding grants and bursaries, started in 1975 by the Welsh Arts Council, has meant that individual artists in Wales now have a reasonable share of state patronage and the consequent prestige that attends it.

Another form of public patronage that is also directly related to supporting individual artists is the growing practice of establishing fellowships. Gregynog Hall, for example, has for several years sponsored an annual Fellowship for writers, artists or craftsmen. Their tenure is not long (usually six months) but the quiet and isolation of Gregynog has enabled the incumbent to produce work high in quality and quantity.

168 When the painter Barrie Cook took up the Gregynog Fellowship in 1978 he had just completed a much longer Fellowship at Cardiff College of Art. Under Derrick Turner, the Principal, an enlightened policy was initiated whereby several teaching posts that became vacant were replaced by a succession of Fellowships, available to artists of standing or promise. This has meant that established artists have been attracted to Wales by the Senior Fellowship, and, by working there for three years, have helped to enrich its artistic life. Cook was the first of these and he was followed in 1977 by Adrian Heath, an outstanding painter with an acknowledged reputation in the art world of London. The College has also encouraged younger, unknown artists by the provision of three Junior
169 Fellowships: two in Fine Art and one in Ceramics.

Jack Crabtree, an earlier holder of the Gregynog Fellowship, subsequently persuaded a large industrial concern to grant him another fellowship. In 1974, the National Coal Board in Wales supported Crabtree for a year while he depicted the mines and miners under their control. This was a rare form of patronage for Wales, equalled only by the Fellowship awarded by the Steel Corporation of Wales to the sculptor, Garth Evans, which exceeded the random commissions given to Keith Vaughan, Harold Foster, Charles Cundall and other painters, by the steel industry in Wales, both before and after it was nationalised.

There is a marked difference in Crabtree's work between the Gregynog and the NCB fellowships. In his earlier period Crabtree had specialised in a stylised form of landscape,
170 sometimes industrial but always romantic in its implications. With the Coal Board commission there was a remarkable, seemingly unconnected change in his work. The emphasis was now on figures: miners and other colliery workers; not simplified as in Josef Herman's work, but detailed, almost caricatured, and showing the unmistakable influence of George Grosz. Crabtree was fortunate in having a tolerant employer in the form of Newport College of Art, which allowed him leave from his teaching post there to devote all his time to his own work.

Another innovation that has fostered the rise of Welsh art in recent years has been the provision of studio space for artists and designers. A pioneer in this respect was Chapter, an enterprising arts centre established in an unfashionable part of Cardiff, and housed in one of its redundant red-brick schools. The building has been imaginatively transformed to provide cinema, theatre, performance and gallery facilities, accommodation for amateur societies, as well as a number of studios available at a modest rent. The number is limited, but the studios do allow some artists and craftsmen an opportunity to take advantage of the more favourable climate of the arts in Wales.

Almost inevitably, the arts centre at Chapter is supported by public money: in the financial year 1976-77, for instance, over £80,000 — virtually its total income — came from public funds, three quarters of it from the Welsh Arts Council. Even with all this support, the artists in Wales had not become so debilitated by official patronage that they were incapable of self-help. In 1975, the Association of Artists and Designers in Wales was formed; partly as a pressure group to raise the voice of professional opinion in national matters of art; partly as a union, committed to the improvement of conditions for its members. Born out of discussions held at Chapter in Cardiff, the Association quickly matured and established itself as a force in Welsh art politics. It soon had branches throughout the country with membership open to all practising artists and designers. Prompted by this open-hearted policy it did not trouble itself about nice distinctions between professional and amateur status, and it has helped to unite artists in Wales, and to diminish the long standing complaint about the hegemony of the south-east.

It has also produced a phenomenon: a magazine about the visual arts in Wales. Its title is *Link* — which symbolises the aspirations of the Association — and it carries an engaging mixture of news and opinion; of the artists, by the artists, and for the artists. Modest in style and appearance, it is a shade parochial with the hint of an earnest sixth-form magazine about it. But it continues to improve, and its unique achievement cannot be disputed. It is financed entirely by the Association, which in turn is financed by members' subscriptions and the virtually mandatory grant from the Welsh Arts Council.

Another equally ambitious enterprise promoted by the Association of Artists and Designers in Wales is the provision of studio facilities for its members. In pursuit of this
171 strategy it has been taking over and converting derelict premises in Cardiff, Swansea, Carmarthen, Aberystwyth, Bangor and other centres. Together with the magazine, this project has done much in recent years to promote the confidence and unity of artists in Wales. It offers the exciting prospect of a change in the pattern of artistic life in Wales, where the custom of isolated studios in suburban front parlours or country cottages could be superseded by a concentration of studios in artists' quarters in the larger centres of population.

This in turn could generate a conspicuously absent factor: the practice of debate among artists, collectors, critics and their like, on topics related to their art, its time and its place. It has never occurred in the history of art in Wales — though there are famous precedents in European and American history — and it is one of the few remaining factors necessary for establishing the autonomy of a School of Wales. For there now exist in Wales more artists than at any time in the past, more studios in which they can work, more galleries to exhibit their work, more patrons (chiefly public) to purchase that work, and an organisation that gives them unity, confidence and a corporate identity.

There is also another promising project that was launched in November 1981. It is called the Welsh Sculpture Trust and, following a custom established around the world in the last 30 years, it intends, literally, to give sculpture a breath of fresh air, and also 'to promote and encourage throughout Wales, for the benefit of the public, a wider appreciation and understanding of sculpture'. Unlike the Association of Artists and Designers — which emerged from a vociferous, rather unruly groundswell among practising artists — the Sculpture Trust is impeccably orthodox and indisputably respectable. Its president is the former Speaker of the House of Commons (Viscount Tonypandy), its trustees include the President of the Royal Academy (Sir Hugh
172 Casson), while the representative sculptors are Henry Moore, Elizabeth Frink, Phillip King and Ivor Roberts-Jones. With such luminaries to guide it, and with 'the active support of ... people of public significance in Wales', its future looks promising. It does, however, recall the worthy and glowing optimism of the establishment figures who launched the Cambrian Academy exactly one hundred years earlier.

But perhaps the Sculpture Trust has wisely kept its sights relatively low. No talk now of a splendid national academy; instead a modest achievement: the creation of Wales's first sculpture park at Margam Abbey in West Glamorgan. Again, alas, an innovation has been located in the south-east of Wales, but the setting is beautiful, and it is to be hoped that the enterprise will aspire to its stirring though apologetic and self-evident motto: 'a nation's culture is expressed in its visual arts as in its music and its literature'.

Seen in the perspective of history, the visual arts in Wales have made remarkable headway in the period since 1850, and all the existing conditions are propitious for further progress. However, not all the possible conditions are present, and so there are no grounds for complacency. Wales still has no national academy of art; there is neither a Welsh Museum of Modern Art nor a Museum of Modern Welsh Art; and there has yet to appear a body of scholarship dedicated to the future as well as to the history of art in Wales. And even if these obvious gaps were to be filled, it would always be necessary to seek, find and foster that elusive ingredient which neither public money nor political organisations can create, which neither wishful thinking nor wishful writing can stimulate. It is the indiscriminate, indefinable factor that produces great art, wherever the artist might be, or however unfavourable the conditions.

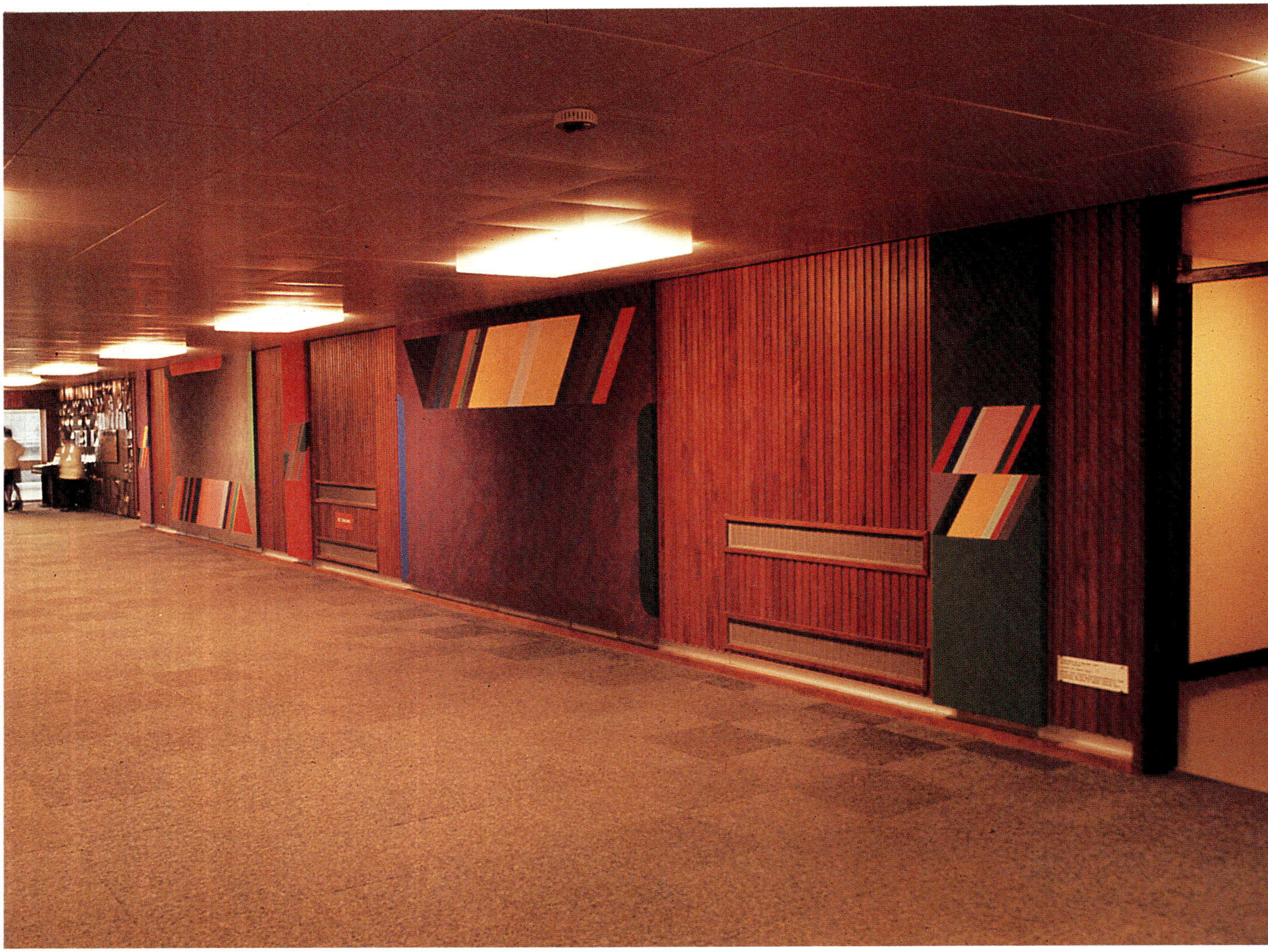

131. Michael Tyzack b. 1933
Mural painting: 'Variations on a ground 1971'
Acrylic on canvas
Heath Hospital, Cardiff
During his period in Cardiff, Tyzack won the first prize in the John Moores Liverpool Exhibition of 1965. Shortly afterwards he was one of the artists commissioned to provide mural decorations for the large, new hospital being built in Cardiff. This large painting is his contribution to the scheme, and it is in the style known as Hard-Edge Painting, or Post-Painterly Abstraction. This was initially an American movement, though derived from European geometric abstraction, and was regarded as the anthithesis and radical alternative to Abstract Expressionism.

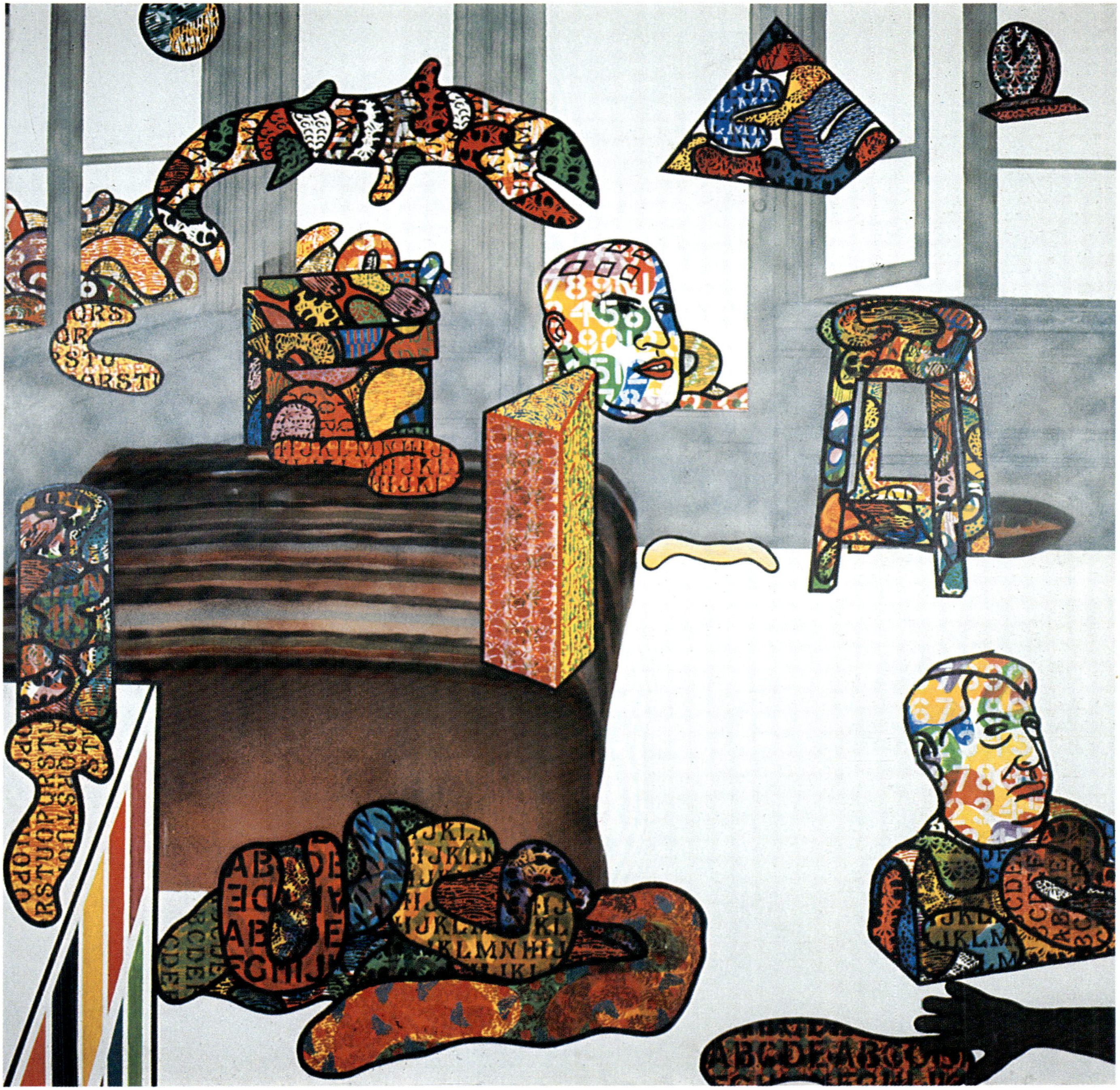

132. Norman Toynton b. 1939
My Room with De Chirico (1963) Acrylic on canvas
213 x 213 cm
Welsh Arts Council

Toynton belonged to the generation of students at the Royal College of Art which included David Hockney, Derek Boshier, Allen Jones and Patrick Caulfield. As the 'enfants terribles' of British art, they dominated the Young Contemporaries Exhibition of 1961, and thrust before the public the third and most sensational stage of English Pop Art. Toynton appeared in Cardiff three years later, and during his five years there, he developed his imagery and his technique. Like Hockney and Boshier, Toynton was at that time fascinated by the world of mass-communication, the imagery of the urban environment, and the graphic style derived from graffiti.

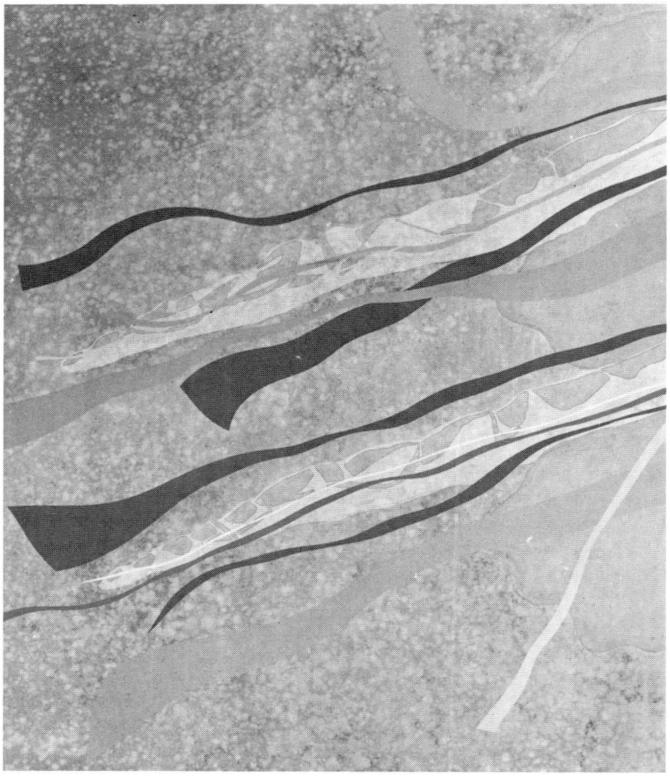

133. Alan Wood b. 1935
Ribbons and Promontories (1968) Acrylic on canvas 183 x 152.5 cm
National Museum of Wales

With Eric Malthouse, the other main contact between Welsh art and the St. Ives school was Alan Wood. Before he settled in Cardiff, he had been working in Cornwall, with a studio in St. Ives. During his seven years in Cardiff he kept those contacts alive and preserved some of the influences of the St. Ives type of abstraction derived from landscape and natural forms. In this picture there is a synthesis of that style with the hard-edged type of abstraction as practised by Tyzack.

134. Tom Hudson b. 1922
Castell Britannica (1965 - 6) Polyester, fibreglass and aluminium 122 x 122 cm
National Museum of Wales

In his earlier work, Hudson had been a constructivist, using conventional materials to create geometric, relief forms. In the fourteen years he spent in Wales, he evolved a striking and original way of working in new materials. Experimenting with fibreglass and synthetic resins, Hudson stretched the potential of these materials, and created a medium as fluent as paint and as durable as bronze. With this he produced a series of highly individual constructions, such as this one, where the brilliance of Pop Art is combined with the austere machine forms of his earlier work.

135. Terry Setch b. 1936 ▷
Blue Poles, Wallscape (1965) Acrylic on canvas 213 x 183 cm
Welsh Arts Council

Setch was one of the first artists in Wales to produce Pop Art. Unlike Toynton (No.132) or John Selway (No.142), Setch's was not typical of the English strain of Pop, but was closer to the American kind. There was a more intellectual bent to his ideas; witty or ironic comments on the consumer society, the urban environment, or the history of art. In paintings such as this, he takes the work of modern artists, and transposes their style into the kind of debased banal images that commercial art produced. In this painting the title refers to Jackson Pollock's masterpiece of Abstract Expressionism, 'Blue Poles'.

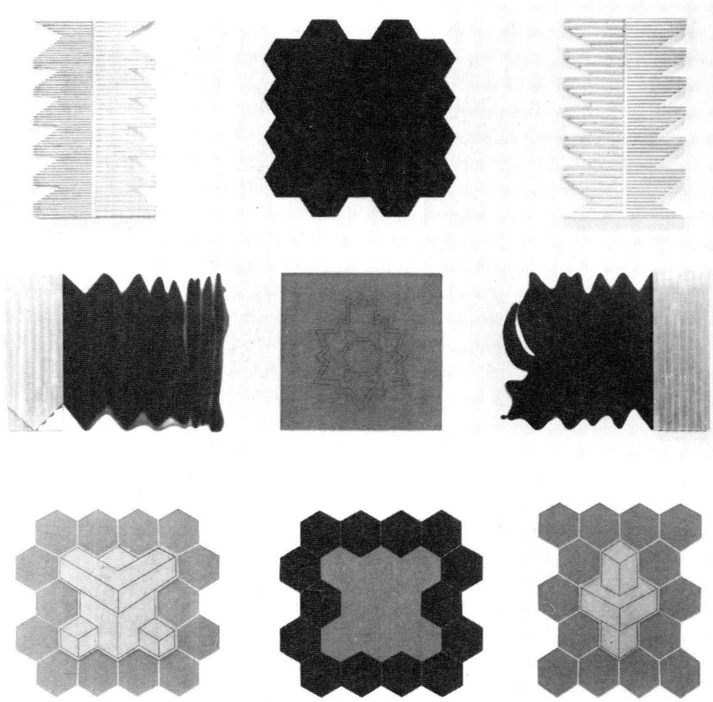

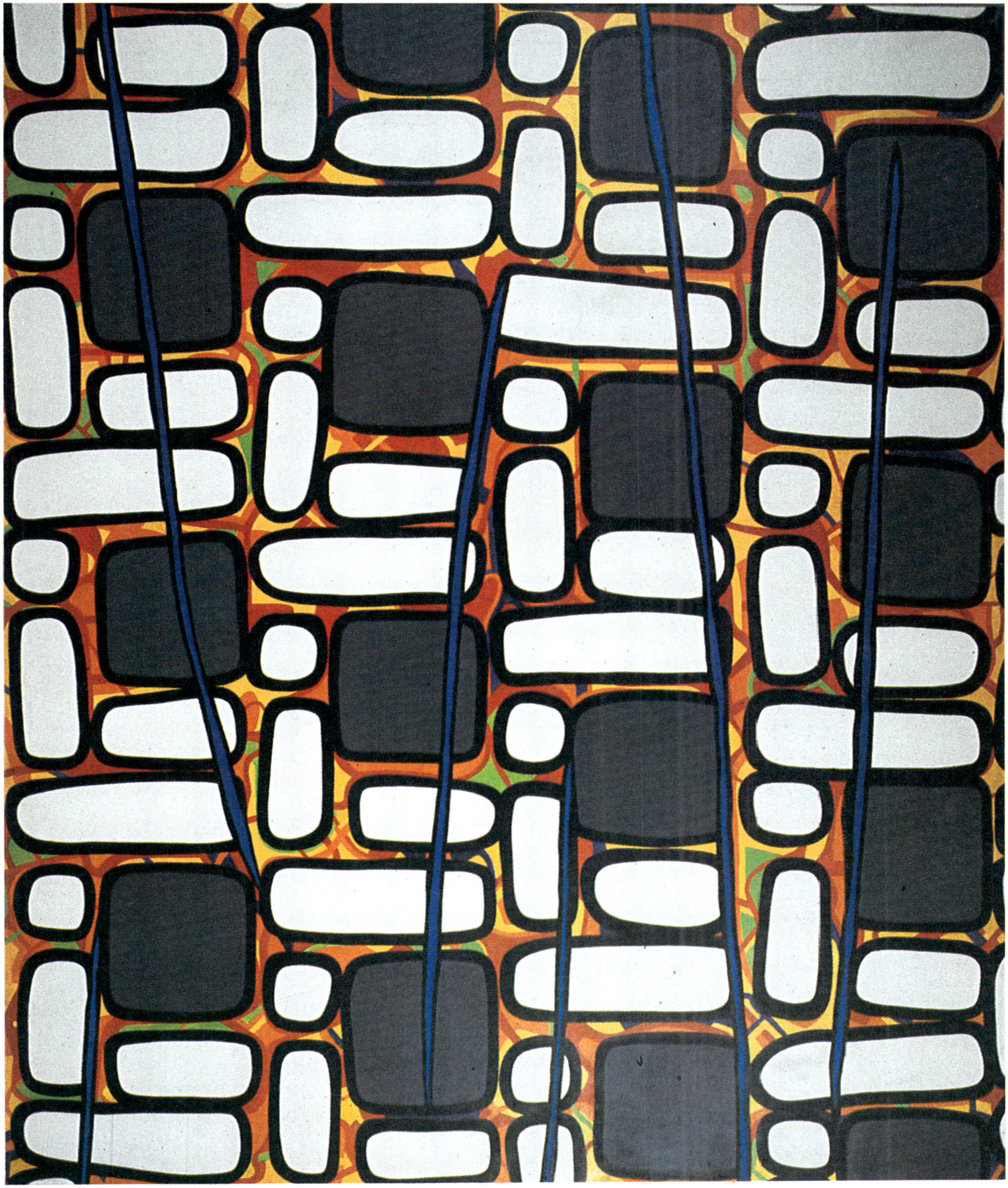

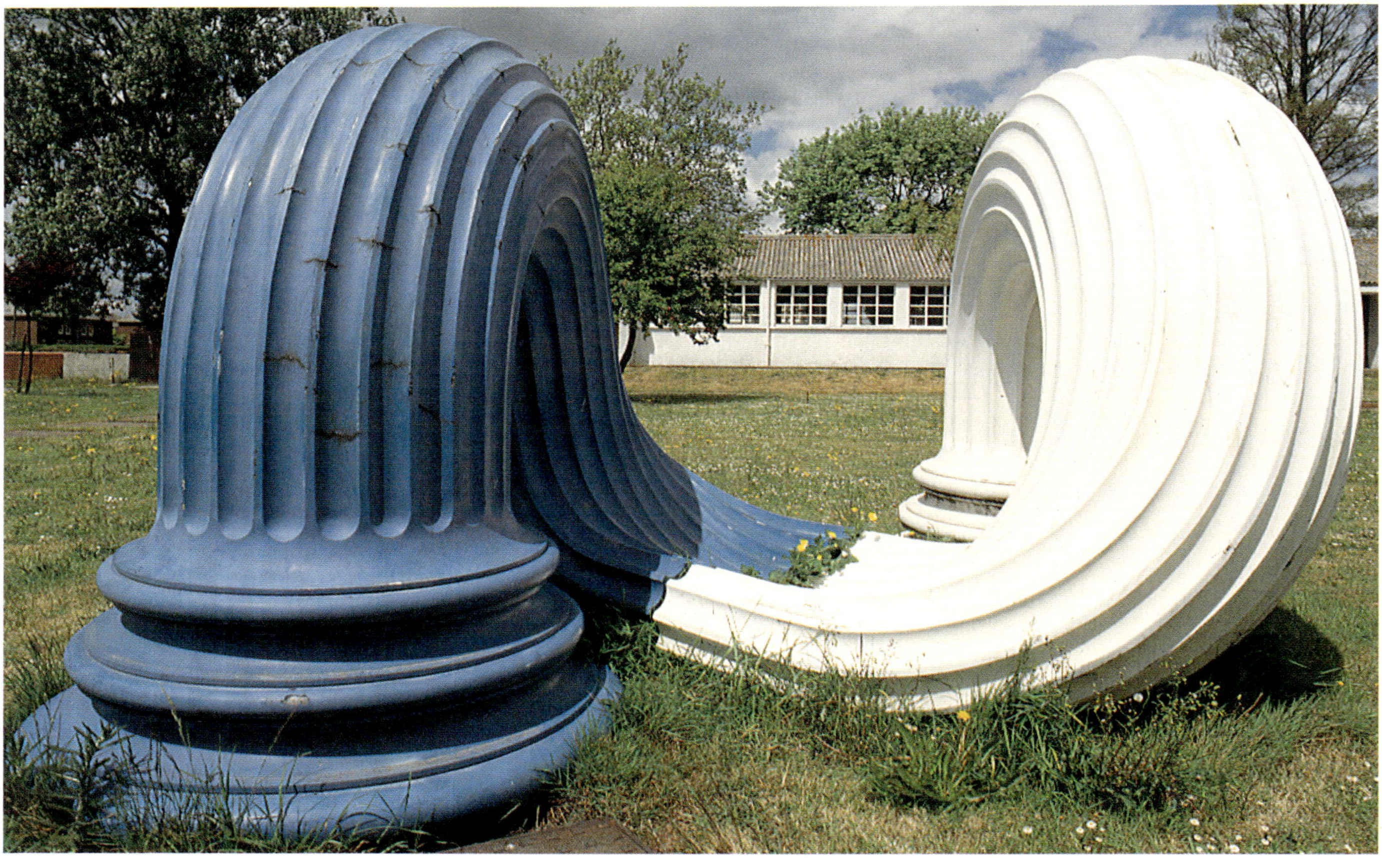

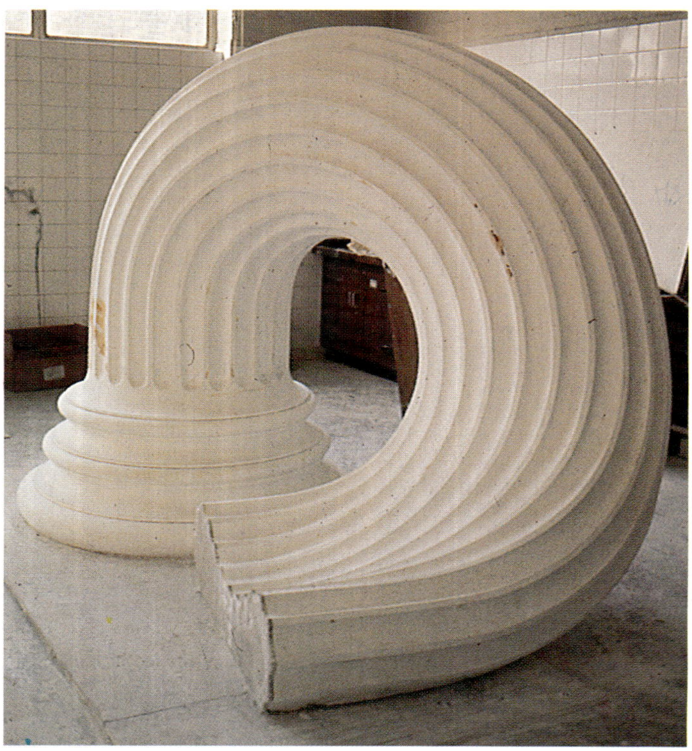

136. Mervyn Baldwin b. 1934
That's the Way the Column Crumbles (c.1968)
Polyester resin and fibreglass

With an attitude, though not a style, akin to Burt's, Baldwin used figurative imagery to propose ironic comments on contemporary society. Among the most enduring and successful of these was a series of sculptures using the classical column as a metaphor for our civilization. Such visual irony was rare in Welsh art, which made it even more effective. Traditionally in sculpture, the rigid broken column was a symbol for a life cut short; using modern synthetic materials, Baldwin was able to create a column that was bent, twisted, torn, limp and deflated, and sometimes metamorphosed into pink, bleeding flesh. Such imaginative treatment greatly extended the potential of this simple symbol.

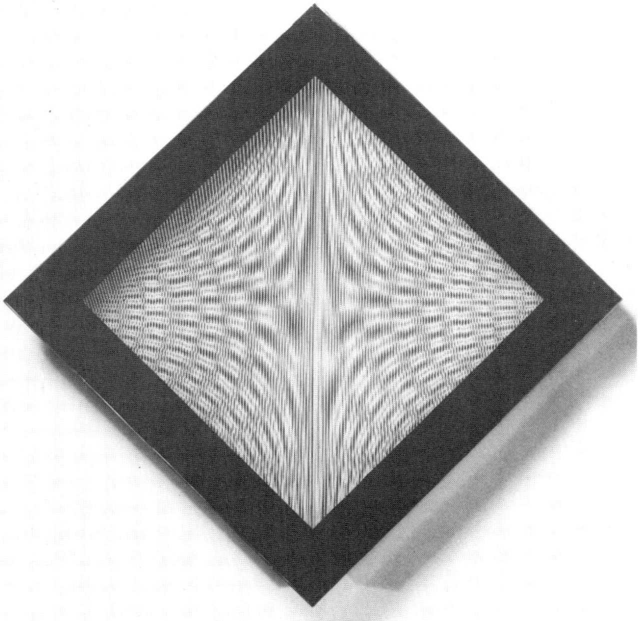

137. Christopher Shurrock b. 1939
Serial No. 30/A/68 (1968) Acrylic Sheets, pigment, wood
86.4 (diagonal) x 7.6 cm
Dyffryn Joint Committee

At the time when this piece was made, Shurrock was one of the leading exponents in Wales of optical abstrction, usually known as Op Art. It took simple principles of perceptual psychology and extended them to produce either ambiguous visual patterns or, as is the case with Shurrock's work, to create disturbing effects on the eye and the mind of the spectator. With this piece, the movement of the spectator is necessary for full appreciation, as the lines begin to shift and dazzle - thus impinging on the category of Kinetic Art.

138. Hubert Dalwood 1924 - 76
Large Object (1959) Aluminium 76 x 89 x 89 cm
Tate Gallery

Born in Bristol, Dalwood worked for a time as an apprentice with the Bristol Aeroplane Company, before studying art at the Bath Academy. He taught for a period at Newport College of Art, during the middle 1950s, at a time when modern art in Wales was neglected, and progressive artists were attempting to influence public opinion. In this activity, Dalwood's uncompromising modernism and his growing reputation added weight to the pressure being exerted on the insularity of establishment opinion about modern art. By joining the 56 Group, during his time in Wales, Dalwood also added his influence to the collective voice of protest.

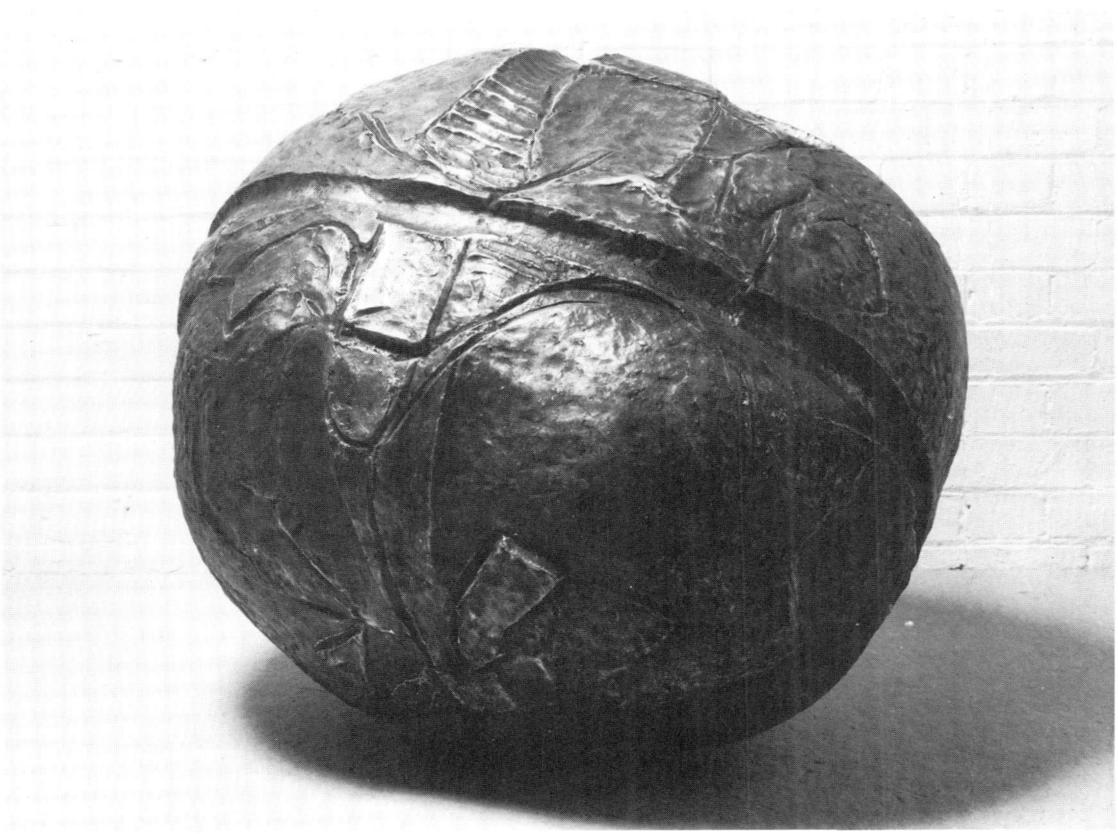

139. Anthony Stevens b. 1928
Crow Wood (1969 - 70) Fibreglass, wood and aluminium
91.5 x 81 x 81 cm
The Artist

As a sculptor, Stevens is difficult to classify, for he has moved through various distinct stages in his career, and has always retained a personal quality. He has touched upon Pop Art, and at one period was producing Funk Art; everyday objects such as telephones and television sets deprived of their precise machine forms and rendered in ciment fondu as soft, drooping images. In later work, such as this piece, he uses images from landscape, animals and people, working in a wide range of materials: fibreglass, wood, latex, aluminium, resin and clay, often in unusual combinations.

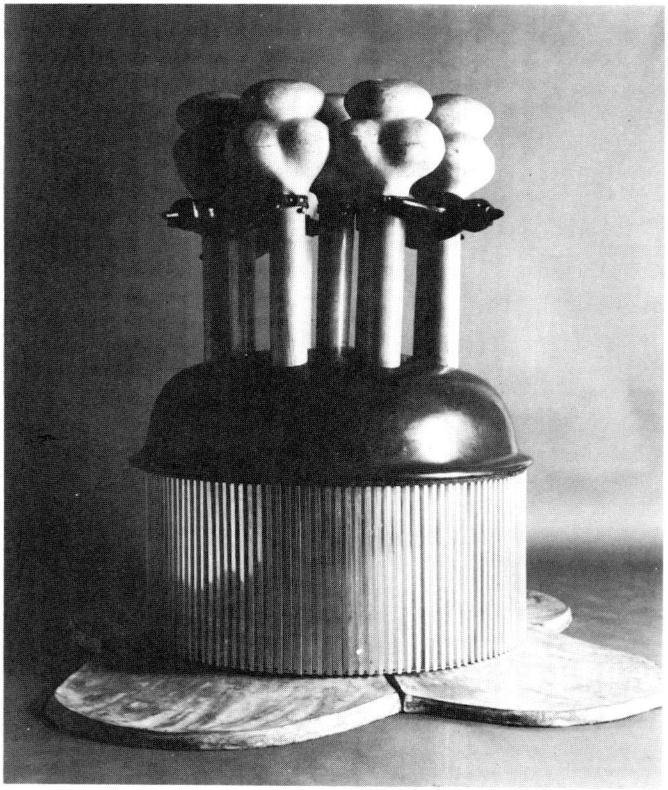

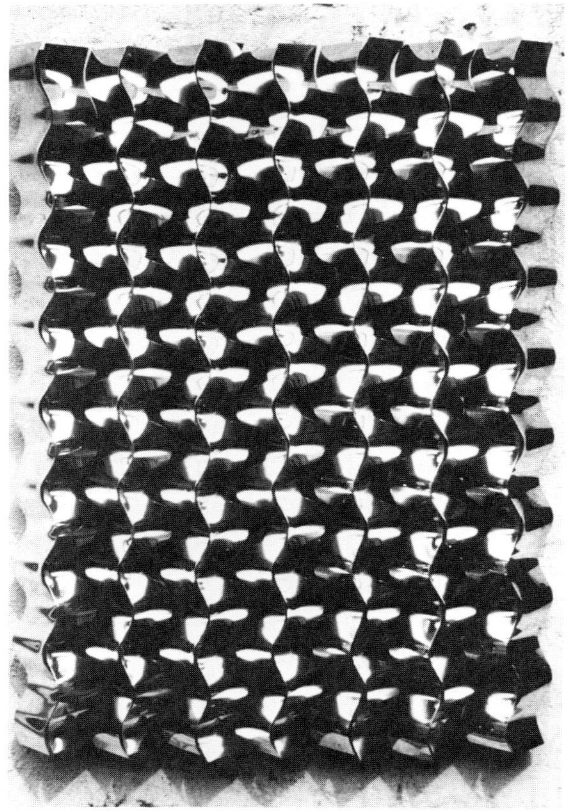

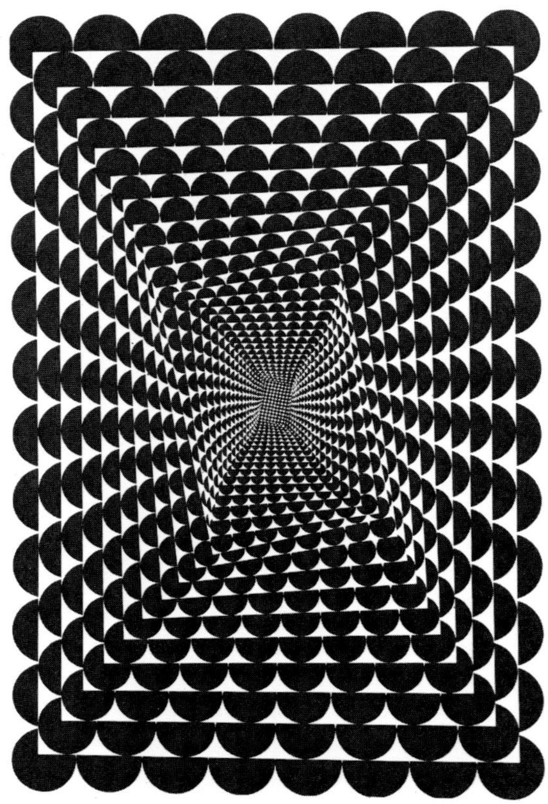

140. Jeffrey Steele b. 1931
Baroque Experiment, Fred Maddox (1964) Oil on canvas
152.5 x 101.5 cm
The Hon. Anthony Samuels

Steele was born in Cardiff, and was one of the best known British Op artists. During a scholarship in Paris, he came across the work of Vasarely and other concrete abstract painters. From this beginning he experimented in optical abstraction, and, during the years he spent teaching at Cardiff and Newport Colleges of Art, he produced many precise, dazzling configurations in black and white. This painting, typical of that period, was Steele's contribution to the international exhibition of Op Art, which was held at the Museum of Modern Art in New York in 1965 under the title 'The Responsive Eye', and which was also shown in St. Louis, Seattle, Pasadena and Baltimore.

141. Keith Richardson-Jones b. 1925
Prototype for a Multiple (1967) Polished aluminium
65 x 49.5 x 7.5cm
The Artist

Richardson-Jones spent a long period working in the area between hard-edge colour abstraction and optical abstraction, and has since moved into the field of system painting. In the late 1960s, in common with several Welsh and European artists, he began creating multiples; a practice of producing many reproductions of sculpture and reliefs that could be sold cheaply and were the three-dimensional equivalents of prints. As such, it was partly a socially motivated art form, and it used new techniques such as vacuum forming of plastics. In 1968, the Welsh Arts Council mounted a comprehensive exhibition of multiples, and one that was among the first in Britain.

142. John Selway b. 1938
The Factory Inspector (1966) Oil on canvas 81 x 81 cm
Welsh Arts Council

After studying at Newport College of Art, Selway completed his training at the Royal College of Art, where he became one of the precocious generation of young Pop artists of the early 1960s. He returned to the College of Art in Newport as a teacher, and began a long series of paintings dealing with beach scenes, and which introduced a note of fantasy into his interpretation of contemporary mores.

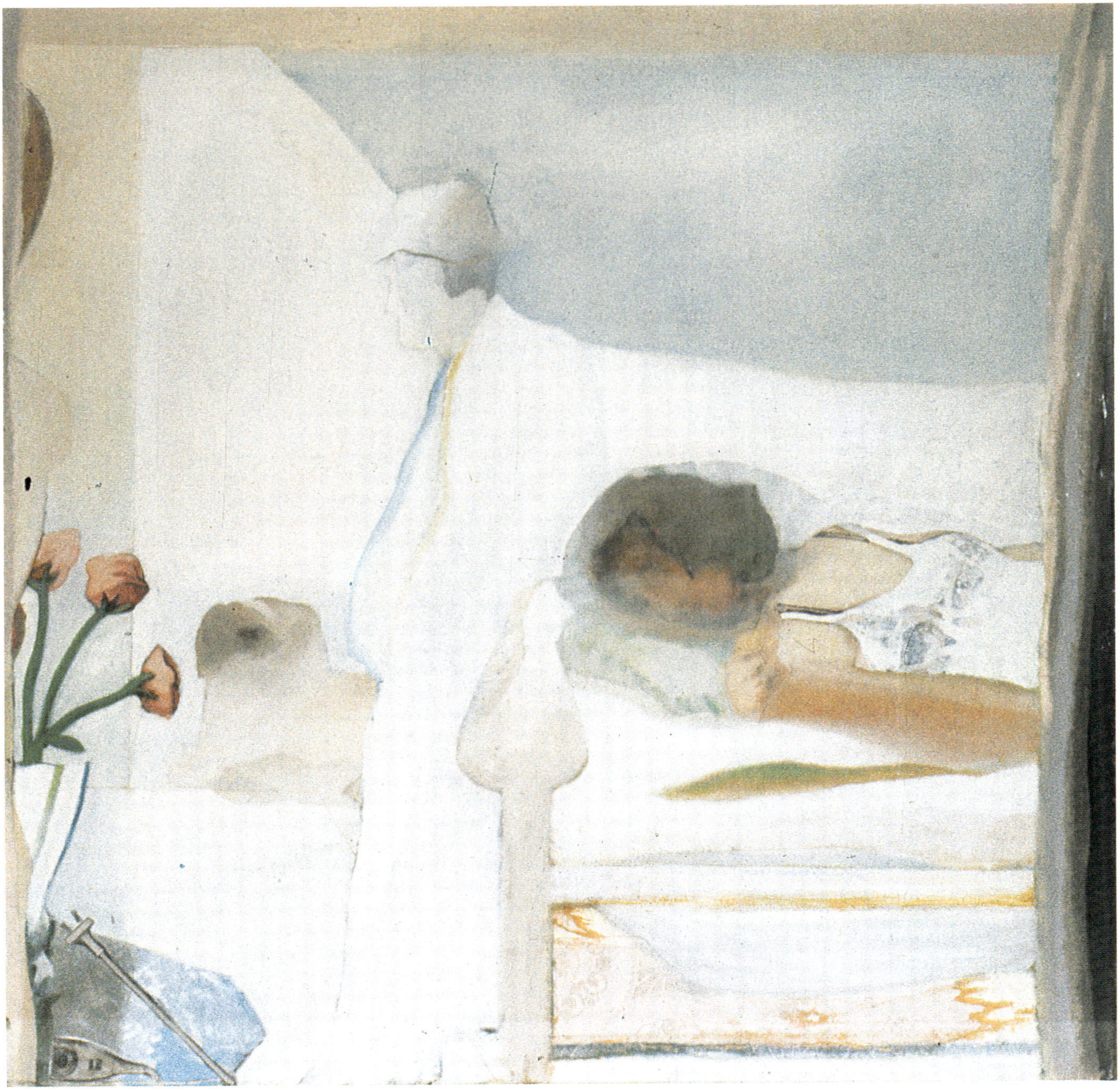

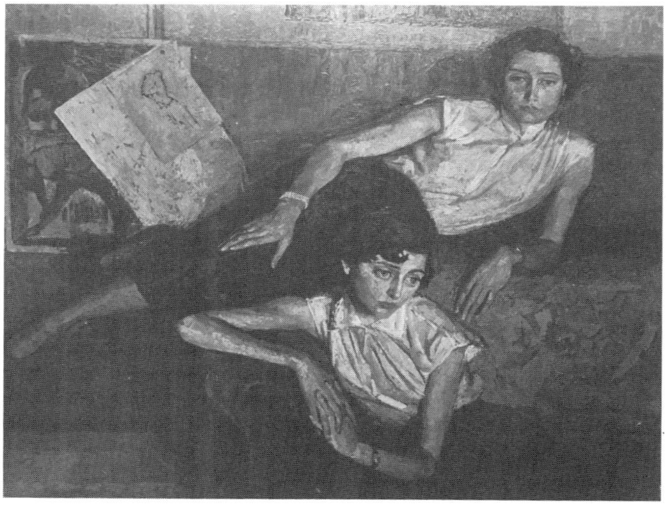

143. Thomas Rathmell b. 1912
The Sisters (1953) Oil on canvas 119.5 x 151 cm
University College of Wales, Aberystwyth

When all about him were investigating the new ideas in the art of the 1960s, Rathmell - then Head of Fine Art at Newport College of Art - was patiently following his own path of exploration. By contrast, this seemed a traditional mode of painting, for it was concerned mainly with figures in interiors, depicted in a painterly style derived from Intimism and the Nabis. It has, nonetheless, a highly distinctive quality and there is a dignified quietude about his pretty girls in domestic settings that sets them apart from related images to be found in Pop Art.

144. Evan Charlton b. 1904
The Crate (1974) Oil on panel 122 x 152.5 cm
The Artist

Although he is often linked with the surrealists, Charlton disclaims any direct ideological connection with the classic forms of Surrealism. He admits that 'there is a certain surrealist feeling but I would like to point out that all my things work; there are no melting watches ... or anything of that sort. They are surrealist in the sense that Leonardo or Giorgione are surrealist'. One artist to whom Charlton feels close is Lucien Freud, though Charlton's work has more of an atmosphere of mystery and enigma than has Freud's. The distant, misty horizons, the interiors, filled with menace or potential drama, and with anxious, expectant people, add up to 'an intense reality of the world, not an imitation of the world but ... a parallel reality'. (Quotations from an interview with Evan Charlton; 'Link', No. 9 Autumn 1977.)

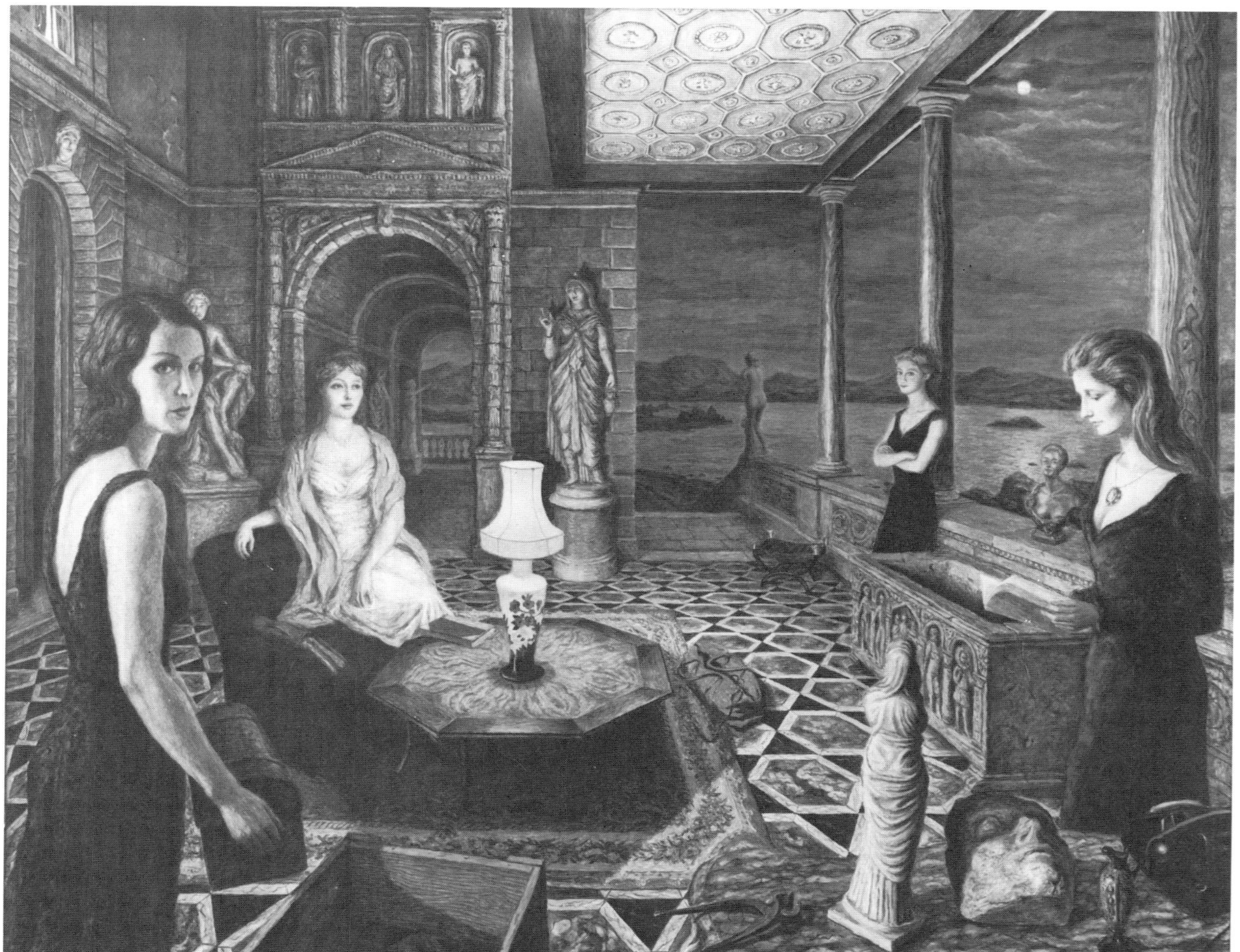

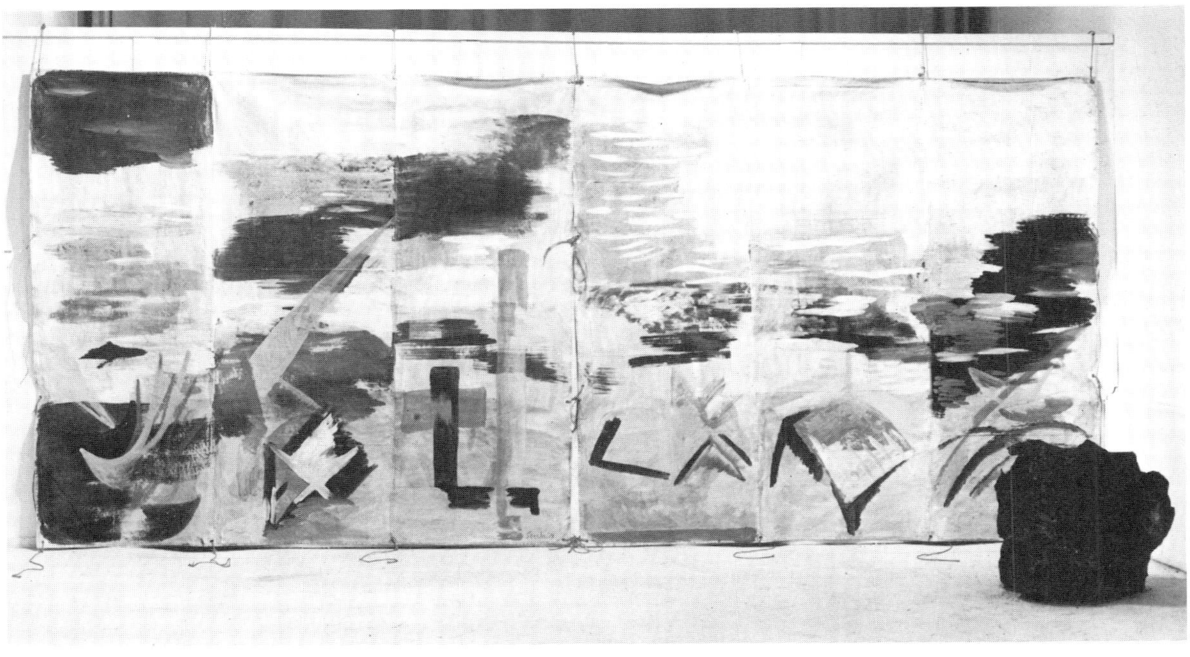

145. Glyn Jones b. 1936
Carmel (1975) Pitch and scrim on canvas 366 x 549 x 23 cm
The Artist

This monumental piece is the largest example of Jones's work in this style. It is, in effect, a movable mural, consisting of stiff panels, mounted onto scaffolding, and forming four horizontal steps. Seen in situ it is daunting in its uncompromising, unrelieved blackness, and is a fitting equivalent to the locale that inspired it - the Taff Vale and the Rhondda Valley. 'At its best I want the work to be as real as many of the objects which characterise my locality ... It is necessary to emphasise that the work is not about making symbols or metaphors for any of these things ... At no time do I wish to suggest that reality is somewhere else, outside the work'. (From the artist's statement in 'The Artist and how to employ him', 56 Group Wales, 1976).

146. Terry Setch b. 1936
Sisley, Marconi - Were Also Present (1973) Shellac and acrylic on unstretched canvas 244 x 518 cm
(Destroyed by the artist)

This large, unstretched canvas was painted on the beach at Penarth, alongside six totem-like structures constructed from flotsam and jetsam found on the tide line. Later, when exhibited at the Grabowski Gallery in London, a floor sculpture, six feet wide, was lashed to the painting. Like the works of Jasper John, Setch's pieces of this period have a metaphysical dimension beyond the declared imagery. In this case the style and technique are deliberately uncouth and provocative; challenging conventional tastes and values. The historical associations of Penarth (where the artist lives) are evident in the title, which, together with the images, is a tribute to his predecessors in art and science.

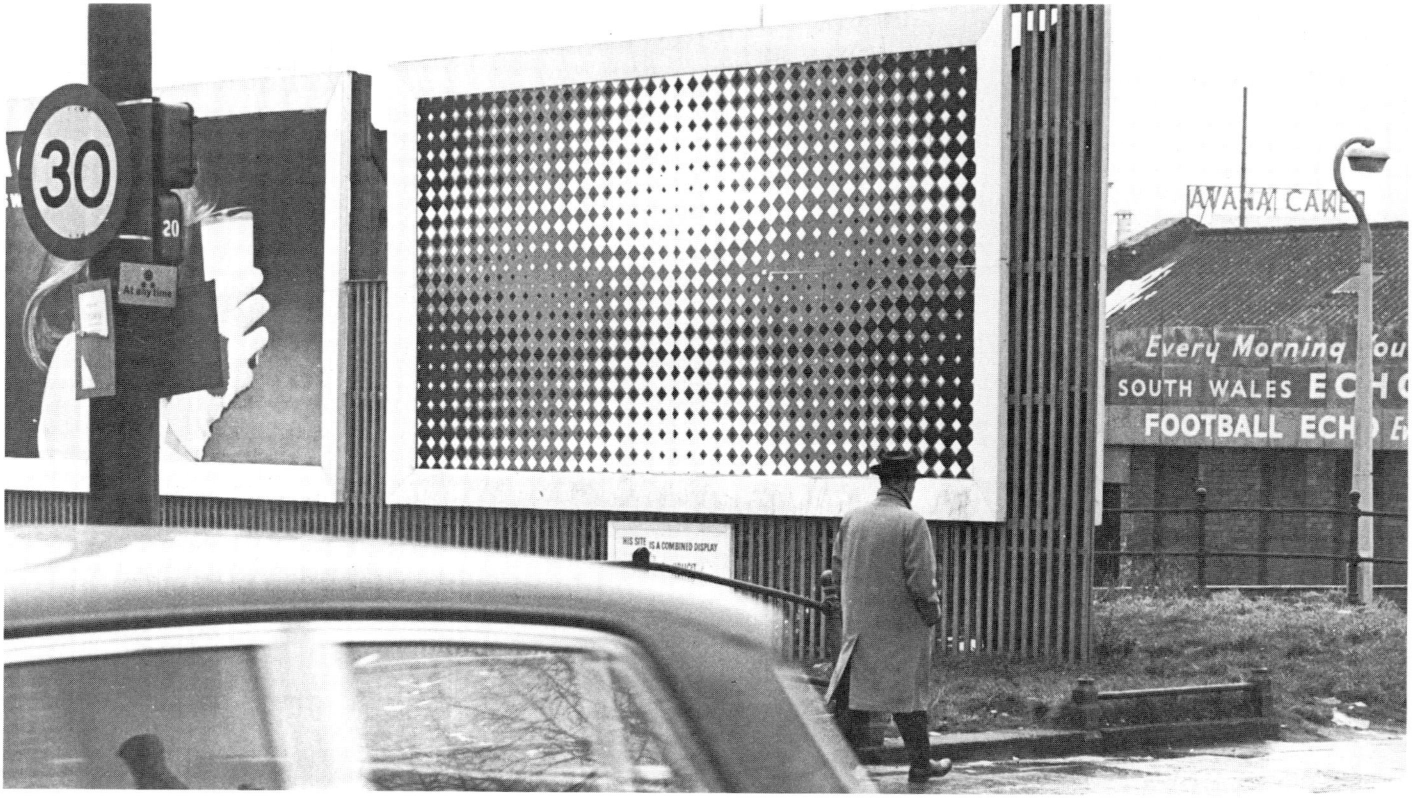
30
20
At any time
Every Morning
SOUTH WALES
FOOTBALL

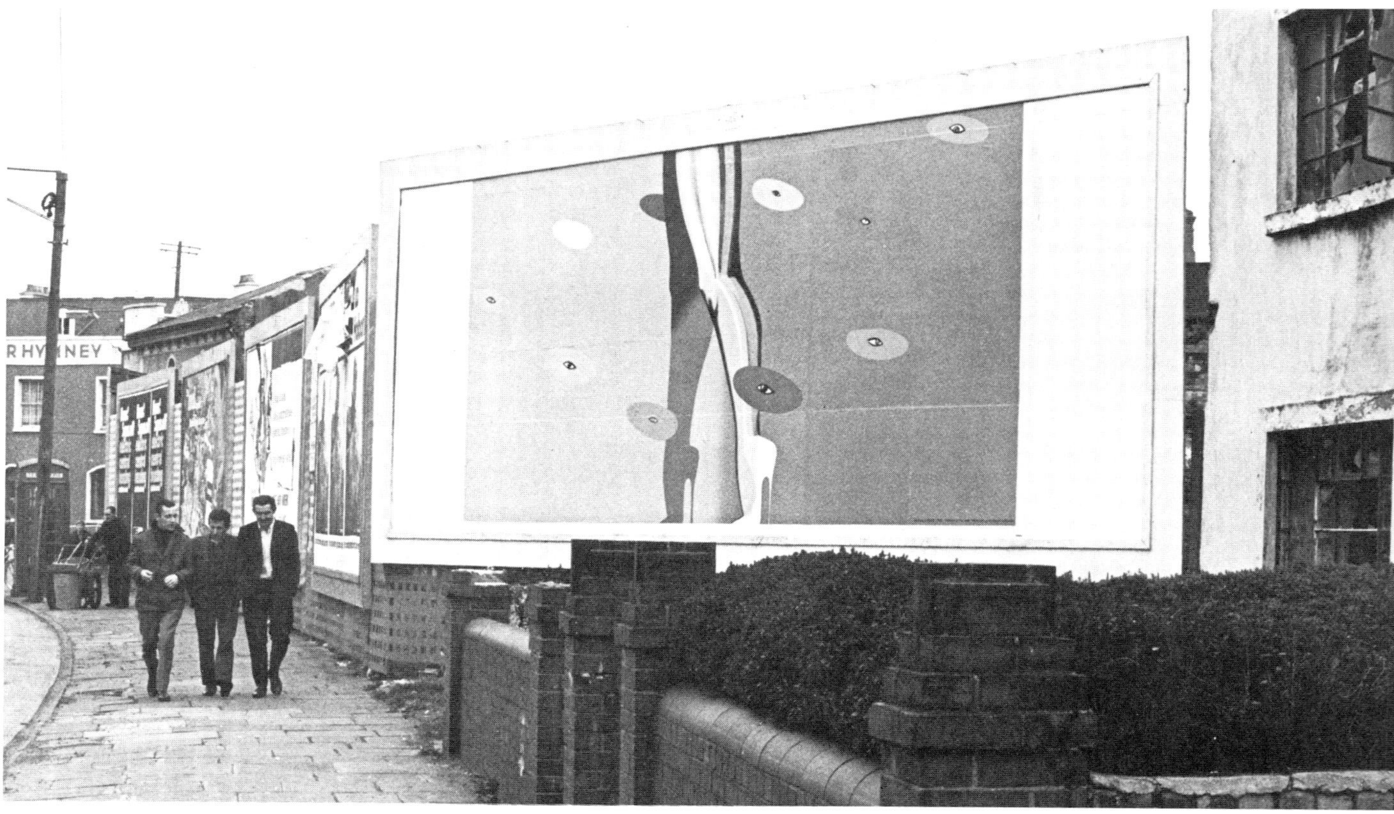

147. Poster Scheme (1967 - 8)
Poster Print by Jeffrey Steele, Cardiff location
Welsh Arts Council

Several artists were commissioned by the Welsh Arts Council to design prints which could be reproduced at a size that would fit commercial hoardings in urban areas throughout Wales. The Council's declared intention was that they should function as a 'casual and easily available stimulus', and serve as a means of 'activating the whole environment'. A television programme made at the time suggested that the public response was mixed and inconclusive, the scheme lapsed after about a year, and a projected series using three-dimensional multiples was never realised. It was, however, an original and potentially fruitful attempt to democratise art, and for those who noticed these monumental prints, they certainly enlivened the whole environment.

148. Poster Scheme (1967 - 8)
Poster Print by Allen Jones, Cardiff location
Welsh Arts Council

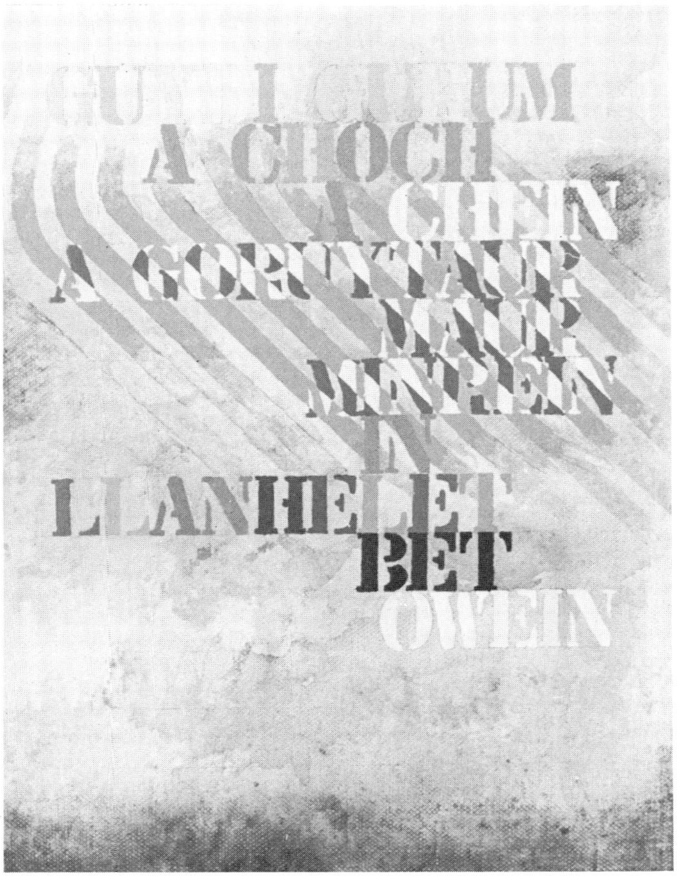

149. Tom Phillips b. 1937
From the Stanzas of the Graves (1972) Acrylic on canvas 20.3 x 15.2 cm
Haags Gemeentemuseum, The Hague

Although Tom Phillips was born in South London, and has always lived there, he is the son of a Welshman, and very conscious of his cultural ancestry. With his intellectual romanticism, Phillips clearly feels considerable affinity with Wales and its history. About this painting he has written: 'Although I do not properly speak Welsh, I am Welsh by origin, physique (if that's what you call it) and, to some extent, character: the language and its sounds has always interested me. Ian Tyson first introduced me to these spare and laconic texts from the Black Book of Carmarthen. I tried to express their meaning through the words alone'. In this manner of transposing signs into symbols, Phillips has much in common with David Jones, whose calligraphy (No. 79) was prompted in a similar way.

150. Kyffin Williams b. 1918
Self portrait (1978) Oil on canvas 112 x 56 cm
Private collection

Kyffin Wiliams was born in Anglesey, and he now lives and works there, with a house and studio overlooking the Menai Straits. Although he is probably best known for his Welsh landscapes, Williams himself set more store by his portraits. In 1968, on a Winston Churchill Fellowship, he visited Patagonia and brought back many paintings of the landscape there. In 1974 he was elected as a Royal Academician.

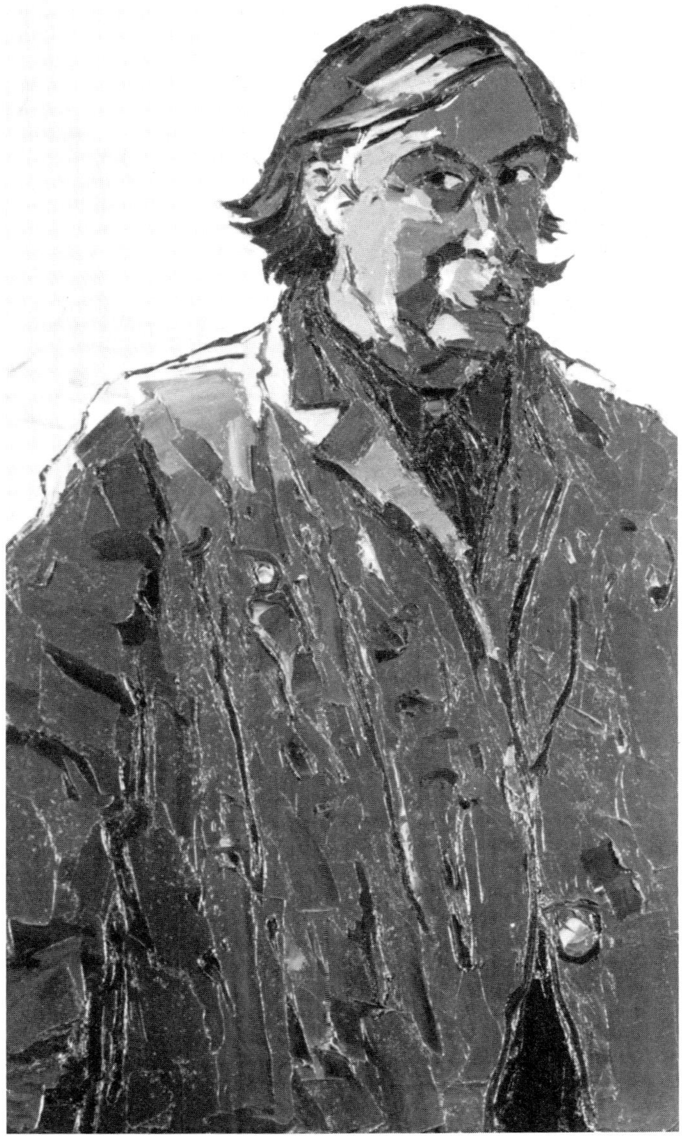

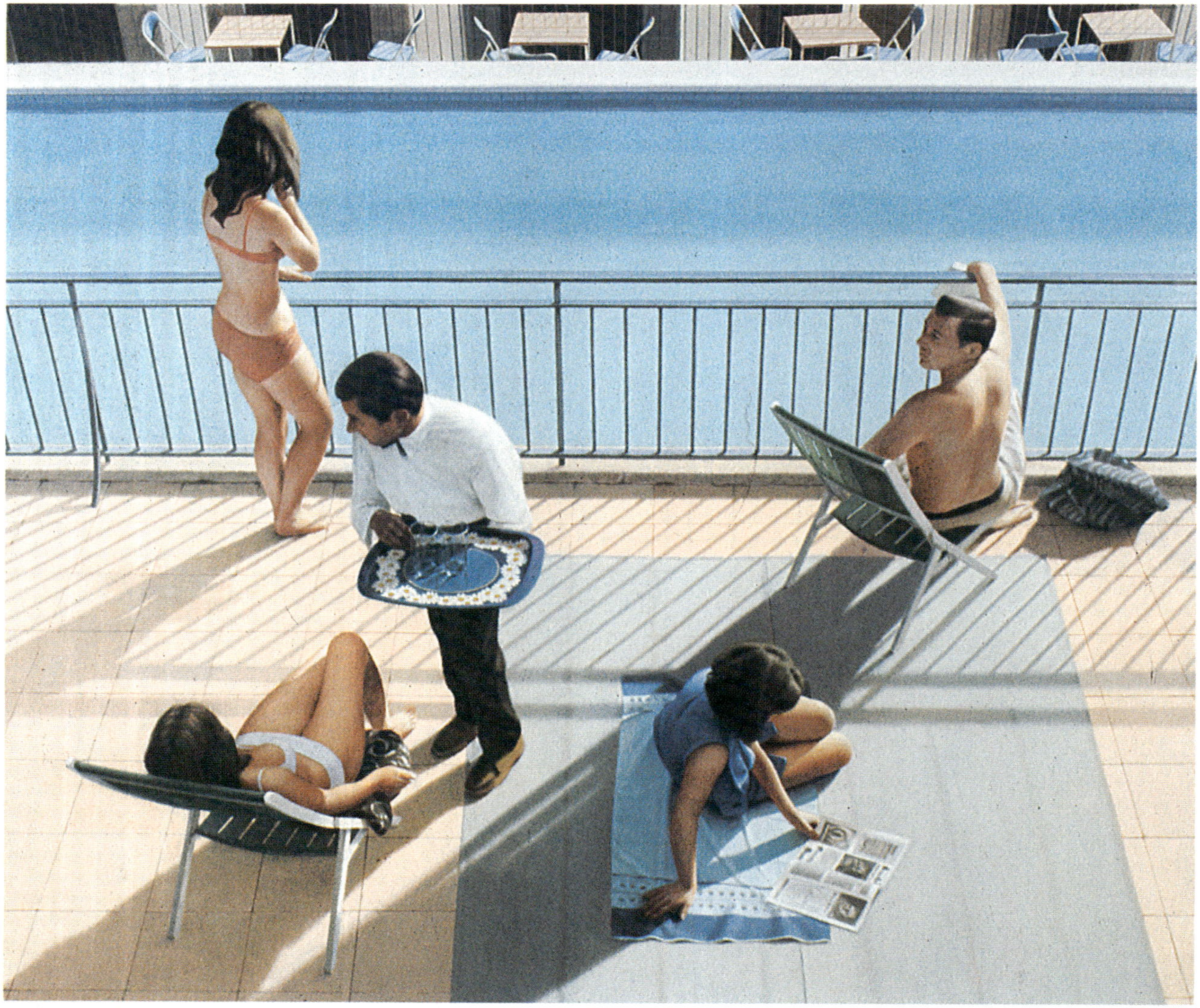

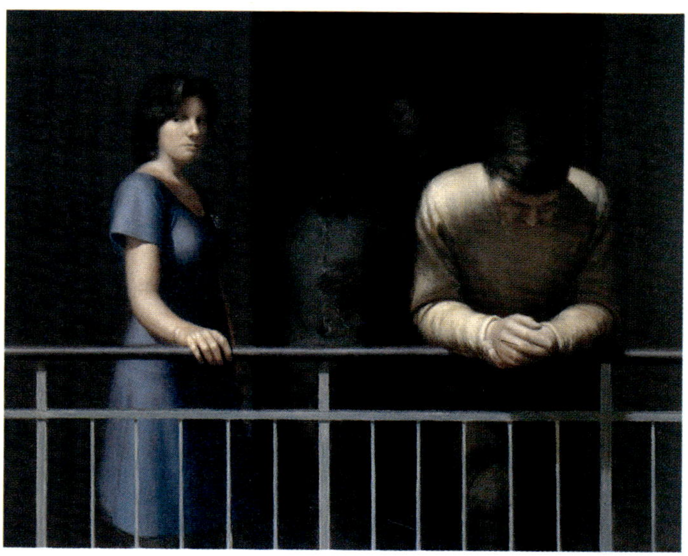

151. Harry Holland b. 1941
The Swimming Pool (1975) Oil on canvas 137 x 152.5 cm
Welsh Arts Council

Holland's paintings of this period bear a resemblance to the style of American Photorealism and French Hyperrealism; subject-matter taken directly from photographic images, with little or no adjustment on the part of the artist. Although this painting has a clarity and immediacy about it, usually associated with photography, it has subtle undertones in the postures and glances of the figures giving a suggestion of some significant relationship between them.

152. Harry Holland
Hatfield Mead (1979) Oil on canvas 155 x 186.8 cm
Denne Hill

In Holland's recent work, the psychological mood has become more dominant. There has been a shift from the hard light and photographic accuracy of his paintings and drawings towards a more traditional use of chiaroscuro in the lighting and a more symbolist note in the subject-matter. In this aspect of Post-Modernism, Holland has also reached the point of using themes from classical mythology, as in his series of drawings (1979) on the theme of Diana and Acteon. In this painting, Hatfield Mead refers to the block of flats in Morden, Surrey, where the artist lived as an adolescent. During the middle 1970s Holland taught at Cardiff College of Art until he resigned his post to become a full time artist, living and working in Cardiff.

153. Ian Grainger b. 1942
A Self-portrait for Dr Trotman Dickinson (1975)
Etching, zinc plate, 60 x 45 cm

Described by the artist as 'an old-fashioned self-portrait for the Vice-Chancellor of the University of Wales', this etching also carries the slogan 'an orinary (sic) scene in Wales' on the inverted drawing pinned to the wall. This modest disclaimer is contradicted by the rest of the etching which is a typical example of Grainger's combination of schematic drawing with trompe l'oeil devices to support his complex, erudite imagery. Drawn from a wide range of sources: the mystical books of the Renaissance, medieval engineering, Pop art, and so forth, his work has infinite variety, and is constantly challenging in its combination of ideas.

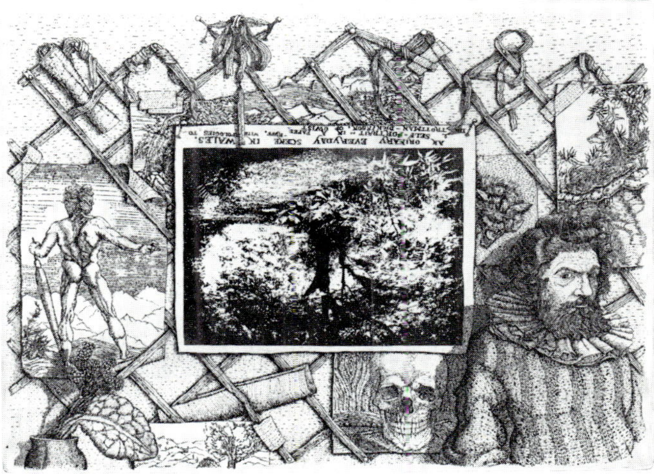

154. William Powell Wilkins b. 1938
Figures with a Landscape (1978 - 9) Oil on canvas 61 x 79 cm
Private Collection

In contrast to the previous four illustrations, the figures in Powell Wilkins's work have a calm, classic repose about them; the result of a patient, painstaking technique. 'My paintings start with a thin wash; thereafter they are built up with small dabs of paint, not quite 'pointes', but nonetheless they are similar in that every dab is separate. There may be six to ten layers of dots and dabs as the right balance of colour and tone is finally established'. In spite of their small scale, 'drawings take days or weeks to finish, paintings take weeks or months'. A discernable French quality in Powell Wilkins's work is perhaps due to the fact that for several years he worked for the French Ministry of Cultural Affairs, advising on the ecclesiastical architecture of Western Brittany. He now maintains a studio near Llandeilo in Dyfed.

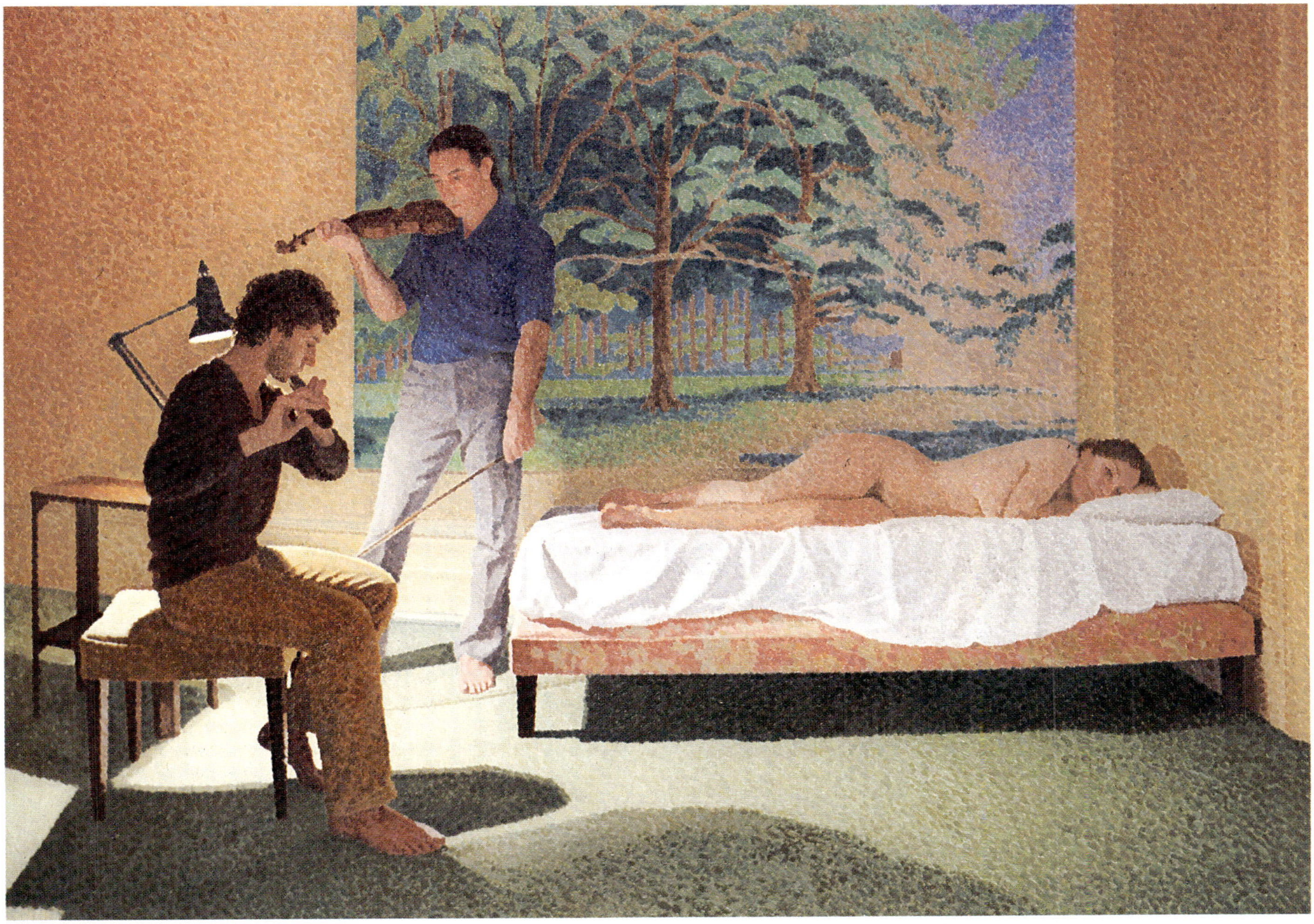

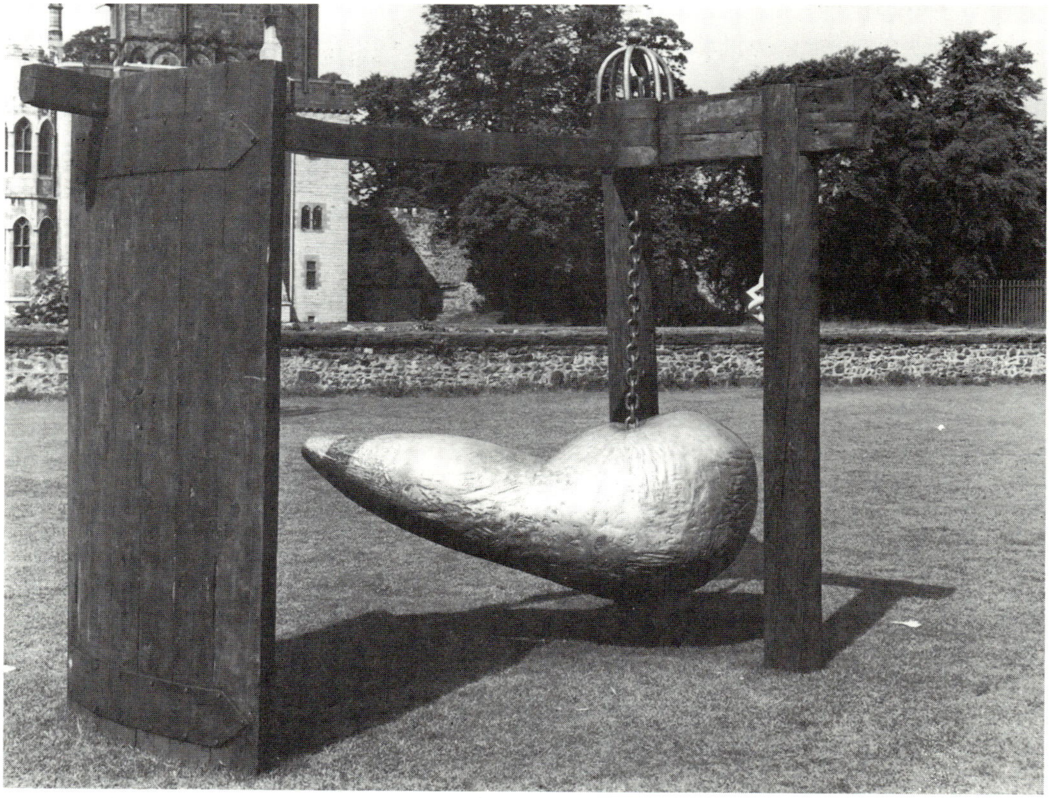

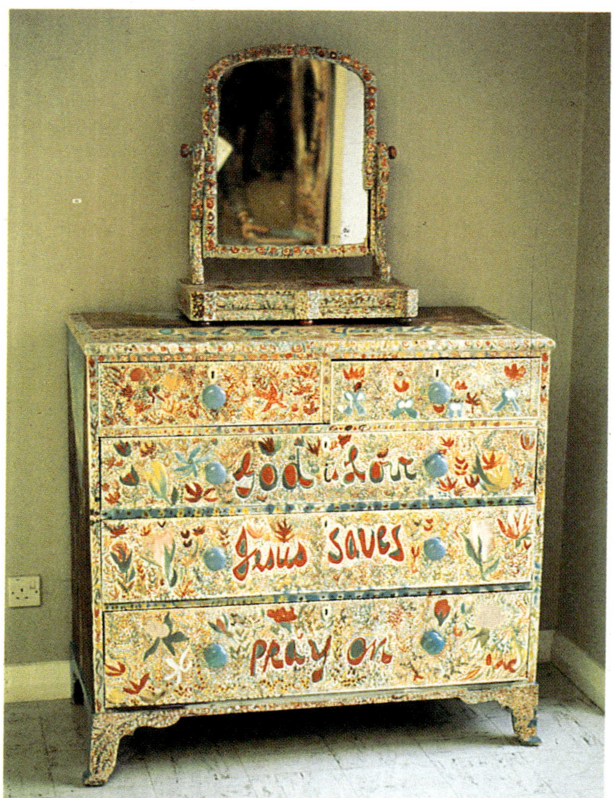

155. William Pye b. 1939
Deity Enshrined II (1965) Aluminium, wood and steel
244 x 305 cm (photograph of the Green in Cardiff Castle, showing part of the outdoor section of 'Structure 1966')

In the summer of 1966, the Welsh Arts Council organised an exhibition called Structure 1966, which gathered together, from all over Britain, a selection of eighty works of sculpture and construction. Although a laborious and complicated exhibition to organise, it succeeded in its two main intentions: to show a wide cross-section of the new developments in the area between painting and sculpture, and to show the work of Welsh artists, working in that area, alongside others from the rest of Britain.

156. Olive Bousfield Rogers 1901 - 80
Chest of Drawers (exhibited 1972) Wooden furniture painted with commercial lacquer
Estate of the Artist

One of the most remarkable exhibitions to be held in Wales during 1972 was called 'An Alternative Tradition'. It was selected by Alun Williams of the National Museum of Wales, though 'selection' is barely adequate to cover the process of investigation and discovery that was an essential preliminary to the exhibition. The alternative tradition was the work of amateur or naïve artists: those who, usually untrained, are more concerned with the joy of creative activity than with any fame or fortune attendant on it. What Williams uncovered was a fascinating body of artists which showed that, whatever other shortcomings there might be in Welsh art, there was no deficiency in the naïve idiom. No single work can be considered typical of the exhibition, though Mrs Rogers was representative of her kind of artist in the sheer obsessive delight she took in her paintings, objects, scrapbooks, tableaux and decorated furniture.

157. David Nash b. 1945
Table with Cubes (1973) Pine 122 x 152 x 122 cm
National Museum of Wales

David Nash works almost exclusively in wood, though he sees his work as 'a direct reaction to the discipline of cabinet making ... I want to touch the wood as little as possible; just enough to get the sense of human presence and human intention'. Having 'constructed an uncarved block', Nash was faced with the problem of how to display them. 'On a plinth they were too precarious, so I ended up making a table for them'. This is one of the several tables he made over a period of five years, each one 'like a domestic altar ... emphasising a different aspect of "table"'.

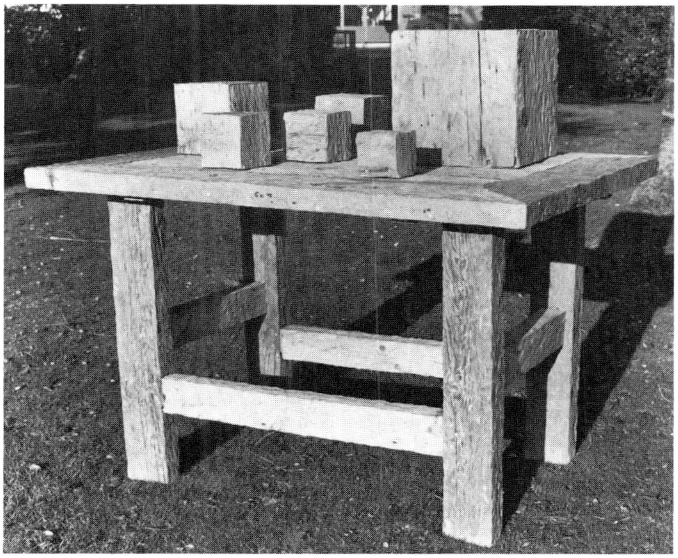

158. David Nash
Fletched-over Ash Dome, Growing ash trees (diameter of circle approx. 12.20 m)
Caen-y-Coed, Maentwrog

As Nash had gradually moved away from prepared wood, 'town wood' he calls it, towards a more natural finish, so he progressed to the idea of using wood that is growing. Having planted a circle of ash saplings, he is now training them to form a living dome - a process that will take about forty years to complete. 'In the winter it'll be a silver structure, and in the summer it'll be like a great green volcano'.

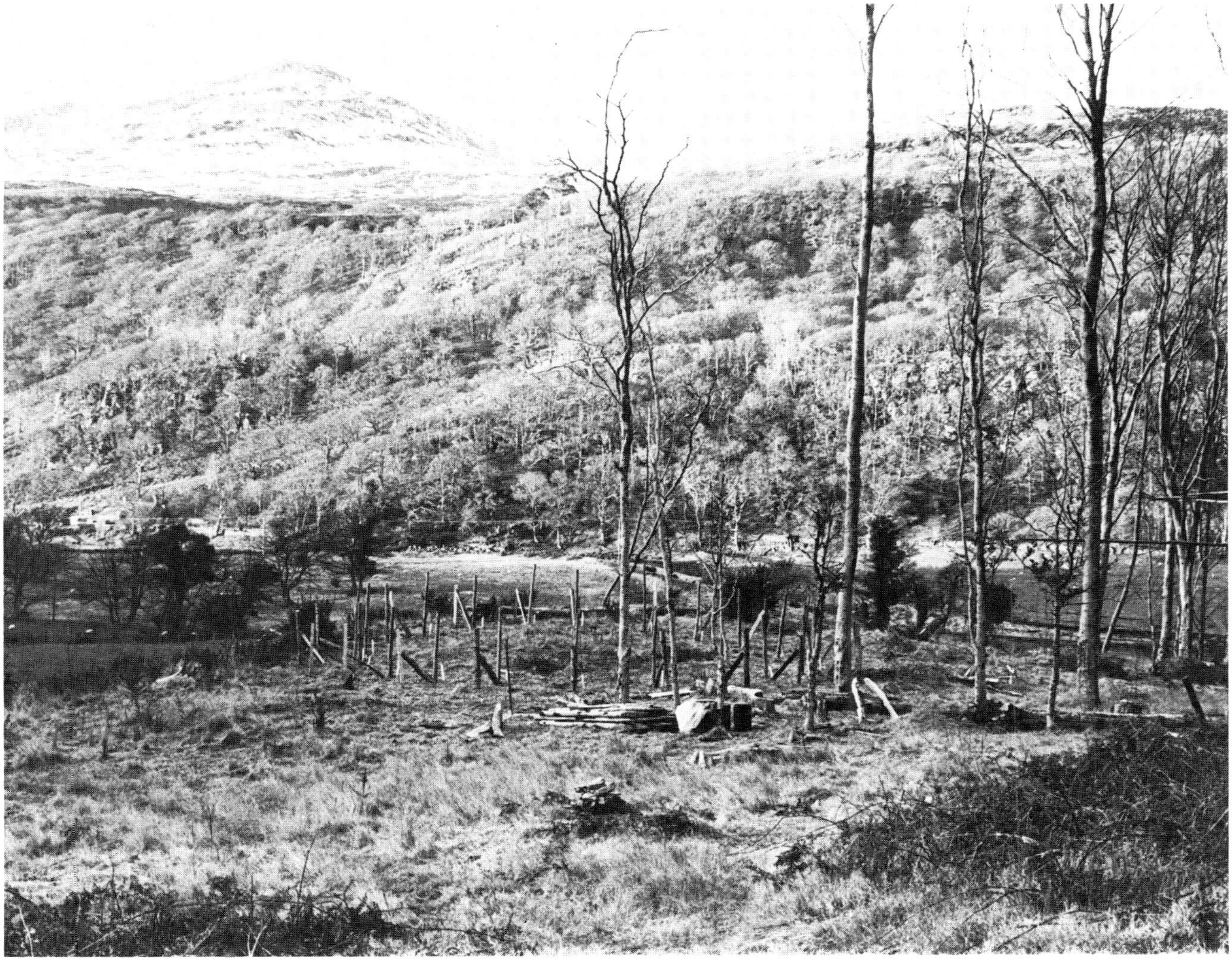

159. David Nash
Drawing for Fletched-over Ash Dome (1980)
The Artist

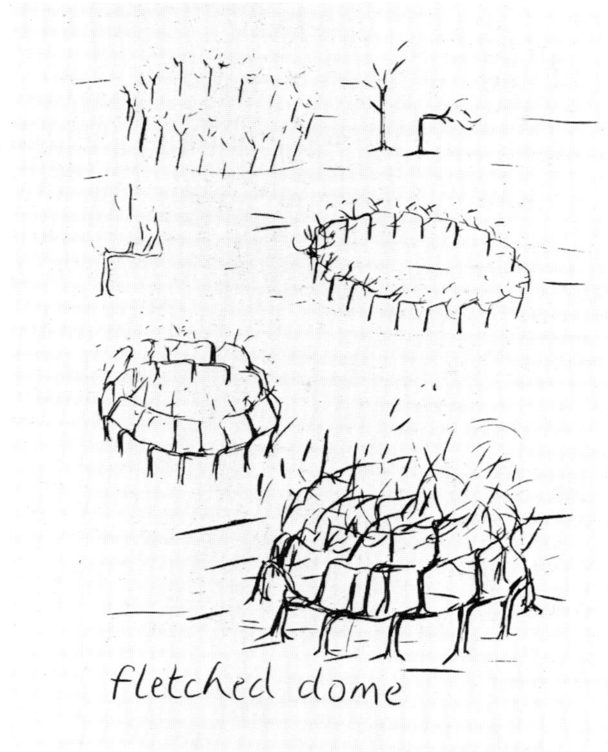

160. David Shepherd b. 1944
Installation Work (1977) Mixed media. Newport Art Gallery, from March 25 to April 15, 1977
Sheppard's installation pieces are ephemeral, being created for a specific location and then dismantled after the exhibition is over. The parts may be used again in another place, but never in the same configuration. Here, in Newport Art Gallery, the artist had to contend with the large, bare gallery and the metal, skeletal frame used to support partitions. Numerous identical units, made in his studio, were arranged on the floor to conform to the proportions of the gallery and to counteract the dominant metal structure over them. The black polythene beneath served to eliminate distracting shadows on the parquet floor and to relate Sheppard's work to the predominantly black paintings by Brian Thomas that were exhibited on the walls.

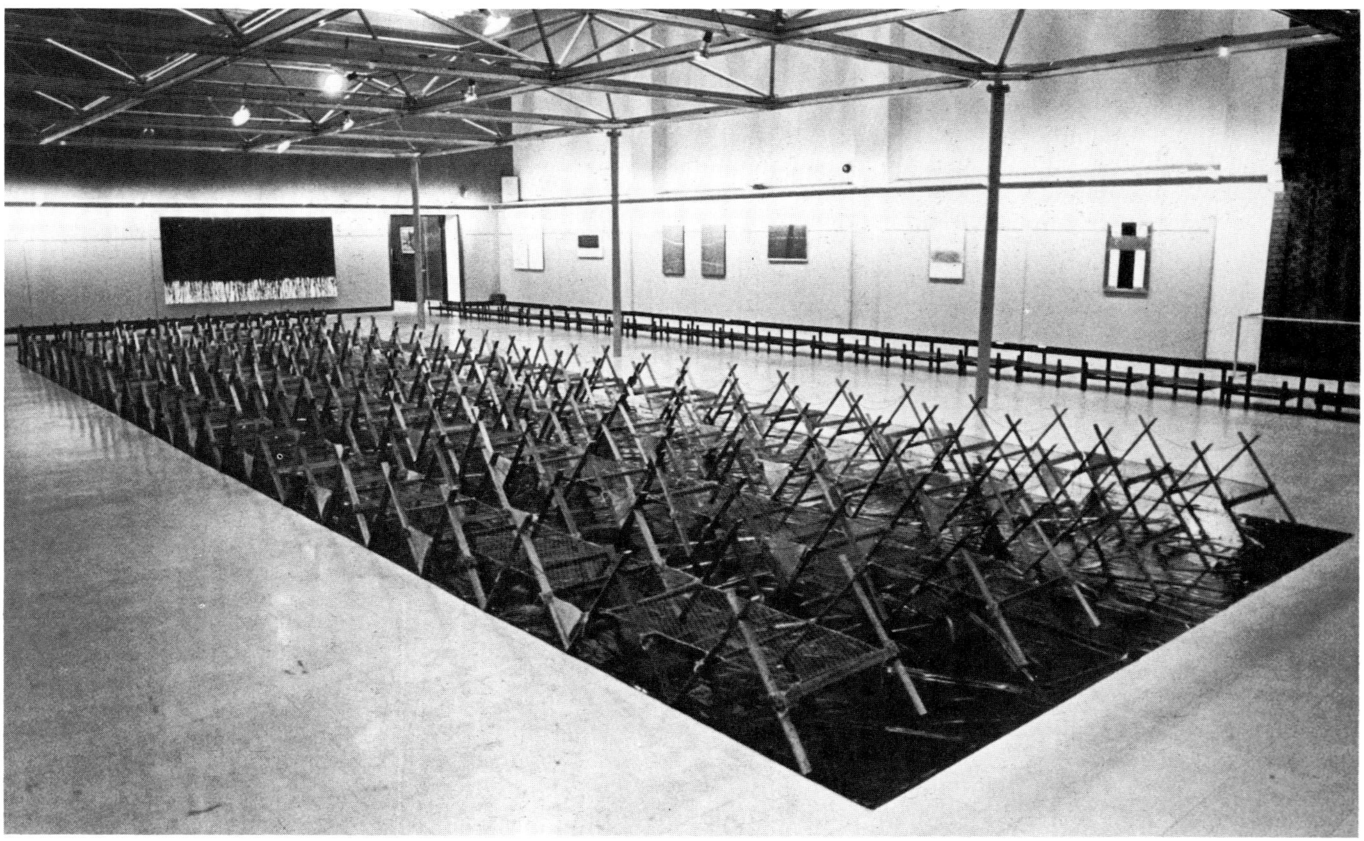

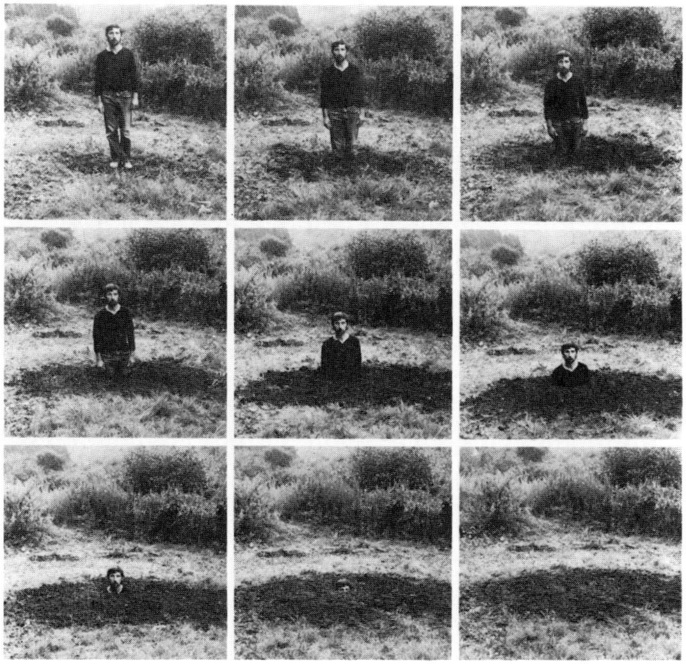

161. Keith Arnatt b. 1930
Self-burial or The Disappearance of the Artist (Tintern, Summer 1969)
Photograph: Tate Gallery

Before this period of his work, Arnatt had been a minimalist painter, and later a sculptor (he was one of the exhibitors in Structure 1966). Subsequently he moved into the area loosely covered by the term conceptual art. This work dates from that period though it is also a combination of land art, happening and installation art. In this instance, the event itself would not have the spare, dramatic effect given to it by this sequence of photographs, since there would be preliminary work such as digging and positioning which would distract the spectator. It was partly this reliance on the camera, partly the example of his colleague at Newport College of Art, David Hurn, that eventually led Arnatt to an interest in photography as an art form in its own right.

162a. David Hurn b. 1934
International Eisteddfod, Llangollen (1972)
Black and white photograph

162b. David Hurn
Epynt (1973) Black and white photograph

In 1971 David Hurn was awarded a grant by the Welsh Arts Council; the first ever given to a photographer. The outcome, over the next few years, was a series of forty photographs depicting various aspects of Welsh life, under the general title of 'Wales Black and White', from which these two illustrations are taken. Hurn's approach was that of a Welshman rediscovering his native land, which accounts for his tender, witty, unsentimental, often ironic view of Wales. In this attitude he also shows the influence of some of his favourite photographers: Kertesz, Brandt and Cartier-Bresson. In 1974 at the Gwent College of Higher Education (the former Newport College of Art), Hurn set up the first high-level photography course in Wales.

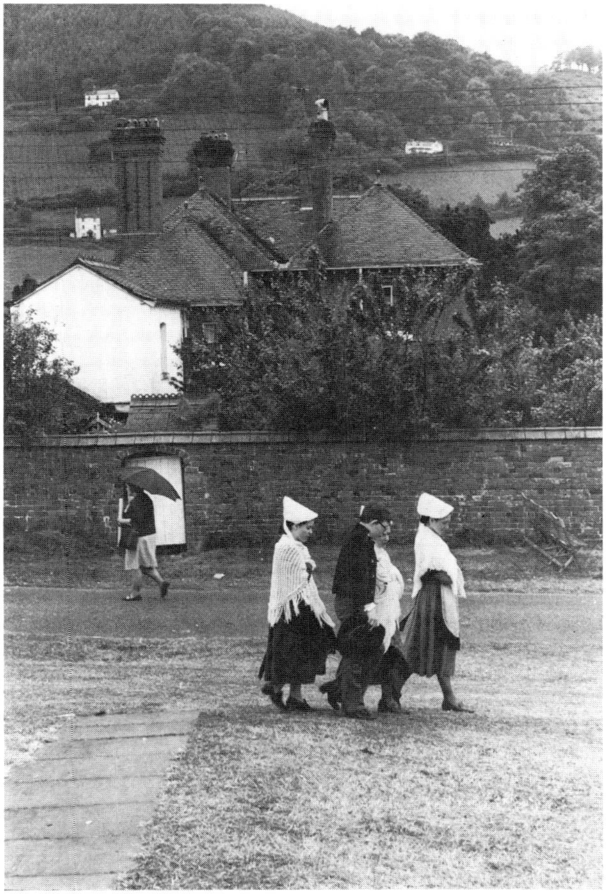

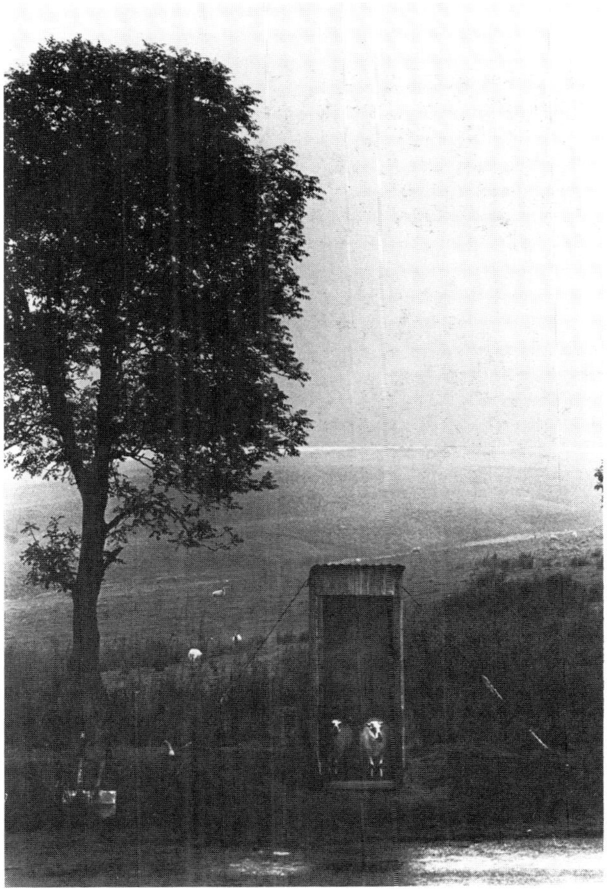

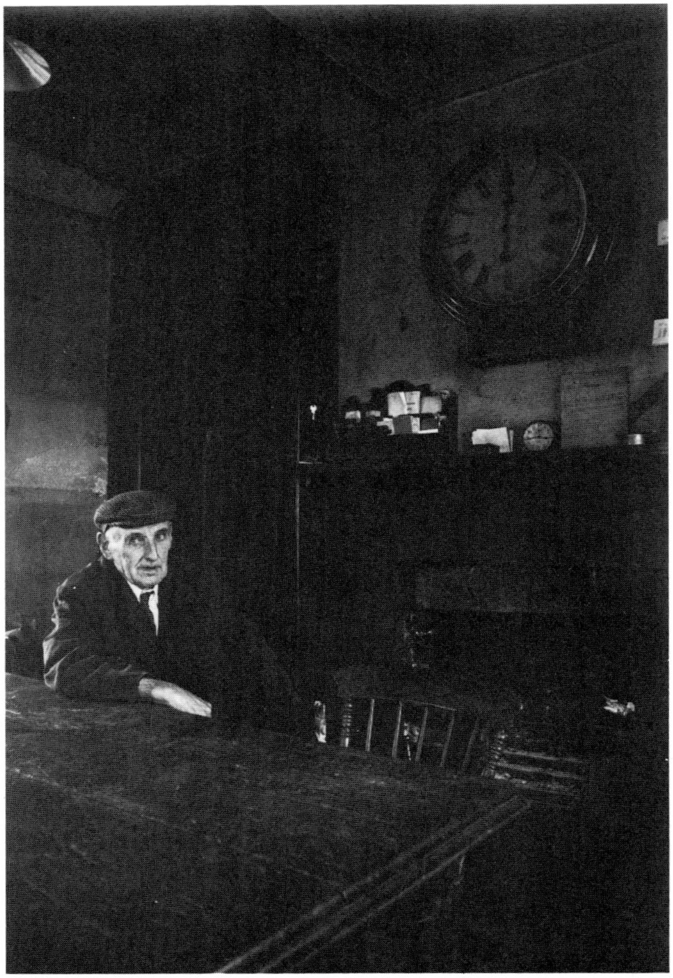

163. Julian Sheppard b.1929
Undermanager, Pen yr Orsedd Quarry (1974)
Black and white photograph

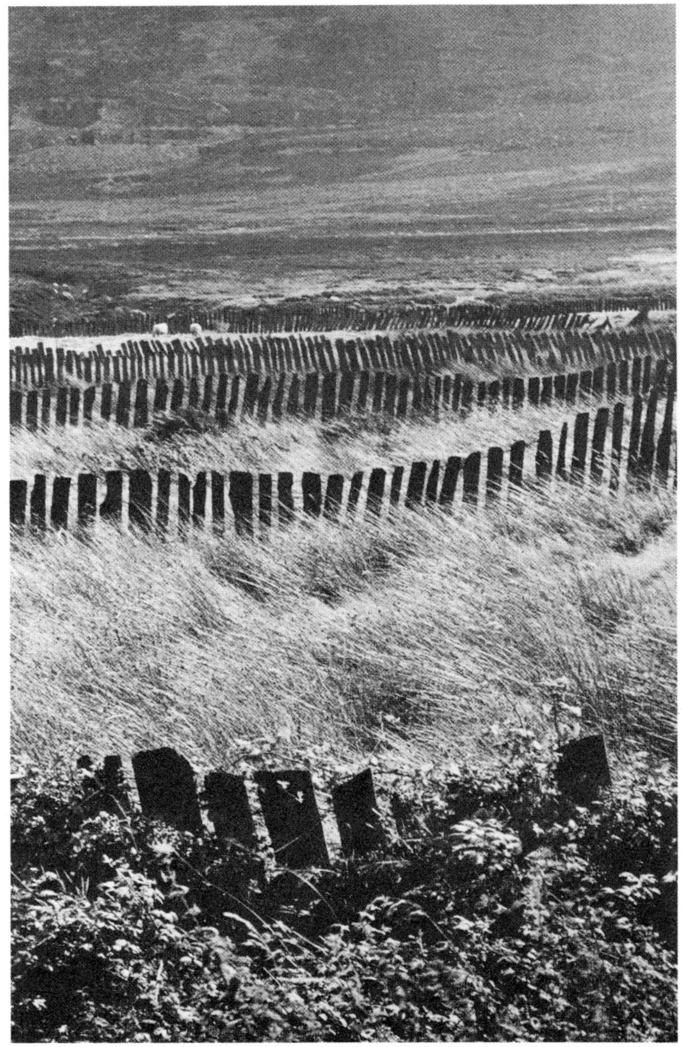

164. John Thomas b.1930
Slate Fences, Bethesda (1974) Black and white photograph

These two photographs are from an exhibition entitled 'Slate', that was sponsored by the Welsh Arts Council to celebrate the centenary of the founding of the North Wales Quarrymen's Union. Nine photographers were eventually selected to record life in the Nantlle Valley during the summer months of 1974, and from six thousand exposures, eighty prints were finally exhibited. The photographers were given complete liberty to portray their view of life in the valley: the people, the buildings, the derelict workings and the four quarries still active. The melancholy and nostalgia that cling to the decline of the industrial age are movingly conveyed in these two samples from the exhibition. The calm resignation in Sheppard's photograph is in complete contrast to his more familiar work for the Welsh National Opera, while Thomas's photograph has a paintlerly view reminiscent of the foreground of Stanley Spencer's painting of 1938 (No.88).

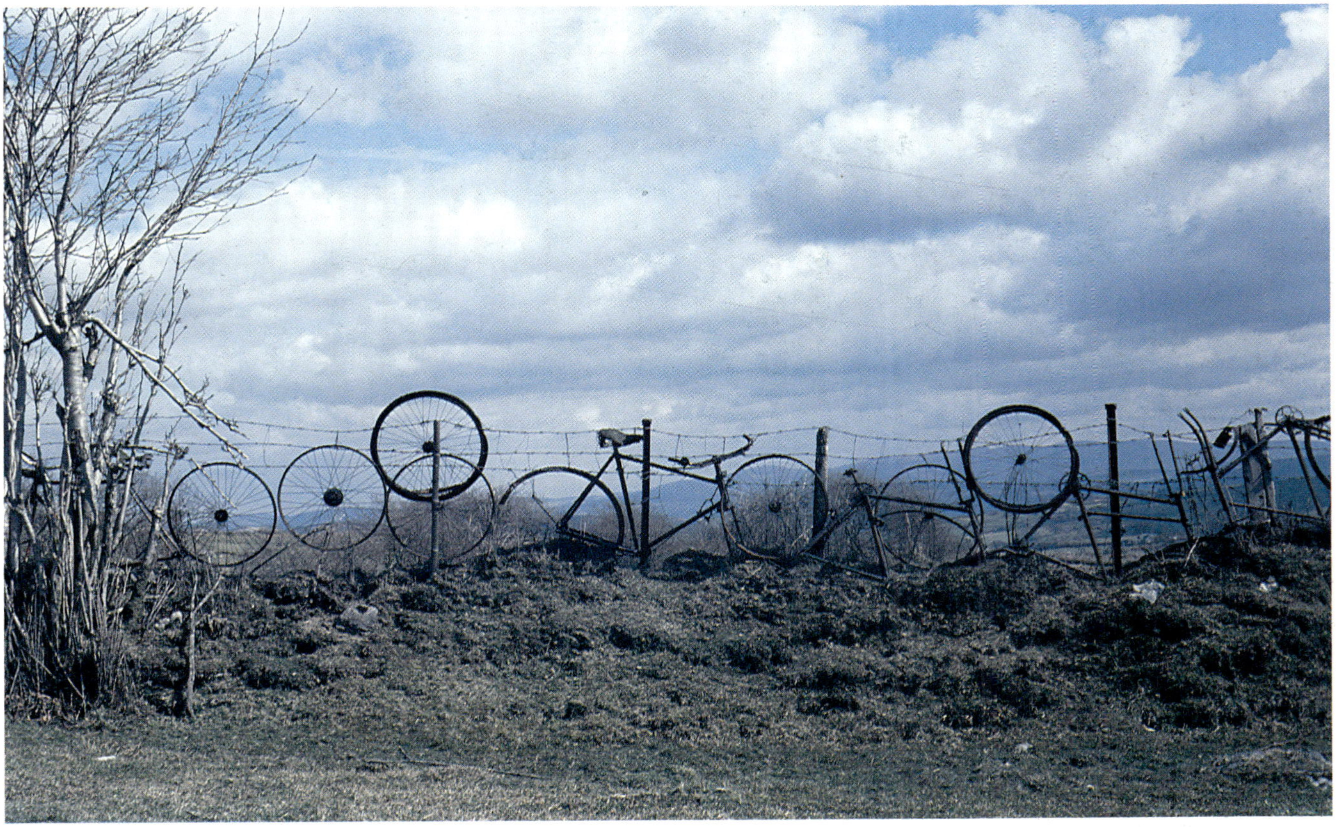

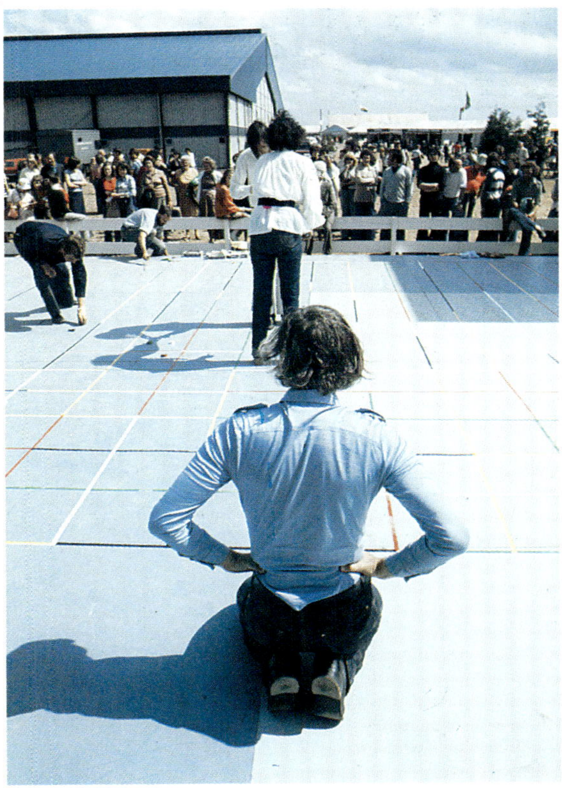

165. Sue Wells b. 1952
John 'Tan y Mynydd' Fence (1976) 35mm colour transparency
Born in Rhodesia, Sue Wells studied at the London School of Printing, from where, in 1973, she moved to Blaenau Ffestiniog. In north Wales, she became fascinated by the landscape, the quality of rocks, stone walls and buildings, and by the contribution made to the environment by man's rural activities. This was represented in an exhibition at Coleg Harlech called 'Ardudwy - Things made by hand, on farms, in quarries, and at sea'. The serendipity aspect of this interest also produced a series of photographs on the fences of a farmer from near Bala, who seemed obsessed with the notion of making fences from almost any abandoned article.

166. Patrick Ireland b. 1934
How the Past Perishes - How the Future Becomes (1970)
Event performance, 3rd August 1977
National Eisteddfod, Wrexham
At the 1977 National Eisteddfod, held at Wrexham, the main feature of the visual arts programme was an international festival of events and performance art. Organised by Caroline Tisdall, artists were invited from many countries, including Patrick Ireland (né Brian O'Doherty) whose contribution was this piece, first devised in 1970 and dedicated to the Welsh language. Subtitled 'Vowel Grid: A Restoration of Language' it has two performers (male and female) who move about on a grid divided into five lengths with five different colours. Each length represents a vowel from the early Celtic alphabet (Ogham), and the performers move from vowel to vowel following a schematic, ritualised pattern, translating the vowels into 'movement, colour, direction, position'. The austere, enigmatic potential of this work was diluted by the addition of a commentary, spoken (in Welsh) by Ifor Davies. It hardly needs saying that the festival was sponsored and financed by the Welsh Arts Council.

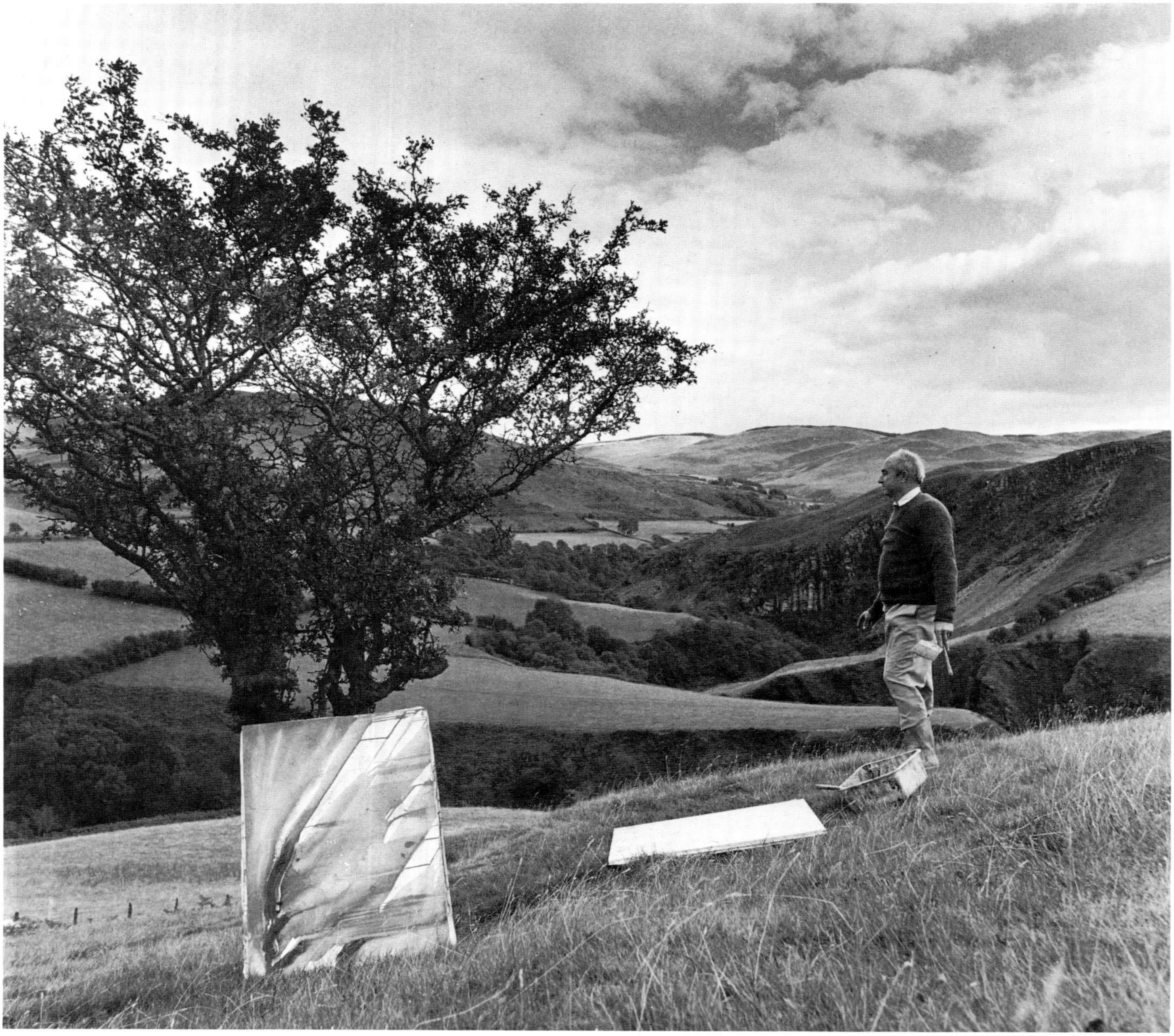

167. Olivier Debré b. 1920
Photograph of Debré at work near Capel Bangor, Dyfed (1976)
Yet another venture by the Welsh Arts Council, though one that has never been repeated, was the International Artist Award. The Council had already awarded such a grant for Literature, to Eugène Ionesco, and in 1976 a French painter, Olivier Debré, was invited to accept a similar award. Under the conditions of the award, the recipient was to spend some time in Wales on his own work, and also to meet Welsh artists and visit their studios - presumably to give them the benefit of an international contact. In this photograph, Debré is shown on location near his base at Capel Bangor, bravely trying to come to terms with the Welsh landscape. The following year, another award was offered to Jim Dine, the American Pop artist; but though Dine provisionally accepted, he was later unable to take up the fellowship, the project was shelved, and the funds allocated elsewhere.

168. Barrie Cook b. 1929
Soft Whites, Hard Blues (1977) Acrylic paint on cotton duck 221 x 267 cm
The Artist
A more enduring form of fellowship for established artists was initiated in 1974 by the Cardiff College of Art (now the Faculty of Art, South Glamorgan Institute of Higher Education). The Principal, Derrick Turner, always enterprising in ways of promoting arts and crafts in Wales, proposed the scheme whereby a vacant senior teaching post would be transformed into a three year Fellowship open to practising artists. The first incumbent (1974-77) was Barrie Cook, an abstract painter of distinction and reputation who came from England to work in Wales; he later held the Gregynog Fellowship in Fine Art. Cook works with spray gun, brush, sponge, rag and the like, on unprimed canvas, to create a highly individual version of soft-focus perceptual abstraction. The holder of the Cardiff Senior Fellowship after Cook was Adrian Heath (1977-80).

169. Peter Prendergast b. 1946
The Road to Bethesda (1977) PVA on paper, 93 x 107 cm
Powys County Council (Brecon)

The antithesis of Barrie Cook's type of painting is represented by Peter Prendergast, a younger artist, who was born at Abertridwr in south Wales, and who now works in and around Bethesda in north Wales. In spite of eight years as an art student at Cardiff College of Art, the Slade School and Reading University, Prendergast has preserved - or acquired - a direct, unsophisticated attitude towards his work, and a spontaneous, expressionistic style of painting. A typical (and complete) catalogue statement by him reads: 'I simply try to paint the best pictures that I can about Bethesda. I am going to have a good go during my lifetime to paint a great picture of Wales'. This landscape is one of a series painted from the front garden of the artist's house outside Bethesda.

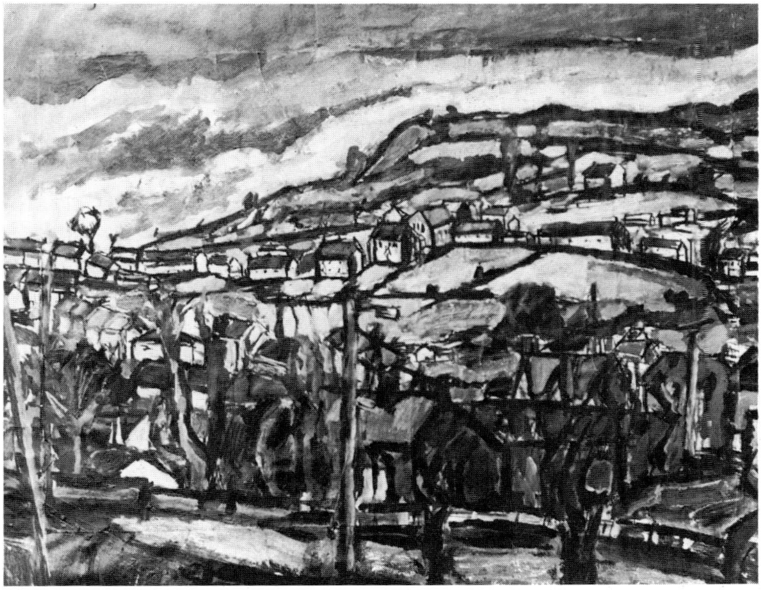

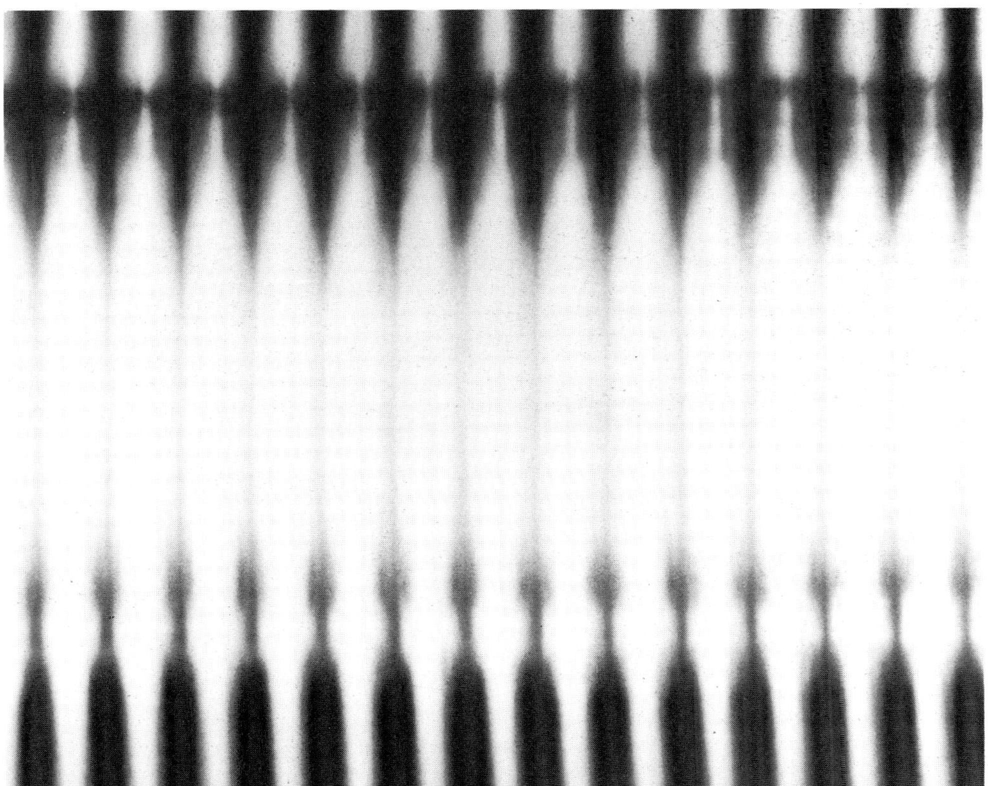

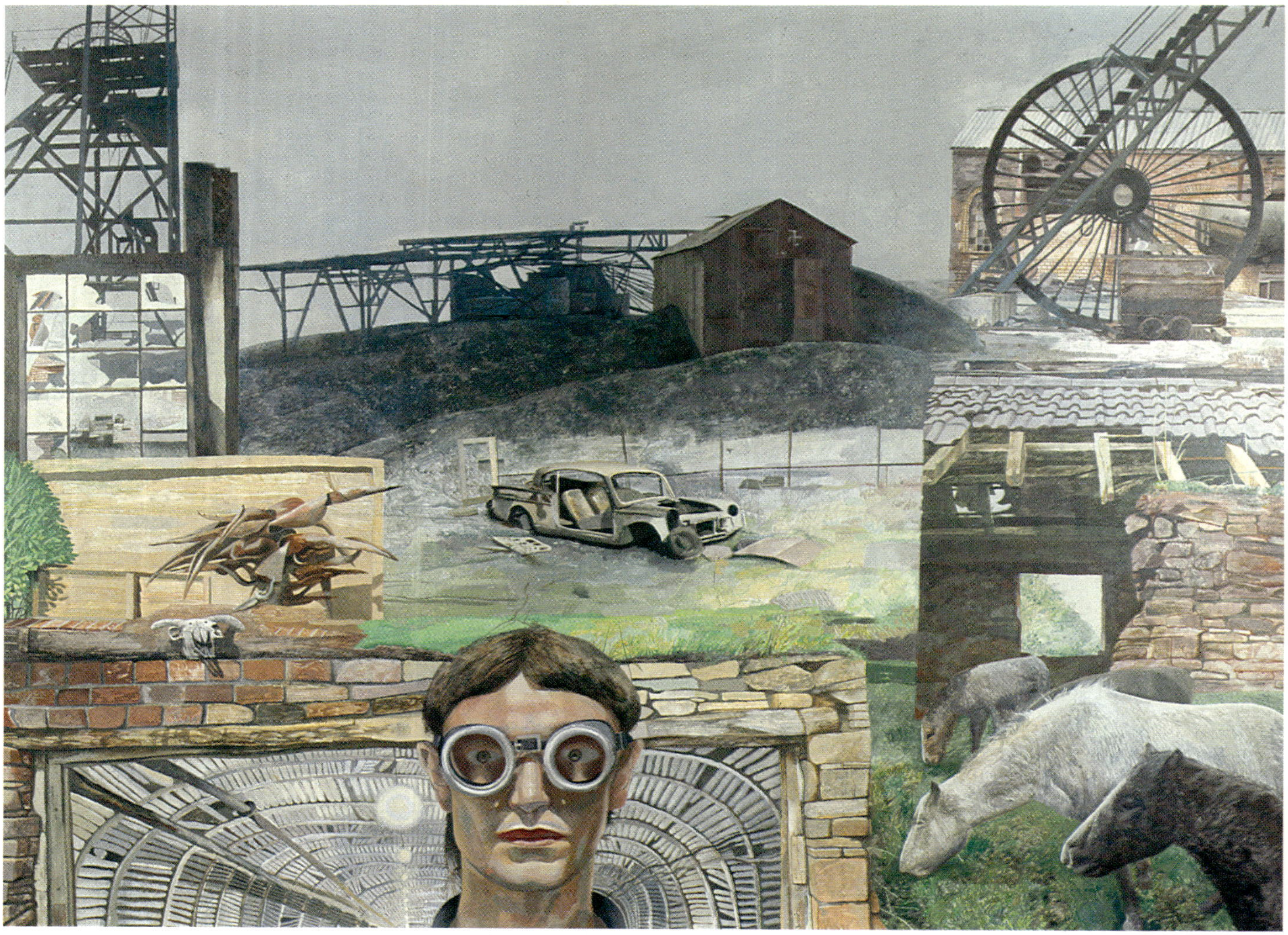

170. Jack Crabtree b. 1938
Where I work (1974) Oil on panel, 76 x 101.5 cm
W.B. Cleaver, Esq.

Crabtree, who comes from Rochdale in the industrial part of Lancashire, was teaching at Newport College of Art in the late 1960s. There he became fascinated by the hybrid landscape of south Wales; its natural appearance transmogrified by the effects of centuries of coal mining. In mining terms, images such as this one - though powerful as landscapes - dealt only with the surface of the subject. Then, in 1974, Crabtree applied to the National Coal Board for a commission to paint for a year down and around the collieries of south Wales. This was granted to him - an uncommon and enterprising form of industrial patronage.

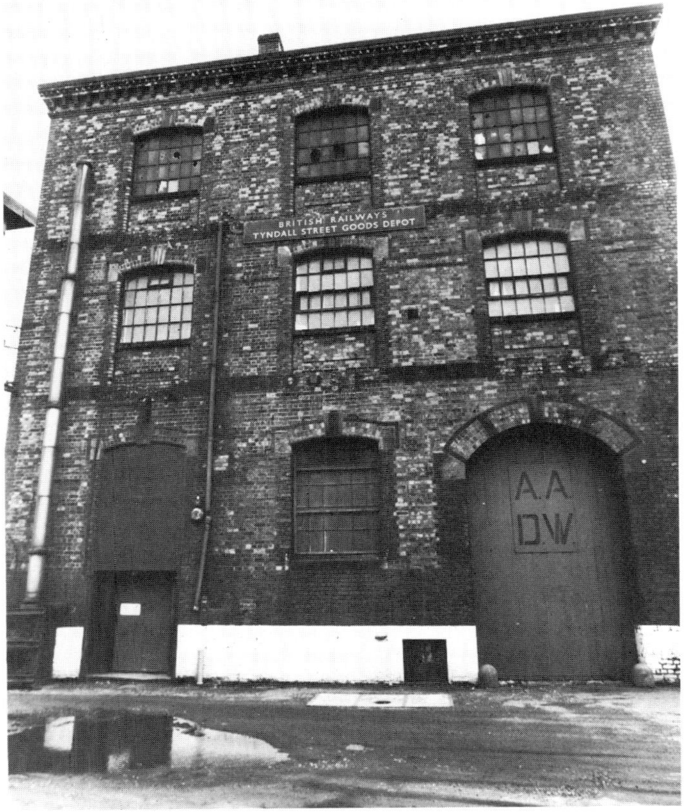

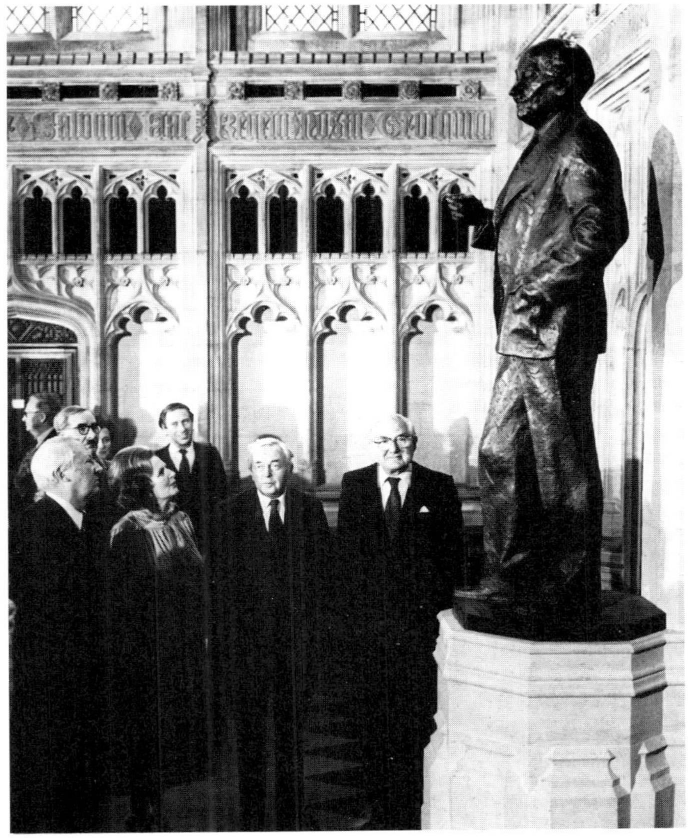

171. AADW Branch Studios
Tyndall Street, Cardiff (1980)
In June 1974, at a meeting in Chapter Arts Centre Cardiff, with representatives from all over Wales, the Association of Artists and Designers in Wales (AADW) was founded. The organisation quickly expanded and multiplied, began to produce a bi-monthly magazine 'Link', and by the first quarter of 1980 had more than 300 members belonging to the ten branches distributed throughout Wales. The next step was to acquire studios for those members in need of them. Because of the Association's limited funds, these studios are often in abandoned, condemned and derelict property, usually available only on short leases. The first studios in Cardiff, for instance, were in a Co-op warehouse, which, though commodious and convenient, was soon demolished to make way for yet another temporary car park in the city. It was replaced by two more warehouses in Cardiff's dockland: one in Bute Street and this one in Tyndall Street. In spite of their uncertain tenure, the studios are in great demand, and this 'Warehouse Bohemia', spread throughout Wales, has produced a milieu similar in principle, if not in scope, to the 'loft culture' of the New York School.

172. Ivor Roberts-Jones b. 1913
Clement Attlee (1979) Bronze, height 2 m 33 cm
Members' Lobby, House of Commons, London
Ivor Roberts-Jones is perhaps the latter-day equivalent of John Gibson (Nos. 1-3), for he produces statues of eminent citizens (albeit in contemporary dress), or historical, mythological and allegorical figures. This statue of Attlee is placed not far from Gibson's Queen Victoria in the Palace of Westminster. Outside, in Parliament Square, stands Roberts-Jones's statue of Attlee's great political rival, Winston Churchill. A famous Welshman portrayed by the sculptor was Augustus John, though his memorial statue was disliked by Dorelia John, and it now languishes in an obscure corner of the park at Fordingbridge. The latest work by Roberts-Jones is a commission by the Welsh Arts Council, a bronze equestrian figure illustrating the 'Mabinogion' legend of Brân, that is to stand outside Harlech Castle.

BIBLIOGRAPHY

GENERAL

BELL, David *The Artist in Wales*, London, 1957

HAFTMANN, Werner *Painting in the Twentieth Century*, London, 1960

HAMILTON, George Heard *Painting and Sculpture in Europe, 1880-1940*, Penguin Books, 1967

NOVOTNY, Fritz *Painting and Sculpture in Europe, 1780-1880*, Penguin Books, 1960

REES, Rev. T. Mardy *Welsh Painters, Sculptors and Engravers, 1527-1911*, Caernarvon, 1912

ROTHENSTEIN, John *British Art Since 1900*, London, 1962

ROWAN, Eric (Ed.) *Art in Wales 2000BC - AD1850*, Cardiff, 1978

THE NINETEENTH CENTURY

Unpublished Manuscripts: **John Gibson and Penry Williams,** *Letters from Rome*, Manuscripts in Victoria & Albert Museum, London

BURGES, William *Art Applied to Industry*, London and Oxford, 1865

CROOK, J Mordaunt *William Burges and the High Victorian Dream*, London, 1981

DAULTE, François *Alfred Sisley, Catalogue Raisonné de l'oeuvre peinte*, Lausanne, 1959

GLENN, Virginia, Catalogue to exhibition: *The Strange Genius of William Burges*, National Museum of Wales, 1981

MATTHEWS, T. *The Biography of John Gibson, R.A., Sculptor, Rome*, London, MCMXI

STALEY, Allen *The Pre-Raphaelite Landscape*, Oxford, 1973

CIVIC PRIDE

BELL, David *The British Empire Panels*, Swansea, 1958

CHAPPELL, Edgar L. *Cardiff's Civic Centre*, Cardiff, 1946

PEARSON, Fiona *Goscombe John at the National Museum of Wales*, National Museum of Wales, 1979

RUTTER, Frank *The British Empire Panels by Frank Brangwyn*, London, 1933

A TIME OF REVOLUTIONS

Unpublished Manuscript: **Charles Hampton,** *Some of the Sources for the Art of J.D. Innes*, BA Thesis Cambridge, 1970

DE BELLEROCHE, William *Brangwyn's Pilgrimage*, London, 1949

EASTON, Malcolm and HOLROYD, Michael *The Art of Augustus John*, London, 1974

FOTHERGILL, John *James Dickson Innes*, London, 1946

FRASER JENKINS, A.D. *J.D.Innes at the National Museum of Wales*, National Museum of Wales, 1975
Gwen John at the National Museum of Wales, National Museum of Wales, 1976

GALLOWAY, Vincent *The Oil and Mural Paintings of Frank Brangwyn, R.A.*, London, 1962

HOLROYD, Michael *Augustus John* (2 Vols.),
1. *The Years of Innocence*, London, 1974
2. *The Years of Experience*, London, 1975

HOOLE, John Catalogue to the exhibition: *James Dickson Innes, 1887-1914*, Southampton Art Gallery, 1977

JOHN, Augustus *Chiaroscuro*, London, 1952
Finishing Touches, London, 1964

ROTHENSTEIN, John *Modern English Painters:*
Sickert to Smith, London, 1952
Lewis to Moore, London, 1956

ROWAN, Eric Catalogue to the exhibition: *Some Miraculous Promised Land*, Mostyn Art Gallery, Llandudno, 1982

SHAW-SPARROW, Walter *Frank Brangwyn and His Works*, London, 1910

'THE LONG-DELAYED REVIVAL'

BETJEMAN, John *John Piper*, Penguin Books, 1944

BLAMIRES, David *David Jones: Artist and Writer*, Manchester, 1971

COOPER, Douglas *The Works of Graham Sutherland*, London, 1961

GILL, Eric
Autobiography, London, 1940
Essays, London, 1947
Letters (ed. Walter Shewring), London, 1947

HOWARD DE WALDEN, Lady Marguerite, *Pages from My Life*, London, 1965

INGAMELLS, John *The Davies Collection of French Paintings*, National Museum of Wales, 1967

IRONSIDE, Robin *David Jones*, Penguin Books, 1949

JONES, David *Epoch and Artist* (ed. Harman Grisewood), London, 1959

PICTON CASTLE TRUST Catalogue to the Graham Sutherland Museum, Picton Castle, 1976

SPEAIGHT, Robert *The Life of Eric Gill*, London, 1966

SUTHERLAND, Graham 'Welsh Sketchbook', *Horizon*, Vol.V, No. 28, April 1942

THOMPSON, David *Ceri Richards*, London, 1963

WOODS, St. John *John Piper, Paintings, Drawings and Theatre Designs, 1932-1954*, London, 1955

YORKE, Malcolm *Eric Gill*, London, 1981

AFTER 1945 CONTEMPORARY ART IN WALES

ALLEY, Ronald *British Painting Since 1946*, Tate Gallery, 1966

BRION, Marcel, and others *Art Since 1945*, New York, 1958

COUTTS-SMITH, Kenneth *The Dream of Icarus*, London, 1970

DUNTHORNE, Kirstine Brander *Artists Exhibiting in Wales, 1945-75*, Welsh Arts Council, 1976

GIARDELLI, Arthur (ed.) *The Artist and How to Employ Him*, 56 Group Wales, 1976

HERMAN, Josef *Related Twilights*, London, 1974

HOPKINSON, Tom *David Hurn, Photographs, 1956-1976*, Arts Council of Great Britain, 1979

LUCIE-SMITH, Edward *Movements in Art Since 1945*, London, 1969

READ, Herbert
Art Since 1945, London, 1959
Contemporary British Art, Penguin Books, 1964
A Concise History of Modern Sculpture, London, 1964

STEPHENS, Meic (ed.)
Artists in Wales, Gwasg Gomer, 1971
The Arts in Wales, 1950-75, Welsh Arts Council, 1979

ILLUSTRATIONS

The location of each work illustrated is given in the relevant caption in the text; in those cases where ownership does not coincide with location, the name of the owner is given in the following list. To all owners, the University of Wales Press and the Welsh Arts Council wish to record their gratitude for permission to reproduce the illustrations. Unless otherwise stated, all photographs have been provided by the owners of the works.

THE NINETEENTH CENTURY

1. John Gibson, 1790-1866, *Aurora.*

2. John Gibson, *Tinted Venus.* Photograph by John Mills Ltd.

3. John Gibson, *Queen Victoria Flanked by Justice and Mercy.* Photograph by Property Services Agency. Crown Copyright.

4. Thomas Brigstocke, 1809-1891, *General Sir James Outram, Bt., 1803-63.*

5. Penry Williams, 1800-85, *View of Rome.*

6. Alfred William Hunt, 1830-96, *View of Nantlle, Gwynedd.*

7. William Dyce, 1806-64, *Welsh Landscape with Figures.* Photograph from *The Pre-Raphaelite Landscape* by Allen Staley, published by Oxford University Press 1973 (c) Oxford University Press.

8. Henry Mark Anthony, 1817-86, *Tintern Abbey.*

9. Dante Gabriel Rossetti, 1828-82, *David Rex.* By kind permission of Dean and Chapter. Photograph by Stanley Travers & Partners.

10. Sir Edward Coley Burne-Jones, 1833-98, *The Nativity.* Photograph by Eric Rowan.

11. Horatio Walter Lonsdale, 1844-1919, *Scenes from the life of Robert Earl of Gloucester, Banqueting Hall of Cardiff Castle.* Photograph by Jarrold & Sons Ltd., Norwich.

12. Thomas Nicholls, 1817-mid 1890s, *The Three Fates.* Photograph by Eric Rowan.

13. Thomas Nicholls, *Bird with Fledglings.* Photograph by Eric Rowan.

14. Plas Mawr, Conwy. Photograph by Welsh Arts Council.

15. Alfred Sisley, 1839-99, *Cardiff Shipping Lane with Penarth Pier.* Photograph by J. Babinot et Cie., Reims.

16. Alfred Sisley, *Bristol Channel, Evening Effect.*

17. Alfred Sisley, *Storr Rock, Lady's Cove, Langland Bay.* Photograph and (c) by Photographie Laurous-Giraudon, Paris.

CIVIC PRIDE

18. Civic Centre, Cardiff: Law Courts and City Hall. Photograph by Eric Rowan.

19. Henry Poole, 1873-1928, *Unity and Patriotism.* Photograph by Eric Rowan.

20. Paul Montford, 1868-1938, *Commerce and Industry.* Photograph by Eric Rowan.

21. Gilbert Bayes, 1872-1953, *The Stone Age; The Bronze Age.* Photograph by Eric Rowan.

22. Louis Richard Garbe, 1876-1957, *The Coal Age.* Photograph by Eric Rowan.

23. Albert Hemstock Hodge, 1875-1918, *Navigation.* Photograph by Eric Rowan.

24. Albert Hemstock Hodge, *Mining* (detail). Photograph by Eric Rowan.

25. Various artists, *Eleven Welsh Heroes.* Photograph by Eric Rowan.

26. J. Harvard Thomas, 1854-1921, *Queen Boadicea.* Photograph by Eric Rowan

27. Sir William Goscombe John, 1860-1952, *Dewi Sant.* Photograph by Eric Rowan.

28. Sir William Goscombe John, *Morpheus.*

29. Sir William Goscombe John, *The Elf.* Photograph by National Museum of Wales.

30. Sir William Goscombe John, *Viscount Tredegar.* Photograph by Eric Rowan.

31. Sir Frank William Brangwyn, 1867-1956, *British Empire Panels.* Photograph by Pete Davis.

32. Sir Frank William Brangwyn, *British Empire Panel.* Photograph by Pete Davis.

33. Sir Frank William Brangwyn, *British Empire Panel.* Photograph by Pete Davis.

34. Sir Frank William Brangwyn, *British Empire Panel.* Photograph by Pete Davis.

A TIME OF REVOLUTIONS

35. Sir Frank William Brangwyn, *Sunday.* Photograph by National Museum of Wales.

36. Sir Frank William Brangwyn, *Entry of The Welsh Division into Jerusalem.*

37. Sir Frank William Brangwyn, *The Wine Press.* Dudley Art Gallery Collection.

38. Augustus Edwin John, 1878-1961, *French Fisherboy.*

39. Augustus Edwin John, *View of Martigues.* Photograph by Eric Rowan.

40. Augustus Edwin John, *Landscape at Chirk.*

41. Augustus Edwin John, *The Rt. Hon. David Lloyd George.* Photograph by Studio Morgan, Aberdeen.

42. Augustus Edwin John, *The Smiling Woman.*

43. Augustus Edwin John, *Lyric Fantasy.*

44. Augustus Edwin John, *Caravan with Horse.* Photograph by National Museum of Wales.

45. James Dickson Innes, 1887-1914, *Canigou in Snow.*

46. James Dickson Innes, *Girl seated by a Lake.*

47. James Dickson Innes, *Arenig.*

48. Augustus Edwin John, 1878-1961, *Llyn Treweryn.*

49. James Dickson Innes, 1887-1914, *Pembroke Coast.*

50. Derwent Lees, 1885-1931, *Evening, Wales.* Photograph by Courtauld Institute of Art.

51. Gwen John, 1876-1939, *Self-Portrait.* Photograph by National Museum of Wales.

52. Gwen John, *The Convalescent.*

53. Gwen John, *A Corner of the Artist's Room.* By permission of Sheffield City Art Galleries.

54. Auguste Rodin, 1840-1917, *Study for the Whistler Memorial* Photograph by Eric Rowan.

55. Gwen John, 1876-1939, *Studio Interior.*

56. Christopher Williams, 1873-1934, *Branwen.* Photograph by Pete Davis.

57. Christopher Williams, *The Charge of the Welsh Division at Mametz Wood.*

'THE LONG-DELAYED REVIVAL'

58. A Loan Exhibition, *February 1913.* Photograph by National Museum of Wales.

59. Claude Monet, 1840-1926, *Crépuscule, Venice.*

60. Edouard Manet, 1832-83, *L'Eglise du Petit-Montrouge.*

61. Paul Cézanne, 1839-1906, *Montagnes, L'Estaque.*

62. Pierre Bonnard, 1867-1947, *Soleil à Vernon.*

63. Greynog Hall, Powys. Photograph by Jon Perry

64. Chirk Castle, Clwyd. Photograph by National Trust.

65. The Monastery, Capel-y-Ffin, Gwent. Photograph by Eric Rowan.

66. Eric Gill, 1882-1940, *Deposition.* Photograph by Messrs. W.L. Entwhistle, Canterbury.

67. David Jones, 1895-1974, *Mr. Gill's Hay Harvest.* All David Jones's works by permission of the David Jones Trustees. Photograph by Anthony D'Offay Gallery.

68. Eric Gill, 1882-1940, *Mankind.*

69. Eric Gill, *War Memorial, Chirk, Clwyd.* Photograph by Eric Rowan.

70. David Jones, 1895-1974, *Crucifixion.* Photograph by Dave Daggers.

71. David Jones, Photograph of *Crucifixion,* taken in 1948, by Edgar Holloway.

72. David Jones, *Sanctus Christus de Capel-y-Ffin.* Photograph by Edgar Holloway.

73. David Jones, *The Annunciation in a Welsh Hill Setting.*

74. David Jones, *Manawydan's Glass Door.* Photograph by David Perkins.

75. David Jones, *Eric Gill.*

76. David Jones, *The Four Queens Find Lancelot Sleeping.*

77. David Jones, *Frontispiece for 'In Parenthesis'.*

78. David Jones, *Tristan ac Essyllt.*

79. David Jones, *Beird Byt Barnant.*

80. Ceri Richards, 1903-71, *Nude.* Photograph by Courtauld Institute of Art.

81. Ceri Richards, *White and Dark.*

82. Ceri Richards, *The Variable Costerwoman.*

83. Alfred Janes, b. 1911, *Salome.* Donated by Contemporary Art Society for Wales. Photograh by Cyfarthfa Castle Museum.

84. Sir Cedric Morris, 1889-1982, *Llanthony.* Photograph by David Perkins.

85. Edward Morland Lewis, 1903-43, *Shendon Church.* Donated by Contemporary Art Society for Wales. Photograph by Pete Davis.

86. David Jones, 1895-1974, *Petra.* Donated by Contemporary Art Society for Wales.

87. Augustus John, 1878-1961, *Portrait of Dylan Thomas. (also frontispiece)*

88. Sir Stanley Spencer, 1891-1959, *Landscape in North Wales.*

89. John Piper, b. 1903, *Welsh Beach Aberayron.*

90. John Piper, *Welsh Nonconformist Chapels.*

91. Hafod, Dyfed. Photograph by John Piper (1939).

92. John Piper, *Hafod.* Photograph by National Museum of Wales.

93. Graham Sutherland, 1903-80, *Estuary With Rocks.* Photograph by National Museum of Wales.

94. Graham Sutherland, *Study for Masonic Hall, Swansea.* Photograph by National Museum of Wales.

95. Merlyn Evans, 1910-73, *The Chess Players.* Photograph by National Museum of Wales.

AFTER 1945

96. Ceri Richards, 1903-71, *Mural Paintings.* Photograph by Dave Daggers.

97. Ceri Richards retouching the 'Norwegian' murals. Original Western Mail & Echo photograph re-photographed by Dave Daggers. *(also page 10)*

98. Ceri Richards, *The Force That Through the Green Fuse Drives the Flower.* Photograph by Courtauld Institute of Art.

99. Ceri Richards, *Blue Vortex in the Primaries.*

100. Ceri Richards, *Cycle of Nature.* Photograph by Courtauld Institute of Art.

101. Ceri Richards, *Trafalgar Square.*

102. Ceri Richards, *Homage to Beethoven.*

103. Ceri Richards, *Blessed Sacrament Chapel, Metropolitan Cathedral, Liverpool.* Photograph by English Counties Periodicals Ltd., Leamington Spa.

104. Ceri Richards, *The Deposition.* Photograph by Pete Davis.

105. Ceri Richards, *Pianist.* Photograph by Douglas Smith.

106. Jacob Epstein, 1880-1959, *Christ in Majesty.* By kind permission of Dean and Chapter. Photograph by Stanley Travers & Partners.

107. John Piper, b. 1903, *The Supper at Emmaus.* Photograph by Pitkin Pictorials Ltd.

108. Rex Whistler, 1905-44, *Harbour Scene.* Photograph by National Trust.

109. John Piper, b.1903, *Rock Face Under Tryfan.*

110. Graham Sutherland, 1903-80, *Road at Porthclais with Setting Sun.* Photograph by National Museum of Wales.

111. John Petts, b. 1914, *Clogwyn du'r Arddu Eryri.*

112. Brenda Chamberlain, 1912-71, *Children on the Sea Shore.* Donated by Contemporary Art Society for Wales. Photograph by Cyfarthfa Castle Museum.

113. Kyffin Williams, b. 1918, *Ogwen.* Photograph by A.C. Cooper Ltd.

114. Josef Herman, b. 1911, *Evenfall, Ystradgynlais.*

115. Josef Herman, *The Bridge at Ystradgynlais.*

116. Josef Herman, *Miners.* Photograph by Tom Scott.

117. Will Roberts, b. 1910, *Farm at Cimla.* Donated by Contemporary Art Society for Wales. Photography by National Museum of Wales.

118. Heinz Koppel, 1919-80, *Lover's Lane.*

119. Ernest Zobole, b. 1927, *Ystrad and People No. 1.* Donated by Contemporary Art Society for Wales. Photograph by Pete Davis.

120. Jonah Jones, b. 1919, *Still Life with Table.* Photograph supplied by artist.

121. Frank Roper, b. 1914, *Station of the Cross.* Photograph supplied by artist.

122. Eric Malthouse, b. 1914, *A Flurry of Pigeons.* Donated by Contemporary Art Society for Wales. Photograph by Cyfarthfa Castle Museum.

123. Eric Malthouse, *Rockpool VII, Twisted Wicker.* Photograph supplied by artist.

124. John Wright, b. 1930, *Cothi Pool.* Photograph supplied by artist.

125. Arthur Giardelli, b. 1911, *Coedwig Sal.*

126. Arthur Giardelli, *The Veil.* Photograph by David Perkins.

127. Robert Hunter, b. 1920, *Banner for Pwyll and Rhiannon*. Photograph by Arthur Williamson.

128. David Tinker, b. 1924, *MJQ*.

129. David Tinker, *Relief Mural, University College, Aberystwyth*. Photograph supplied by artist.

CONTEMPORARY ART IN WALES

130. Laurence Burt, b. 1925, *'Machine AD 65...'*. Photograph Hylton Warner & Co. Ltd.

131. Michael Tyzack, b. 1933, *Mural Painting: 'Variations on a Ground 1971'*. Photograph by Peter Jones.

132. Norman Toynton, b.1939, *My Room with De Chirico*.

133. Alan Wood, b. 1935, *Ribbons and Promontories*.

134. Tom Hudson, b. 1922, *Castell Britannica*.

135. Terry Setch, b. 1936, *Blue Poles, Wallscape*. Donated by Contemporary Art Society for Wales. Photograph by Welsh Arts Council.

136. Mervyn Baldwin, b. 1934, *That's the Way the Column Crumbles*.

137. Christopher Shurrock, b. 1939, *Serial No. 30/A/68*. Photograph by Julian Sheppard.

138. Hubert Dalwood, 1924-76, *Large Object*.

139. Anthony Stevens, b. 1928, *Crow Wood*. Photograph supplied by artist.

140. Jeffrey Steele, b. 1931, *Baroque Experiment: Fred Maddox*. Photograph by M.D.Trace.

141. Keith Richardson-Jones, b. 1925, *Prototype of a Multiple*. Photograph supplied by artist.

142. John Selway, b.1938, *The Factory Inspector*.

143. Tom Rathmell, b. 1912, *The Sisters*. Donated by Contemporary Art Society for Wales. Photograph by Godfrey G. Taylor.

144. Evan Charlton, b. 1904, *The Crate*. Photograph supplied by artist.

145. Glyn Jones, b. 1936, *Carmel*. Photograph by Roy Chamberlain.

146. Terry Setch, b. 1936, *Sisley, Marconi – Were Also Present*. Photograph by Hylton Warner & Co. Ltd.

147. Poster Scheme (Steele), Photograph by Julian Sheppard.

148. Poster Scheme (Jones), Photograph by Julian Sheppard.

149. Tom Phillips, b. 1937, *From the Stanzas of the Graves*.

150. Kyffin Williams, b. 1918, *Self-Portrait*. Photograph by Prudence Cuming Associates.

151. Harry Holland, b. 1941, *The Swimming Pool*.

152. Harry Holland, *Hatfield Mead*. Photograph by Nicholas Treadwell Galleries.

153. Ian Grainger, b. 1942, *A Self-Portrait for Dr. Trotman Dickinson*. Photograph supplied by artist.

154. William Powell Wilkins, b. 1938, *Figures with a Landscape*.

155. William Pye, b. 1939, *Deity Enshrined II*. Photograph by Welsh Arts Council.

156. Olive Bousfield Rogers, 1901-80, *Chest of Drawers*. Photograph by Peter Jones.

157. David Nash, b. 1945, *Table with Cubes*. Donated by Contemporary Art Society for Wales. Photograph supplied by artist.

158. David Nash, *Fletched-Over Ash Dome*. Photograph supplied by artist.

159. David Nash, *Drawing for Fletched-Over Ash Dome*. Photograph by Sue Wells.

160. David Shepherd, b.1944, *Installation Work*. Photograph supplied by artist.

161. Keith Arnatt, b. 1930, *Self Burial*.

162a. David Hurn, b. 1934, *International Eisteddfod, Llangollen*. (c) David Hurn.

162b. David Hurn, *Epynt*. (c) David Hurn.

163. Julian Sheppard, b. 1929, *Undermanager, Pen yr Orsedd Quarry*. (c) Welsh Arts Council.

164. John Thomas, b. 1930, *Slate Fences, Bethesda*. (c) Welsh Arts Council.

165. Sue Wells, b. 1952, *John 'Tan y Mynydd' Fence*.

166. Patrick Ireland, b. 1934, *How the Past Perishes – How the Future Becomes*. Photograph by Peter Jones.

167. Olivier Debré at work near Capel Bangor, Dyfed. Photograph by Colin Molyneux.

168. Barrie Cook, b. 1929, *Soft Whites, Hard Blues*. Photograph by Colin Molyneux.

169. Peter Prendergast, b. 1946, *The Road to Bethesda*. Donated by Contemporary Art Society for Wales. Photograph supplied by artist.

170. Jack Crabtree, b. 1938, *Where I work*.

171. AADW Branch Studios, Tyndall Street, Cardiff. Photograph by Dave Daggers.

172. Ivor Roberts-Jones, b. 1913, *Clement Attlee*. Photograph by Gerald Pudsey.

INDEX

Italic figures denote illustration numbers;
n indicates a note.

Art in Wales
An illustrated history 1850–1980.

First edition published in 1985 by the University of Wales Press and the Welsh Arts Council.

Paperback edition published in 1996.

Designed and typeset by Peter Gill Associates Cardiff. Printed in Wales by South Western Printers, Caerphilly.

British Library CIP Data

A catalogue record for this book is available from the British Library.

ISBN 0-7083-0854-6
0-7083-1408-2 (pbk)